Can Japan Globalize?

Arne Holzhausen
Editor

Can Japan Globalize?

Studies on Japan's Changing Political Economy and the Process of Globalization in Honour of Sung-Jo Park

With 30 Figures
and 32 Tables

Springer-Verlag Berlin Heidelberg GmbH

Dr. Arne Holzhausen
Institute for East Asian Studies
Freie Universität Berlin
Podbielskiallee 42
14195 Berlin
Germany
arne2c@zedat.fu-berlin.de

ISBN 978-3-7908-2485-8

Cataloging-in-Publication Data applied for
Die Deutsche Bibliothek – CIP-Einheitsaufnahme
Can Japan globalize?: studies on Japan's changing political economy and the process of globalization; in honour of Sung-Jo Park; with 32 tables / Arne Holzhausen ed.

ISBN 978-3-7908-2485-8 ISBN 978-3-662-11285-4 (eBook)
DOI 10.1007/978-3-662-11285-4

Originally published by Physica-Verlag Heidelberg New York in 2001

Hardcover Design: Erich Kirchner, Heidelberg

SPIN 10796394 88/2202-5 4 3 2 1 0 – Printed on acid-free paper

Preface

On September 30th 2000, Dr. Dr. h. c. Sung-Jo Park, university professor for economics, politics and Japanese studies at the Institute for East Asian studies at the Freie Universität Berlin celebrated his 65th birthday. At this occasion, friends and colleagues from Europe, Asia and America joined in writing this book as an expression of the great appreciation that his works, his inspiration and his personality have won in many places around the world.

It is a great pleasure for me as the editor to wish my academic teacher and mentor many more years of happiness, exciting projects and love with his family, friends and colleagues to come in the name of all contributors.

This book is about Japan and about the process of globalization, bringing together two of the topics Sung-Jo Park has published on widely. After the end of the cold war and the burst of the stock market bubble, Japan entered years of lingering economic crisis and half-hearted reform projects. While U.S. American and increasingly European companies are shaping the new global economy, Japanese firms, which have long been admired – or feared – for their high productivity and ruthless market strategies, are trailing far behind. At the start of the 21st century, hardly anyone is talking about the "Pacific Century" with Japan at its centre anymore. The papers of this volume analyse the causes of the Japanese malaise and discuss the new challenges brought forth by the process of globalization from different viewpoints and different strands of social science. As the legacy of nearly 130 years of catching up and learning from the West is certainly shaping Japan's effort to adapt to the globalization process, arguments about the need of deregulation and transparency or about establishing shareholder and consumer sovereignty are often influenced by general beliefs whether further Westernization is desirable or not. Today, Japan is thus not only discussing recipes to get itself back on growth, but its position in the global political economy in general.

Many so-called "Festschriften" include a photograph of the honoured person, his or her long list of publications and at least one chapter describing his or her academic vita, achievements and merits at length. But as Sung-Jo Park is not just one of many professors but an exceptional person – who rather dislikes this kind of academic self-reference –, his Festschrift, too, is rather unusual in this aspect. Instead of these laudatory parts the three appendices shed some light on Sung-Jo Park's multifarious activities, discussing fields so diverse as the German re-unification, university reform and Japanese studies in Germany.

For their help in editing the numerous papers I would wish to thank Barbara Fense, Sierk Horn and especially Benjamin Lunau. Finally, I would also like to acknowledge the generous support for the publication of this book by Folker Streib, the DaimlerChrysler AG and the Schering AG.

Berlin, December 2000 *Arne Holzhausen*

Contents

Introduction

Part One: The Internal Preparations

I The Economy: Towards the Market Principle?

II The Firm: Towards Open Structures?

V Global Markets: The New Paradigm

VI Japan and Globalization: Who Shapes Whom?

Epilogue

Appendices

INTRODUCTION

Is Japan Changing?

Malcolm Trevor

1 Introduction

The present volume's theme is where Japan lies in relation to other political economies both in Asia and in Europe, North America, Australia, New Zealand etc: loosely referred to as the *West*, used here in italics because of its imprecise lumping together of e.g. the member states of the EU, whose political economies show considerable differences, and because the term has frequently been used in Japan to set up dichotomies of doubtful intellectual rigour for national ideological reasons, as in the *nihonjinron* (Dale 1986:38). In the space available, the question of whether Japan is changing is taken in the context of, to use another shorthand term, Anglo-Saxon capitalism, for reasons that should become apparent.

The prime example of Anglo-Saxon capitalism is America, which is also Japan's largest export market and historically a major source of technology, such as Bell Labs' transistor, and of inputs into techniques of quality and cost management (Hopper 1982, Ikari 1991, Wood 1989). Since Perry's arrival in 1853, the Occupation of 1945-1951, and in economic and strategic relations ever since, America's relations with Japan have been characterised by a depth and breadth that Europe's purely economic relations do not match. Yet as a co-founder of Honda Motor Co. put it, "Japanese and American management is 95 per cent the same and differs in all important respects." Japanese speakers to EU managers at the EU-Japan Centre in Tokyo, for instance, concentrated on the latter, leaving no reason to doubt that business and industry in Japan were indeed different.

Whether they are changing, as a popular view seems to think in spite of the judgments of respected commentators (Krugman 2000, Samuelson 2000), is a crucial question for the EU (Moorhouse 1986, Moorhouse and Teasdale 1987), America and others because of long-standing trade imbalances and the imbalance in direct investment: at least nine to one in the European case. The former European Commissioner Sir Roy Denman wrote that the, "variety of devices from technical standards to cartels and arrangements between companies at the heart of Japan's one way street trading practices [were] a problem for the world trading community." (Financial Times June 2nd 1995) To accountants sitting thousands of miles away from Japan and without any first hand experience on the ground this may seem like a purely economic problem, but to think that it is anything other than a problem of political economy, with its identity of interests between the ruling groups of political kingmakers, big business and influential bureaucratic circles (Johnson 1982, 1995, Koh 1989, Rothacher 1993), is to be a prisoner of concepts that are not applicable to Japan: especially Anglo-Saxon concepts.

Nevertheless in the aftermath of the bursting of the bubble economy, we are yet again hearing that Japan is changing, or indeed must change. The Wall Street Journal, one of the *West's* leading business newspapers commented that "Japan has changed utterly", because the cabinet's political figures had changed (Wall Street Journal June 21st 1993). Dan Quayle, the former American Vice-President, attacked in a speech the idea that the Japanese economy was not "subject to the same market forces as American or European companies" (quoted in Sakakibara 1993:ix). Following the June 1995 US-Japan automobiles and parts agreement, the American President stated that Japan "had taken a significant step to fundamental change" and that the agreement was "specific". Simultaneously, the Japanese Prime Minister was saying that, "Japan had adhered to the principle that we oppose managed trade (...) we have successfully excluded all the numerical targets" and that the companies belonging to the Keidanren, the big business organisation, and to the keiretsu were "beyond government reach": a disingenuous remark in view of the government priority in building up a strong national economy but evidently designed to fit in with Anglo-Saxon, and especially American, notions that governments have no business to interfere with the free market. The reference to excluding numerical targets referred to the Japanese government's priority in avoiding another agreement like that made with the US in 1986 that did set such figures for the sales of American semiconductors in Japan (Fallows 1995:449, Huber 1994:93-157). This clear discrepancy between what the two parties thought they had agreed led one experienced US Trade Representative, himself a Japanese American, to wonder "do trade agreements work?" One reason is the use of what is known in Japanese as language of the *tamamushi iro* variety i.e. language which like the iridescent colours of the jewel beetle changes from purple to green to brown, depending on the angle that one views the beetle from. This can make a trade agreement for instance a source of further mutual recriminations (Fukushima 1995).

Market forces may indeed affect Japanese companies but, with certain exceptions widely publicised in the *Western* media, as far as bankruptcy is concerned it is the small Japanese companies that are far and away the main sufferers (MITI: annual). It may be true that ultimately one can not disregard the market but recent history shows many examples of regimes that have tried to manipulate the market, such as the Communist system and the British Labour Party's system of nationalising industries in 1945-1951. These examples are well known but some still find difficulty in accepting that the Japanese economy is not a free market economy in the Anglo-Saxon sense, shown by its successful pursuit of national economic goals and the official favouring of the big combines, or keiretsu.

2 Anglo-Saxon Capitalism and Japan's Developmental State

Anglo-Saxon capitalism owes its inspiration to Adam Smith but Japanese official thinking owes its inspiration to Friedrich List and his concept of the national economy. Unfortunately many educated people in Britain, and perhaps also in America in spite of List's activities and influence there in the last century, appear not to have heard of List's concepts of political economy. It is one difficulty for some in understanding that there are different ways of running an economy and that the Japanese economy, despite its high rates of bankruptcy among small firms and the competition among large firms – but generally only up to the point of ranking among the makers or service providers in a given industry rather than leading to bankruptcy and going out of business altogether – is not a free market economy in the Adam Smith sense.

Some might think that this is just a foreign view but some of those who have been most influential in helping the Japanese economy to prosper have said exactly the same thing and it is contended here that we should pay careful attention to them. A famous and sophisticated postwar Vice-Minister, or de facto head, of the Ministry of International Trade and Industry (MITI) made the pithy statement that, "the realisation of the myth that if you entrust things to the market mechanism, the invisible God's hand will bring about a rational result is quite limited". Obviously Amaya was acquainted with the philosophy of Adam Smith and, in reference to Smith, the same quotation categorically states that, "we violated all the traditional economic concepts": a clear rejection of the view quoted earlier expressed by Dan Quayle (quoted in Prestowitz 1989:248). Another MITI official bluntly stated that, "free competition has a stifling effect. We must not allow it to be used in distributing the benefits of high growth, wages and profits." (Sakakibara 1993:9)

Referring to official policy, Amaya remarked that, "post-war Japan defined itself as a cultural state holding the principles of liberalism, democracy and peace but these were only superficial principles (*tatemae*); the fundamental objective (*honne*) was the pouring of all our strength into economic growth." (quoted in Thomas 1989:151) *Tatemae*, meaning the facade, and *honne*, meaning the real intention, are the two most important words in the Japanese language and their ubiquity is absorbed by Japanese children in the socialisation process. The distinction between the two is seen as a natural, not a moral, question but officially expressed views for international consumption, as Amaya frankly indicated, normally contain more tatemae than anything else. This again tends to obscure the nature of the Japanese economy. What strikes many who spend time in Japan, and some Japanese, such as the management consultant Ohmae Kenichi, is the effect of the education system in inculcating uniform statements that reflect the official or orthodox view. "Ask any Japanese to describe his country and he will deliver the same stock phrases about Japan's tiny paucity of resources, using almost the same words in the same order. Anyone who has had to deal with the Japanese has heard it repeated countless times." (Ohmae 1987:3)

Reinforcing Amaya's criticism of the limited effectiveness of Adam Smith's *unseen hand*, unless given a powerful nudge by official policy or intervention, another MITI Vice-Minister, Ojimi Yoshihisa, explained in a speech to the OECD that the Japanese authorities had "not entrusted (Japan's) future to the theory of comparative advantage". Instead, Japan had not "adopted the simple doctrine of free trade" and had "in consideration of competitive cost" promoted industries that "should be the most inappropriate for Japan, such as steel, oil refining, petrochemicals, automobiles, aircraft, industrial machinery of all sorts, and electronics, including electronic computers". This policy would in the short run "seem to conflict with economic rationalism" but in the long run it would promote rising labour productivity and raise the standard of living from its modest pre-war level (quoted in Eatwell 1982:89-90). This detailed public explanation of Japanese policy to a major economic forum makes it all the harder to understand why there is still reluctance to see that the model followed was not that of Adam Smith.

It is hardly necessary to point out that Japan has become a leader in several of the above industries, such as cars, machine tools and electronics, while this policy of infant industry protection and import substitution has not just been in force since the Second World War. It originated during the time of the new oligarchic regime from the start of the Meiji Period in 1868 onwards and therefore has an established tradition (Pyle 1996:97-133). Chalmers Johnson has used the phrase "developmental state" to characterise the basic assumptions about how an economy should be run; so how likely is it that those who control the policy that has brought Japan power through economic strength would be willing to make an abrupt turn towards the Adam Smith model, with its threat to the existing political and economic order? As the social changes in Britain, America and elsewhere in the 1960s showed, there is also the question of Max Weber's famous "unintended consequences".

3 What Kind of Changes?

Rather than simply asking the question whether Japan is changing, it is better to ask who usually raises the question and what motivates them. Do people elsewhere in Asia ask it? Probably not in this way – and they are closer to Japan, and not just in a geographical sense. Those who pose the question are normally in the *Western* world and their motivation is that it would be convenient for them if Japan changed in their direction. In colloquial language, it would be easier for businessmen and officials if their Japanese counterparts became *more like us*.

Intellectually, there is the assumption of the so-called "convergence theory" that modern industrial development will inevitably lead to social and political changes that will lead to societies conforming to the same model. Since the theory itself arose out of an Anglo-Saxon intellectual tradition, this can be taken that modernisation equals *Westernisation* on the free market and liberal democratic model. Japan's history so far suggests that this is an oversimplification, while present day Russia could be another case in point.

More recently, there has been the "End of History" approach (Fukuyama 1992), from the same intellectual background. This again argues that the Anglo-Saxon models of free markets and liberal democracy have won the main argument in world political economy, following the end of the Cold War, and that therefore history is at an end. This euphoric and, depending on one's viewpoint, over-optimistic vision has been rebutted by e.g. Williams (1994), who successfully demonstrated that the Japanese power elites' skilful realisation of a "nationalist economic programme, structured in its tools and mercantilist in its ends" means that it will be a long time before Fukuyama's dream is realised – if it ever is. Perhaps the theory should be revised to read that democracy without free markets is unlikely but that free markets by themselves do not guarantee democracy. Meanwhile democracy itself can be threatened by menaces such as Political Correctness.

3.1 The Manufacturing Sector

It is easy to see why the perennial questions about Japan *changing* – as if other societies did not! – have arisen with renewed speculation in the aftermath of the bursting of the bubble economy and the apparently dramatic events that it has produced in both manufacturing and finance. Because of Japan's conspicuous successes in manufacturing, quality management and the export of sophisticated and reliable manufactured products since the 1960s, it is here that the effect seems most striking.

The most sensational case to date has been Renault's 1999 acquisition of a 36.8 per cent stake in Nissan, giving the right of veto but not outright control, and the despatch to Japan of *le cost killer*, Carlos Ghosn, to restore the company to profit as part of Renault's international strategy. A similar deal had previously been rejected by DaimlerChrysler, understandably fearing that Nissan's accounts did not reveal the true extent of its losses and that resistance to the bitter medicine of change might be insurmountable (The Economist March 20th 1999). In 1999-2000 Nissan's losses were announced as \$5.6 billion: the seventh loss in eight years and the company's worst performance (Financial Times March 30th 2000).

The Nissan news was a sensation for the European and American media, doubtless good for French national pride and an encouragement for those who believe that "Japan is finished". In fact it was not the first time that Nissan, far behind Toyota in market share in Japan even if it was number two, had been in deep trouble (Cusumano 1985, Halberstam 1987) but this was forgotten. This time the difference was that other Japanese companies were unprepared to help and that the burden was given to a foreign company, ultimately underwritten by the French taxpayer: an interesting speculation in itself.

And what was the official view? A MITI official described the Renault deal as "a national disgrace" and a blot on the whole Japanese motor industry (Financial Times March 23rd 1999). Nissan's president resigned amid criticisms for putting the company up for sale, or *miuri*, "selling one's body" in the traditional ideology (Gibney 1999). These were not auspicious or welcoming comments for this new venture; in contrast to European and American investment incentives and the rolling out of red carpets to attract Japanese inward investors. Meanwhile Toyota, having invested in Britain, was investing in a new factory in France: not to be judged presumably by the same criteria as Renault's investment in the opposite direction. DaimlerChrysler finally settled for 34 per cent of Mitsubishi Motors, another loss-making company, but at a price said to be excessive and without getting its hands on Mitsubishi's commercial vehicle business (Financial Times March 28th 2000).

In fact the Nissan case followed Ford's earlier participation of 33.4 per cent in another financially troubled manufacturer, Mazda (Financial Times 23rd 2000), and the despatch to Japan of William Miller as chief executive, who had tried to end the system of cosy relations with suppliers in favour of terminating relations with those judged insufficiently competitive. Complaints filtered back to Ford's American headquarters that he was not sensitive enough to the *Japanese way* and he was replaced by a 39 year old marketing executive, Mark Fields (Financial Times March 17th 2000). According to traditional thinking in Japan, he would have been considered too young and unsuitable to be put in a position over older senior executives.

Carlos Ghosn had some acclaim as Nissan's potential saviour but his October 1999 plan to close no fewer than five factories with job losses of 21,000 at a time of higher than usual unemployment led to union protests in January 2000 at the company's Tokyo headquarters. Carlos Ghosn promised to find alternative work for those laid off but there was scepticism that this was realistic (Financial Times January 25th 2000). A union complaint was that, "in the Japanese way of thinking, Ghosn's plan is unforgivable (...) There has never been anything like this before. Companies have gone bankrupt rather than do this." Okuda Hiroshi, chairman of Toyota – a much stronger company – and president of Keidanren, also criticised Ghosn's plan, apparently in favour of a *third way* between Japanese capitalism and laissez-faire capitalism: often represented in orthodox Japanese ideology as a dog eat dog creed. But another keiretsu manager stated that, "managers at other Japanese companies would probably like to do a similar thing (to Ghosn's plan), but for the moment it is still difficult." (The Guardian February 15th 2000)

An anxiety here is that, once the necessary actions have been taken to restore companies to profit, other consequences unintended by management and not in management's interest could follow, leading in the worst case to the system unravelling. What happens, for instance, to the great emphasis placed on loyalty, commitment to the company and the prevention of a free labour market for the employees of large companies, which has been of great benefit to management control, if the company is seen not to be keeping its part of the bargain and forces even *permanent* staff out well before the company's retirement age of sixty? There have already been mutterings of discontent.

Carlos Ghosn gave Nissan's 1,145 suppliers until the end of January 2000 to explain how they would cut costs, in itself a normal procedure for assemblers, who expect constant reductions, though less comfortable for Japan's extensive small business sector. His plan aimed at reductions over the three following years. Through Nissan, Renault has had an influence on Japanese suppliers by the French component maker Valeo entering into joint ventures with Unisia Jecs in engine and transmission parts and with Zexel in fuel injection and air conditioning systems: something unheard of in Japan until recently. The advantage for these Japanese parts makers in being able to expand their sales into Europe via the Renault route has received less publicity than Renault's dramatic purchase of its stake in Nissan (Financial Times April 17th 2000). Neither the Nissan, Mazda nor Mitsubishi cases are entirely favourable from the foreign partners' viewpoint. Nonetheless some people in Murayama, the site of one of the Nissan plants for closure, see Renault's move on Nissan as more like a hostile takeover.

3.2 The Banking and Finance Sector

Given the strength of *Western* financial institutions and that even in Japan their methods of accounting have more credibility than those so far used locally, what has happened in banking and finance may appear less dramatic than those in manufacturing, where many Japanese firms are world class competitors. Indeed the scale of the fall-out from the bubble economy has persuaded those who have faith in the *bean counter* approach of basing deductions on columns of figures without regard to their context that Japan is "finished".

As many reports show, the scale is of course huge. The Financial Times for instance reported that the seventeen largest banks had written off Y51,000 billion, or £300 billion, in an eight year effort to clean up their balance sheets: a sum slightly larger than the South Korean economy, or slightly smaller than the Canadian economy, amounting to no less than ten per cent of Japan's GDP (Financial Times March 2nd 2000). Another injection of taxpayers' money, this time to prop up the banks, became increasingly unpopular.

Since the initial shock of the bankruptcy of the Hokkaido Takushoku Bank, in itself a milestone in Japan's post-war financial history, there has been a wave of mergers in the banking sector e.g. the Mitsubishi Bank and the Bank of Tokyo; Fuji Bank, the Industrial Bank of Japan and the Daiichi Kangyo Bank, itself a previous merger of two banks; the Sanwa, Asahi and Tokai Banks; and the two heavy hitters of rival keiretsu, the Sumitomo and Sakura (i.e. Mitsui) Banks (Financial Times March 15th 2000). Similarly, the merger of the country's third and fourth largest non-life insurers, Sumitomo and Mitsui Marine and Fire respectively, creating a giant with assets of $53.6 billion has not passed unnoticed (Financial Times March 28th 2000). But those who hasten to see the demise of keiretsu structures, rather than their strengthening by these strategic alliances, may be too quick.

These bank mergers, apparently confirming the received wisdom that Japan just had too many banks, were however less newsworthy than the irruption of foreign institutions into Japan's closely guarded financial sector. The most striking was the American Ripplewood's purchase of the bankrupt and then nationalised Long Term Credit Bank (LTCB): one of the three jewels in the crown of the mechanisms for promoting Japan's post-war industrial growth on a long term policy basis. Ripplewood was then reported to have raised $1.3 billion to buy Japanese industrial companies in the diverse fields of chemicals, industrial electronics, telecommunications and automobile components (Financial Times April 12th 2000).

3.3 Hostile Takeovers

The LTCB case may seem epoch making – but one is reminded of the old saying that "one swallow does not make a summer" – and the Anglo-Saxon capitalist concepts of hostile mergers and acquisitions and shareholders' rights are not part of the *Japanese way*. Most mergers that have taken place since the war have been the absorption of financially embarrassed companies into a stronger one e.g. the trading company Ataka into C.Itoh, or Heiwa Bank into the Sumitomo Bank. These have been rescue operations.

In February 2000 what was billed as "Japan's first domestic hostile bid" (sic) was defeated. Shoei, the target, an electronics and real estate company, was defended by the Fuyo keiretsu, who criticised the Japanese bidder for being "unnecessarily aggressive" and for "undermining traditional Japanese loyalty". The bidder retorted that, "Japan Inc. is not a market; it's a member's club", confirming what many foreign businessmen have long thought (Time February 7th 2000). The case again underlined the incompatibility between the Anglo-Saxon and Japanese capitalist systems (van Marion 1993).

The first foreign company to win a hostile bid – in 1999! – was the British Cable and Wireless, which beat NTT for the IDC telecommunications group. The Cable and Wireless case was said to have displeased the supervising Ministry but perhaps discriminating against a foreign company in favour of NTT, a company with a long history of official support, would have looked too obvious in view of the Japanese government's theoretical opposition to managed trade.

By February 2000 the German pharmaceutical firm Boehringer Ingelheim had increased its stake in the Japanese SSP, with whom it had had relations for some time, to 36 per cent and had made an unsolicited offer. A Japanese investor acquired 20 per cent of the restaurant chain Totenko but the board "refused to meet him". Following the LTCB case, the Financial Reconstruction Commission (FRC) of the Ministry of Finance passed over a higher bid from the American company Cerberus in favour of a lower bid from the Tokyo-based Softbank. Foreign observers wondered whether the FRC was swayed by "nationalist concerns" (Financial Times February 25th 2000).

Because Anglo-Saxon capitalism frequently looks at the financial side rather than, as in Japan, at the manufacturing side (Fingleton 1999) and because the sums of money are clearly huge, there is the danger that the recent foreign advance into the Japanese market of American financial institutions in particular will create a distorted impression. Goldman Sachs, Morgan Stanley, Cerberus, Lonestar and Merrill Lynch have actively bought up an estimated Y25,000 billion, or £150.2 billion, of distressed assets sold by Japanese banks and others since the banking crisis of 1997 (Financial Times April 19th 2000).

GE Capital in January 1999 spent £4.2 billion on leasing and other companies and its president was clearly pleased that this deal, described at the time as "the largest ever by a foreign buyer", meant that his company had "been allowed (sic) to take one hundred per cent control". GE Capital was supposed to be ring fenced against any possible hidden losses that might surface later, due to local accounting practices such as *tobashi*, or the shuffling of losses around different parts of corporate structures, and what is known in Japan as the *window dressing* of accounts: another part of the facade, or *tatemae* (Financial Times January 25th 1999, February 23rd 1999).

4 But What About the Long Run?

These figures may seem impressive but what happens in five or ten years time? An old Japanese joke is that it is only after the contract is signed that the real bargaining begins; contrasting with the Anglo-Saxon theory of the sanctity of the contract. What happens in the hypothetical case of one of GE Capital's life companies going bankrupt, because of hidden losses etc that later come to light, and the Japanese public considers that GE Capital is morally bound to cover the cost? In a political economy where the law, to make another contrast with Anglo-Saxon theories, plays a minor role and can be used by the state as it pleases (van Wolferen 1993:265-297), the companies could be under pressure when, as the

Japanese saying has it, "the bamboo that bends with the wind snaps back." As has already happened in the case of Carlos Ghosn's plans for factory closures and job losses at Nissan, it is not difficult to imagine the criticisms that would be levelled at the *cold* and legalistic foreigners: criticisms that would reinforce the reasons for staying with Japanese capitalism as it is, with the added emotional distaste for the cold and hard methods of the foreigners.

It is frequently said that economic and business policy in Japan is oriented towards the long term and some foreign companies that are enthusiastic now need to remember that, "virtually every acquisition in the financial sector has run into problems," not only about hidden losses but very much about who is to run the firm and how it is to be managed (Financial Times February 4th 1999). Even with a hundred per cent GE Capital, for instance, is still in an environment which from the points of view of regulation, personnel management structures, law and public expectations etc is very different from that of its home country. In reply to my question of why he thought there was not more interest in Japan, the world's second largest economy, among European businessmen, my ultimate superior at the EU-Japan Centre, the late Viscount Davignon, former Vice-President of the European Commission and one of Europe's leading businessmen experienced in the ways of Japanese business, immediately replied that it was because "it is so difficult to make money there": as simple as that.

This brings one back to the fundamental character of Japan's political economy as a *national economy* of the type put forward by Friedrich List, with a way of operating based on the recommendations of the classic "The Art of War" by Sun Tzu: a short but pithy work on how to outwit and defeat the enemy or competitor that should be required reading for any *Western* manager concerned with Japan (Krause 1995). In the present context, Sun Tzu on the competitive advantage to be gained by misleading others as to one's own situation and intentions is expressed by official encouragement of the view that the Japanese economy is in much greater trouble than it really is. "Japanese officials and business leaders" – two important constituents of "the Japanese Power Elite" (Rothacher 1993) – "have found that it is good strategy to play down Japan's economic strengths. They are practiced hands at acting out pantomimes of exaggerated anxiety that serve not only to spur Japanese workers to ever greater efforts but to foster complacency among foreign rivals." (Fingleton 1995:3)

Whose cars, audio equipment, computers, watches and office automation hardware of all sorts etc etc are we all buying? Who is the world's biggest creditor, especially in relation to its major market, America, on whom it can therefore exert political pressure? Who continues to rack up huge trade surpluses? In 1999, in the middle of what were supposed to be such difficult times for Japan, the surplus against the EU was up 26 per cent; with imports down 12 per cent. With America the surplus reached Y6,700 billion, the highest since 1987, leading it to be described by the Deputy US Trade Representative as a "serious global issue and an extremely serious issue in our relationship with Japan" (Financial Times January 26th 1999). In April 2000 Japan had foreign currency reserves of $300 billion (Sunday Times April 16th 2000). The Yen is still strong at the present time and the Japanese government has been trying to get others to cooperate in its depreciation in order to help Japanese exports. These sound like *problems* that quite a few governments would be envious of.

In spite of the tendency to play down these strengths, there are those knowledgeable people in Japan who represent a more realistic point of view. Among them is Sakakibara Eisuke, former director-general of the International Finance Bureau of the Ministry of Finance, popularly known as "Mr Yen". He argued in The Economist (March 22nd 1997) that "pessimism about the Japanese economy was overdone," in addition to writing the book entitled "Beyond Capitalism", in which he extolled the superiority of the Japanese system, using the orthodox arguments of Japanese capitalism as the avoidance of the twin pitfalls of inflexible Communist style planning and the dog eat dog approach of Anglo-Saxon capitalism (Sakakibara 1993). In more bullish style, the then managing director of the Keidanren, and later chairman of the Japanese members of the EU-Japan Centre's supervisory board, Nukazawa Kazuo, stated that, "we Japanese feel we have been pretty successful. Why should we change? Others who are doing worse than us should change, not us." (quoted in Fingleton 1995:49) These are attitudes that find wide echoes in Japan. The frequently used expression "we Japanese" (*wareware nihonjin*) might strike some in Europe, which has experienced its share of destructive nationalism, as unashamedly nationalistic or worse, but the ideology is an integral part of the Japanese system, expressed for example through what is taught to schoolchildren (Fingleton 1955:145). It is one of the things that worries people from other Asian countries.

Until the end of 1950s many in the *West* underestimated Japan's industrial capacity and the ability and commitment of its population to make notable economic advances. Especially up to the bursting of the bubble economy and to some extent afterwards, this underestimation was replaced by overestimation, except for those who subscribe to the new fashion of thinking that Japan is "finished". At the root of all these attitudes is the insufficient attention paid to Japan and to the significance for their own economies of Japanese business behaviour. For Anglo-Saxon capitalist economies, especially the all-important American economy, which are most at variance with the Japanese system, there is the temptation, increased by the convergence theory and others, to believe that theirs is the only way to run an economy and that the Japanese economy will eventually recognise this – at some unspecified date. Alternatively, there is the temptation to see the Japanese system as some kind of exotica and to believe the myths that support it.

5 Change. What Change?

Given these failures of attention on the *Western* side, which companies, industrial organisations and governments would do well to think more seriously about, it is not surprising that many seem to think that the Japanese economy "responds more or less in the same way and to the same stimuli as the US economy" (Horsley & Buckley 1990:163-168) or as European economies do to consumer-oriented, rather than production-oriented, objectives. It is one factor in the recurrent trade disputes and the immense amount of talk that has produced such meagre results.

Mention has been made of the use of *tatemae*, facade, and *honne*, or real intention, in Japanese society in general. The distribution system is an important issue for foreign exporters to Japan because chain stores are more likely to handle imports than the hundreds of small, family run businesses that are to be seen in all Japanese towns. For many years this sector was subject to MITI's Large Scale Store Law (*Daitenhô*), which favoured the small shops, whose owners are an important constituency for the Liberal Democratic Party, which has been in power almost without a break since the Second World War. Consequently the *Daitenhô* became an issue in international, principally US-Japan, trade negotiations. In 1998 the regulatory authority, which had severely restricted the growth of chain stores to the benefit of the small shopkeepers, was passed from MITI to the local authorities; in other words, to the people with whom the small shopkeepers were most hand in glove. A Japanese retail sector analyst commented that, "on the surface things have changed. Japan can say to the US that deregulation has occurred. In reality, nothing has changed, and in fact the regulations have actually become more strict." (Financial Times July 14th 1998)

Japanese people living abroad are accustomed to using foreign products but once they are to be imported into Japan they have to be regulated and the interests of the domestic producers protected. In March 1995 a Japanese government deregulation programme was published containing 1,091 items but it was denounced by the president of Rhone-Poulenc in Tokyo as "meaningless", since it contained such phrases as "will be considered" and "to be reviewed": "we are afraid that things under consideration will remain under consideration for many years." (Japan Times April 4th 1995)

The following year the EU Commission published a 99-page "Summary of Market Access Problems in Japan" and a 127-page "List of Deregulation Proposals for Japan" but experience showed the endless possibilities for protecting the local producers. There were for instance the stories about "Japanese snow is different" to keep out the French and Italian ski manufacturers, the alleged discovery of the "Mediterranean fruit fly" by Japanese officials in Rotterdam harbour to hinder and delay for years the Dutch bulb and cut flower exporters, who eventually agreed to onerous inspection procedures; the eventual acceptance of Dutch peppers and tomatoes but the refusal to accept the same products from a short distance away in Belgium, or "even to give a clear indication of the procedure to be followed to obtain import authorisation." (van Marion 1993:49-50)

A former US Trade Representative and current businessman in Japan wrote that, "the Japanese bureaucracy has no background of liberalism towards foreigners, foreign business, or foreign products where foreigners have the edge. Discrimination has long been the rule," to the benefit of local producers and local electors (Fukushima 1988). Here the Japanese authorities continue to play off one EU country against another, in the absence of a common EU policy on Japanese trade and inward investment, and to benefit from the EU and America pursuing different policies, despite the many interests they have in common. In these circumstances, is it realistic to expect change?

In the meantime, the official information machine continues to create the impression that deregulation, now a fashionable word along with restructuring – and one that will please the US – is in train, though it may take a little longer. "There may have been an impression that we are backsliding recently but that is not the fact," according to Tanigaki, head of the FRC and minister of banking reform (Financial Times March 7th 2000). His predecessor, Ochi Michio, had the month before been indiscreet enough to say to bank and credit union officers that they would receive considerate treatment "if audits by the Bank of Japan and the government's bank watchdog were too strict": a view said to reflect those of government party colleagues. An American analyst expressed a widespread fear among foreign institutions that "the LDP is seriously putting aside any serious reform agenda." (Financial Times February 26th-27th 2000) Ochi was obliged to resign for his indiscretion.

Problems with traditional Japanese accounting methods have been briefly mentioned e.g. hidden losses concealed by *tobashi* methods, dubious criteria for valuing company assets, use of auditors inside the firm itself, lack of enforceable independent standards etc: what a Financial Times editorial once referred to as "Wonderland accounting", though we are now told that changes are in the pipeline (Financial Times March 28th 2000). At the national level, economic statistics have been prepared by two different bodies, MITI's Economic Planning Agency, and the Management Co-Ordination Agency respectively, employing about 1,000 people altogether. These "statistics have been presenting conflicting signals" as to whether the economy is actually in recession or not and have been criticised as "dangerously inaccurate". The political implications are clear (Financial Times March 13th 2000). The Financial Times reported that the Ministry of Finance was preparing to publish the "first full balance sheet of (national) assets and liabilities for complete transparency in describing (the) fiscal position," hitherto said to be "one of the most opaque in the industrialised world" (Financial Times February 8th 2000). We shall see. The problems in doing so include capturing "the full extent of hidden government liabilities in the complex financial structure", the exclusion or otherwise of regional government accounts, and the accurate assessment of pension liabilities. No wonder the Japanese economy enjoys the advantages of being largely unknown.

Since April 2000 Japan has a new prime minister, Keizo Obuchi's career having been cut short by a sudden illness. This might lead to some people making renewed speculations of change but the new incumbent, Mori Yoshiro, is very much in the old LDP tradition of the head of a faction, involved in the pork barrel politics of lobbying for a high speed train line to his constituency, linked to two financial scandals and apparently more at home in "the familiar smoke-filled rooms" than in international affairs (Financial Times April 4th 2000, Sunday Times April 16th 2000). His May 16th reference to Japan as "a divine country centred on the Emperor" evoked sinister memories of the State Shinto ideology of the1930s and 1940s (Daily Telegraph May 17th 2000).

In the Italian novel "The Leopard" written by Giuseppe di Lampedusa about Sicily at the time of the Risorgimento there is the famous line that "we must change in order to remain the same": the impression given by Japan at the levels of its national economy, politics, bureaucracy and ideology (Garon 1997:237).

But the last word must go to Lee Kuan Yew, the distinguished Senior Minister of Singapore. Speaking of the new global competition, he remarked that, "Singapore, unlike Japan, did not have that same irreversible attachment to the blueprint by which it was built." (Financial Times March 28th 2000)

References

Cusumano, M. (1985), *The Japanese Automobile Industry*, Harvard: Harvard University Press.

Dale, P.N. (1986), *The Myth of Japanese Uniqueness*, London: Croom Helm.

Eatwell, J. (1982), *Whatever happened to Britain?*, London: B.B.C.

Fallows, J. (1994), *Looking at the Sun*, New York: Vintage.

Fingleton, E. (1995), *Blindside*, New York: Simon & Schuster.

Fingleton, E. (1999), *In Praise of Hard Industries,* Boston: Houghton Mifflin.

Fukushima, G.S. (1988), Law and Trade Issues of the Japanese Economy, in: *Journal of Asian Studies*, 47,4: 21.

Fukushima, G.S. (1995), It's tamamushi iro again!, in: *Tokyo Business Today*, September 1995: 48.

Fukuyama, F. (1992), *The End of History and the Last Man*, London: Hamish Hamilton.

Garon, S. (1997), *Molding Japanese Minds*, Princeton: Princeton University Press.

Gibney, F. (1999), Nissan calls for a Tow, in: *Time Magazine* March 15th 1999.

Halberstam, D. (1986), *The Reckoning*, London: Bantam Books.

Hopper, K. (1982), Creating Japan's new Industrial Management: the Americans as Teachers, in: *Human Resource Management*, Summer 1982: 13-33.

Horsley, W. & Buckley, R. (1990), *Nippon: New Superpower*. London: B.B.C.

Huber, T.M. (1994), *Strategic Economy in Japan.* Boulder, Colo.: Westview Press.

Ikari, S. (1991), American Know-how and the Miracle, in: *Japan Update*, October 1991: 18-19.

Johnson, C. (1982), *MITI and the Japanese Miracle,* Tokyo: Tuttle.

Johnson, C. (1995), *Japan: Who Governs? The Rise of the Developmental State*, New York: Norton.

Koh, B.C. (1989), *Japan's Administrative Elite,* Berkeley: University of California Press.

Krause, D.G. (ed.) (1995), *Sun Tzu: the Art of War for Executives,* London: Brealey.

Krugman, P. (2000), The Japan Syndrome, in: *New York Times*, February 9th 2000.

Ministry of International Trade and Industry (Annual), *Small Business in Japan,* Tokyo: MITI, Small and Medium Enterprise Agency.

Moorhouse, J. (1986), *Report on Trade and Economic Relations between the EC and Japan,* European Parliament Working Documents A 2-86/86. PE 101.033. July 1986.

Moorhouse J. & Teasdale, A. (1987), *Righting the Balance: a New Agenda for Euro-Japanese Trade,* London: Conservative Political Centre.

Ohmae, K. (1987), *Beyond National Borders,* Tokyo: Kodansha.

Prestowitz, C.V. (1988), *Trading Places,* Tokyo: Tuttle.

Pyle, K.B. (1996), *The Making of Modern Japan,* Lexington, Mass.: D.C. Heath.

Rothacher, A. (1993), *The Japanese Power Elite,* London: Macmillan.

Sakakibara, E. (1993), *Beyond Capitalism,* Lanham, Md.: University Press of America.

Sakakibara, E. (1997), The Once and Future Boom, in: *The Economist*, March 22nd 1997.

Samuelson, R.J. (2000), Japan's harsh Reality Check, in: *Newsweek*, January 10th 2000.

Thomas, R. (1989), *Japan: the Blighted Blossom,* London: I.B.Tauris.

van Marion, M.F. (1993), *Liberal Trade and Japan: the Incompatibility Issue*, Heidelberg: Springer.

van Wolferen, K. (1993), *The Enigma of Japanese Power,* Tokyo: Tuttle.

Williams, D. (1994), *Japan: Beyond the End of History,* London: Routledge.

Wood, R.C. (1989), A Lesson learned and a Lesson forgotten, in: *Forbes Magazine*, February 6th 1989.

PART ONE: THE INTERNAL PREPARATIONS

THE ECONOMY: TOWARDS THE MARKET PRINCIPLE?

The Government-Industry Relationship in Japan: What the History of the Electric Power Industry Teaches Us

Takeo Kikkawa

1 Introduction

In 1998-1999 winter semester the author of this paper had a chance to teach Japanese Economy and Management at the Ostasiatisches Seminar of Freie Universität Berlin. As deregulation was a hot topic at that time, some students in the class wanted to know the real state of the relationship between government and industry in Japan. The purpose of this paper is to answer their questions to a certain extent.

This paper will examine the government-industry relationship in Japan by reviewing the history of the electric power industry. Japan's electric power industry has basically been under private ownership and management, and kept autonomous from the government.

By contrast, the telecommunication business in Japan had been wholly owned and controlled by the government until recently. The petroleum industry, which belongs to the private sector, has been on the other hand subject to strong government intervention. This paper, focusing on Japan's electric power industry, will concern itself with a comparison of the electric power industry with the telecommunication business in the first half and with the petroleum industry in the latter half.

2 Nationalization or Privatization: Comparison with the Telecommunications Business

2.1 Overview

This section will examine how the privatization of public utilities relevant to electricity developed in Japan through making a comparison of two industries, i. e. the electric power industry and the telecommunications business. The two industries were governed under the same government agency, the Ministry of Communications, before Second World War; however, there was a remarkable contrast between them in respect to the enterprise forms. Japan's electric power industry has basically been under private ownership and management except for a period of state management before and after Second World War. By contrast, the telecommunications business in Japan had been wholly owned and controlled by the government until the privatization of 1985. This section attemots to make clear the reasons for the differences between the two industries.

It was 1883 when Tokyo Electric Light, the first electric power company in Japan, was established. Thereafter, Japan's electric power industry has gone through the following five periods (Kikkawa 1995):

1) the period of independent urban electric light companies based on thermal generation (from 1883 to 1906),
2) the period of competition by regional electric power companies based on waterpower generation (from 1907-1931),
3) the period of cooperation after the establishment of a cartel organization, the League of Electric Power Companies, in 1932 (from 1932 to 1938),
4) the period of state management before and after Second World War (from 1939 to 1950) and
5) the period of the privately managed, regionally integrated nine big companies, which monopolized electric power service (from 1951 till now).[1]

This new postwar system started through the reorganization of the industry during the occupation era. After 1960, the nine companies changed their main power sources from waterpower to thermal generation.

As stated above, only in the period from 1939 to 1950 Japan's electric power industry was controlled by the government. During the other four periods, however, private enterprises have played major roles in the industry.

In Japan the telegraph business began in 1869, and the telephone business started in 1890. From the viewpoint of enterprise forms the history of Japan's telecommunications business consists of the following three periods:

1) the period of direct management by the government (from 1869 to 1951),
2) the period of a public corporation, Nippon Denshin Denwa Kosha (Nippon Telegraph and Telephone Corporation, NTT), which was wholly financed by the government (from 1952 to 1984) and

---

1 Since the late 1990s deregulation of the electric power industry has been progressing step by step in Japan.

3) the period of competition after the privatization of NTT in 1985 (from 1985 till now).

Consequently, it may be safely said that Japan's telecommunications business has been owned and controlled by the government until quite recently. On the part of the government, the Ministry of Communications, which was established in 1885, managed the telecommunications business directly for most of the entire pre-war period.

This Ministry was also the competent authority over the electric power industry but did not manage the industry by itself until 1939, the eve of Second World War.

The following section, then, mainly examines the reasons for the difference of enterprise forms between Japan's electric power industry and the telecommunications business. There are four phases, which should be analyzed separately: The Meiji era, the eve of Second World War, the occupation period, and the 1980s.

2.2 Difference of Policies in the Early Years

Policies concerning the two industries, electric power and telecommunications, differed considerably in the early years. During the Meiji era the government consistently attached more importance to the telecommunications business than to the electric power industry.

Immediately after the Meiji Restoration of 1868, the government took the initiative in establishing a telegraph network all over the country. Early in 1869, public telegraph business started between Tokyo and Yokohama, and by 1877, telegraph lines were running all across the Japan Islands.

There were two reasons why the government made much of the telegraph business. Firstly, the general opinion is that the government recognized the importance of telegraphy from the viewpoint of public order and military affairs: Communication through telegraph lines helped the government to win the civil war of 1877 which was one of the most serious political crises in the Meiji era. Secondly, the government feared foreign companies would enter the Japanese telegraph business. In those days, Great Northern Extension China and Japan Telegraph Co. of Denmark and Great Eastern Extension Australia and China Telegraph Co. of the United Kingdom watched for chances to enter the Japanese market.

Therefore, the Meiji government decided from the start to monopolize the telegraph business and to manage it directly. Even under the deflation policy in the 1890s, which privatized many state-operated factories and mines, government management of the telegraph business was not changed in the least.

In the meantime, at the beginning of Japan's telephone business in 1890, there was a severe controversy over its enterprise form. Some parts of the government advocated private management for financial reasons.[2]

But the Ministry of Communications, which was the competent authority over the telephone business, maintained state operation for the following three reasons. Firstly, private companies could not raise the necessarily enormous funds. Secondly, government management would maintain the secrecy of the military authorities, government offices, and the police. Finally, state operation would also make it easy to exercise strict control over telephone calls disturbing public order.

Ultimately, the opinion of the Ministry of Communications won a triumphant victory. The government decided to manage the telephone business directly in the same way as the telegraph business.

By contrast, the Japanese government was generally unconcerned about the electric power industry during the Meiji era. Factly, the policy for the industry was limited to the preservation of safety. The government gave telegraph and telephone lines priority over electric power lines in those days. Concrete reasons why the government virtually ignored the electric power industry during the Meiji era were as follows. Firstly, the government was not able to foresee the future development of the industry. Secondly, at that time the electric power network was technically restricted to individual urban communities and did not encompass the whole country.[3] Finally, no foreign companies planned to enter Japan's electric power industry.

In contrast to the case of telecommunications, the government did not set up a policy to manage the electric power industry directly in the early years. The Ministry of Communications just supervised the industry indirectly. Therefore, Japan's electric power industry was managed by private companies in the main and by the municipal authorities in part until 1938.

2.3 Influence of the War Structure

In 1938, the Japanese economy had changed into a wartime one. In Japan's war setting the government intervened in almost all main industries. A typical case of intervention was the placement of the electric power industry under state management by the Electric Power Control Law of 1938 which was implemented

---

2 It was thought that providing funds for the telephone business would worsen government finances. Construction of a telephone network was expected to cost much more than construction of the telegraph network.

3 In pre-war Japan some cities and prefectures managed the electric power business directly. However, as the electric power network spread, the role of the municipal authorities in the electric power industry decreased.

with the establishment of Nippon Electric Generation and Transmission Co. in 1939 and that of nine regional electric distribution companies in 1942.

Here we cannot fail to notice that managers of privately operated electric power companies voiced exceptionally strong opposition against the state management. They asserted that private management was more efficient than the state control, and that the role of the government ought to be limited to supervising the electric power industry indirectly.

The opinion leader of the opposition group against the state management was Yasuzaemon Matsunaga, who was the president of Toho Electric Power Co., one of the five major electric power companies in pre-war Japan. Early in 1928 Matsunaga advocated a reorganization plan for Japan's electric power industry, which was called "Denryoku Tôsei Shiken" (A Personal View on Regulating the Electric Power Industry) and consisted of the following four main points (Matsunaga 1964):

1) to establish nine regionally divided companies, which monopolized electric service in each region,
2) to merge wholesalers and retailers; in other words, to integrate power generation, transmission, and distribution,
3) to maintain private management and
4) to establish a Public Utilities Commission in order to supervise the electric power industry.

At the time Matsunaga advocated his "Denryoku Tôsei Shiken" few of the other managers in the industry could fathom the significance of his grand design.[4] Thus, in pre-war Japan Matsunaga's plan had not yet been put into effect. As Matsunaga himself recalled, however, when Japan's electric power industry was reorganized in 1951 (Kikkawa 1993a, 1993b), his ideas were adopted almost completely. That is to say, "Denryoku Tôsei Shiken" was a historical document, perceiving the post-war reorganization of the industry twenty-three years before it occurred.

Matsunaga thoroughly resisted the government management of the electric power industry since 1939, which denied private operation and integration. However, owing to a rise of totalitarism under the wartime economy, his opposition had no effect. Ultimately, privately managed electric power companies in Japan were obliged to dissolve by 1942.

Meanwhile, Japan's telecommunications business had continuously been under the government management during the Second World War.

4 On the role of Matsunaga concerning the regulation of the electric power industry in pre-war Japan see Kikkawa (1986).

2.4 Changes under the Occupation

Japan was under the control of GHQ/SCAP (General Headquarters/ Supreme Commander for Allied Powers) from 1945 until 1952. During the occupation period the electric power industry was fundamentally reorganized from state control to private management in 1951, while on the other hand the telecommunications business changed only slightly from direct operation by the government to management by the public corporation, NTT, in 1952.[5]

In the electric power industry, as a result of a severe controversy, Nippon Electric Generation and Transmission Co. and the nine electric distribution companies were dissolved in 1951, and the government management of the industry came to an end. In its place nine regionally divided and privately operated electric power companies were constituted in May of the same year.

The post-war system of Japan's electric power industry is different from those in European countries because private management is prevalent, and also from the American counterpart on the grounds that privately managed companies are gigantic there (McCraw 1986:11-12, Vietor 1986:196).

The nine privately operated electric power companies were established in 1951 and integrate power generation, transmission, and distribution, and monopolize electric service in their respective region. Parallel to them the Public Utilities Commission was founded in 1950 for the purpose of supervising the industry[6]. Therefore, it is not too much to say that the reorganization of the electric power industry of 1950-1951 really put into practice Matsunaga's "Denryoku Tôsei Shiken" of 1928. Matsunaga actually played the leading part in the process of the reorganization as the chairman of the Council for the Reorganization of the Electric Power Industry in 1949-1950, and as the acting chairman of the Public Utilities Commission in 1950-1952.

On the other hand GHQ/SCAP was limited to the role of a supporting actor. For example, after some differences GHQ finally complied with the opinion of Matsunaga on how to establish regionally divided electric power companies.[7]

As stated up to here, it was the ex-managers of pre-war electric power companies like Matsunaga, who had managerial capability based on experience of private management, that enabled the privatization of the electric industry in 1951. In this

---

5 Strictly speaking, NTT was established three months after the end of the occupation.

6 The Public Utilities Commission was abolished in 1952. Since then the Ministry of International Trade and Industry (MITI) has been the supervising authority over the electric power industry until now. Incidentally, the Ministry of Communications was dissolved in 1949.

7 GHQ originally envisioned a plan for seven or ten companies, but ultimately accepted Matsunaga's plan for nine companies.

case, the experience of private management was of importance to a considerable degree.

During the occupation period, privatization of the telecommunications business was also examined. In the case of Japan, however, there was no experience of private management at all. Ultimately, this brought privatization of the telecommunications business to dead halt, and the change was confined to a trifling one. That is, instead of the direct management by the government, a public corporation, NTT, was established in 1952.

2.5 Deregulation in the 1980s

The international wave of privatization in the 1980s reached Japan too. In the middle of the decade Nippon Telegraph and Telephone (NTT), Japan National Railways (JNR), and Japan Monopoly Corporation (JMC) were privatized one after another.

The privatization of NTT in 1985 was combined with the introduction of competition to Japan's telecommunications business with the aim of increasing efficiency and improving service.

Japan's electric power industry has consistently been under private management since 1951. Accordingly, the reorganization of the industry more than thirty years ago was thought of as a model for the privatization of NTT, JNR, and JMC.

2.6 Summary

Throughout its one hundred and eighteen year history, Japan's electric power industry has basically been under private management except for the wartime state control from 1939 to 1951. On the contrary, Japan's telecommunications business had been owned and controlled by the government until quite recently. There were two reasons for the different enterprise forms of the electric power industry and the telecommunications business.

The first reason is the difference of policies in the early years. The Meiji government regarded the telecommunications business to be of grat importance from the viewpoint of public order and military affairs. By contrast, it was not concerned with the electric power industry at all. Therefore, from the beginning the telecommunications business was nationalized, while the electric power industry was left under private management.

Secondly, managerial capability increased steadily in privately managed electric power companies. Yasuzaemon Matsunaga's "Denryoku Tôsei Shiken" of 1928 was definitic proof of this fact. This managerial capability was a crucial factor in the early abolishment of the wartime state management of the electric power industry in 1951. However, in the case of telecommunications business, due to the lack of such capability privatization had to be delayed more than thirty years.

3 Government Intervention or Autonomy: Comparison with the Petroleum Industry

3.1 Overview

One may assert that the private management of Japan's electric power industry should be considered as state control in disguise as it ows its existence to a public utility law, the Electric Power Industry Law, which regulates the industry. This kind of assertion, however, is not correct, because it ignores the following two points.

Firstly, through the wholesale revision of 1931, the Electric Power Industry Law became fully characterized as a law governing a public utility industry. Although the enacting of the Electric Power Industry Law dates back to 1911, there had been no full-scale public regulation to Japan's electric power industry before 1931. Actually until 1931, the power companies were severely competing with each other.

Secondly, even after 1931, it was possible for the industry to keep its autonomy from government intervention. In the case of Japan's electric power industry, this possibility was realized during periods of 1931-1938 and 1951-1973.

This section will focus on the second point. The purpose of Section 3 is to examine the role of the government by asking the following question: What sort of circumstances was conducive to government intervention in a specified industry?

3.2 Two Sets of Laws

For answering the above question it is useful to compare the role of the government defined under two sets of laws, the old (prewar) Electric Power Industry Law and ist new (postwar) version on the one hand, and the old (prewar) Petroleum Industry Law and its new (postwar) version on the other hand.

The two sets of laws have at least three features in common:

1) they were all meant to deal with energy- or public-utility related industries, and had clauses binding the industries' activities from the standpoint of the public interest,

2) they were all meant for application to specific industries and

3) both sets were established almost simultaneously, with the 1931 revision of the old Electric Power Industry Law followed closely by the enacting in 1934 of the old Petroleum Industry Law, and with the new Petroleum Industry Law of 1962 followed by the new Electric Power Industry Law of 1964.

In their conception of the government's role, however, the two sets of laws are in striking contrast.

The 1931 revision of the old Electric Power Industry Law[8] was in part characterized by stepped-up government control, exemplified by the institutionalization of a procedure for government approval of electricity charges. However, the idea of nationalizing the firms supplying electric power and the idea of placing these firms under joint government-private control were abandoned during the deliberations. The revised law firmly upheld the principle of leaving the task of intra-industry coordination to the industry itself, which was dominated by private companies, while the government had only indirect and limited functions to fulfil.

The Electric Power Industry Law of 1964 gave legal confirmation to the prevailing situation of the industry being regionally divided up by nine private companies. The new law simply honored the principles established through the 1951 reorganization of the electric power industry, which terminated the government control over power supply.[9]

In contrast, the enacting of the old Petroleum Industry Law of 1934, which placed the oil refining and distributing industry under strong government control, was a landmark in the history of the industry. Typical examples of the government intervention under this law included a quota system for the sale of petroleum products and a system of placing oil refiners and importers under obligation to maintain stocks of oil against emergencies.

The new Petroleum Industry Law of 1962 was designed to allow the government to continue intervening in the industry. It gave the government much leverage, including the authority to approve oil refining companies' proposals for building or expanding facilities, the authority to take steps to readjust the industry's output, and the authority to set the standard price. As such, the new law governing the oil refining industry's operations proved to be a "powerful instrument of

---

8 As mentioned before, the enacting of the original Electric Power Industry Law dates back to 1911. It was, however, through revision of this law in 1931 that it became a law governing a public utility industry. This is why we are discussing here not original law of 1911, but its revised version of 1931.

9 As mentioned before, the electric power industry in Japan, which had been basically in the hands of private-sector operators since its inception in 1883, was placed under government control in 1939 as part of the wartime economic control, and remained in that situation until 1951.

administrative intervention in business activities of private firms in a specific industry" (Nihon Sekiyu Kabushikigaisha 1988:639).

3.3 When the Government Intervenes

Table 1 summarizes the characteristics of the four laws regulating the electric power and oil refining and distributing industries, and also the features of the deliberation processes leading to their enactment.

Table 1: Patterns of Regulating Laws in the Electric Power and Petroleum Industries

	Electric Power Industry Law		Petroleum Industry Law	
	1931	1964	1934	1962
additional leverage for government **intervention**	–	–	+	+
industry-led **deliberation** process	+	+	–	–

Source: Own Analysis.

A glance at the table reveals the following pattern: when the industry proved competent to regulate itself or to conduct necessary intra-industry coordination, and thus took the initiative in the deliberations leading to the enacting of the law, the resulting law restricted government interference. When, on the other hand, the industry failed to demonstrate self-regulating or coordinating capability, and thus was hardly involved actively and effectively in the deliberations on the proposed law, the enacted law placed in the government's hand greater leverage for intervention.

Let us first look at the role which the government was expected to perform under these laws. The role assigned to the government by the two laws on the electric power industry and that assigned by the two laws on the petroleum refining and distributing industry were different. Both the revision of the old Electric Power Industry Law of 1931 and the new Electric Power Industry Law of 1964 basically restrained government intervention in the industry. By contrast, both the old Petroleum Industry Law of 1934 and the new Petroleum Industry Law of 1962 were characterized by stepped-up government intervention.

This stark contrast in the government role envisioned by these different sets of laws calls into serious question the conventional arguments about the government-industry relationship in Japan.

There are two opposing views about the government's role in Japan: one is unreservedly acknowledging its importance, and the other is almost totally denying it. However, from our observations about the different roles assigned to the government by the two sets of laws, it is clear that both views are one-sided. The former view is contradicted by the laws on the electric power supply industry which restrain government intervention, while the latter view fails to hold water in the face of the laws on the petroleum refining and distributing industry which provide for active government intervention.

What sort of alternative and viable approach to the study of the government-industry relationship can we take, if the conventional approaches are found wanting? Our answer is that it will be far more appropriate to focus on the self-regulating or self-readjusting capacity of the industry itself as the primarily important factor. The government's role should be regarded as secondary, supplementing this capacity when it is found deficient. Unlike the conventional approaches which are preoccupied with the presence or absence of government intervention, our proposed approach pays attention to the presence or absence of the industry's self-regulating or self-readjusting capability.

The electric power industry played an active role in the deliberations both for the 1931 revision of the old Electric Power Industry Law and for the enactment of the new Electric Power Industry Law of 1964. This statement may invite the argument that the power industry, made up of regional monopolies as it is now, should have little difficulties in organizing intra-industry coordination. It should be kept in mind, however, that when the 1931 revision of the old law was under deliberations, the regional monopolies as we know them today had not yet been established, and the power companies were competing fiercely with each other in the so called "Electric Power War". It was in spite of such cutthroat competition that the industry performed its coordinating function. Epitomizing the industry initiative is the publication, in 1928, of "Denryoku Tôsei Shiken" by Yasuzaemon Matsunaga. His policy proposal foreshadowed the major features of the postwar reorganization of the power industry.

During the deliberations on the new law of 1964 – which took place after the regional monopoly system had been established – the electric power industry dared to defy objections raised by the Ministry of International Trade and Industry (MITI), the government office having jurisdiction over its operations, and carried out its own rationalization plans. These plans included proposals to switch its technology of power generation from a hydraulic-based one to thermal-based one and to replace coal by petroleum as the main fuel for thermal power generation. The demonstration of its ability to keep its internal affairs in order and put through its rationalization plans on its own proved to be an important force for the enactment of the new law, which legally confirmed the dividing up of the industry among the nine private-sector operators with their designated service districts.[10]

Unlike the electric power industry, the oil refining and distributing industry did not speak with on voice during the delibarations of either the old Petroleum Industry Law of 1934 or the new law of 1962. On both occasions, some firms of the industry saw the stepping up of government regulations as a convenient means of containing rivals. In particular, locally owned companies looked forward to the enactment of the old law as a chance to contain their foreign competitors, while foreign affiliates looked forward to the enactment of the new law as a chance to stop Idemitsu Kosan, a rapidly growing local firm. The companies, which tried to use these laws in their own interests, however, had to acknowledge some clauses detrimental to their own interests.[11]

Having thus demonstrated its lack of self-regulating or self-readjusting capability, the oil refining and distributing industry subjected itself to stronger government regulations under both the old and new Petroleum Industry Laws.

3.4 Summary

A comparison of the two sets of laws of the electric power industry and the petroleum industry gives us an important insight into the role performed of the government vis-à-vis industry. The greater the ability of an industry to organize itself and coordinate its member firms, the less frequently and less heavily government intervenes. On the other hand, the less it has this ability, the more frequent and heavier the government's intervention is likely to be. This kind of relationship between an industry's self-regulating or self-adjusting capability and government interference in its affairs, which has been borne out by our case studies on the electric power and petroleum industries, can be expected to be observed in many other industries as well.

---

10 It should be kept in mind, however, that the self-regulating capability of the electric power industry in the 1930s had its limitations, as is evident from the fact that Matsunaga's proposals had to wait a few more decades before being fully realized. The industry's limited capability is a factor in explaining why the electric power industry was forcibly brought under the government control in 1939, despite fierce objections raised by the industry.

11 For instances, the old Petroleum Industry Law's obligation that oil refiners and distributors have to maintain stocks of oil against emergencies put local refiners at a great disadvantage, while the new postwar law restricted foreign affiliates in their plans to build or expand facilities.

4 Concluding Remarks

In Japan, the electric power industry was fundamentally reorganized in 1951 from state control to private management. By contrast, "in early post-war Europe, demands to nationalize industry and the energy sector gained strong support in many countries. France and Britain, in fact, nationalized their electricity supply industry between 1946 and 1948" (Myllyntaus 1991: 110).

This paper explained why Japan's electric power industry headed for the opposite direction than its European counterpart during the period just after the Second World War. In Japan's privately managed electric power companies managerial capability had increased. Yasuzaemon Matsunaga's "Denryoku Tôsei Shiken" of 1928 definitely proved it. This managerial capability made it possible to abolish the wartime state management of Japan's electric power industry as early as in 1951.

Generally speaking, the greater the ability of an industry organize itself and coordinate its member firms, the less frequently and less heavily it is likely to be intervened in by the government; and the less it has this ability, the more frequent and heavier the government's intervention is likely to be. In Japan, the electric power industry stand for the former, and the telecommunications business and the petroleum industry for the latter type of industry.

References

Kikkawa, T. (1986), Management and Regulation of the Electric Power Industry: 1923-1935, in: *Japanese Yearbook on Business History*, Vol. 3, Tokyo: Japan Business History Institute.

Kikkawa, T. (1993a), On the Reorganization of Japan's Electric Power Industry in 1951, in: *Aoyama Keiei Ronshu* [Aoyama Journal of Business], 28, 2, Tokyo.

Kikkawa, T. (1993b), La réorganisation de l'industrie électrique au Japon en 1951, in: *Bulletin d'histoire électricité*, 22, Paris.

Kikkawa, T. (1995), *Nippon Denryokugyo no Hatten to Matsunaga Yasuzaemon* [The Development of Japan's Electric Power Industry and Yasuzaemon Matsunaga], Nagoya: Nagoya University Press.

Matsunaga, Y. (1964), Watashi no Rirekisho [My Life Story], in: *Nippon Keizai Shinbun*, January 28th, 1964.

McCraw, T. K. (1986), From Partners to Competitors, in: T. K. McCraw (ed.), *America Versus Japan*, Boston: Harvard Business School Press.

Myllyntaus, T. (1991), *Electrifying Finland*, London: Macmillan Press.

Nippon Sekiyu Kabushikigaisha (1988), *Nippon Sekiyu Hyakunenshi* [One Hundred Year History of Nippon Oil Co.], Tokyo.

Vietor, R. H. K. (1986), Energy Markets and Policy, in: T. K. McCraw (ed.), *America Versus Japan*, Boston: Harvard Business School Press.

Buyer-Seller Interaction and Relationship Development in the Japanese Business Market

Sam Dzever

1 Introduction

The present study analyzes the nature of buyer-seller interaction and relationship development in the Japanese business market. Its objective is to contribute to enhancing knowledge about buyers' decision process and supplier relationship development with regard to raw materials, equipment, and component parts. The following factors are central in the study: the decisive factors in the selection of a supplier and development of long-term buyer-seller interactions and relationships; the role of intermediaries (trading companies, manufacturer's representatives, and marketing agents) in the development of these interactions and relationships; and the effects of environmental factors (culture, market structure, and government industrial policy) on the purchase decision process of buyers and the development of these interactions and relationships. These issues relate particularly to what Robinson, Faris & Wind (1967) have referred to in their well-known *buygrid* model of organizational buyer behavior as *new task* purchasing situation. The study has important managerial implications in the sense that it provides foreign suppliers of industrial products with the basis for developing appropriate market entry and growth strategies in this highly competitive environment. The paper is divided into seven sections as follows: 1 introduction, 2 review of the literature, 3 objective of the study , 4 research methodology, 5 hypotheses , 6 the findings and 7 conclusion and direction for future research.

2 Review of the Literature

The study of purchase decision-making and buyer-seller relationship development occupies an important place in business-to-business marketing literature. A number of variables have been selected which constitute the basis of such studies. These are generally grouped in accordance with whether they relate to the vendor, the product, or the purchasing organization. Vendor's variables have generally included: dependability, service, technical ability, financial strength, geographic location, and reciprocity history (Dickson 1966, Hill 1972, Webster & Wind: 1972, Hill et al. 1975, Corey 1976, Dzever 1993, 1996). Product variables include:

price, quality, and purchase class (i.e. *new task, modified rebuy*, and *straight rebuy*). Research in this area has included the work of Robinson, Faris & Wind (1967), Lehman & O'Shaunghnessy (1974), Dzever (1993, 1996), Dzever & Quester (1999), Chetty, Dzever & Quester (1999). Purchasing organization variables often cited include: Size and formality of decision-making, motives, type of choice process, risk preference or avoidance, past experience with vendor (Webster & Wind 1972, Sweeney et al. 1973, Hill et al. 1975, Baker 1983, 1985). With increasing globalization of economies more recent studies have also included variables such as culture (Carter & Narasimhan 1990, Chang & Ding 1995, Deng & Wortzel 1995, Dzever 1997, Dzever & Zhengyi 1999).

Research has in recent years also focused on better understanding the impact of buyer-seller relationships on the purchase decision process of organizational buyers. The IMP Group (International Marketing and Purchasing Group) developed an interaction methodology (Håkansson 1982) that has since brought to bear a new perspective of studying these issues from an empirical point of view. The approach, based on data from several European firms, was regarded as revolutionary since, for the first time, it was understood that buyers value, to a great extent, the nature of relationships they develop with suppliers. Suppliers were no longer seen simply in terms of sellers of products but rather as partners in business since it was only through this partnership purchasers could achieve their goal of developing products with the best quality standards while at the same time ensuring customer satisfaction. Buyer-seller interaction and relationships became thus one of the most important determinants of supplier selection.

Attempts have also been made to model organizational buyer behavior based on the knowledge of purchase decision process and supplier selection criteria for both new and replacement products. Dzever (1996) has identified three main approaches in the literature as: marketing as exchange, organizational buyer behavior, and interaction perspective. Of these, four groups of models have been further identified within the organizational buyer behavior approach as: task-oriented, non-task oriented, decision process, and complex models (Moriarty 1983, Webster & Wind 1972, Robinson, Faris & Wind 1967). Task-oriented models are, in general, concerned with situation specific factors associated with a particular purchase, while the non-task ones are, in general, based on risk perceptions or on the notion of diffusion of innovation (Bauer 1960, Zaltman et al. 1973). Decision process models are generally concerned with a description and analysis of the decision process involved in organizational purchasing. Robinson, Faris & Wind (1967) further modified these processes in their well known *buygrid* model. The *buygrid* model was further expanded upon by Baker (1983, 1985) in his "composite model" of buyer behavior. Complex models of organizational purchasing and buyer behavior vary greatly from being highly conceptual to emphasizing operationalization. Among the most frequently quoted in the literature are the following: Robinson, Faris & Wind (1967), Webster & Wind

(1972), Sheth (1973), Bonoma et al. (1977), Choffrey & Lilien (1978), and Anderson et al. (1987).

Perhaps one of the main shortcomings of a great number of the models reviewed here is their general inability to sufficiently address the problem of organizational purchasing from an interactive perspective. Apart from the IMP Group model, nearly all of the models reviewed assume that interaction with potential vendors have no significant bearing on buyers' decision process and supplier selection. This is rather important particularly in light of the fact that it is today generally acknowledged that organizational purchasing is a complex and multidimensional activity encompassing many factors, a significant number of which cannot be fully comprehended without a careful consideration of the nature of interaction and relationship development between buyers and sellers in the business market. In the present paper we argue that this fact is one of the most central determinant factors in supplier selection.

Purchase decision process of organizational buyers has become increasingly complex as the traditional role of the purchasing executive has significantly changed during the past few years as organizations increasingly globalize their sourcing activities. Because of this, purchase decisions of buyers have become increasingly more complex, multidimensional, and multifunctional involving not only members of the purchasing organization's DMU (Decision Making Unit) but a host of other important players on a global basis. These include intermediaries (trading companies, independent purchasing agents, manufacturer's representatives, marketing agents, and consultants). Such intermediaries are often very familiar with decision routines of both the purchasing and the supplying organizations and very often facilitate in developing long-term close interactive relationships between the two. It is thus clear that models of organizational purchasing and buyer behavior can no longer ignore this important fact.

Dzever (1996) has proposed an empirical model that helps explain the most important factors influencing the decision process of organizational buyers. The model, together with the IMP Group's interaction model, constitute the theoretical basis for the present paper. Several factors have been identified in the empirical model which are said to impact the decisions of organizational buyers. These factors, which are both of a firm-specific nature as well as environmentally determined, include the following: the composition and functional specialization of the members of the DMU, patterns of buyer-seller interaction and relationships, the role of intermediaries in the decision process, and the influence of environmental factors such as market structure, technology, economic, and culture on the decision process. Moreover, decisions are influenced by three dimensions of organizational buyer behavior identified as technical, commercial, and social (Dadfar 1990, Dzever 1996). By having a correct understanding of these factors one can fully appreciate the decision process of organizational buyers in a global sourcing environment.

3 Objective of the Study

Little is know about the nature of purchase decision making and buyer-seller relationship development of organizational buyers in the Japanese market. Although earlier writers (Campbell 1986) have suggested that Japanese marketing is largely interactive and relational in character this question has yet to be sufficiently addressed empirically within the context of business-to-business marketing. The objective of the present study therefore is to attempt to fill this gap. More precisely, we wish to contribute to enhancing knowledge about the factors organizational buyers in this market consider central in their purchase decision process and the development of long-term business relationships with foreign suppliers.

The study has important implications for foreign suppliers of various types of industrial products whose strategy is to enter and maintain a viable competitive presence in this marketplace.

4 Research Methodology

As indicated earlier the theoretical framework upon which the study is based is derived from the IMP Group's conceptual model of buyer-seller interaction and relationship development in the industrial market (Håkansson 1982), as well as Dzever's empirical model of purchase decision process and buyer-seller relationships developed (Dzever 1993, 1996). As earlier mentioned, the model identifies company-specific problems in the decision process as well as environmentally determined ones. The company-specific problems include the nature of decision process of the interacting parties (i.e. the buying and the selling firms), the role functional units within the interacting organizations play in their decision process, the role various executives of the interacting parties play at different stages of the decision process (these have been referred to respectively in the model as purchasing and marketing decision process), and how these factors together affect the outcome of the final decision. The company-specific determinants of decision-making also include issues such as the role of intermediaries (e.g. trading companies, marketing agents, manufacturer's representatives, etc.) in the decision process, as well as patterns of buyer-seller interaction and relationship development of the interacting parties. The impact of environmental factors in the decision process include the role which economic, technological, cultural, and market structure factors play in the decision process of the interacting parties. Both firm-specific and environmental factors referred to in the model relate particularly to *new task* purchasing situations (Robinson, Faris & Wind 1967). The decision process of the interacting parties can be seen as eminating from three hierarchical levels of the organizational structure identified as strategic, managerial, and operative. The model emphasizes, however, that this hierarchical structure in the decision process should be regarded as rather artificial since although the executives making the decisions are drawn from different levels of the organizational structure they speak with one voice and their final decision is always a unanimous endeavor. In addition to these factors, the model also proposes three dimensions of organizational buying behavior identified as technical, commercial, and social dimensions. The general assumptions of these dimensions are in line with the postulations of Dadfar (1990) who suggests that we can better understand the behavior of organizational buyers if we studied it in relations to these dimensions.

Data collection procedure for the study was based on an integrated research approach known as *triangulation methodology* first proposed by Jick (1979), Reichart & Cook (1979), Johnston & Spekman (1982), and Deshpande (1983). Data was collected through the use of a structured mail questionnaire, in-depth face-to-face interviews, and analysis of secondary material obtained from the respondent organizations, trade and employer organizations, as well as governmental sources. The structured questionnaire was sent to a selection of one hundred organizations (of all sizes) in Japan that were known to regularly purchase materials, component parts, and equipment from foreign suppliers (the list of the respondents was compiled from several trade directories in Japan and Scandinavia). A corresponding questionnaire was sent to an equivalent number of Scandinavian organizations that were known to be active in the Japanese business market. Usable responses were received from 40 of the purchasing organizations and 40 suppliers. An analysis of the published materials in both Japan and Scandinavia (Norway and Sweden) reduced the number of respondent firms participating in the indept face-to-face interviews to 30 organizations (i.e. 15 purchasing organizations and 15 suppliers) distributed as follows:

Purchasing organizations:

> 1 Hi-Silicon Company Limited, 2 Eisai Company Limited, 3 NKK Corporation, 4 Shin-Etsu Chemical Company Limited, 5 Matsushita Electric Industrial Company Limited, 6 Hitachi Zosen Corporation, 7 Mazda Motor Corporation, 8 Mitsubishi Kasei Corporation, 9 Ishikawajima-Harima Heavy Industries Company Limited (IHI), 10 KAO Corporation, 11 Kokushin Company Limited, 12 Mitsui Toatsu Chemicals, Inc., 13 Catalysts and Chemicals Inc., Far East, 14 Asahi Glass Company Limited, 15. Jujo Paper Company Limited.

Supplying organizations:

> 1 Elkem International A/S, 2 Elkem Japan KK, 3 Raufoss A/S, 4 Fesil Group, 5 Nycomed Pharma A/S, 6 Kvaerner Eureka A/S, 7 Unitor Ship Services A/S, 8 Borregaard Lignotech A/S, 9 Aker Stord International A/S, 10 Mascot Electronic A/S, 11 Norcontrol A/S, 12 Norsk Hydro A/S, 13 Kamyr KK, 14 Haag A/S, 15 Asea A/S (Later ABB Limited).

Individual respondents to the in-dept personal interviews were selected on the basis of the answers they provided in the structured mail questionnaire. The participating executives were interviewed individually or as a group. In the mail questionnaire, respondents were asked to indicate if they would be willing to meet with the researcher for two face-to-face interviews each lasting approximately one and a half hours. It was explained that this would provide respondents with the opportunity of elaborating on some of the answers they provided in the structured questionnaire. The findings outlined in tables 1 through 3 are thus based on the three procedures of data collection in the triangulation methodology (i.e. structured mail questionnaire, document analysis, and in-depth face-to-face interviews).

Based on the material received from the structured mail questionnaire as well as document analysis, a semi-structured interview guide was developed and used as the basis for the face-to-face interviews with the selected group of respondents. Two interview sessions (each lasting 1.5 hours) were undertaken with each of the respondent organizations. All interviews were recorded on tape. In addition to the factors listed earlier, the interviews also dealt with the following:

- the structure of the respondent organization,
- its principal products, principal markets, and market development strategies,
- its most recent industrial purchases,
- the nature of its purchase decision process and
- the nature of buyer-seller relationship development criteria.

These factors provide the basis for developing purchase decision typologies which represent: 1. need recognition (for a product to be purchased), 2. purchase decision process of the buying organization, and 3. buyer-seller interaction and relationships for materials, component parts, and equipment purchasing. (For the purpose of space these typologies and a detailed explanation of their validity within the broader context of organizational buyer behavior literature have been excluded in the present paper).

Interviewees in the respondent organizations held the following executive positions: director of international operations, purchasing director, marketing director, director of production, divisional head, sectional head and other executives. As indicated earlier, 90 managers participated in the face-to-face interviews.

5 Hypotheses

Based on the preceding problem definition, study objective, review of the literature, and research methodology, the following hypotheses were developed as the basis for the study:

H1: Technical and commercial factors play an equally important role in developing close buyer-seller interaction and long-term relationships in the Japanese business market. This is particularly the case with regard to *new task* purchasing situations.

H2: Intermediaries such as trading companies, marketing agents, and manufacturer's representatives play an equally important role in developing close buyer-seller interaction and long-term relationships in the Japanese market. This is particularly the case with regard to *new task* purchasing situations.

H3: Environmental factors such as culture, market structure, and government industrial policy play an equally important role in developing close buyer-seller interaction and long-term relationships in the Japanese business market. This is particularly the case with regard to *new task* purchasing situations.

6 The Findings

Table 1 enumerates both commercial and technical factors influencing the development of close buyer-seller interaction and long-term relationships in the Japanese business market. The commercial factors are the first eight, while the technical ones are listed in the second half of the table. These factors were contained in both the structured mail questionnaire and the in-depth interview guide. They were selected on the basis of secondary material obtained from both official and non-governmental sources and pretested on 10 purchasing and supplying organizations in Japan before being integrated in the data collection instruments.

Starting with purchasing organizations, the following were ranked as the most important (15 respondents): contract terms, delivery schedule, after sales service, the image of the supplier in the marketplace, the supplier's references, the supplier's technical ability, the supplier's product performance (in accordance with earlier agreed specifications), the nature of technical services the supplier was willing to offer the purchasing organization (this generally related to both the product supplied by the selling organizations as well as products which the buyer may have acquired from other suppliers prior to the establishment of a relationship with the present supplier). As table 1 shows, all fifteen respondent organizations indicated that these were important attributes in developing long-term relationships with suppliers. Five of these factors were commercial, while three were primarily technical. The remainder of the factors which buyers considered important were ranked in the following order: supplier's technology (14 respondents); supplier's financial situation; the nature of technical training the supplier was willing to provide the purchasing organization (13 respondents); product's technical attributes (11 respondents); price, and the level of supplier's technical innovation (10 respondents); warranty, and supplier's technical quotation (9 respondents). It is interesting to note that price was ranked second last as a significant factor in developing close buyer-seller interaction and long-term relationships in this market. This finding seems to confirm Robinson, Faris & Wind's postulation that organizational buyers are generally willing to pay a premium price for a product for which they have a need in a *new task* purchasing situation. It is only in *modified rebuy* and *straight rebuy* situations that attention tends to be generally focused on price since buyer-seller interaction is at this stage close and long-term relationships have already been well established.

Table 1: Factors Affecting Buyer-Seller Interaction and Long-Term Relationships in the Japanese Business Market

Factor	Purchasing firm	Supplying firm
Price	10	13
Warranty	9	5
Contract terms	15	13
Delivery schedule	15	8
After sales service	15	13
Partner's image	15	12
Partner's references	15	9
Partner's financial situation	13	8
Partner's technology	14	7
Partner's technical ability	15	7
Product's performance	15	2
Technical quotation	9	3
Technical service	15	8
Technical training	13	6
Partner's technical innovation	10	5
Product's technical attributes	11	3

Looking now from the supplying organization's point of view, the following were considered among the most important factors in developing these relationships: price, supply contract term, and after sales service (13 respondents). Next was the image of the purchasing organization in the marketplace (12 respondents); followed by the purchasing organization's references (9 respondents); delivery schedule, financial situation, technical service (8 respondents for each of the three factors). Other factors (recorded in order of importance) were: partner's technology, and technical ability (7 respondents); technical training (6 respondents); warranty and partner's technical innovation (5 respondents); technical quotation and product's technical attributes (3 respondents); and product's performance (2 respondents). Seen from the point of view of commercial and technical criteria, it appears that suppliers valued more highly the commercial factors in developing close buyer-seller interaction and long-term relationships in this market.

There are important differences to be observed in the way the buying and selling organizations viewed factors they considered important in developing relationships in this market. For example, whereas price was of no particular importance to purchasing organizations, suppliers considered it at the very top of the list of factors decisive for such relationships. But there are important similarities too, that can be observed between the interacting partners. These relate particularly to: contract terms, after sales services, and partner's image in the marketplace.

These findings mean that hypothesis 1 is largely supported. It is important to note, however, that the perception of the importance of these factors is largely dissimilar between the purchasing and supplying organizations, confirming once again the need for foreign suppliers to study closely factors organizational buyers in this environment consider to be most essential in their purchase decision process, buyer-seller interaction, and long-term relationship development with foreign suppliers before embarking on detailed market entry and growth strategies for the Japanese market.

Next to the commercial and technical factors is the importance of intermediaries in developing these relationships. Table 2 provides a summary of the findings. From this table it can be observed that all 15 purchasing organizations considered the role of trading companies as very important in establishing these relationships, while 7 indicated the importance of manufacturer's representatives, and 6 the importance of marketing agents. In addition to these responses, 10 purchasing organizations indicated that intermediaries other than those listed in the data collection instruments were important to them in developing these relationships.

From the supplier's point of view, manufacturer's representatives were clearly the most important intermediaries in developing these relationships. This was closely followed by marketing agents (11 respondents), trading companies (7 respondents), and other intermediaries (3 respondents). It is important to note that while purchasing organizations considered trading companies to be important, suppliers on the other hand had a completely different viewpoint, confirming the widely held opinion among foreign marketers that the role of Japanese trading companies in facilitating business relationships between Japanese firms and foreign companies is at times grossly overrated.

Table 2: The Importance of Intermediaries in Developing Close Buyer-Seller Interaction and Long-Term Relationships in the Japanese Business Market

Intermediaries	Purchasing firm	Supplying firm
Trading companies	15	7
Marketing agents	6	11
Manufacturer's representatives	7	12
Other	10	3

From these findings we can see that hypothesis 2 is only partially supported. Intermediaries do seem to play an important role in developing close buyer-seller interaction and long-term relationships in this environment. However, their role is not as significant as hypothesis 2 suggests. For Japanese buyers, the role of trading companies is more important than any other type of intermediaries. On the other hand, for the foreign suppliers manufacturer's representatives and marketing agents are the most important intermediaries in facilitating these relationships. This finding is perhaps not very surprising since most purchasing organizations that participated in the study had trading companies within their corporate structure who played a key role in the development of close interaction and long-term relationships with foreign suppliers. By the same token it appears that most respondent supplier organizations preferred to let their representatives and marketing agents handle the responsibility of developing these interactions and long-term relationships with their Japanese partners since it was felt that these intermediaries had better experience and requisite knowledge of dealing with Japanese companies. These findings underline the need for foreign suppliers of industrial products to be aware of the importance Japanese organizations attach to trading companies especially when it comes to dealing with foreign businesses. Japanese trading companies have the necessary knowledge and experience of dealing with foreign organizations. They have thus the full trust of the organizations they represent. They are powerful entities quite capable of facilitating or breaking a potential relationship between a Japanese buyer and a foreign supplier. It is important to note that since they largely control the distribution channels in this market and provide the necessary financial backing for Japanese and other companies, their influence in this environment is truly without rival.

Finally we look at environmental factors considered to be of the outmost importance in facilitating these relationships. These, as table 3 shows, relate to culture, market structure, and government industrial policy. Twelve purchasing firms considered government policy as the most important factor in developing these relationships. This was followed by market structure (10 respondents); and culture (6 respondents). These results confirm earlier findings (Dzever 1995) that due to the conclusions of the Structural Impediments Initiative (SII) policy between Japan and the United States, the Japanese government exerted significant pressure on Japanese firms to increase their purchasing activities from American and other foreign suppliers of industrial products. SII was put into place as a measure of correcting the enormous trade imbalances that existed between Japan and the United States. The Reagan administration was of the opinion that SII would significantly help in reducing Japan's trade surplus with the USA. It is important to note further that buyers in this environment did not consider culture as an important factor in establishing long-term business relationships with foreign suppliers, confirming the general notion that Japanese firms are generally willing to do business with any foreign partner provided the partner has a product that meets the Japanese demand and is willing to invest time and energy in developing long-term business relationships with its Japanese counterparts. It is thus of no surprise to see that Japanese companies are today at the forefront of business globalization.

Table 3: The Importance of Environmental Factors in Developing Close Buyer-Seller Interaction and Long-Term Relationships in the Japanese Business Market

Environmental factors	Purchasing firm	Supplying firm
Culture	6	8
Market Structure	10	12
Government industrial policy	12	9

The trend observed among purchasing firms is also true for supplying organizations. Most suppliers considered market structure to be an important factor in establishing strong long-term relationships with buyers in the Japanese market. This finding also confirms the established viewpoint that because of the complexity of industrial and market structure in Japan, a detailed understanding of how it works is of the outmost importance in succeeding in this environment. The next most important environmental factor to suppliers in establishing these long-term relationships is government policy (9 respondents); followed by culture (8 respondents), confirming once again that in contrast to popular opinion, cultural differences is often not a hindrance to establishing business relationships in international markets.

These findings show that hypothesis 3 is only partially supported. Environmental factors do indeed exert an important influence in developing close buyer-seller interaction and long-term relationships. There are, however, significant differences between the importance of these factors. But both purchasing and supplying organizations did not consider cultural differences as an impediment to developing relationships with one another. Purchasing organizations, on the other hand, considered the effects of government industrial policy as an important factor in developing these close interactions and long-term relationships. To foreign suppliers, however, it was the thorough understanding of the complex Japanese industrial and market structure that was the most decisive environmental factor in developing these relationships. These findings suggest the need for foreign suppliers to have a detailed understanding of the effects of market structure and government industrial policy when developing appropriate market entry and growth strategies in this highly competitive environment.

7 Conclusion and Direction for Future Research

This study has demonstrated the need for foreign suppliers to study carefully factors which organizational buyers in the Japanese market consider to be the most decisive in developing close buyer-seller interaction and long-term relationships. The Japanese market is clearly one of the world's most competitive markets. But it is also among its most lucrative. Succeeding here can be very rewarding and may even signal success in other markets. However, success would certainly not come overnight. Foreign marketers must be prepared for a long-term engagement before they could see their effort bear fruits. The Japan External Trade Organization (JETRO) has described the Japanese market as follows:

> Japan is a well supplied, sophisticated and mature market. Generally speaking, a successful new product takes market share from a competitor rather than create new demand, unless the product is unique. This means that a product needs to fill a gap in the market, or a specialized niche. Alternatively, it needs to be technologically superior to competing lines. (JETRO 1987)

These attributes coupled with a keen understanding of the factors necessary in developing long-term buyer-seller relationships are the recipe for success in this marketplace. The importance of close buyer-seller interaction and long-term relationships is also emphasized in Mazda's purchasing policy:

> The days of suppliers simply delivering parts to car manufacturers are gone. To Mazda suppliers are partners, and we enter these relationships with our eyes on the long term. (...) The suppliers we work with in Japan and overseas are involved in

product development right from the beginning (...) and their ideas are reflected in every Mazda vehicle. (Mazda 1992)

This study is limited, however, by the fact that only a small sample of purchasing and supplying organizations were included in the survey. Future studies should be able to build on this base to include a larger sample of respondent organizations both in Japan and Europe. These limitations notwithstanding, however, it is our hope that this study has made a small contribution toward enhancing our understanding of the importance of purchase decision process, buyer-seller interaction and long-term relationships in the Japanese business market.

References

Anderson, E., Chu, W. & Waitz, B. (1987), Industrial Purchasing: An Empirical Explanation of the Buyclass Framework, *Journal of Marketing* 51.

Baker, M.J. (1983), *Market Development: A Comprehensive Survey*, London: Penguin Books.

Baker, M.J. (1985), *Marketing Strategy and Management*, London: Macmillan Press.

Bauer, R.A. (1960), Consumer Behavior as Risk Taking, in: Hancock, R. S. (ed.), *Dynamic Marketing for a Changing World*, Chicago: American Marketing Association.

Bonoma T.V., Zaltman, G. & Johnston, W. J. (1977), *Industrial Buying Behavior*, Cambridge, Massachusetts: Marketing Science Institute.

Campbell, N. (1986), *Japanese Marketing as an Interaction System*, Manchester Business School, Working Paper 131.

Carter, J. R. & Narasimhan, R. (1990), Purchasing in the International Market Place: Implications for Operations, in: *Journal of Purchasing and Materials Management* Summer.

Chang, K. & Ding, C. G. (1995), The Influence of Culture on Industrial Buying Selection Criteria in Taiwan and mainland China, in: *Industrial Marketing Management* 24.

Chetty, S., Dzever, S. & Quester. P. (1999), Country of Origin Perception and Industrial Purchase Decision-Making in New Zealand, in: *European Journal of Purchasing and Supply Management* 5.

Choffrey, J. M. & Lilien, G. (1978), Assessing Responses to Industrial Marketing Strategy, in: *Journal of Marketing* 42.

Corey, E. R. (1976), *Industrial Marketing: Cases and Concepts*, Englewood Cliffs, N.J: Prentice-Hall.

Dadfar, H. (1990), *Industrial Buying Behavior in the Middle East*, Linköping: Linköping University.

Deng, S. & Wortzel, L. H. (1995), Importer Purchase Behavior: Guidelines for Asian Exporters, in: *Journal of Business Research* 32.

Deshpande, R. (1983), Paradigm Lost: On Theory and Method in Research in Marketing, in: *Journal of Marketing* 47.

Dickson, G. W. (1966), An Analysis of Vendor Selection Systems and Decisions, in: *Journal of Purchasing* 2.

Dzever, S. (1993), Towards an Integrated Conceptual Model of Organizational Buyer Behavior Analysis, in: *ENBS Academic Review* 2.

Dzever, S. (1995), Measuring the Effects of Government Policy on Organizational Procurement Activities in Japan: The Case of Japan-USA Structural Impediments Initiative, in: *Japon in Extenso* 42.

Dzever, S. (1996), *Le Comportement d'Achat Industriel*, Paris: Economica.

Dzever, S. (1997), Industrial Procurement Practices of Taiwanese Firms in the Chinese Market, in Dzever, S. & Jaussaud, J. (eds.), *Perspectives on Economic Integration and Business Strategy in the Asia-pacific Region*, London: Macmillan.

Dzever, S. & Quester, P. (1999), Country-of-Origin Effects on Purchasing Agents' Product Perceptions: An Australian Perspective, in: *Industrial Marketing Management* 28.

Håkansson, H. (ed.) (1982), *International Marketing and Purchasing of Industrial Goods: An Interaction Approach*, London: John Wiley & Sons.

Hill, R. M. (1972), The Nature of Industrial Buying Decisions, in: *Industrial Marketing Management* 2.

Hill, R. M., Alexander, R. S. & Cross, J. S. (1975), *Industrial Marketing*, 4th Edition, Homewood Ill.: Irwin.

JETRO (1987), *The Japanese Market: A Compendium of Information for the Prospective Exporter*, Tokyo: JETRO.

Jick, T. (1979), Mixing Qualitative and Quantitative Methods: Triangulation in Action, in: *Administrative Science Quarterly* 24.

Johnston, W. J. & Spekman R.E. (1982), Industrial Buying Behavior: A Need for an Integrated Approach, in: *Journal of Business Research* 10.

Lehman, D. R. & O'Shaughnessy, J. (1974), Differences in Attribute Importance for Different Industrial Products, in: *Journal of Marketing* April.

MAZDA (1992), *Annual Report*, Hiroshima: Mazda.

Moriarty, R. T. (1983), *Industrial Buying Behavior*, London: Lexington Books.

Reichardt, C. S. & Cook, T. D. (1979), Beyond Qualitative versus Quantitative Methods, in: Cook, T. D. & Reichardt, C. S. (eds.), *Qualitative and Quantitative Methods in Evaluation Research*, Beverly Hill: Sage.

Robinson, P., Faris, J. & Wind Y. (1967), *Industrial Buying and Creative Marketing*, Boston: Allyn and Bacon.

Sweeney, T. W., Mathews, H. L. & Wilson, D. T. (1973), An Analysis of Industrial Buyers' Risk Reducing Behavior: Some Personality Correlates, in: *AMA Proceedings*, Chicago: AMA.

Webster, F. E. & Wind, Y. (1988), A General Model for Understanding Organizational Buying Behavior, in: Enis, B. M. & Cox, K. K. (eds.), *Marketing Classics: A Selection of Influential Articles*, Boston: Allyn and Bacon.

Zaltman, G., Duncan, R. & Holbek J. (1973), *Innovation and Organization*, New York: Wiley-Interscience.

Restructuring à la Japonaise: Supplier Relationships in the Japanese Car Industry in the 1990s

Arne Holzhausen

1 Introduction

Since the MIT study on the future of the automobile has trumpeted the superiority of the Japanese car manufacturers and has coined the phrase "lean production" (Womack, Jones & Roos 1990), things have dramatically changed for the Japanese automotive industry. Hit by a severe recession in its home market and plagued by a rising yen during the first half of the 1990s, the Japanese automotive industry is now in poor shape and causes hardly any American or European car maker sleepless nights.

On the contrary, amid the global fever of consolidation Japanese car makers are perceived as take-over-objects which play the role of the missing Asian part of the global strategy-puzzle of American or European car makers. The fall of Nissan, Japan's second largest car manufacturer, very clearly illustrates the new image of the Japanese car industry: Nissan, which in the past pursued a strategy of sales growth and challenged Toyota to become number one in Japan, has fled this year from its horrifying debt into the arms of Renault, after DaimlerChrysler was prompted to back off after a closer view into the mess of Nissan.

However, it would be too easy to attribute the recent problems of the Japanese car industry only to the business cycle of the Japanese economy or to the fluctuations of the exchange rate. After all, Japanese car makers responded with several restructuring phases to control costs as well as by shifting production capacity overseas to reduce the vulnerability to floating exchange rates. But during this process of restructuring the Japanese car industry revealed itself in a state that has hardly anything in common with the ideal of "lean management".

Admittedly, the Japanese car makers still operate some of the world's most productive car factories, but despite this edge in production management the organization of Japanese automotive firms is rather fat. First, there is the organization of R&D which excels in short development times due to the practice of simultaneous engineering but has continuously failed to consolidate the range of products and parts: the unlucky Nissan boosts no less than 50 models which are based on 25 platforms (VW sales 50% more cars but uses only four platforms). Second, personnel structures have to considered: under Japanese employment patterns redundancies are prevented by any means; this results not only in rising personnel costs but in inflexible and over-staffed hierarchies: prior to its engagement with Renault, Nissan had afforded having 37 directors on its board.

And finally, Japanese car makers command a vast network of dealers and suppliers. During the heydays of the Japanese automotive industry when sales were steadily moving upward, these networks, especially on the supplier side, were viewed as a competitive advantage: "vertical-keiretsu" or "keiretsu-networks", as these supplier networks are often called, are conducive to a stable supply of high-quality parts at moderate prices and are a prerequisite of just-in-time-deliveries without stocks. But as the car-sales began to plummet, car makers realized that maintaining their keiretsu-networks during the prolonged recession is a heavy burden and decided therefore that restructuring should also aim directly at their relationships with suppliers.

This paper focuses on this process of restructuring supplier relationships in the Japanese car industry since the burst of the bubble at the beginning of the 1990s.[1] Its aim is to overview the recent developments within the supplier system and to consider the consequences these changes may have for the competitiveness of the Japanese car industry.

The rest of the paper is organized as follows. In chapter 2 the *old* model of Japanese supplier relationships is analysed; this analysis makes clear that reform was inevitable should the favourable circumstances change as they did indeed in the 1990s. The restructuing efforts of the car and parts makers are sketched in chapter 3; furthermore, the influence of new patterns of supplier relationships on keiretsu-networks is discussed. Chapter 4 winds up by providing some conclusive remarks regarding the competitiveness of the Japanese car industry.

2 Japanese Supplier Networks Before the Crisis Hit

There is already a large volume of literature on Japanese subcontracting relationships or vertical keiretsu. Their characteristics such as exclusivity, mutual dependency, trust[2] and long-term orientation of business relationships are well

1 This paper is based on the findings of FU-Automotive-Research-Group to which – besides the author – Sung-Jo Park, Gabrielle Hennig and Natascha Haehling von Lanzenauer belonged.

2 There is some disagreement in the literature whether trust is merely a characteristic of Japanese keiretsu networks (i.e. the outcome of the close and intensive co-operation by the partners) or whether trust is an important condition for the establishment of these structures (i.e. the external explaining factor). On the one side, Fujimoto (1994) differentiates the logic of system emergence, which can mainly be explained by entrepreneurial visions or environmental constraints (historical imperatives), from the logic of system stability which requires trust between the partners as the result of a learning process. On the other side, Dore (1987) argues that goodwill trust belongs to

known facts that are often discussed in opposition to the European or American approach of parts procurement (Asanuma 1989, Helper 1990, Smitka 1991, Richter & Wakuta 1993, Nishiguchi 1994).

2.1 Superior Performance of Keiretsu-Networks

Based on the works of Williamson on the conditions of markets and organizations (Williamson 1985), many authors have argued that a structure like Japanese keiretsu, which is located between pure market and pure organization principles as an *intermediate organization* (Imai & Itami 1984:296), achieves a superior cost performance because of the higher degree of *asset specificity*. Knowing the long-term character of their relationships both partners are willing to invest further in this relationship to improve its performance: a supplier could for example decide to build its new factory in the vicinity of the customer. In general, Japanese suppliers and car makers develop business transactions into co-operative partnerships in which both sides invest through sharing *all* information, which leads to joint development programmes and joint foreign direct investments, synchronized production schedules and exchange of engineers and managers. During the course of interaction the partners improve their *relational-specific skills* (Asanuma 1989:19ff.) and yield a *relational quasi-rent* (Aoki 1988:208ff.); they are not prepared to end the relationship because this would imply the loss of the additional profits that are available only in this specific relationship due to relational investments.

But although the intensive co-operation of the partners is instrumental in lowering the costs and simultaneously rising the quality of the procured parts, its inner logic results not instantaneously in higher long-term competitiveness. On the contrary, the inherent growth orientation which epitomizes Japanese firms and the closeness of the relationship may potentially change the fruits of co-operation to drags on the further development of competitiveness.

2.2 Drags on Long-Term Competitiveness

Even if their dependency is mutual, the car makers and suppliers are not equal partners.[3] Though the practice of single sourcing is the dominant procurement

---

the core set of Japanese values and has led to the spreading of co-operative relationships in the Japanese industry.

3 Nevertheless, this imbalance of power has also a positive aspect for the dependent supplier as its risk is partially absorbed by the car maker. (Asanuma & Kikutani 1992). This kind of risk-sharing, however, is not a free service of the car maker, but comes at a premium: a higher stability of the profit rate coincides with a lower level of the profit rate which implies that the car maker is getting a part of the profit from the supplier as a premium. (Okamuro 1995:214ff.). Furthermore, this risk-sharing

strategy in the Japanese automotive industry (Fujimoto 1994:6), the car makers have one or two other suppliers inside their keiretsu networks that are capable of producing the same part. This means that suppliers do business in a rather competitive environment and are potentially threatened with losing their business to their competitors if they fail to deliver the required quality. Suppliers react to this threat by investing even more into their relationship with the car maker to become an indispensable partner. This is one reason why these partnerships are mostly exclusive. There is only a minority of suppliers in Japan that can afford to engage in this kind of intensive relationship to different customers at the same time. Normally, the chunk of their sales is directed to one car maker; options outside their established networks are limited because becoming the core supplier to another car maker would require huge additional investment for this new relationship. But exclusivity means also that the only way to grow is to expand the existing partnership. As the car maker itself has a genuine interest in strong suppliers, he is hardly reluctant to intensify a successful partnership. This might be the hidden reason behind the proliferation of new models and the shortening of model cycles by the Japanese car industry during the 1980s when the growth of sales volumes had begun to slow down. By steadily introducing new models with originally designed parts the suppliers were able to secure rising orders.

Further, mutual dependency and exclusivity could work in another way to undermine long-term competitiveness. The close interaction of the partners leads to a growing stock of accumulated common knowledge which can be easily used to optimize the operation of the partnership in terms of better communication, improved logistics and synchronized production. On the other hand, this stock of knowledge defines the boundaries of action: shared experience and memories can translate in conservative behaviour; changes and new ideas which are sure to alter the nature of the relationship are intentionally or un-intentionally blocked by the partners. This is particularly important in the development stage where access to advanced knowledge outside the firm or group plays a crucial role. Richter and Wakuta (1993:264) conclude therefore, that "design and engineering functions at Japanese firms (...) have been inferior to those of their Western competitors. (...) The organizational memory acted as a hindrance to change."

This intrinsic danger of Japanese supplier networks to become self-absorbed and ignorant about technological, strategic or managerial advancements outside the network's boundaries will undermine the competitiveness of Japanese car makers in the long run even under stable market conditions. But if circumstances are less than favourable, demanding prompt reaction to new challenges, these short-comings of Japanese network behaviour can rather quickly weaken the market position.

---

mechanism applies only to core suppliers which are closely connected to the car maker. (Okamuro 1995:217)

The majority of the literature on the Japanese supplier system ends at the point when it has discussed the pros and cons of these perceived essential characteristics of exclusivity, mutual dependency, trust and long-term orientation of business relationships – normally strongly biased toward stressing the cost advantages of close co-operation. But the analysis of the relationships between core suppliers, which are more than often big companies, and the car maker is far from giving a complete picture of the Japanese supplier networks; instead, it is narrowly focused on the first-tier of the hierarchical pyramid consisting of thousands of suppliers which are predominantly small- and medium-sized firms.

2.3 The Bottom of the Supplier Pyramid

The situation of these small suppliers on the second- or third-tier of the supplier hierarchy differs fundamentally from the stable position of large, first-tier suppliers which are embedded in long-term and co-operative relationships with the car maker. As most of the smaller suppliers lack the technological capacity for development or design, they manufacture parts on the basis of provided drawings from their customers. Yet, this exclusion from the development process lowers not only the potential for profitable growth, but also the need for intensive communication and the exchange of engineers and managers; moreover, the influence of the smaller part makers on the price of their products is substantially reduced. Whereas first-tier suppliers and car makers are intertwined by mutual dependency, second-tier suppliers are unilaterally dependent on their customers although some aspects of co-operation like *kyôrokukai* (suppliers forums) and a long-term orientation of business relationships are recognisable on the second-tier, too. (Fujimoto, Sei & Takeishi 1994:15ff.).

At the bottom of the supplier pyramid, the picture is even bleaker. Not surprisingly, part makers on third- or fourth-tier – according to the findings by Fujimoto, Sei & Takeishi (1994:15ff.) who studied small automotive suppliers in the Kanagawa prefecture – are very small firms with 10 employees on average. These firms carry out labour-intensive or small-lot production processes that bigger part makers deem unprofitable. But these smallest suppliers are rarely integrated into the supplier networks of their customers: long-term business relationships are exceptional; co-operative structures like *kyôryokukai* and technical or managerial support by the customers are almost non-existent. Instead, transactions are characterized by hefty fluctuations of prices and volumes.

It thus is certainly no exaggeration to say that the situation of smaller suppliers on lower tiers of the supplier hierarchy resembles the notion of industrial dualism. Like in the first days of subcontracting in Japan during the 1930s and the post-war era, firm-size related wage differences prompts bigger firms to use smaller ones as low-cost workbenches. As the big firm is not dependent on the inputs of the subcontracting firms that can offer nothing else than physical work, it does not feel restrained from exploiting them and treating them as buffers in business fluctuations. The swings of prices and volumes at the bottom of the supplier pyramid suggest that industrial dualism has not yet completely disappeared from the industrial landscape of Japan.

2.4 Summary: Dichotomy of Keiretsu-Networks

To sum up, the pyramidal supplier hierarchies of the Japanese automotive industry are far from being homogenous structures but encompass a spectrum of different modes of inter-firm relations which represent different stages (and economic theories) of the development of supplier relationships. Whereas co-operation and reciprocity prevail on the one end of the spectrum between car makers and first-tier suppliers (making them perfect examples of network analysis), on the other end of the spectrum dependency and persisting wage differences are overshadowing the business relations of the small subcontractor to their customers (making them cherished targets of Marxist critique on capitalism). Yet, the necessity to reform which might be self-evident for the latter relationships applies also to the co-operative partnerships: due to their close nature and their indisputable success in the past, new product concepts as well as growth strategies turned complacently inwards, inevitably sowing the seeds of the loss of international competitiveness which were finally brought up by the recession of the Japanese economy after the burst of the bubble in 1991.

3 Restructuring Efforts of Car and Parts Makers

In the aftermath of the bubble economy the first objective of chief executives of Japanese car makers was to cut costs. Even if in the early 1990s the notion of increasing shareholder value was not yet – at least in Japan – a much heard phrase as today, it was well understood that the excessive investments of the bubble era have escalated costs that now have to be curtailed out in order to avoid ever falling profits.

Besides personnel structures and reorganized assembly operations[4], cost-reduction plans are aimed mainly on part purchasing. Cost reductions in this field could be

4 Regarding personnel costs, instead of radical downsizing, which is difficult to put through under Japanese employment patterns, the focus was on delayering and new schemes of promotion and wage determination in order to reduce the influence of the seniority rule. For further discussion see Holzhausen (1998:137 ff.). Regarding assembly operations, new factories like the Miyata Plant of Toyota Motor Kyûshû Inc. are featuring simpler plant and equipment designs and lower assembly automation ratios than their predecessors which were designed during the heights of the bubble economy. The new assembly concept aims not only at high customer and

achieved by two overlapping strategies. One is the lowering of the purchasing price, the other is the reorganization of the development and design process of new products.

3.1 Purchasing Price Reductions

The simplest form of a purchasing price reduction strategy is to demand that suppliers have to cut their prices; these demands which set ambitious targets of 30% price reductions within three years were made by all car makers[5]. The first-tier suppliers responded by squeezing their costs carrying out value analysis and value engineering, by slimming their workforce, by optimizing their production processes – and by themselves demanding equivalent price reductions from their suppliers. Despite heroic work on this matter on all tiers of the supplier pyramid – one interviewed supplier admitted that he had tried to cut costs by shutting off the air condition during lunch breaks in summer –, many suppliers had, however, to suffer declining profits on yet larger scales than the car makers; generally speaking, the lower the rank of the supplier, the sharper the decline of profits[6]. This transfer of responsibility for cost reductions shows that the issue of unequal powers inside the supplier hierarchies, which was seldom felt as problematic in the booming years, matters a lot during business downturns. Thereby, the pressure accumulates on the lowest tiers of the supplier pyramid. This was further confirmed by a survey of the Small and Medium Sized Enterprise Agency in which 68% of the respondents pointed to extra price reductions when asked what their biggest problems to cope with were (Chûshô-kigyô-chô 1998:96).

The situation improved somewhat at least for first-tier suppliers when the so-called strategy of "common parts" (*buhin tôgôka* or *buhin kyôtsûka*) began to work. As discussed in chapter two, owing to the growth incentives of exclusive co-operative partnerships, the Japanese car industry witnessed in the latter half of the 1980s an explosion of new models and model variations that led to a double-digit increase in the number of necessary parts. All car makers therefore declared at the beginning of the crisis that they would reduce the models and variations by some 20% to 35% in the next few years and that they would on the other hand nearly double the share of used parts in new models which were slightly euphemistically called "common parts". The rationale behind this strategy was not only to cut costs in the development stage but also to enable suppliers to grab

employee satisfaction, but equally at low fixed costs to improve the cash flow. For further discussion see Fujimoto (1996).

5 That Japanese car makers are not reluctant to squeeze profits of their network partners by extracting lower prices, indicates that the risk-sharing mechanism of former years becomes ineffective in hard times when the car makers too suffer falling profits and thus cannot afford to absorb additional risks.

6 This phenomenon of increasing rates of profit slumps was confirmed in interviews by the FU-Automotive-Research-Group.

economies of scale (and thus reduce prices further) through streamlining their product menu.

3.2 Reorganization of the Developement Process

But the reorganization of the development and design process did not stop at a mere reduction of models, variations and parts. The practice of joint development with suppliers was enforced. Suppliers were involved in the development process at an earlier stage and had to carry out more tasks. In addition to the responsibility for their own products, first-tier suppliers were expected to shoulder the co-ordination of the development process of part units, a task that car makers normally fulfilled themselves. This prompted the bigger suppliers – in spite of general efforts to cut personnel costs by redundancies – to increase the number of engineers in their development departments in order to strengthen their own technological expertise.

This enlarged development duties of first-tier suppliers resemble in a way the strategy of "modularization" which is by now common in the European automotive industry. In comparison with their European competitors the Japanese approach is, however, much more cautious. Though some sub-lines have been moved from the assembly plants of car makers into the factories of suppliers and though some suppliers have emerged as leaders in the development process, an overall concentration on *system suppliers* cannot be proven yet. Throughout the interviews of the FU-Automotive-Research-Group, car makers showed some reluctance to push the idea of modularization further because they fear that the bundling of too many parts into systems would drive some of their distinguished business partners out of business.[7] Most of them seem to be satisfied with the degree of modularization the Japanese automotive industry has already achieved within its layered supplier networks (this represents, admittedly, a higher degree than usual in Europe before the radical reorganization of supplier relationships has started few years ago).

Therefore, the recent increase of M&A in the automotive parts industry should not be interpreted as attempts to create genuine *system suppliers* in Japan which may eventually become global players. As most cases of M&A – like the merger between Calsonic and Kansei – have so far taken place inside the established keiretsu-networks, it seems reasonable to assume that the objectives of these M&A activities are more moderate. Supplier networks are reshaped to remove

[7] In a survey conducted by the Small and Medium Sized Enterprise Agency, 28% of big firms said that they had carried out an "intensification of subcontractors" (*shita-uke kigyô no shûyaku*; Japanese bureaucracy's way of saying that they have concentrated orders on fewer suppliers), but only 11% (of this 28%) did so because of modularization (Chûshô-kigyô-chô 1998:92).

redundant production capacity of same parts so that the merged firm can benefit from economies of scale.

3.3 Use of Outside Suppliers

So far only those strategies of purchasing cost reductions have been considered that are confined to the existing supplier pyramid. But on the other hand, car makers are making increasing use of suppliers *outside* their established keiretsu-networks as well. Particularly, they take advantage of the strong yen by importing parts: import volumes of automotive parts grew by 75% between 1990 and 1995 (Böttcher 1999:236). Whereas the market share of imported parts is still negligible, their sharp rise and the accompanying centralization of purchasing departments which track world-wide prices of automotive parts have, however, added extra pressure on domestic suppliers to cut prices.

Equally, buying parts from outside domestic suppliers even if they are members of keiretsu-groups of competitors is no longer unthinkable. Anecdotal evidence can be found to back this up all across the Japanese automotive industry. Even some suppliers of Toyota and Nissan which both demarcated their fiefs jealously from each other in the past have started business with the former arch-rival.[8] Car makers generally encourage efforts of their suppliers to enlarge their customer base. Nissan is said to urge its suppliers to obtain about 30% of their sales outside the Nissan-keiretsu (Richter 1997:53). Car makers thereby calculate that increasing sales improve capacity-use-rates so that prices – first and foremost the price that they have to pay themselves – can be lowered.

3.4 Opening or Closing of Keiretsu-Networks?

On the one hand, these efforts by car manufacturers to reduce purchasing costs have more than often caused profits of first-tier suppliers to fall – pushing some of them into financial distress –, but have, on the other hand, also the effect of strengthening the position of first-tier suppliers: these suppliers now play a greater role in the development process and have better business opportunities as car makers have opened their purchasing departments to outsiders. Some observers have therefore concluded that a dismantling of keiretsu-structures is in the making, or that, more cautious, former close networks develop into "permeable networks" (Richter & Wakuta 1993:265-266). But this seems a rather premature conclusion. Although some suppliers are expanding rather independently into new

8 The willingness to buy parts outside the own keiretsu-network is often a result of overseas production owing to the fact that network suppliers have no local capacities but, however, Japanese suppliers are prefered; this is mirrored in the rising degree of fluctuation of business partners with rising rates of overseas production (Chûshô-kigyô-chô 1998:93).

markets that have not much to do with the automotive industry, it is much harder for suppliers to capitalize on their technological strength inside the automotive industry. Information and know-how regarding state-of-the-art-technologies do not flow freely beyond the boundaries of keiretsu-networks; new business relationships with competing car makers are more like old-style subcontracting arrangements: suppliers carry out the production of standardized parts (though modified to the needs of the customer) but are not involved in research and development of new technologies. Car makers are aware that their competitiveness depends on their technical capabilities that are embedded in their supplier network; therefore, they are not prepared to let these capabilities leak to competitors.

The recent tensions between Toyota and Denso illustrate the dilemma that strong suppliers can pose for car makers if they strive to enlarge their customer base. The conflict between the two partners broke out when a new technology of engine management which Toyota and Denso had developed in close co-operation from 1991 to 1995 had finally been sold to Fuji Heavy Industries by Denso – without Toyota's consent. Toyota was so upset about this that it excluded Denso from the development process of the hybrid engine of its new concept car "Prius". Furthermore, in an attempt to take a firmer grip on the management of Denso, it has this year for the first time sent a Toyota-man as vice-chairman to the board of Denso. Even if car makers diversify their sources of supply (and suppliers thus enlarge their customer base) the heart of keiretsu-networks, i.e. the free and open exchange of information and know-how between the partners, and the joint development of new technologies, is not going to become open; on the contrary, it seems that supplier relationships inside established keiretsu-networks are becoming even closer in this regard.

3.5 Changing Relationships with Small Suppliers

This enforcement of keiretsu-relationships can be observed on the lower tiers of the supplier pyramid, too. As mentioned above, big suppliers were by no means hesitant to squeeze their suppliers as price-cuts were demanded on them by car makers. Furthermore, some big suppliers have started to re-insource production processes as a measure to prevent a fall of the capacity-use-rate (and to keep their employees busy).[9] But above all, the nature of the relationships with smaller suppliers have changed.

In the past, simple, labour-intensive processes were outsourced to subcontractors on terms of CQD (cost, quality and delivery). The smallest suppliers were regarded as cheap workbenches and as buffers in business fluctuations. So, as

9 Most of suppliers which are practising re-insourcing see this strategy rather as a provisional measure than a long-term strategy (interviews by the FU-Automotive-Research-Group).

could expected, the crisis forced large numbers of them to leave the car industry, many of which are prone to go bankrupt; and nearly 50% of these suppliers which could somehow manage to survive in the car industry had to face diminishing orders. Yet on the other hand, a quarter of surviving small suppliers succeeded in getting rising orders (Chûshô-kigyô-chô 1998:94). This is a clear signal that competition among small suppliers is becoming not only harder and more selective but more rewarding. As throughout the Japanese industry, firms of the same sector are being divided into winners and losers by severe competition.

The crisis and its following downward pressure on prices and volumes triggered this competition, but its outcome is mostly defined by changing attitudes towards low-tier suppliers. Instead of choosing simply the cheapest subcontractor, bigger suppliers have begun to apply selection criteria that reflect the managerial and technological capabilities (Chûshô-kigyô-chô 1998:91). Small suppliers that are able to take part in the development process, to cope with short-term demands of product variations and to manage logistics by their own, are very likely to win additional orders from their fellow suppliers that fail to keep pace with these new requirements.

This consolidation process which will re-form the foundation of the supplier hierarchy from pyramidal shape to igloo shape is therefore a rather revolutionary change in the role small parts makers are used playing in supplier networks. Small suppliers are given by the crisis the opportunity to expand and upgrade their business; they are gradually becoming integral parts of keiretsu-networks. During the field research by the FU-Automotive-Research-Group it could be observed that many of them are investing in new machines, are introducing production management tools like *kaizen* and quality circles, and are training their employees to become multi-skill workers. The wide gap in productivity and wages that has separated the small suppliers from the rest of the supplier network is getting narrower.[10]

From an evolutionary perspective, it can be argued that the development of supplier relationships which transformed arm-length subcontracting relationships into close co-operative partnerships has finally reached the bottom of the supplier pyramid. The ongoing restructuring of small suppliers might therefore help to overcome the supplier network's dichotomy which has until now made the Japanese car industry an example of industrial dualism. But it should not be forgotten that this reshaping commands a price: many small suppliers do not find ways to fulfil their new technological and managerial responsibilities; they go bankrupt as far as they did not diversify successfully into new markets. Thus, the

10 For a detailed discussion of the dramatic changes of low-tier suppliers, including case studies of different future outlooks, see Hennig & Holzhausen (1997:10ff.). These changes are underpinned by the fact that on the level of low-tier suppliers the number of produced parts per firm and the number of variations per part are increasing – contrary to the trend of the first-tier suppliers (Hennig & Holzhausen 1997:12).

enforcement of keiretsu-relationships at low tiers of the supplier pyramid has far-reaching consequences because it is carried out more radical than the similar process at the level of first-tier suppliers. Furthermore, as it will be discussed in the next concluding chapter, the implications for the overall competitiveness of the Japanese car industry are different.

4 Conclusion

The downturn in the Japanese economy during the 1990s has thrown the automotive industry in its severest crisis since the second world war; it has compelled the industry to rigorously reduce costs that had swollen up owing to the inherent logic of exclusive and co-operative supplier relationships and owing to complacency during the years of the bubble economy. Inevitably, the cost-cutting measures have had tremendous impact on the nature of supplier relationships. Squeezing profits, forcing weaker parts manufacturers to merge with stronger suppliers and even causing some suppliers to leave the industry: these are the more or less typical circumstances to proceed consolidation of an industry in. What is remarkable in the Japanese case, is that supplier relationships have been simultaneously enforced by enlarging the tasks that both partners carry out jointly. This holds with regard to the relationships between car makers and first-tier suppliers in which suppliers emerge as co-leaders in the development process; and this is even more pronounced at the lower tiers of the supplier pyramid because small suppliers have been integrated for the first time in co-operative partnerships which cover design and development programmes, harmonization of production schedules and logistics.

What do these enforced keiretsu-relationships imply for the competitiveness of the Japanese automotive industry as a whole? First-tier suppliers can improve their technological expertise and become therefore theoretically more independent. That would surely boost competitiveness as big suppliers could use their freedom to aggressively pursue strategies of building up capabilities of system suppliers and global players. But it is rather doubtful, however, whether the car maker as the core firm of the keiretsu-network would approve.

As long as suppliers acquire new customers to sell standardized parts or expand into new markets outside the automotive industry, the car maker sees no reason to interfere because he is speculating that he shall benefit from lower prices. But if keiretsu-members start to supply technology, the car maker gets alarmed. Because large amounts of technology, due to the practice of joint development, are rather embedded in the network than well-defined properties of firms, the transfer of technological information and know-how which are perceived sensitive for the future of the car maker will be hindered by the car maker.

This has two negative effects on long-term competitiveness of the Japanese car industry. First, the reluctance to open their keiretsu-networks and to allow know-how to overthrow the limits of keiretsu-networks deprives in consequence the car makers themselves of much needed access to outside advanced technology – as far as domestic suppliers are concerned. Foreign part manufacturers and car makers which can offer new ideas and technologies are therefore esteemed as white knights that have the magic power of reviving ailing car makers and their supplier networks. Second, keiretsu-membership constrains Japanese suppliers to advance into the global major league of parts makers. On a long-term perspective, this could harm their competitiveness because they might be treated as junior partners in strategic alliances which are becoming more and more important in the future for the development of new technologies.

Contrary to these potential competitive damages by maintaining closed keiretsu-structures on the upper level of the supplier pyramid, the restructuring of relationships with small suppliers should be viewed in a more favourable light. Because in the past these relationships were based mainly on wage differences without any significant interaction between the business partners, turning them more co-operative should create some synergy with the prospect of rising productivity and profits in the future (putting it in transaction-cost jargon: the fostering of relational-specific skills leads to relational-quasi rents). That should improve not only the competitiveness of the car industry but also the still marginalized position of small firms in the Japanese industry.

References

Aoki, M. (1988), *Information, Incentives and Bargaining in the Japanese Economy*, Cambridge: Cambridge University Press.

Asanuma, B. (1989), Manufacturer-Supplier Relationships in Japan and the Concept of Relation-Specific Skill, in: *Journal of the Japanese and International Economies* 3: 1-30.

Asanuma, B. & Kikutani, T. (1992), Risk Absorption in Japanese Subcontracting. A Microeconomic Study of the Automobile Industry, in: *Journal of the Japanese and International Economies* 6: 1-29.

Böttcher, M. (1999), *Marketing im japanischen Investitionsgüter-Produktgeschäft*, Wiesbaden: Gabler.

Chûshô-kigyô-chô (1998), *Chûshô Kigyô Hakusho* [White Paper on Small and Medium-sized Enterprises], Tokyo: SMA.

Dore, R. (1987), *Taking Japan Seriously. A Confucian Perspective on Leading Economic Issues*, London: Routledge.

Fruin, W. M. & Nishiguchi, T. (1990), The Toyota Production System. Its Organizational Definition in Japan, in: *Keizai Kenkyû* 42,1: 42-55.

Fujimoto, T. (1996), *An Evolutionary Process of Toyota's Final Assembly Operations. The Role of Ex-post Dynamic Capabilities*, Discussion Paper Series 96-F-2, Research Institute for the Japanese Economy, Tokyo University.

Fujimoto, T. (1994), *Buhin Torihiki Kankei to Suparaiyâ Shisutemu* [Parts Transaction Relationships and the Supplier System], Discussion Paper Series 94-J-19, Research Institute for the Japanese Economy, Tokyo University.

Fujimoto, T. & Takeishi, A. (1994), *Jidôsha Sangyô 21 Seiki e no Shinario* [Scenario for the Car Industry in the 21st Century], Tokyo: Seisansei Shuppan.

Fujimoto, T., Sei, S. & Takeishi, A. (1994), Nihon Jidôsha Sangyô no Supuraiyâ Shisutemu no Zentaizô to sono Tamensei [The Whole Picture of the Supplier System of the Japanese Car Industry and its Diversity], in: *Kikai Keizai Kenkyû* 24: 11-36.

Helper, S. (1990), Competitive Supplier Relations in the U.S. and Japanese Auto Industries. An Exit/Voice Approach, in: *Business and Economic History* 19: 153-161.

Hennig, G. & Holzhausen, A. (1997), *Neue Kooperationsformen in der Automobilzulieferindustrie in Japan*, Occasional Paper Series 123, Ostasiatisches Seminar, Freie Universität Berlin.

Holzhausen, A. (1998), *Das japanische Beschäftigungssystem in der Krise*, Wiesbaden: Gabler.

Holzhausen, A. (1996), *Restrukturierung der Zulieferbeziehungen in der japanischen Autoindustrie*, Occasional Paper Series 115, Ostasiatisches Seminar, Freie Universität Berlin.

Ikeda, M. (1996), *Transformation of Japanese Subcontracting System amid Extreme Appreciation of Yen*, Occasional Paper Series 103, Ostasiatisches Seminar, Freie Universität Berlin.

Imai, K. & Itami, H. (1984), Interpenetration of Organization and Market. Japan's Firm and Market in Comparison with the U.S., in: *International Journal of Industrial Organization* 2: 285-310.

Nishiguchi, T. (1994), *Strategic Industrial Sourcing. The Japanese Advantage*, New York, Oxford: Oxford University Press.

Okamuro, H. (1995), Changing Subcontracting Relations and Risk-sharing in Japan, in: *Hitotsubashi Journal of Economics* 36,2: 207-218.

Richter, F.-J. (1997), Vertical Co-operation in the Automotive Industry. Perspectives from Japan, in: *Euro Asia Journal of Management* 14: 51-56.

Richer, F.-J. & Wakuta, Y. (1993), Permeable Networks. A Future Option for the European and Japanese Car Industries, in: *European Management Journal* 11,2: 262-267.

Smitka, M. (1991), *Competitive Ties: Subcontracting in the Japanese Automotive Industry*, New York: Columbia University Press.

Williamson, O. (1985), *The Economic Institutions of Capitalism. Firms, Markets, Relational Contracting*, New York: The Free Press.

Womack, J. P., Jones, D. T. & Roos, D. (1990), *The Machine that Changed the World*, New York: Rawson.

Japan's Financial Reform

Kurt Görger

1 Reasons for the Crisis of Japan's Banks

1.1 The Slump in the Stock and Real Estate Markets

Since the 1990s, the Japanese financial market has been undergoing revolutionary changes, preceded by an overheated stock and real estate market, the so-called "bubble-economy". From the beginning until the end of the 1980s, not only the economy posted a growth of 5% in average, but also the stock and real estate market experienced a spectacular boom, that was fuelled by a heavily expansive monetary policy and almost uninhibited lending by the banking sector. Of predominant significance for the bubble-economy to burst was the tightening of the monetary policy by the Bank of Japan as of mid-1989, in order to slow down overheating. This resulted in a massive slump of the stock and real estate prices. That initiated the falling market for Japanese equities in autumn 1989. The Nikkei-225 index fell from 38,900 in October 1989 to less than 13,000 in October 1998. Simultaneously, the Dow-Jones-index boomed from 2,400 in 1989 to more than 10,000 – at times even above 11,000. As a result, Tokyo – by market capitalisation in 1989 still the largest stock-exchange in the world (Y385 trillion) – fell to rank three behind New York and London. During the same decade not only the number of foreign companies quoted at the Tokyo Stock Exchange fell considerably, but also the total number of the companies quoted remained nearly unchanged, whilst the New York Stock Exchange showed an increase of about 45%. Recovery started only in 1999, when the benchmark Nikkei 225 index powered ahead, spurred by hopes in recovery of the Japanese economy. With that performance, which reached its peak in mid-April 2000 with an index ranging above 20,000, Japanese stocks had indeed detached themselves from the general economic development. Stocks were driven by companies that moved aggressively on restructuring and committed to shareholder value, showing high profits in spite of the economic environment. Many Japanese corporations' efforts to curb down cost and their willingness to accept direct foreign investment may further assure the stock market. A continuous rally along a wide front, however, requires an economic turnaround. This, however, is being put at risk as of the Nikkei's latest fall that commenced in April 2000. At first, this fall of the Tokyo Stock Exchange was considered to be in consequence of consolidation tendencies at Wall Street, however, meanwhile the lasting decrease down to around 16,000 by the end of May 2000 is dampening hopes for a domestic economic recovery.

Whilst the stock market during the past years from time to time showed signs of recovery, real estate prices are still today falling. This deflation of real estate value over the past ten years has added up to a total loss of 80% in the urban areas, which equals roughly three-times worth the Japanese GDP. In contrast to the stock markets, the further deterioration of the real estate prices has not stopped in 1999. 1999 showed a further decline of 4.9%, which was even an acceleration in comparison to the previous year. This development was due to many companies' restructuring and selling property in the frame of consolidation. Furthermore, there was a downturn in housing demand due to unemployment fears. In comparison to 1990, the peak of the bubble-economy with its inflated real estate and equities prices, commercial real estate in Tokyo was available at 28% and in Osaka at 24% of the price at the time. During the current year, there have been no signs that this downturn will stop. In consequence, this means that the crisis of Japan's banks, that is closely linked to the steep fall of real estate prices, has not yet ended.

Against the background of the spiral of deflation, the Japanese financial sector already started to suffer during the early 1990s. Following a high volume of bad loans resulting from the sharp fall in prices, banks started to trim their lending towards commercial businesses. It is true that the licensed banks extended only 20% of their total loan book to the real estate and construction sector, however, around 80% of the total loans were secured by real estate collateral alone. Japan's banks crisis therefore can be considered in the first place a crisis of the real estate sector. Against all odds, Japan's banks have yet managed to tackle the increased pressure for disposal of their problem loans. They have been supported by the Cooperative Credit Purchasing Company (CCPC), that was founded in March 1993. CCPC has bought a large number of bad loans and has been selling off properties that were forming the collateral for such loans purchased. Real estate sales realised by CCPC, however, have led to a further deterioration of real estate prices and consequently of the Banks' balance sheets quality.

1.2 Structural Banking Problems: Lack of Transparency and Slow Financial Reform

Whilst the aftermath of the bubble economy can be considered the trigger of Japan's banks' crisis, deep rooting problems and structural aspects are still besetting the Japanese banking system. The crisis was intensified by unsatisfactory transparency and control mechanisms within the banking industry. Therefore, it is not surprising that investors in the Japanese securities market are still suspicious about each bank and its future development. During so-called "black November" in 1997, when the forth largest securities firm, Yamaichi, the tenth largest commercial bank, Hokkaidô Takushoku, one middling securities firm, Sanyô, and a regional bank, Tokuyô City Bank, failed, Japan's financial crisis gained international momentum. Since, international markets' worries over the stability of the entire financial system of the world's largest net-creditor never stopped, in spite of the alarming writings on the wall that had been clearly visible already much earlier. Beginning in December 1994 until black November 1997, yet 14 regional banks and credit cooperatives failed. Further, the entire industry of housing loan companies (so called *jûsen* companies) and Nissan Life, a life insurance company, collapsed. Only against the background of unsatisfactory transparency and control, banks' balance sheets fraud was made possible and – for example – became the fate of Yamaichi. Generally speaking, due to far-reaching choices in assessment of assets and liabilities, banks' balance sheets were only little meaningful. Lack of transparency was also reflected in the number of non-performing assets disclosed, which gradually sharply increased. Resulting from the on-going weak economy and reoccurring corporate collapses, the level of bad loans at financial institutions is still not clear. In fiscal 1999 (as of March 31st 2000), three large commercial banks alone – Industrial Bank of Japan, Fuji Bank and Dai-Ichi Kangyô Bank – were still holding a volume of Y4,700 billion bad loans on their books.

Japan's banks' crisis is also a result of a drawn-out financial reform process, that until the end of the 1990s never really gained momentum. The Japanese financial system was distinguished by a high degree of specialisation, that was developed in the 1940s in order to finance wartime industry, and in the 1950s to finance economic revival. A number of specialised institutions were founded, each for an individual purpose. Such, in 1971 the *jûsen* were founded as a union of seven housing loan companies, offering housing finance loans that ordinary banks were not able to extend due to the long-term nature of the business. Traditionally, Japanese financial institutions by law were designated to very precisely defined areas of activity. Banks in Japan, as in the United States, were prohibited in principle from conducting securities business. Securities business was only allowed to so-called "securities-houses". Chief focus of ordinary banks were deposit-taking and lending activities. It was intended that way to avoid problems in one particular area of business to infect another. Furthermore, as formerly in France or Italy, Japanese financial institutions were classified as either short-term, or long-term in their deposit-taking or lending, in order to avoid the risk of a gap between maturing assets and liabilities.

This double demarcation of financial institutions was unique among the world's leading industrial nations financial systems and resulted in 147 licensed banks in Japan operating in highly specialised groups. Still today the Japanese financial system is highly *overbanked* with a number of 842 operating financial institutions. Moreover, the old system was not led by market mechanism, but by a system of *financial socialism*.

1.3 Other Serious Weak Points of the Financial Market

Two additional drawbacks of the Japanese financial system have to be mentioned: the dependence of the Bank of Japan (BoJ) and the low capital base in the banking sector.

The BoJ had no freedom to take own decisions. It operated as an agency only to carry out the monetary policy ordered by the government. The BoJ was probably the only central bank world wide that had to present detailed plans about its future activities to the government. The central government, in contrast to particularly most federally governed states, had great economic power. Considering these circumstances, timely intervention by the central bank, for example to avoid Japan's banks' crisis, was nearly impossible .

Banks have traditionally low net worth. Moreover, they hold a relatively large portion of their capital base in the form of shares (between 6% and 10% for city and trust banks). Thus a falling market influences the net value of banks and their collateral quality. Not least because of shrinking net worth and severe under-capitalisation, a dangerous liquidity crisis (credit-crunch) was looming over Japan. However, this credit crunch proved to be an unexpected benefit to the underdeveloped investment banking sector. Issuing asset-backed securities turned out to be a true alternative for those companies, that had faced credit cuts. This boom resulted in a thriving securitisation market.

2 Infection of the Real Economy

In addition to the domestic liquidity crisis, the banks faced severe losses from Russia, the emerging markets as well as from hedge funds, that resulted in even firmer restraint in extending loans. Since the banks over years massively shrank their loan books in order to stabilise their eroding balance sheets, more and more companies were driven into bankruptcy. The inability of Japan's banks to extend new loans accelerated the downturn of the country's economy.

Spring 2000 was raising hopes for an economic upturn in Japan, which was stimulated by expansive monetary and fiscal policy, stabilisation of the banking industry and an unexpected rapid recovery of the Asian economies. A turnaround is becoming possible for Japan's economy. After Japan's real GDP showed modest growth of 0.3% in 1999, the economists of the IMF were raising hopes in their spring issue of World Economic Outlook for a GDP growth of 0.9% in 2000. Optimism was fed by improved corporate profitability, increasing production levels in the nation's industrial sector and a generally improved business confidence. As deflationary effects seem to have slowed down, the IMF expects an increase of prices of 0.1% in 2000. This would liberate Japan from the country's deepest and longest recession since the Second World War. During the first quarter of 2000, GDP grew 2.4% compared to the previous quarter, which was the strongest growth in four years. The Japanese Economic Planning Agency (EPA) is expecting a GDP growth of 1.0% for the current fiscal year 2000/2001. From January until March, domestic demand has risen by 1.5%, foreign demand by 0.9%. Consumer spending, which accounts for 60% of Japan's economic activity, increased by 1.8% against the previous quarter. This too was the first time in three years that the indices stopped deteriorating. The rate of corporate investment expanded by 4.2%, led by IT-industries. It does now depend largely on the future development of the stock and real estate market whether the hopes of a GDP rebound will be disappointed or not. The latest falling stock market in May 2000 could sweep away early signs of recovery. During the last decade, experience has shown that a sudden crash of the stock market – as it happened lately in May 2000, entails a credit curb and a slow down in investment.

3 Measures to Deal with the Banks' Crisis

If the bubble economy had not occurred, the traditional structure of the financial market could have survived for some more decades – though working inefficiently. Due to the massive problems and the long-lasting economic crisis, international financial markets pressured step by step into a reform of the banking system. Moreover, Japan had to realise that several economic packages of the past had failed to spur growth. Japan has been the last stronghold of Keynes' theories, which teaches anti-cyclic governmental fiscal policy to steer the economy. In Japan, Keynes' concept to increase domestic demand by expansive budget policy has meanwhile led to substantial fiscal imbalance. Public spending has resulted in Japan's public debt level soaring. Already back in late 1997, a "Plan for Financial System Stabilisation" was announced, which set aside additional equivalent of DM140 billions to the pool of funds already in place to recapitalise weak banks. This measure (bank recapitalisation by state capital injections) was politically highly disputable, as it inflated – together with general tax cuts – the public sector debt dramatically. The public deficit rose excessively from 2.3% of GDP in 1994 to 7% of GDP in 1999. Japan's gross debit reached 105% of GDP in 1999. The government thus has nearly no more scope for bold action.

3.1 The Financial Rehabilitation Law

For that reason, in 1998 the government jointly with businesses tried to overcome the banks' crisis and the related economic weakness by a more demand-driven policy. The financial rehabilitation law issued in spring and further enhanced in autumn 1998 had in principle three elements:

- state funding to shore up defaulting institutions,
- establishment of state-controlled bridge banks to take over insolvent banks and
- agreement on deposit insurance fund.

Moreover, giving in to international pressure, it was announced that taxpayers' money was to be used to fund these measures. There was strong criticism among taxpayers over the use of public money to recapitalise the financial industry, as the banks had suffered a severe loss of public confidence. Originally, Y60,000 billion were set aside to support the banking system, which were allotted as follows:

- Y17,000 billion for the Deposit Insurance Funds,
- Y18,000 billion for state purchase of failed banks and
- Y25,000 billion to recapitalise weak but viable banks.

In spring 2000, fresh Y10,000 billion were set aside to protect depositors. To summarise, yet the total public money backing the process amounts to Y70,000 billion. That way, an comprehensive net of public protection was set up, that covered individual depositors as well as the general risk of a renewed panic in the financial markets. Generally, *calm before the storm* has settled since over the banking industry. Banks accepting government funds must also dispose and write down their non-performing loans (NPLs) and sell their collateral, such as properties or securities, in order to at least partly compensate the losses.

Another major new development was the formation of the Financial Supervisory Agency (FSA), performing transparent and fair financial supervision and classification of financial institutions as an independent agency.

3.1.1 Details of the Recapitalisation of Banks

Apart from undercapitalised banks, also solvent banks with a capital adequacy ratio (CAR) of 8% or more could ask for public funding through state purchases of preferred shares. However, such funding was restricted to three conditions: the solvent bank is taking over a failed institution, or the solvent bank is involved in a merger or any similar kind of reorganisation within the industry, or the solvent bank would be threatened to stop booking new loans 'suddenly and massively' if public funds were not granted.[1] Undercapitalised banks operating internationally with a CAR over 4% but less then 8% (over 2% less then 4% domestically) could seek capital injection through state purchases of preferred shares. For banks with a CAR of less then 4% but more then 2% operating internationally, (less then 2%

1 For defining the CAR, the bank's assets, especially securities held, were not strictly valued at the lowest either book or market value, but *adequately*, with the intention to restore the financial markets' confidence in the banks' balance sheets. Similarly, the definition of NPLs and required reserves was not based on clear rules, but reserves were required *adequately*.

but more then 1% domestically), capital injection could be made through state purchases of common or preferred shares. Banks extremely undercapitalised with a CAR less then the numbers quoted above, but which debts that did not exceed the assets could also seek state capital injection. However, only such banks were to be considered for government help if their survival was considered vital for local businesses. At the same time, the "Financial Revitalisation Committee" would order an increase of the CAR, reduce the scope of the bank's operations or merge it with another bank. For banks which debts that exceed their assets, a legally defined procedure would deal with the failed institution, either appointing a Financial Disposal Trustee, or if necessary handing over operations to a publicly owned bridge bank with limited life span, or taking over the bank completely, as it happened in the case of Long-Term Credit Bank of Japan and Nippon Credit Bank. This way, the government avoided that a bank failure entailed the bankruptcy of sound borrowers.

3.1.2 Weaknesses of the Reform Plan

Although now a legal framework and financial resources for mastering the financial crisis are in place, there are still doubts whether the measures will carry the desired effects as the application for public funds is based on the banks' voluntary decision.

According to many critics the major fault in dealing with the long-term structural banking problems is the government's waiver to enforce the increase of the banks' capital base. Injection of public funds is subject to the voluntary submission of a "Management-Improvement-Plan", that should include improved efficiency of operations, reduction of staff, cost-cutting measures, reform of the senior management, reduction of senior management positions, reduction of dividends and bonuses, or even a reduction of capital at the cost of the shareholders. For that reason, it was expected that there would be only very few applications. From today's point of view it can be said that those worries – for the time being – were groundless. On the other side, the alternative to force public money on all banks without asking for their voluntary application would have carried the risk that even fatally weak banks were held alive artificially. Yet, the effects of the first round of financial injections to all banks of spring 1998 had fallen far behind the expectations.

Another doubt regards the fact that public money injections do not guarantee that commercial banks are not trimming their lending. The difficult situation in the banking industry, that the Bank of Japan's extremely loose monetary policy tried to counteract, will for the time being overshadow the real economic development of Japan.

3.2 First Results of Injection of Funds

By end of March 1999, 15 of 18 banks have received capital injection for Y7,460 billion, of which Y5,560 billion were convertible preferred stock, Y600 billion were other preferred and Y1,300 billion were subordinated debt. Additionally, Y2,150 billion were raised from private funding to stabilise the banking industry, which resulted in a total capital injection for Y9,600 billion (see figure 1).

Figure 1: Capital Increase for 15 Banks in Fiscal Year 1998, Billion Yen

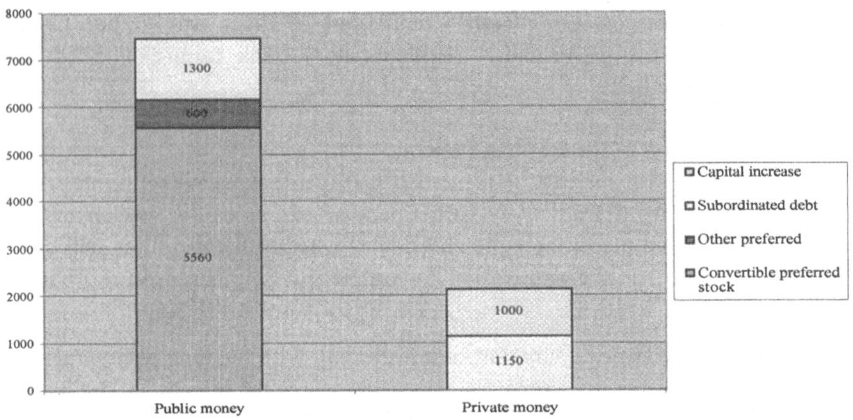

Source: Financial Reconstruction Commission (1999), *Annual Report 1999*, Tokyo: FRC.

So, the banks were less hesitant over aid than expected. A further scheme to help the ailing banks was announced in March 1999: 15 commercial banks received additional public injections between Y150 billion and Y1,000 billion against which the banks directly placed preference shares to the FSA. The total public funds for Y9,600 billion resulted in a drastic improvement of the banks financial strength. Furthermore, the capital base, following the BIS guidelines, expanded by Y7,000 billion due to a strong stock market. In total, Japan's banks were able to raise their BIS-Capital-Adequacy ratio by the end of September 1999 to 11.8% (1990: just above 8%). The figure represents the capital base in relation to the total of loans outstanding. By using a total of Y70,000 billion and virtually partly nationalising nearly all leading banks, Japan has made good progress during 1999 in stabilising the faltering banking system (see figure 2). At the same time, the roots of instability never really vanished. Three major problems are still lurking over the banking sector:

- In the light of the enormous size of the banking problems, the whole system is still quite weak. The banks therefore still do not properly fulfil their duty in loan supplies. Moreover, they are facing the difficult task of repayment of their public fund injection within three years.
- In addition, a lot of small and middle-sized local and regional banks are in a critical state and not likely to be able to survive. For those institutions, the forthcoming discontinuation of 100% government protection for bank deposits will be crucial. After the relevant date of implementation, only deposits for Y10 million will be insured. Weak banks, therefore, are in danger of a run on their deposits.
- A third dilemma in the Japanese financial system represents the life insurance sector in the light of Japan's lasting zero interest rate policy and the resulting negative interest margins. Thorough consolidation is to be expected in this industry. Following the massive government aid to Japan's banking system, the same is to be expected for the life insurance industry.

Figure 2: Non-Performing Loans and Total Cushion of 17 Major Banks (as of September 1999, Billion Yen)

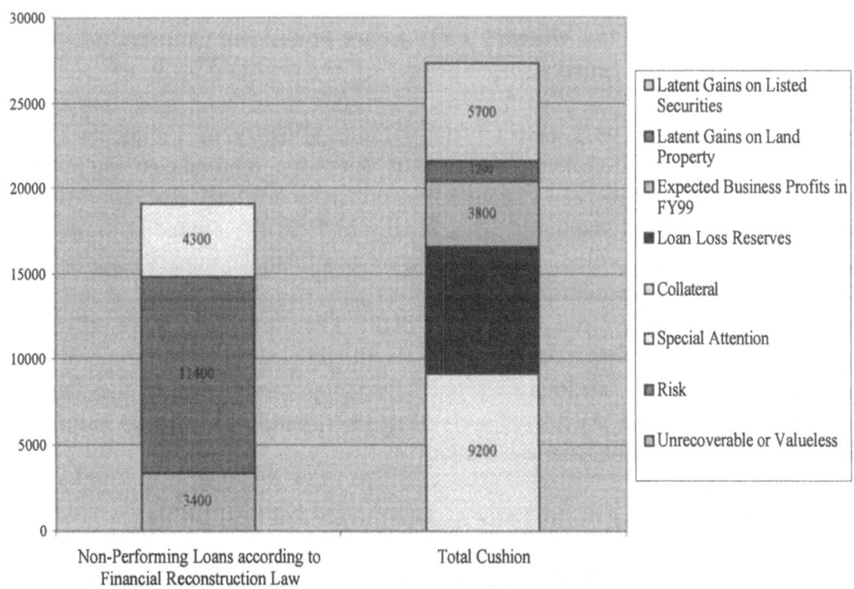

Source: Financial Reconstruction Commission (1999), *Annual Report 1999*, Tokyo: FRC.

3.3 Indirect Solution: Ways to the "Big Bang"

When the Japanese government in the early 1990s failed to revitalise the economy, a severe loss of confidence in previously well-known methods to regulate the economy emerged. Gathering speed since the mid-1990s, deregulation was now considered not only to be a measure to revive the domestic economy, but also to reform the financial sector. As opposed to the London "Big Bang", the Tokyo "Big Bang" reforms will be completed in several stages until 2001. This way, Japan is facing the challenges of global competition. This is crucial as the 1990s was a decade virtually lost, compared to other parts of the world such as the US, which experienced the IT-revolution, or Europe, which prepared for the common market. It can be said, however, that during the past two years of liberalising the financial markets, increased global competition and a massive growth of IT-investment, significant progress was made: there is a massive shake-up in Japan's banking, broker and insurance industry.

Dealing with liberalisation and deregulation, the financial sector has the following four objectives: reduction of the Ministry's of Finance power and constitution of an independent supervisory agency; independence of the Bank of Japan from political influence; adoption of internationally accepted standards and desegmentation and consolidation of the banking industry.

3.3.1 Reduction of the Ministry's of Finance Power and Constitution of an Independent Supervisory Agency

In this context, not only restructuring of the Ministry of Finance's (MOF) organisation was undertaken, but also of operating methods of the banking supervision. Those had been characterised rather by arbitrary discretion than by mandatory, numerical standards. That is why in 1998 the Financial Supervisory Agency (FSA) was formed, which took over the financial supervision from the MOF. However, bureaucratic connections are still very tight, as all FSA-employees were recruited from the MOF. The new agency is of utmost importance, as it can find a bank to be insolvent and place it under temporary state control. The FSA is anxious to return investors' confidence to the Japanese financial market. Thus it declared early May 1999, that it will step up its balance-sheet audits on all major Japanese Banks.

3.3.2 Independence of the Bank of Japan from Political Influence

The Bank of Japan had been under control of the MOF for several decades (exactly since 1942). With effect from 1. April 1998, it received greater independence. Until that day, the Bank of Japan had no right of own decision-making; it worked solely as executive organ for the government. The BoJ was probably the only central bank world wide that had to present detailed plans about its future activities to the government. After 18 months years of independence, the Bank of Japan has in the meantime taken over the major role in reforming Japan's financial system. At the same time, the MOF has lost its importance. According to analysts, the bank reform under the guidance of the central bank has made better progress than expected.

3.3.3 Adoption of Internationally Accepted Standards

Apart from the aforementioned structural reforms, owing to international pressure, important decisions of financial deregulation that adapt to international standards were taken. When the "Big Bang" will be completed, brokerage commissions on stock trading and on insurance premium will be fully liberalised, curbs on using financial instruments such as derivatives will be lifted and foreign currency can be freely exchanged. This will lead to an increased competition in the financial sector.

3.3.4 Desegmentation and Consolidation of the Banking Industry

The most important objective, however, is to abolish firewalls between banks, securities, and insurance business and permit institutions to develop to efficiently operating, universal financial institutions. Although competition has increased during the past years between the different financial groups and activities of banks have spread, there is still a certain division. This shall now be abandoned completely in order to create an internationally accepted standard.

The elimination of the firewalls between the different types of financial institutions will entail a concentration within the industry. Therefore, mergers and acquisitions within the banking, securities and insurance industry will be imminent. This will additionally accelerate the reform of the financial sector. Moreover, holding companies for financial institutions will be permitted. Before this background, preparations for mergers and acquisitions are under full steam. Also, institutions preparing to merge will benefit from the revised employment laws that make it easier to lay off staff. In the whole banking industry, a staff reduction of at least 15 to 20 per cent is expected during the next few years, which equals a total number of workforce of over 100,000. First steps to overcome the firewalls between the different types of institutions were the merger between the Bank of Tokyo and the Mitsubishi Bank in September 1998, the alliance between Industrial Bank of Japan and Nomura Securities in May 1998 and the union of Dai-Ichi Kangyô Bank with Kankaku Securities.

Winners following this vital and desired change of structure could be three types of groups:

- Large city banks, that maintain a large and profound branch network serving private as well as local corporate customers and offering a wide range of financial products.

- Large regional banks, that equally maintain a strong local branch network connected to private customers and as well as to small enterprises. They could well adopt a valuable economic role in the future.
- Shinkin-Banks (Savings-Banks) with their roots in the retail market. They have a strong local basis and their activities are aimed at providing easily accessible services for small and medium enterprises and for the general public.

Losers following this restructuring process could be the below mentioned banking groups:

- Long-term-credit banks (specialised in long-term commercial lending), as shown by the collapse of Long-Term-Credit Bank of Japan.
- Trust banks, as these institutions do not maintain a branch network. They are mainly restricted to wholesale banking. Some of the long-term-credit banks as well as some of the trust banks are expected to merge with banks that maintain a wider branch network.
- Small regional banks (such as Hyôgo and Taiheiyô), that will be subjected to increasing competition by the local-regional and city banks.
- Credit cooperatives, as the rural sector will further loose importance. Following latest reports, the reform of the credit cooperatives proceeds in a very slow pace. This sector represents around 13% of the total loan outstanding in Japan. In 1996 this part of the industry declared to reduce the number of 3,000 rural credit cooperatives to 530 in March 2001. In April 2000, still 1,411, more than twice as many cooperatives as originally intended, are in operation. The delay in reorganising the rural credit cooperatives concerns the large commercial banks, as they see the danger of a fresh market disturbance as the reorganisation fails.
- Japan's securities firms, as since October 1999 banks' brokerage subsidiaries will have access to the securities business. Also other industries, such as Sony, and foreign financial institutions, that are interested to participate in this attractive business, can enter the market. Foreign financial institutions, that have gained ground in Japan during the recent years, will be able to attract a bigger market share due to ongoing liberalisation. Looking some years ahead, large US financial institutions could well have positioned themselves strongly in the market.

3.4 Japan's Banking Industry after the "Big Bang"

When Japan's Big Bank will complete in 2001 six separate universal bank-holdings could emerge.

The first new group is the giant-alliance between the leading Japanese financial institutions Industrial Bank of Japan (IBJ), Dai-Ichi-Kangyô Bank (DKB) and Fuji Bank under the holding named "Mizuhô". These three institutions, ranking among the 15 largest banks of the country, will form after the proposed marriage the largest banking group in the world with assets of about Y140,000 billion. Whilst DKB and Fuji Bank represent traditional commercial banks, IBJ stands out as the country's only institution with certain experience in investment banking. During the last business year 1999/2000, all three banks could return to black figures after heavy losses suffered in the year before. However, they still suffer from a burden of bad loans. There was no immediate pressure for the alliance. Some analysts doubt the economic value of the alliance, as size alone will not guarantee for international competitiveness. However, on the other hand, strong investment needs in IT will be eased by large size. Generally, information technology in Japan is considered to be the key to revitalisation of the banking sector as well as to recovery of the entire economy.

The second group is built from the merger of the city banks Sumitomo and Sakura, that is expected to be completed by April 2001. This merger is even more spectacular than the Mizuhô alliance as it tears down the walls between the rival Mitsui and Sumitomo corporate groups. This signals the end of a system, that has been in place since the Second World War. The following imminent concentration and reorganisation in the financial world has led to a split of the traditional corporate groups (Keiretsu). This core element of Japan's economic system, characterised by cross share-holding, regularly sitting committees and a joint *house-bank* as a co-ordinator has started to deteriorate.

Other emerging banking groups include the alliance of Asahi Bank, Sanwa Bank and Tôkai Bank which agreed in autumn 1999 on the establishment of a financial holding company[2], the merger of Chûô Trust & Banking and Mitsui Trust & Banking into Chûô Mitsui Trust & Banking as of April 1st, 2000. Furthermore, two more large mergers have been announced.

Another milestone in Japan's process of financial reform illustrates the re-privatisation of the previously – due to insolvency – nationalised Long-Term Credit Bank (LTCB) (now called: Shinsei Bank) to a consortium of around ten foreign investors assembled by Ripplewood, an US private equity group. The consortium comprises influential names such as Deutsche Bank, GE Capital, ABN AMRO, Mellon Bank and other high-graded financial and industrial companies. Likewise, Nippon Credit Bank, which was nationalised in the end of 1998, is expected to be sold to a consortium of investors led by Softbank, including the insurance group Tokyo Marine & Fire and leasing group Orix. As part of the agreement, the government is planning to remove clearly bad assets so that Nippon Credit Bank will be already *clean* at the time of sale. That Japan is now

---

2 In June 2000, however, Asahi Bank pulled out of the planned merger after disputes about management strategy.

heading for reform is also proved by new licences granted for new entrants from non-financial industries, such as new Itô-Yokado Bank (see table 1).

Table 1: Some Non-Financial Corporations Entering Japan's Banking Industry

Corporation	Contents to enter into financial industry
Itô-Yokado	Bank for individuals specialising in settlement
Sony	Internet banking which is specialised for individuals: •Getting deposits by using Internet and •Settlement service for individuals via Internet
Softbank, Tokyo-Marine, Orix (Buying Nippon Credit Bank)	Core aim is to support venture corporations: •Loan to venture corporations depending on their intellectual property •Search and invest in hopeful venture corporations •Settlement service for electric commerce trading via Internet

4 Summary

The reform process as it now has taken off has not quite yet reached the roots of financial instability. However, it can be said that the financial *crisis* is over. Tokyo will not turn over night into a new world financial hub, but further damage to the power of the Tokyo financial centre can be avoided. If Japan goes ahead with the planned mergers, by size of assets, Japan's banks will again be topping the list of the world's leading banks. The "Big Bang" is pointing into the right direction. In the long run, it will not only tear down the firewalls between the different sectors of the Japanese financial markets, but it will also split up the traditional corporate groups (Keiretsu). In the light of earlier mergers in the banking industry, commercial success of new alliances can not be considered as guaranteed, as different corporate cultures include a large conflict potential. Particularly, *big is beautiful* does not seem to be a reasonable strategy in times of radically changing corporate finance and IT-revolution.

Japanese consumers as well as businesses will profit from increased competition in the Japanese financial market. On the one hand, due to consolidation in the banking industry, creditors will gain influence on their borrowers with regard to the enforcement of structural changes; on the other hand consolidation will bring more efficiency to the terms and cost of credit. This means a more rigid selection of borrowers as a consequence of fewer commercial banks. Moreover, radical changes in deposit taking and lending business are to be expected. Thus, financing in the capital market, such as raising funds by selling stocks or bonds, will more and more take the place of classical loan financing. In the long run, we can expect that Japan, too, will adopt the Anglo-Saxon, capital market driven financial models.

When the NASDAQ was formed not long ago, the Tokyo Stock Exchange followed with a market for venture capital called MOTHERS (Market of the High-growth and Emerging Stocks). It offers Japanese depositors who are traditionally very conservatively-minded new prospects of investment in high-risk companies. Up to now, the largest portion of private savings for about Y1,300 trillion is being placed in the postal savings system and in bank deposits. Lately, interest in more attractive investments is rising. During the next two years, Y106 trillion postal savings will mature and are expected to be shifted to alternative investment forms. In all probability, foreign investment firms based in Tokyo will profit from this process, due to their know-how and wide range of financial products.

Modes of Employment in Japan

Michio Nitta

1 Regular Employees and Non-Regular Employees

According to Suzuki (1998) who surveyed the European and Japanese literature on the topic, regular employment (or typical employment in the literature) is generally defined as "employment for full-time work without a fixed employment term." Non-regular employment, therefore, denotes modes of employment other than those in the previous definition. Suzuki (1998) also pointed out that these criteria were insufficient for an accurate understanding of the actual circumstances of regular and non-regular employment. For instance, there are many workers in Japan who work the same or almost same hours as "regular" employees, but are nonetheless differentiated from regular employees and treated as "non-regular" employees.

Table 1 shows the distribution of the hours worked weekly by employment types based on the Basic Survey of the Employment Structure in 1997. This includes "regular" employees (working a minimum of 200 days annually), "part-time" employees, and "arubaito" employees. As shown in the table, those working fewer than 35 hours per week as "part-time" employees accounted for no more than 56.8% of the total. Many "part-time" workers in Japan work fulltime or almost fulltime.

Furthermore, Table 2 shows the distribution of employment status defined by types of contracts broken down by the types of employment, based on the same survey. The table shows that only 41.2% of the "part-time" workers were employed under contracts with a clearly-specified term of employment. This percentage rises to the 63% level for "arubaito" employees. It shows that this type of employment is more of an interim nature than that of "part-time" workers. Regrettably, the lack of available data prevents us from determining the percentages of "part-time" workers and "arubaito" workers working more than 35 hours per week under contracts without a fixed term. Assuming that 50% of "part-time" workers under employment contracts with no particular term limitations work 35 hours or longer in a week, this would correspond to about 1.5 million workers. Those working under contracts without fixed terms may be likely working longer hours than those under fixed term contract. If this is true, it would be more realistic to assume the ratio would be 60% instead of 50%. This would mean that more than 1.8 million people fall under this category, namely working under non-limited term contract and longer than 35 hours per week.

Table 1: Employee Status and Weekly Working Hours (%)

	< 35	35 – 42	43 – 48	49 – 59	60 <
Regular Employees	1.9	37.8	34.1	16.8	9.2
Part-timers	56.8	29.1	10.5	2.7	0.8
Arubaito Workers	35.3	33.3	20.4	7.6	3.2

Notes: 1) Part-timers: Those who are called as parttimer or by similar name.

2) Arubaito Workers: Those who are called Arubaito or by similar name. Arubaito traditionally meant student workers but are now used more widely, meaning young no-regular employees.

Source: Management and Co-ordination Agency (1997), *Shûgyô Kôzô Kihon Chôsa 1997* [Basic Survey of Employment Structure 1997].

Table 2: Employee Status and Types of Employment Contract

	Total Number (1000 persons)	%	Non-limited term	Limited term: 1 month – 1 year	Limited term: less than 1 month
Total	51,147	100	87.3	9.8	2.8
Regular Employees	38,542	100	99.1	0.5	0.4
Parttimers	6,998	100	58.8	33.4	7.8
Arubaito Workers	3,344	100	35.1	52.0	12.9
Shokutaku Workers	966	100	66.7	30.6	2.7
Agency Workers	257	100	54.5	40.5	4.7
Others	1,025	100	38.6	36.6	24.7

Notes: 1) Shokutaku Workers: Those who are called shokutaku or by similar name. Shokutaku means special assignment and implies senior workers.

2) Agency Workers: Those who are employed and dispatched to client users by manpower dispatching service agencies.

Source: Management and Co-ordination Agency (1997), *Shûgyô Kôzô Kihon Chôsa 1997* [Basic Survey of Employment Structure 1997].

A similar calculation leads us to estimate that there are about 1.25 million “arubaito” workers working under non-limited term contract and longer than 35 hours per week. Therefore, the workers in these two categories exceed three million people. They are "regular" employees by generally used definition because of the nature of employment contract and working hours. It is clear, however, that they are differentiated from typical "regular" employees in terms of actual status. Thus, those group of workers can be categorized as "non-typical" non-regular employees.

There are types of non-regular employees other than "part-time" and "arubaito" workers according to the survey. They include agency workers, contract workers and so on. Those types of workers account for about 18% of total "non-regular" employees. We will discuss those group of workers later in more detail.

2 The Diversity in Regular Employment

We have already noted there is some diversity among "regular" employees too, although most of them work full time without term limitations according to table 1 and table 2. From the standpoint of Japanese law, the most important meaning of employment contracts without term limitations is that the legal range for limiting employee dismissal is clearly regulated, in which Japanese courts would curb "abuses of the employer's right to dismiss employees". Nevertheless, there are cases in which workers employed under contracts without term limitations enjoy quite different levels of employment protection.

2.1 Small Firms

For example, Table 3 shows the substantial differences by company size in the percentages of the workers discharged for disciplinary reason among all workers who left employment during 1994. This may be partly attributable to the capability of large companies to attract, select and retain better, disciplined workers as a result of the success of their rigorous recruitment procedures and various tools of personnel management. Another possibility is that smaller enterprises are more liable to dismiss employees than larger companies as a means of penalizing workers for their shortcomings. It may sound contradictory with the strong legal protection for employment provided by court that large number of workers in small firms are dismissed for disciplinary reasons. In reality, it is very likely that large numbers of legally unjustifiable dismissals exist particularly in the small firm sector. The reason for this lies in the fact that there are extremely fewer lawsuits in Japan than in Europe and the U.S. The number of labor disputes taken to court is no exception. The cost and time for court action should be taken into account. Many of the actual dismissals in Japan would very likely be judged to be abuses of the right of dismissal on the part of employers if they were brought to court. This action would require workers to invest a lot of money and time, however. It is much easier for workers to avoid lawsuits and seek another chance of employment. Therefore, the number of dismissed workers who actually take their cases into court is limited.

Table 3: Disciplinary Discharge Ration by Size of Company

Total	> 1000 employees	300 – 999 employees	100 – 299 employees	30 – 99 employees	5 – 29 employees
4.6	1.9	2.9	3.7	3.5	8.1

Note: Disciplinary Discharge Ratio: Number of discharged workers for disciplinary reasons * 100 / number of workers who left a company for any reason.

Source: Ministry of Labour (1994), *Koyô Dôkô Chôsa 1994* [Survey of Employment Trend 1994].

A reason for the fewer dismissals in large companies is that workers in these companies have a higher percentage of union membership, and labor union activities inhibit dismissals, including discharges for disciplinary reasons. The lower unionization rate in small businesses makes the actual level of employment protection for workers under contracts without fixed terms lower than in larger companies.

Table 4 provides support for this through reverse reasoning. The table shows the employment contract relationship for part-time workers broken down by company size, based on the 1990 Ministry of Labor survey of part-time workers. The "Part-time workers A" in the table are typical "part-time" workers working shorter hours than regular workers. "Part-time workers B" are non-typical "part-time" workers who are treated as non-regular employees but work the same or almost same hours as regular employees. For both types of "part-timers", the smaller the size of the company, the higher the percentage of employment contracts without fixed terms.

This does not mean that "part-timers" in large companies are less assured of continued employment than their counterparts in smaller firms, however. Indeed, the opposite is the case. Many "part-time" workers in large companies have worked for a long time under contracts with fixed terms through contract renewal. Though terminating these employment contracts for "part-time" workers is not as difficult as discharging regular employees, it is not very easy, either. From a legal viewpoint, courts have expanded the interpretation of the legal principle of the abuse of the right of dismissal to those "part-time" workers who have continuously worked for a long period under contracts with term limitations.

Table 4: Limited Term Contract Ratio for Parttime Workers by Size of Company and Type of Parttime

	Total	>1000 empl.	500–999 empl.	300–499 empl.	100–299 empl.	33–99 empl.	5–29 empl.
Type A	30.4	71.6	67.2	70.2	41.2	27.3	16.8
Type B	44.6	80.1	79.5	70.0	57.9	37.7	16.9

Notes: 1) Type A: typical part-time worker working less than regular workers.

2) Type B: no-typical part-time worker working the same or almost same hours as regular workers.

Source: Ministry of Labour (1990), *Pâto-taimu Rôdôsha Sôgô Jittai Chôsa 1990* [Survey on Part-time Workers 1990].

The difficulty of dismissal is not only a legal issue. If any large company responded to economic downturns by simply canceling employment contracts with workers under contract with fixed terms (normally not organized in a labor union), the company's reputation as a good employer would suffer and it could have a negative impact on the business. In contrast, small business owners are less aware of their obligation to consider employment protection even for regular employees and often lack knowledge of the legal aspects of dismissal. They are also not under social scrutiny of conduct as strictly as in the cases of large employers. Thus they tend not to care about the types of employment contract, keeping many "part-timers" under non-fixed term contracts.

Needless to say, not all small business owners lack awareness of ensuring employment for their employees. For one thing, there are many types of small companies, so discussing them as if they were alike would lead to erroneous conclusions. Compared as a group, however, small businesses have obvious differences with big businesses. It may well be true that the regular employment at small businesses includes a substantial number of workers employed under "non-typical regular employment" relationships.

2.2 Female Workers

Though it is not a question of direct dismissal, some argue that many female workers are forced to forego long-term continuous employment and are de facto shut out from regular employment by several factors. These include the implicit encouragement of voluntary severance (by giving preferential treatment for the severance pay on quit due to marriage or childbirth) and discrimination in actual treatment (for instance, fewer opportunities for promotion). Of course, it cannot be proven that all female workers who leave a job due to marriage or childbirth do so for foregoing reasons. It is certain, however, that this is at least one persuasive hypothesis for explaining the lower numbers of long-term regular female employees in Japan in comparison to other countries. There has long been an argument based on this aspect that female workers be defined as "peripheral" workers among the regular employees (Furugori 1997:9). This argument holds that a certain portion of the female regular employees should be classified as being in the category of "non-typical regular employment" and not "typical regular employment".

3 Agency Workers, Quasi-Agency Workers and Construction Workers

3.1 Agency Workers and Quasi-Agency Workers

As shown in table 2, the Basic Survey of the Employment Structure in 1997 shows that there are less agency workers than often supposed – at most, only about 260,000. This, however, includes only those workers subject to the Labor Dispatching Service Law.

Many workers not subject to the law work at offices, shops or factories other than their employer's one through subcontracting agreements between the relevant companies. Typical examples include salespersons dispatched to department stores by wholesalers or manufacturers, subcontractors' employees at steel plants and shipyards, and employees of building maintenance companies and security guard service companies. Legally, agency work and those quasi-agency work are strictly differentiated but the distinction between the two is sometimes blurred in reality. To reach more comprehensive understanding of these categories of workers, Sato (1998) cites the Establishment and Enterprise Census of 1996 as an index for a comprehensive understanding of the number of employees working in workplaces other than their emplpyer's ones. The survey shows that approximately 1,917,000 employees were working as dispatched, subcontracted, or as loan employees. This estimate may be too small, however.

According to the census, there were 689,000 building maintenance service workers and 273,000 security service workers, for a total of nearly one million. Most of the employees in both industries are likely working at the host company. If the workers dispatched by outside companies or subcontractors in the manufacturing and other industries were added, the total number could be larger. Since it is not easy for host companies to accurately estimate the number of workers from other companies based on sub-contracting contracts, an underestimation of the total may be inevitable.

3.2 Construction Workers

Furthermore, if one focuses on flexibility in places of work and resulting instability and complexity in employment relationships, many workers in the construction industry do not work at a fixed site but move from one construction site to another. According to the Basic Survey of the Employment Structure in 1997, the construction industry employs 6,867,000 workers (Management and Co-ordination Agency 1997). Major construction projects are undertaken by general contractors who organize the work and oversee a large number of subcontractors. Employees of those subcontractors are working under somewhat similar relationships with general contractors to those of the quasi-agency workers referred to above.

3.3 Working Conditions

It should be noted, however, that employment conditions including wage level of these workers working in host companies under subcontract relations are quite different from those of non-regular employment workers such as "part-time" workers. For instance, wage levels of the workers from subcontracting firms in the steel industry are similar to those of the workers of small manufacturing companies (Nihon Rodo Kenkyu Kiko 1997), even though the latter category of workers could be classified as "non-typical regular employment".

It should also be noted that employment conditions of about half of the agency workers under the Labor Dispatching Service Law, who are employed by labor dispatching agencies on contracts without a fixed term, are similar to those of the regular employees of small businesses.

4 Quasi-Employed Self-Employed, Semi-Independent Employed and Typical Self-Employed

According to the Suzuki paper, the types of employment discussed in Europe as non-regular employment include not only part-time work, fixed-term employment and agency temporaries, but also telework, work at home, and contract labor. These fall in an intermediate area between self-employment and employment, according to the conventional understanding of employment issues in Japan. Although telework can include those working under an employment contract, the actual situation in Japan is that most people engaged in telework, who are still small in number in this country, work under subcontracting agreements with ordering firms (Hirata & Nitta 1985).

4.1 Quasi-Employed Self-Employed

The debate from the viewpoint of Japanese labor law has focused on employed-like characteristics (thus considered to be under protection of labor law) of some groups of self-employed workers. In traditional labor law discussions, one primary criterion for the employment relationship between an employer and an employee is an established relationship for giving directions and orders. In fact, however, the boundaries in this relationship are rather blurred, and it is difficult to make an accurate determination. Specifically, the issue has been discussed whether these workers in an intermediate area between self-employment and employment are covered by the Labor Standards Law and the Labor Union Law, and whether they are eligible for workers' accident compensation.

Work at home is classified as self-employment in the statistics. The Basic Survey of the Employment Structure counts "pieceworkers at home" as part of the self-employed population. There were 575,000 pieceworkers at home in the 1997 survey, of which 548,000 or 95.3% were women (Management and Co-ordination Agency 1997). The number of pieceworkers fell by half from 1,047,000 during the 15-year period starting in 1982. Most workers at home work in the textile industry and other manufacturing industries. Although they work under subcontracting agreements, they actually have attributes as employed workers. Based on this policy assumption, they are defined as "workers" at home, and are regulated by Home Workers Law. An advisory council for the Minister of Labor establishes minimum rates for piecework and other conditions for these workers. The rates are enforced by the Ministry of Labor.

In this narrow sense of the term, there are limited numbers of people engaged in work at home. Yet the same survey shows that there are as many as 5,313,000 self-employed people with no employees. Of these, 26.6% or 1,411,000 are women (Management and Co-ordination Agency 1997). Owners of very small retail shops are typical of this category. Also, it is estimated that many workers with no significant difference from workers at home are included in the self-employed population engaged in a variety of service industries. They include the operators of private "exam preparatory" schools of a larger chain.

Considering the contractual relationship with those who place the orders, many people work in what may be called "quasi-employed self-employed" working mode in addition to the workers at home. For instance, 1,276,000 (18.6%) people were either self-employed or family workers in the construction industry. In addition, some of the 735,000 executives in private-sector companies in the construction industry are de facto self-employed business operators or their families (Management and Co-ordination Agency 1997). Legally, they are executives of a company, because their business is incorporated because of tax regulation or other business considerations but in reality there is no clear difference between large part of those "executives" and self-employed masters. The powerful National Federation of Construction Workers' Unions comprising more than 700,000 members not only controls the job classified wage system for construction workers but also operates its own health insurance society under the national health insurance program, which is different from workplace-based health insurance programs for employed people. The union members include self-employed business operators with or without employees who are called "oyakata" (masters) in the industry. Moreover, musicians, professional baseball players and other people working under contract are occasionally regarded as "workers" in labor law and their right to join labor unions has been authorized (Sugeno 1995:422-423).

Thus, there is a broad range of self-employed business operators similar to employed workers in terms of the applicable laws governing labor-management relations, social insurance systems, and the Labor Standards Law, though the workers to whom these laws are applied differ by the terms of the legislation.

4.2 Semi-Independent Employed

In contrast to those "quasi-employed self-employed" workers, there may be "semi-independent employed" workers. For instance, there are many life insurance salespersons, mostly women, called "Seiho Lady" (life insurance canvassers), in Japan. Most Japanese have a life insurance policy of some saving and investment nature, and the canvassers try to promote the sale of these policies by visiting customers' homes and places of work. According to the 1995 National Census, there were 521,900 people classified either as insurance agents or canvassers, of whom 353,500 were women (Management and Co-ordination Agency 1995). Presumably, the majority of these women were "Seiho Lady" or canvassers.

These canvassers are considered employed sales staff for the purposes of personnel management in life insurance companies. They are differentiated from in-house staffers but are treated as company employees. They are counted as employees in government statistics. In the previously-noted national census, 96.0% (339,200) of the female insurance agents and canvassers were employees (Management and Co-ordination Agency 1995). The National Federation of Life Insurance Workers' Unions comprising 350,000 workers is one of the major industry-wide organizations in the Japanese Trade Union Confederation (Rengo). Of the life insurance union members, nearly 280,000 correspond to these salespersons.

Most life insurance canvassers work on a commission basis and most of their remuneration is paid as a commission of the contract. They are clearly differentiated from the ordinary employment relationship under the tax system. Unlike ordinary employed people, they pay income tax as a "business income" earner, the same category as that for self-employed business operators.

There are still other workers who work under payment by results arrangements. Even if they work under an employment contract instead of on a subcontract basis, their actual employment status is scarcely different from that of those life insurance canvassers as long as they are paid on a commission basis with a small guaranteed salary. Since union membership generally is low among workers in this category, their employment relationship may be more unstable than that of an insurance canvasser.

Taxi drivers are a typical example of this category. According to the Transportation Ministry, there were approximately 400,000 taxi drivers in 1994 (Ministry of Transportation 1994). Most drivers were paid by taxi companies based on a percentage of the drivers' revenue, while the other drivers were self-employed operating owner-driver taxis.

In a sense, registration-based agency workers, which are thought to account for half of all agency workers, can be classified to this "semi-independent employed" category. They are registered at temporary staffing agencies. Every time they are allotted work, they conclude an employment contract with the staffing agencies but actually are sent to work at other (host) companies. Many registration-based agency workers are registered with several staffing agencies to get better jobs. As it is often the case, they join the national health insurance program operated by municipal governments as self-employed business operators do.

4.3 Typical Self-Employed

Finally, there are the typical self-employed business operators who are different either from the "quasi-employed self-employed" or "semi-independent employed" people. However, reorganization and restructuring are underway in this sector, too. A convenience store owner, for example, is self-employed but his or her independence is strongly limited because the franchiser of the convenience stores has an upper hand in the contractual relations. Such store owners may be called the "non-typical self-employed". Self-employed retail shop operators dealing with goods of a particular manufacturer or wholesaler in the traditional keiretsu arrangement may be included in this category, too.

Of course, there are also many typical self-employed business operators in the original sense of the term with no keiretsu relationship. A closer look at these operators in a socioeconomic context will, however, disclose that these proprietors are involved in the networks of social division of labor which centers on large companies, thus, they are not completely independent.

5 Conclusions

Table 5 shows changes in the composition of Japan's employment modes by industry, compiled from the Basic Surveys of the Employment Structure.

I have quoted the 1982 survey because the government survey added "part-time" and "arubaito" workers category, which are important for a quantitative understanding of Japan's non-regular employment, in its statistics for the first time that year. There is not enough space left to discuss this table in detail. However, I would like to point out that the percentage of "regular" employees in the total working population remains rather stable at around 57% for the whole labor force. Excluding the agriculture and forestry industry, the percentage dropped only 2%, from 62.4% to 60.3%. This suggests that the proposition that non-regular employment is increasing its share at regular employment's costs should be reconsidered.

Yet, it is true that the percentages of "part-time" workers and "arubaito" workers increased from 8.1% to 15.4% during this period. It may be more appropriate, however, to attribute the increase to a corresponding sharp decline in the self-employed population (self-employed business owners and their families) from 26.6% to 17.8% in the same period than to attribute it to the encroachment in the regular employees share by non-regular employees.

Table 5: Changes in Shares of Employment and Self-Employment Status

	1982		1997	
	Total	Non-agriculture	Total	Non-agriculture
Total	100	100	100	100
Self-employed Owner	16.5	13.5	11.8	10.0
Family Worker	10.1	6.4	6.0	4.1
Company Executive	4.8	5.2	5.7	6.0
Regular Employee	57.0	62.4	57.5	60.3
Parttimer/Arubaito Worker	8.1	8.8	15.4	16.1
Shokutaku Worker	1.2	1.3	1.4	1.5
Agency and other Non-regulars	2.3	2.4	1.9	2.0

Source: Management and Co-ordination Agency (1982, 1997), *Shûgyô Kôzô Kihon Chôsa 1982, 1997* [Basic Survey of Employment Structure 1982, 1997].

A typical example that may support the above postulate is the structural reform that has caused small retail shops to lose in the competition with large retail stores such as supermarkets. Also, small retailers are forced to give up their business due to a lack of younger family members to inherit the business. Consequently, this has reduced the number of self-employed business operators and greatly boosted the number of part-time workers employed by large retailers.

It should be noted that this statement on rather unchanged balance between regular and non-regular employment has significant limits because it lacks sufficient quantitative analyses of such diverse subtypes such as "non-typical non-regular" employees, "non-typical regular" employees, "quasi-agency workers", "quasi-employed self-employed" or "semi-independent employed" workers. In-depth analyses of these employment modes will be necessary for discussing the directions of the changes we are seeing.

References

Furugori, T. (1997), *Hi-seiki Rôdô no Keizai Bunseki* [Economic Analysis of Non-regular Labor], Tokyo: Tôyô Keizai Shimpôsha.

Hirata, S. & Nitta, M. (1985), Zaitaku Kinmu [Teleworking], in: *Nihon Rôdô Kyôkai Zasshi* 318: 26-33.

Management and Co-ordination Agency (1997), *Shûgyô Kôzô Kihon Chôsa 1997* [Basic Survey of Employment Structure 1997], Tokyo: Statistics Bureau, Management and Co-ordination Agency.

Management and Co-ordination Agency (1995), *Kokusei Chôsa 1995* [National Census 1995], Tokyo: Statistics Bureau, Management and Co-ordination Agency.

Ministry of Labor (1996), *Shûgyô Keitai no Tayôka ni kansuru Sôgô Jittai Chôsa Hôkoku* [Report on the Comprehensive Survey of the Diversification of Working Styles], Tokyo: Printing Bureau, Ministry of Finance.

Ministry of Transportation (1994), *Riku-un Tôkei Yôran 1994* [Summarized Land Transportation Statistics in 1994], Tokyo: Printing Bureau, Ministry of Finance.

Nihon Rôdô Kenkyû Kikô (1997), *Tekkôgyô no Rôshikankei to Jinzai Keisei* [Industrial Relations and Human Resources Development in the Steel Industry], Toyko: Nihon Rôdô Kenkyû Kikô.

Sato, H. (1998), Hi-Tenkei Rôdô no Jittai [The Realities of Atypical Work], in: *Nihon Rôdô Kenkyû Zasshi* 462: 2-14.

Sato, H. (1999), Kigyô no Risutorakucharingu no Genjô to Kadai [Present Status of and Challenges for Corporate Restructuring], in: *Jurisuto* 1149: 30-37.

Sugeno, K. (1995), *Rôdôhô* [Labor Law], 4th ed., Tokyo: Kobundô.

Suzuki, H. (1998), Senshinkoku ni okeru hi-tenkei koyô no kakudai [Dissemination of Atypical Employment in Developed Countries]", in: *Nihon Rôdô Kenkyû Zasshi* 462: 15-26.

The Firm: Towards Open Structures?

Recent Arguments on Corporate Governance in Japan

Kazuo Shibagaki

1 Introduction

The aims of this short essay are twofold: to examine the final report of the Japan Corporate Governance Forum which was issued on May 1998, and to criticize its assertion which recommend a management strategy to maximize shareholder's profit or to maximize the share prices of the firm. The conclusion of my examinations is that such a management strategy will force, through monetary manipulations, speculative management upon Japanese firms which will risk to lose their excellent skills of productivity.

2 The Inauguration of the Japan Corporate Governance Forum

Until the end of 1980s, a time when the Japanese economy out-performed most other advanced economies, arguments over corporate governance in Japan were concentrated on the managerial control systems in large firms. Supported by both the monitoring functions of main banks and the bottom-up decision making system within firms, presidents of big firms were in a very comfortable position. Shareholders, including cross-shareholders from other corporations, were considered as silent bodies in connection with corporate governance. As it is well known, under the Japanese management system, customers or users were the most important stakeholders of the firm; employees ranked second whereas shareholders had hardly any influence on management.

However, after the bubble economy ended at the beginning of the 1990s, a new trend of thinking on corporate governance emerged. Now it was deemed useful or even necessary that shareholders should monitor firms. This new assertion resulted from the following new economic and managerial circumstances.

On the one hand, with the slowdown of the economic growth rate after the first oil crisis, the ratio of indirect financing through bank loans decreased gradually, and thus the monitoring function of banks was weakened. In addition to this, under the asset inflation in the late 1980s, many firms eagerly engaged in speculative investment in real estate and shares supported by affluent money supply from banks and other financial organizations. This brought about a bubble that eventually had to burst. Since then, a whole row of scandals incited by unethical behaviour of top managers of banks and other financial organizations has caused the complete loss of their monitoring functions in corporate governance.

On the other hand, in economic thinking, market fundamentalism which had been strengthened in Anglo-American economies under the Thatcher and the Reagan Administration, gained widespread acceptance in Japan in the 1990s. This anachronistic economic thinking rapidly overwhelmed Japan, and deregulation and liberalization measures have been implemented with reference to the pressure of globalization. And consequently Japan has seen a strengthened discussion of corporate governance. In November 1994, the Japan Corporate Governance Forum was founded by interested parties both in business and academic circles. Kaneo Nakamura, then executive councillor of Industrial Bank of Japan, and Takayasu Okushima, the President of Waseda University, were nominated as the two representatives of the Forum. The Forum organized the Draw-up Committee for Corporate Governance Principles[1] and its final report was announced on May 26 in 1998 (Nihon Kôporeito Gabanansu Gensoku Sakutei Iinkai 1998). This is one of the representative works of the new arguments over corporate governance in Japan.

3 The Message of the Final Report

The most important point of the mentioned report is to stress the change of Japanese corporate governance from managerial control to shareholders' control. Let me quote from the report to highlight this. Firstly, on the present situation:

> In Japan, until now, there was no clear distinction between the roles of director as a governor and as a managerial executor. (...) It is hard to believe that directors of almost all corporations in Japan have the ability and function as governor independent from their ability as managerial executor. As a result, the board of directors does not fulfil its original function. (...) The corporate auditor system also become nominal and shareholders' control is actually absent. (Nihon Kôporeito Gabanansu Gensoku Sakutei Iinkai 1998:6)

Then, regarding the future the final report gives the following proposals:

> The first thing we have to do is to build a consensus among people that the joint stock company (corporation) is owned by its shareholders and its aim is to make

1 The Committee had 17 members including top managers, professors, journalist and lawyers; Tadao Suzuki (President of Merushan Co.) and Yoshihiko Miyauchi (President of Oryx Co.) served as chairman and vice chairman, respectively.

> profits. [In order to make this possible *K.S.*] we propose a new system of corporate governance, that is, the distinction between governance and management on the basis of shareholders' interest and to establish superintendence or governance on managerial executors by the board of directors. (Nihon Kôporeito Gabanansu Gensoku Sakutei Iinkai 1998:11)

As it is well known, such a view on the joint stock company is based on an understanding of the fictional theory of corporation, which was founded by F.K.von Savigny in the 19th century. The Commercial Law and company laws both in Japan and America are also based on this theory. Therefore, the report is only asserting, at first sight, that the present *reality* of corporations has moved far from the old *ideal*. If so, such an assertion is rather meaningless, because there are some historically necessary reasons for the discrepancy between the *reality* and the *ideal*. But, the final report pays no attention to this point. However, it is interesting to analyze why such an assertion is rehashed at this time. In order to investigate this point, we must examine the proposals for the future system of corporate governance in more detail.

4 Two Proposals for the Future of Corporate Governance in Japan

The concrete proposals of the final report consist of the following two points. The first point is the attempt to settle the main objective of the joint stock company as maximization of shareholder value. According to the report, the shareholder value is reflected by the share price; therefore, the most important task of the top management of the company is to keep the share price of the company at high levels. For instance, on the one hand, the report agreed with the idea that "the company is a system of stakeholders which is composed of shareholders, managers, employees, suppliers and users, and creditors" (Nihon Kôporeito Gabanansu Gensoku Sakutei Iinkai 1998:6-7). But, on the other hand, the report holds that the co-ordination of interests among them should be "trusted on the market" (Nihon Kôporeito Gabanansu Gensoku Sakutei Iinkai 1998:7) depriving managers of their role. This shows the criticism of the traditional values of Japanese management that puts customers first, employees second and shareholders last, as mentioned before. The only role managers have to fulfil under the proposed paradigm is to pay for the environmental problems caused by market failure.

The second point is the outline of a new system of corporate governance. It aims at the above-mentioned principles of distinction between governance and management and of establishing superintendence or governance of managerial executors by the board of directors. In order to realize that, the report suggests "to concentrate the auditing function into the hands of the board of directors and to give the outside directors who stand only for the shareholders' interest the leading role in this regard" (Nihon Kôporeito Gabanansu Gensoku Sakutei Iinkai 1998:11-12).

The latter point is an adaptation from the US-model, but the substance is different from the reality in America. In America, outside directors are elected from different kind of stakeholders of the company. Directors who represent shareholders' interest are used to occupy only some of the director's seats. In addition to this, especially since the 1970s when people were engaged in hot debates about the social responsibility of firms, outside directors in big firms have been recruited from representatives of the public interest.[2]

But in Japan, "independent outside directors who have no direct interest in the firm" insinuates the inauguration of directors who "stand for the shareholders' interest" – as it is evidenced by the report's understanding of the term "independent" as "independent from stakeholders' interest except shareholders'" (Nihon Kôporeito Gabanansu Gensoku Sakutei Iinkai 1998:20). Though the report continues to assert that "it is necessary to reflect various viewpoints in the society on the board of directors; therefore, composition of outside directors should not be one-sided but should be well-balanced," (Nihon Kôporeito Gabanansu Gensoku Sakutei Iinkai 1998:20) it is evident that outside directors of the kind the report proposes would overwhelmingly represent shareholders' interest.

5 The Meaning of Shareholder Value

The question is whether it is possible to create such a structure of corporate governance in the near future in Japan. We are unable to answer this question without an examination of why the old regime of shareholders' control had to give way for the managerial control in the process of capitalist development.[3]

However, it is important, too, to analyze what kind of situation would appear if the corporate governance by shareholders' would be realized. Let us focus on the term "shareholder value". As I quoted from the report before, the shareholder value is reflected on the share price of the company. Therefore, shareholder value means company's price or company's value. In order to maximize the shareholder value, managers of a company always must make all efforts to increase its share price. However, I think such management necessarily becomes speculative because share prices are determined by various factors in which the efforts of managers

2 During the 1970s, many social movements including consumers' movements had been active in America, and one of the issues of these movements was the pursuit of the social responsibility of firms. Thus, many corporations introduced the system of outside directors who represent interests of stakeholders except shareholders.

3 This examination has been undertaken by Shibagaki (1979) and thus is omitted here.

play only a limited role. As it is well known, the share price of a company is fundamentally determined by the present discounted value of its profits. Additionally, many factors such as political and economic circumstances and expectations of market participants have a great impact on the share price which fluctuates frequently. These additional factors can hardly be influenced by the management.

Furthermore, the fundamental factors that determine the share price are profits and the discount rate. As for the latter, the interest rate is normally used as discount rate. But the interest rate is a given by conditions in the money market. If interest rates are raised share prices fall regardless of good or bad management of managers. Therefore, only profits can be influenced by the capability and effort of managers. Yet, there are many sources of profits. They are produced from the core business of the firm or from financial transactions of which success is determined by fluctuations of exchange rates, interest rates and share prices. Therefore, setting the managerial target as the maximization of shareholder value induces a speculative management, because factors beyond the impact of managers become overwhelmingly important.

However, the recent globalization of the world economy has brought a new situation in which the high levels of profit made possible by financial transactions are overshadowing the small profits in manufacturing. Today, there is an enormous amount of excessive money in the global economy that has been accumulated by increasing current balance deficits of America that is the one and only supplier of the international key currency, the American dollar. The excessive money is *dancing for joy* on the stages of capital markets, money markets and foreign exchange markets. The fluctuation of prices does not function to allocate materials and funds to the optimal use, but reflects speculative investments. It is rather cynical that the final report recommends Japanese firms to change their management style adapting to this new situation of global economy mentioned above.

6 A Comparison with America

Lastly, I have to comment a popular belief that the power of shareholders exceeds the power of management in America. Fukao & Morita (1997:55-56) showed in their detailed investigation that the legal rights and real power of shareholders in America is weaker than in Japan from an institutional viewpoint. Only a generation ago, Chandler (1977) wrote on what the *managerial* control had accomplished in America: “In making administrative decisions, career managers preferred policies that favoured the long-term stability and growth of their enterprises to those that maximized current profits.” (Chandler 1977:10) This assertion can be applied to Japanese managerial control, too.

And what constellation fascilitates the belief that American top managers are in a more unstable position than top managers in Japan? More than often, this conviction is confirmed by the boom of hostile take-overs since the beginning of the 1980s.

However, Fukao & Morita explain this phenomenon not from the strength of the shareholders but from their indifference:

> In the US and the UK, being only a few investors (shareholders) who monitor the management of firms, it is necessary to make a hostile parches of firms in order to correct the inefficient firms. (Fukao & Morita 1997:55)

I think that the boom of hostile take-overs in America is related to the developed labour market for top managers. In striking contrast to Japan where managers often are making their entire career within the same firm, America has a wide and deep market for top managers who are graduated from business schools. Therefore, the frequent change of CEO does not confirm the instability of his (or her) status, but is a sign of high mobility among top managers who have extraordinary high outside career chances.

Yet, Miwa (1995) has shown that the change of CEO by hostile take-overs has indeed increased in recent years. According to her investigation, until the early 1980s, institutional investors who were unsatisfied with the management of the firm used to sell their shares. Such a behaviour of institutional investors was called the *Wall Street Rule*; institutional investors mostly did not intervene in the management of the firm. However, as computerized index operations of shares suddenly increased, it became difficult to replace individual shares. At that point, most institutional investors abandoned the *Wall Street Rule* and began to exercise their right of shareholders. Considering that this new attitude of institutional investors began in the early 1980s, the behaviour of American top managers who put more emphasis on short-term profits than the long-term growth of firms is almost a recent phenomenon. Thus, the reflection of shareholder value on management worked in a way to strengthen the speculative nature of management.

7 Concluding Remarks

Many scandals involving executive managers have triggered the debate about shareholders' sovereignty and the necessity of supervision of management by shareholders. However, if we consider the fact that there are at least as many scandals involving shareholders as well, it is difficult to belief that control by shareholders should be the best solution of Japan's recent management woes.

References

Chandler, A. D. Jr. (1977), *The Visible Hands: The Managerial Revolution in American Business*, Harvard: Harvard University Press.

Fukao, M. & Morita, Y. (1997), *Kigyô Gabanansu-Kôzô no Kokusai Hikaku* [International Comparison of Corporate Governance Structures], Tokyo: Nihon Keizai Shinbunsha.

Miwa, Y. (1995), Beikoku Kikantôshika to Kôporeto Gabanansu [US Institutional Investors and Corporate Governance], in: *Shôken Keizai Gakkai Nenpô* 30: 23-35.

Nihon Kôporeito Gabanansu Gensoku Sakutei Iinkai (1998), *Kôporeito Gabanansu Gensoku – Atarashii Nihongata Kigyô Tôchi wo Kangaeru – Saishû Hôkoku* [Principles of Corporate Governance – Ideas for New Japanese Enterprise Rule – Final Report], Tokyo: Nihon Shôken Keizai Kenkyûjo.

Shibagaki, K. (1979), Dissolution of Zaibatsu and Deconcentration of Economic Power, in: *The Annals of the Institute of Social Science* 20.

Foreign Capital and the Recent M&A Environment in Japan

Shinobu Muramatsu

1 The Steady Increase of Foreign Capital in Japan's M&A Market

Foreign capital in Japan's M&A market has become common today. Starting in the American and in the European markets, the trend has lastly engulfed Japan. In the 1980s, Japanese firms were aggressively buying foreign companies in the overseas M&A markets, mainly in America, especially during the bubble economy in the latter half of the 1980s and the very beginning of the 1990s. After the collapse of bubble economy the economy is still sluggish up to now.

It would be worthwhile to look back on the trend of Japan's Out-In market in the 1980s and the 1990s. The Out-In market implies M&A transactions in which foreign companies acquire Japanese capital in Japan. No one can deny that such an acquisition is attractive for foreign investors, because acquisition is the preferred mode of entry into a highly developed market like Japan. Things are steadily changing in the arena of the Out-In M&A market in recent years, even though the level remains low relative to In-Out and In-In markets. As table 1 depicts, the total number of M&A deals in this market stood at 608 (6.3% of the total M&A deals) in the period 1985–2000 (for the year 2000 the first six months only). Although the number of deals in this market was still modest, it has been increasing steadily, and more so for the period 1997–2000. Many of the Out-In deals are aimed at securing sales routes in Japan and Asia in general through the purchase of interest in Japanese companies. This makes it likely that foreign business expansion into Japanese market will touch off a wave of industrial reorganizations. Concerning Out-In deals by country, Germany ranked first, followed by America, Switzerland, France, South Korea and Taiwan. By industry, pharmaceutical, chemical, electrical machinery, transport equipment and precision instrument industries are leading the league table.

As we can see in table 1, the increase in the Out-In market is apparently one characteristic of the recent increase in M&A deals in general. Compared to establishing a new company from scratch, the benefits to foreign firms of M&A are (1) reducing time required to start a business, (2) sidestepping permits and licensing procedures.

Table 1: M&A Deals by Market after 1985

Year	In-In	In-Out	Out-In	Out-Out	Total
1985	160	77	22	1	260
1986	223	178	14	3	418
1987	207	156	17	2	382
1988	218	285	14	6	523
1989	247	384	11	8	650
1990	271	461	19	8	759
1991	312	293	18	18	641
1992	255	179	29	21	484
1993	236	108	23	29	396
1994	249	188	33	35	505
1995	255	206	33	35	529
1996	325	226	31	43	625
1997	455	216	51	33	755
1998	488	213	85	348	834
1999	718	248	129	74	1169
2000	492	155	79	18	744

Note: For 2000, only data for the first six month are recorded.

Source: Recof (2000), *Merger & Acquisitions Research Report (MARR)*, 6,6: 23.

Japanese companies increasingly realize that tying up with foreign companies offers a way to become part of a global strategy that they might not be able to achieve on their own. Linking up with foreign companies in many cases provides Japanese companies with needed expertise in corporate restructuring, profit-making, technology implementation and other areas where they have not been able to lead so far.

Before, no company in Japan was accessible for would-be foreign buyers. As it has been true for domestic mergers, non-legal barriers such as industrial group membership, mutual shareholdings among Japanese companies, and nepotism associated with M&A activities in Japan have hampered the development of Out-In acquisitions. Another constraint on acquisition in Japan was the relatively high price of Japanese corporate shares with high price-earning-ratios. High share prices reflected the fact that Japanese companies usually have high hidden asset values which are not reflected on the balance sheet because real estate and other investments are carried on the balance sheet at historical costs. The collapse of the bubble economy which triggered the fall of land prices and corporate share prices has eased the constraints mentioned above to a great extent. More specifically, increased M&A deals in Japan reflect an increase in selling-off of unprofitable divisions and subsidiaries by Japanese companies, the reorganization and elimination of cross-shareholding and restructuring of operations of troubled companies.

The following example illustrates how a company which has once tried to diversify its business had to sell off unprofitable divisions to a foreign company. Nippon Steel Semiconductor Corp., an affiliate of New Nippon Steel Corp., was bought by United Microelectronics Corp., Taiwan's second largest semiconductor foundry in January 1999. By using its new owner's expertise, Nippon Steel Semiconductor plans to minimize manufacturing of its in-house brand dynamic random-access memory and transform itself into a foundry specialist.

Originally, the semiconductor business has nothing in common with steel business. After Nippon Steel bought the majority of the company's stock from Minebea Co. in 1993 as a part of diversification effort, it learned its lesson. Now Nippon Steel is concentrating on its core business in an effort to raise profitability.

Nippon Steel Corp. is one of Japanese companies which sold its peripheral businesses to foreign companies. They realized that their attempts during the bubble economy to deviate from their core business have not paid off.

2 The Role of Foreign Capital in Some Industries

In the past few years, a flurry of acquisitions of Japanese companies by foreign capitals took place. This represents a major change in the M&A landscape. Foreign companies have struck one major deal after another with Japanese companies: some involving complete buyouts and others involving acquisition of major equity stakes.

2.1 The Renault – Nissan Case

In March 1999, Renault, a French auto-maker, decided to pour Y646 billion into the Nissan Group, the second largest Japanese auto-maker, as a rescue operation. At this point, Renault owned about one-third of all Nissan's outstanding shares, and held control over it. Now CEO Carlos Ghosn who was formally appointed among 18 French executives in June 2000, is using strong leadership to restructure the management system and Nissan's entire operations. Up to now, restructuring plans were clearly insufficient for the ailing company. In 2000, the so-called "Revival Plan" was adopted as the last and most drastic plan. Its main purpose is a reduction of non-performing assets. A reduction of capacity is also a target, with the goal of producing more closely in line with real demand. If Nissan were to cut 25% of its capacity to 1.5 million cars a year as the plan envisaged, that meant closing some factories. Actually it has already been announced that the Kodaira plant, one of Nissan's major factories, is to be closed.

Nissan's new parts procurement policy is symbolized by the slogan "The best at the lowest cost." Ghosn believes that Nissan's rigid keiretsu network of affiliated suppliers was pushing purchasing costs higher. Under this new policy, there will inevitably be some losers among the company's current suppliers.

Ghosn has been preceded by another foreign capital-led restructuring case in the same industry: the mammoth Mazda-Ford tie-up. Ford has had a capital stake in Mazda since 1979, and it raised its stake in Mazda from 25% to 33.4% in 1996. Mazda's president, James Miller, who was sent from the Ford Group announced its best consolidated net profit – Y38.7 billion – in 14 years in March 1999. It reversed a trend of six consecutive years of net losses since 1993. The market and professional analysts have given the foreign capital-led restructuring effort postive appraisal.

Recently, both Nissan and Mazda have made drastic changes at the operation level as well as the top strategy level. Mazda adopted a performance-oriented personnel system. In August 1999, it made an unusual announcement of a mass promotion of 500 female employees into higher positions. It used to be very difficult for female workers in Japanese companies to advance in their careers. But since the company decided to give female workers a chance to be promoted based on ability and merits, many of them started pursuing career goals more sincerely.

In Nissan's case, the move was more drastic. In spite of the fact that there were only 18 new executives, it made English its official language. The main reason why it has done so is that 18 foreign executives are taking managerial positions and will be a part of the company's decision-making process, so most of the company's documents need to be written in English. These drastic changes are almost unimaginable for tie-ups among genuine Japanese companies. In that sense, teaming-up with a foreign partner is beneficial for Japanese companies in changing their old style of management.

2.2 The C&W – IDC Case

Cable and Wireless PLC, a major British telecommunication group has spent Y55.2 billion to buy IDC (International Digital Communications) through an aggressive takeover bid in June 1999. Long before C&W decided on acquiring IDC as a part of its new strategy to concentrate on core businesses, NTT (Nippon Telephone & Telegram) had been attempting to acquire IDC through an operational alliance without revealing its intention. C&W kicked off the contest by asking IDC's major shareholders such as Toyota, Chu-Ito and Air-Touch Int'l to sell their shares to C&W. IDC's immediate reaction was to ask C&W and NTT to show their bid prices openly. C&W and NTT accordingly disclosed their buying conditions including prices, Y100,000 per share and Y105,769 per share respectively. C&W and NTT fought a fierce fight by repeatedly upping the other's bid price in three months. In the meantime, C&W threatened NTT through a TOB attempt. The drawn-out bidding came to a close in June 1999 with C&W's price of Y11,577 per share.

In the beginning stage of the bidding, Toyota and Chu-Ito favored NTT because they are Japanese companies which share common corporate culture. However, after C&W outbid NTT decisively, their attitudes towards the deal have changed. They decided on selling their shares to C&W, based on economic rationality. C&W ended up owning as much as 97.69% of IDC's outstanding shares. This result illustrates the trend that the traditional coalition of Japanese corporate shareholders is on the decline, and a more Anglo-American market for corporate control is being developed.

Japan's telecommunications market was liberalized in 1985, but only nominally. The market has been virtually monopolized by NTT, providing little room for foreign entry to the market. In January 1999, NTT was broken up into two regional carriers and one long-distance and international carrier, thereby opening the door a little wider for foreign players. In 1999, foreign direct investment in the telecommunication sector increased 19.7 times over the previous year to Y330 billion. C&W's acquisition of IDC accounted for one sixth of the total value of deals.

BT and AT&T, too, jointly invested in Japan Telecom in May 1999. It was the first time a Japanese telecommunications company formed a comprehensive alliance with foreign counterparts. Under the agreement which came only after a great deal of hard negotiation behind the scenes, BT and AT&T took a 15% stake in Japan Telecom respectively, which meant a total investment of Y220 billion. At the same time, Japan Telecom was able to structure the deal in a way that leaves it with a considerable degree of management autonomy as it intended.

2.3 The Ripplewood Holdings – LTCB Case

One of the biggest foreign buyers in the finance industry has been Ripplewood Holdings, a U.S. investment fund, which, as the principal player in an international investment consortium, has acquired the operations of the nationalized LTCB (Long-Term Credit Bank) for about Y120 billion in 1999. First, Ripplewood Holdings LLC formed the Amsterdam-based consortium and named it New LTCB Partners CV. This international consortium was then renamed LTCB Shinsei Bank, effective June in 1999. The new name reflects a resolve to create a new bank and is readily understandable to clients. Shinsei means "new birth" in Japanese. The LTCB had been under state control since October 1998 when it collapsed due to massive losses stemming from a huge amount of bad loans. The LTCB began operating under its new management in

March 1999. The new LTCB filed an application with the Financial Reconstruction Commission for an injection of Y240 billion in public funds to strengthen its capital base immediately after it began to operate in March. The injection pushed up the bank's capital adequacy ratio to 12.05%. The new top management appeared to be confident about gaining around Y70 billion in net operating profit in the year through 2003. The Bank plans to list on the Tokyo stock exchange again within three to five years time. The Bank also plans to establish joint ventures for brokerage and asset management services with Mellon Bank of the U.S. and other institutions.

One of the incidents that revealed the new corporate culture and strategy of Shinsei Bank's operations recently occurred with the handling of loans to the troubled department store chain Sogo Co. In June 2000, Sogo Co. started off with gaining acceptance of a massive and costly restructuring plan. A total of 72 Japanese banks, including Sogo's main bank, Shinsei Bank, eventually agreed to forgive debts valued at Y631.9 billion. The biggest hurdle for the cooperative debt waiver was Shinsei Bank. Shinsei Bank initially disapproved of the debt forgiveness plan, and asked the DIC (Deposit Insurance Corp, run by the government) to purchase Shinsei's liabilities. DIC decided to purchase debt valued at Y200 billion, and abandon Y97 billion owed to Shinsei. The DIC's decision stirred controversy. Some observers have raised eyebrows at the idea of the state paying for private company management mistakes. As the DIC deal collapsed Shinsei Bank refused to approve of the debt forgiveness plan. It became evident that management sharply differs between Shinsei Bank, led by the U.S. investment fund Ripplewood Holdings, and other Japanese banks which tend to follow a softer line.

Immediately after the collapse of LTCB in October 1998, another big bank, Nippon Credit Bank (half in size compared with LTCB) declared bankruptcy. Like LTCB, it was also nationalized and kept by the government. In an early stage of the game, Ripplewood showed interest in NCB by signing a contract to have an access to its management information.

In the case of LTCB, Japan's business leaders had strongly supported Ripplewood Holdings group as a buyer of the bank. However, the government hesitated to sell two national banks to the same U.S. investment fund, because it was apparently against Japanese mentality. Fortunately a consortium was formed by some Japanese companies. Two of the three consortium members, Softbank and Orix, a leasing group, planned to buy the overhauled bank. Besides this consortium, Cerberus Capital Management LLC of the U.S. had been the other contender in the race to gain control of the bank. After it kept the pressure on for a deal that minimized the public burden of cleaning up the failed bank, the commission finally agreed on the sale of NCB to the Softbank-Orix consortium.

More recently, the commission approved a transfer of a failed regional bank, Tokyo Sowa Bank, to WL Ross & Co., a U.S. private equity fund, in June 2000.

The deal will be conducted by the end of September. Total public funds to be injected into Tokyo Sowa will likely be just over Y700 billion.

As we have observed so far, a number of foreign financial firms have been taking over failed Japanese financial institutions. The finance and insurance sector saw direct investment totaling Y515.5 billion in 1999: a 12% increase compared to the previous year. Eight large deals in that sector raised the total to Y208 billion. The Out-In deals in that sector increased from 23 in 1998 to 27 in 1999, a 17% increase.

2.4 The Boehringer – SS Pharmaceutical Case

Japan once was the second largest national market for drugs. In per capita terms, Japanese drug consumption is still the highest in the world. Competition in Japan was highly fragmented. In the early 1980s, over 2,000 firms competed in the market. Until the early 1980s, pricing was set by the Kôseishô (Ministry of Welfare) and drug-makers were strictly regulated by the Kôseishô.

Only three (Bayer, Roche and Sandoz) of eighteen foreign pharmaceutical companies operating in Japan have achieved sales volumes comparable to those of the Japanese drug makers. With respect to the Japanese market for drugs, it was most economical for foreign makers to specialize in product development and for domestic companies to specialize in marketing and distribution. A good example is the Merck-Banyu case. Not until 1982, under the liberalized Foreign Exchange Law, Merck acquired a direct 5% equity interest in Banyu and a 30% interest in a smaller firm, Torii, both through purchases of common stock in the market. Banyu controlled a large and effective sales force that had well-established relationships with doctors. For its part, Merck offered a number of widely efficacious drugs that could be sold in large volume. Since Merck-Banyu liason worked well, their brilliant performance has been serving to inspire foreign pharmaceutical companies to expand into Japan.

In 2000, a hostile takeover bid was made by Nippon Boehringer Ingelheim Co., a wholly owned subsidiary of Germany's Boehringer Ingelheim GmbH on SS Pharmaceutical Co. It successfully bought a 33.4% stake in the company. SS Pharmaceutical is strong in distributing drugs in nationwide markets. To deal in SS Pharmaceutical products, managers of drugstores and dispensaries were required to participate in a scheme known as SS Chain-Store Club. One condition of participation was that the outlet should purchase at least 1,000 shares in the company. At one stage, these customer/shareholders held at least 26 million shares, or more than 20% of the outstanding shares. These shareholders were supposed to serve as fortress blocking any hostile takeover bid.

Nonetheless, in February 2000 an unexpected takeover bid was made. The target SS Pharmaceutical had enjoyed a steady growth after hitting the bottom in the fall of 1998. The acquirer, Nippon BI, offered Y1,100 per share, a 40% premium. This generous bid price encouraged individual shareholders to lock in gains by taking up the offer. The hostile take-over bid was unexpected because Boehringer Ingelheim had a capital and business relationship with SS Pharmaceutical. While the Japanese company remained officially neutral on the bid, the management seemed taken aback by the suddenness with which the bid was made. Executives secretly hoped the bid would fail. In the end, Nippon BI ended up with more than 30% of SS Pharmaceutical, and had the power to control it virtually. This was done with the help of individual shareholders. The executives must have overlooked the strength of individual customer/shareholders, concentrating defensive measures on corporate shareholders who in fact did not respond to the offer.

It is interesting to see that today individual shareholders respond to bid prices quite differently compared to the way they did 15 years ago. Not only individual shareholders but also corporate shareholders respond more rationally than they used to, as the case of C&W-IDC indicated.

3 Corporate Restructuring and Deregulation

After the bursting of the bubble economy, almost all of Japanese companies had to go through a restructuring process to reduce costs and labor force and regain profitability. To help such restructuring strategy of companies, the government has been revising legislation since 1998 to make it easier for companies to realign themselves. These revisions would work with the legislation passed in 1997 that allowed holding companies for the first time since the Second World War. Further, a piece of legislation passed in August 1999 that cleared the way for stock swaps, a key part of mergers and acquisitions.

3.1 Spin-off

The Diet passed a bill to revise the Commercial Code in June 2000. It should make it easier for companies to spin off unprofitable divisions, and corporations could actually be able to start using the new system from the beginning of 2001. The revision, the last in the series aimed at facilitating corporate realignments, follows the 1997 lifting of a ban on holding companies and the 1999 introduction of a stock swap system to streamline mergers and acquisitions of subsidiaries by parent companies. Under the revised code, companies will be allowed to spin off divisions, branches and plants after securing a broad approval and submitting spin-off plans or written contracts for approval by general shareholders meetings. The new bill specifies two types of corporate breakups: a spin-off of a division into a new company for which a spin-off plan is required, and a takeover of a division by an existing company which will be formalized by a written contract. Before these revisions were made, a court-appointed lawyer had to assess the value of a company that planned to spin off a part of itself. The assessment usually took six months to a year, and the part being spun off had to stop operations during that time. The revised code would speed up this spin-off process because it would free the company from getting approval for the spin-off from all its creditors. Also it would promptly make more divisions, branches and plants available for sale to foreign companies as well as Japanese companies.

The revised law would immediately affect the plans of companies such as Mizuho Financial Group. The group, which consists of Dai-ichi Kangyo Bank, Fuji Bank and Industrial Bank of Japan, plans to consolidate under a holding company structure. The group's realignment plan anticipates spinning off independent entities in bank retailing, wholesale banking and other specialized businesses. It is certain that the ability to spin off divisions and units allows companies to make their operations more efficient because they can offer different wages and benefits at different companies.

3.2 Stock Swap

As it was mentioned above, a stock swap system was introduced in 1999. The business community was calling for this system because foreign countries already had it. A more liberal method for financing acquisitions was needed as more companies sought to get involved in M&A deals. In America, nearly 60% of the value of large deals – those over $100 million – were paid for entirely in cash in 1988. Less than 2% were paid for in stock. But just ten years later, the profile was almost reversed: 50% of the value of all large deals in 1998 was paid for entirely in stock, and only 17% was paid for entirely in cash.

This shift has profound ramifications for the shareholders of both acquiring and acquired companies. In a cash deal, the roles of two parties are clear-cut, and the exchange of money for stock completes a simple transfer of ownership. But in a stock swap, it becomes far less clear who is the buyer and who is the seller. In some cases, the shareholders of the acquired company can end up owning most of the company that bought their stock. The main distinction between cash and stock deals is that in cash transactions, shareholders of an acquiring company take the entire risk that the expected synergy value will not be realized. In stock deals, that risk is shared with shareholders of the acquired company. More precisely, in stock deals, the synergy risk is shared in proportion to the percentage of the combined company that both the acquiring and selling shareholders will own. Although we have to take a cautionary approach for the complexity a stock swap system has, we are not advocating that companies should always avoid using stock to pay for acquisitions. Stock issues are a natural way for companies with limited access to other forms of financing to pay for M&As. In those cases, a high stock valuation in the market can be a major advantage.

3.3 Holding Companies

As stated earlier, in 1997 holding companies became legal in the revised code. Before that it had been prohibited to establish a company whose principal objective was to control the business activities of other companies through majority stockholdings. Under the revised law, holding companies issue shares in order to raise funds for the acquisition of major equity stakes in a limited number of firms (subsidiaries). The intention to hold control over these firms distinguishes holding companies from investment companies and investment trusts. The holding company itself consists of a small team of managers. Each manager presides over or is a member of a subsidiary's board of directors. The ties between the holding company and subsidiaries are limited to financial and personnel relations. As a result, new subsidiaries can easily be separated through divestments, and by the same token, integrated into existing organizational structure through acquisitions.

Recently in Japan, the holding company structure has begun to be adopted among financial institutions as well as business enterprises. In July 2000, Sanwa Bank, Tokai Bank and Toyo Trust & Banking Co. announced that they have agreed to integrate their operations under a single holding company to be formed in April 2001. Besides this financial group, the Bank of Tokyo-Mitsubishi, Nippon Trust & Banking Co. and Nippon Trust Bank will operate under a common holding company formula. The biggest planned group is the Mizuho Financial Group which is comprised of Fuji Bank, Dai-Ichi Kangyo Bank and IBJ (Industrial Bank of Japan). It also will be integrated in the form of a holding company in 2001. It is certain that the adoption of the holding companies system would accelerate the speed of reconsolidation and spin-off among banks and businesses.

4 Other Main Factors to Promote M&A

4.1 The Decline in Land Prices

Besides deregulation and tax cuts, there are other factors which are promoting foreign firms to enter the Japanese market through M&As. Falling land prices are apparently stimulating foreign companies to invest in Japan. Real estate prices which were once ridiculously high posed a major obstacle to foreign firms. They have been steadily declining since the burst of the asset-price bubble at the beginning of the decade.

Land prices in Japan are now approaching international standards. In 1999, Japan's average property price dropped 3.6% from the previous year for the ninth consecutive year-on-year decline according to the survey of the National Land Agency. The average price of plots in commercial districts fell 40.4% from its peak in 1991, while that in residential areas has sunk 14.6%. The decline has been particularly sharp in the three major areas, Tokyo, Osaka and Nagoya. Commercial land prices in those areas have dropped to the levels below those in 1983, well before the bubble started forming. Therefore, land prices in Japan are approaching those of other economic centers in Asia, and downward pressure still remains strong, because many companies undergoing restructuring efforts are on a selling spree while individuals remain cautious about buying due to concerns about stagnating take-home income and job security. Falling land prices contributed to lower stock prices of companies in Japan, which in turn offer a favorable environment to foreign firms attempting to acquire Japanese companies.

4.2 Government's Efforts to Promote Foreign Investment

The government is hoping that foreign direct investment will create new jobs in Japan. About 3,000 foreign businesses now operating in Japan employ a total of 230,000 workers. On the other hand, Japanese companies have close to 2.75 million workers overseas on their payrolls. An increase in the number of foreign companies doing business in Japan will help lower Japan's unemployment rate, which is at a record high of well above 4%, and provide a boost to the economy as a whole.

The prolonged recession and the high unemployment rate have made the Japanese government more eager to encourage foreign direct investment than before. In 1994, the government set up a special council headed by the prime minister to promote investment. The council issued a general policy statement in June 1995 and another with regard to M&As in April 1996. In April of 1999 the council published a new statement stressing the importance of efforts to attract foreign direct investment.

JETRO (Japan External Trade Organization) is another government-backed body in the front line of the investment promotion drive. The Development Bank of Japan, a government-affiliated bank, is offering various types of information about Japanese markets and businesses to foreign firms and investors. DBJ also supplies consulting services to foreign companies about capital investment in Japan and refers them to potential Japanese partners.

5 Concluding Remarks

Foreign direct investment in Japan continues to rise rapidly. According to the announcement by the Ministry of Finance, foreign direct investment in 1999 increased 79% from the previous year to a record high of Y2,3993 trillion in a second annual rise. Typically, foreign direct investment takes the form of acquiring stocks as a way of gaining a major influence on its operations.

Japan had been traditionally an unpopular destination for M&As. However, after the collapse of bubble economy, the growing importance of M&As and strategic alliances for surviving the extremely competitive, global business environment is certainly changing the situation. As we have observed, the main factors leading to the major change in Japan's business climate are:

- lower business costs in Japan due to falling land and stock prices,
- reduced barriers to entry in the financial and information sectors and many other sectors due to deregulation, and
- expected cuts in corporate taxes to levels found in other highly industrial nations.

Japan is still suffering from a prolonged sluggish economy. Japanese economists who are worried about weak investment and consumption are still pessimistic about the comeback of the Japanese economy. Unlike these Japanese economists, foreign investors have been fairly optimistic, betting boldly on Japan's economic comeback. The upswing of stock prices in the past several months has been led by such foreign investors. It is not surprising that, after about ten years of recession, both private investment and consumption are weak in Japan. But the tide could turn quickly since structural changes have begun to take place in the Japanese business arena. The Japanese market is now a fertile ground for excellent M&A opportunities for foreign firms.

It should not be overlooked that the bold M&A strategies that many foreign companies have sought in Japan have made executives of Japanese firms more willing to make similar moves. Foreign M&A techniques with highly sophisticated financial measures are certainly providing a strong impetus to companies looking to restructure their operations. As Table 1 indicates, the number of M&As involving Japanese companies in 1999 increased by over 40% from the previous year.

Lastly, it is worthwhile noting that Japanese are generally reluctant to have foreigners play a dominant role in any company. We use the term "Wimbledon effect" to describe such Japanese mentality. A good example is found in the financial service field. When the financial Big Bang first started, many foreign business people thought it was a bold government move to open up the market.

But it turned out that the real purpose was to make Japan's financial institution more competitive globally.

This strong Japanese emphasis on nationality of capital is the reason why Industrial Bank of Japan, Dai-Ichi Kangyo Bank and Fuji Bank decided to band in together, creating a huge institution that would be globally competitive. In many other countries, it may be more natural for such banks to look for a foreign partner. Yet, there are a few exceptions also as in the case of Ripplewood Holdings which we have already analyzed.

References

Dietl, H. M. (1998), *Capital Markets and Corporate Governance in Japan, Germany and the United States*, London: Routledge.

Muramatsu, S. (1998), Cross-boarder M&A in Japan and Asia, in: *The Sixth Pacific Basin Symposium, Development and Equality*, Soka University & Thammasat University: 128-137.

Muramatsu, S. (2000); Shihon Chôtatsu to Shiharai Shûdan no Sentaku [Financing and Selection in Payment Methods], in: Muramatsu, S. (ed.), *Kigyô Hyôka no Riron to Gihô* [The Theories and Methods of Valuation] Tokyo: Chûô Keizaisha: 114-144.

Human Resource Development of Professional Workers in Large Manufacturers in Britain and Japan: A Comparative Study

Kazuo Koike

1 Introduction

1.1 Problem and Methods

This paper aims to clarify the Japanese features of human resource development of professional and managerial workers or college graduates in industry by comparing the three cases of two British and one Japanese frim.

The reason of why the focus is put on professional workers in industry needs a little explanation. In many industrialized countries, this group of workers is growing fast and it has become one of the largest groups in several countries such as Japan and Britain. This clearly implies that their skills are now crucial to the competitiveness of an economy. Yet, few in-depth studies have analyzed the human resource development of this group. Consequently, opinions lacking any empirical evidence prevail, such as that Japanese college graduates in industry are usually generalists without specialized skills, while the counterparts in the West are specialists with high levels of skills.

The research method adopted here is to survey the breadth of individual work experience or the series of jobs an individual worker has experienced over a long term which implies focusing on long-term on-the-job-training (OJT). The following three types of career are defined to provide a measuring of the breadth of work:

- single-function type,
- main- and sub-function type and
- multi-function type.

Here, the phrase "single function" is used in the broadest sense, meaning accounting or finance for instance, which is divided furthermore into three sub-functions: financial accounting, managerial accounting, and finance. A single-function type of career thus is called "narrow" when it is confined to only one of these three sub-functions; it is called "broad" when it covers two or three sub-functions. The main- and sub-function type of career implies long-term experience of one function and rather short-term experience of another function. A multi-function type, or so-called generalist, classifies a worker who has experienced several functions.

Another indicator of importance is the level of the organization in which the work experience takes place, and whether the career covers not only jobs at the division level and headquarters, but also groundwork at the plant or branch level. It is noted, in particular, if those targeted for promotion to central managerial positions have experienced groundwork. Such experience may strongly affect the skill formation and hence skill distribution in the organization. Whether the career mostly develops within a firm or across firms is a traditional indicator, and is considered here too. The noteworthy differential in this indicator is not if there is external experience in the initial few years of career, but if managers are recruited directly from outside, since external experience during the first few years hardly affects human resource development in the long run.

For this research, five intensive interviews for each firm were conducted. One interview was with the personnel managers, enquiring the outline of human resource development policy of their firms, and the practices in both accounting and marketing departments viewed from the personnel department. In the other four interviews – two with an accounting manager and two with a marketing manager – the practices of their departments and individual careers of close co-workers were researched. Although the targeted departments were both accounting and marketing in the original survey, in this evaluation analysis is confined to the accounting department.

1.2 Three Cases

The two British and one Japanese firm are all large, long-established manufactures, and are abbreviated hereafter as BA, BB, and JA, respectively. Considering only large, long-established manufacturers should make international comparison fruitful, since similar conditions within the selected firms will clarify the differences by country – if there are any. All three firms employ a large number of employees (from forty-five to seventy-five thousand).

Another similarity is that the three firms are all manufacturers of investment goods. In selling of investment goods engineers constitute a part of the marketing staff. Although the three firms differ in their product range, comparing them should explore the variances and similarities in human resource development systems between Britain and Japan.

This paper is organized as follows. The following section 2 summarizes the overall findings; sections 3 and 4 focus on the essence of professional workers' skills, i.e. the breadth of work experience. Section 5 tries to explain reasons for similarities as well as differences between the three. The final section discusses the future trend.

2 Overall Findings

Let me begin with summarizing the findings in three features, concerning the breadth of work experience, the most vital component of human resource development.

- For all three firms, the extent of work experience for most professional employees is of the **broad single functioned type** of career. That is different, of course, for senior managers, who are mostly multi-functioned. Japanese careers are not particularly broad. That clearly contradicts popular arguments claiming that Westerners are specialists, while Japanese are generalists.
- As expected, many employees in the British firms have worked in other companies, whereas very few in the Japanese firm have. Yet, the **external work experience** for employees in the British firms is usually as short as two to five years and most of these employees are recruited into non-managerial positions. Promotion from within is common practice for managerial posts in both British firms as well as in the Japanese one.[1]
- Most of the employees of the Japanese firm who are university graduates have experienced **groundwork**, whereas only some of their counterparts in the British firms have similar experience. Although the two British firms once followed this practice, too, it had become unpopular at the time of our investigation.

1 Accounting employees face the necessity for external experience in the British firms. As it is well known, certain professional certifications issued by several professional accountant associations prevail in contemporary British industry. Particularly, Chartered Accountant, the most traditional title among them, requires two to three years of work experience in accounting firms. On the other hand, the Japanese firm recruits mostly new university graduates, as is common for large firms in contemporary Japanese industry. It is extremely difficult to become a legally qualified Japanese accountant, and very few of those who succeed remain in ordinary firms; many prefer careers in accounting firms.

3 Breadth of Work Experience: The Japanese Case

3.1 Accounting in the Semiconductor Division

With seventy-five thousand employees in Japan, the Japanese case JA was originally a manufacturer of electrical machinery. Today its products range from heavy electrical machinery, industrial machinery, semiconductors and computers to atomic energy plants. Each of the ten divisions is in charge of one particular group of products. We interviewed accounting and marketing managers in the division of semiconductors, and personnel managers in the headquarters.

Like other divisions, the semiconductor division has its own accounting department that is divided into 10 sections. Five sections are in charge of budget control of five subdivisions dealing with certain kinds of semiconductors manufactured by a couple of factories; four sections handle related companies, overseas activities and other offices, and one section is the supervising section. Individual career information has been collected for nine employees including the department head and section and sub-section chiefs.

A rough description of the accounting organization at the headquarters of the corporation is also necessary, since individual careers could extend to that office. Headquarters have several departments, including an accounting department and a finance department. The accounting department is composed of a managerial group (managerial accounting), a financial accounting group (preparing balance sheets), a tax group and a planning group (planning and personnel administration in the field of accounting across the whole corporation). The finance department consists of a finance group, an administrative group and an international exchange group. In addition, each factory has an accounting group to handle cost accounting, and each branch has an accounting group to collect payment for bills.

3.2 Transfer of Employees

New university graduates start their careers in accounting with cost accounting at one of the factories for their first four or five years. In his or her first year a new graduate is in charge of one manufacturing section, fully engaged in cost accounting; the next year he or she is moved to the next section; the third year he or she is put in charge of more than one section. This career development gives the employee the opportunity to acquire knowledge about a variety of semiconductors and their manufacturing processes. Many of these graduates move to the accounting department of the division, where they firstly handle manufacturing costs in their subdivision and secondly sales costs. Finally they are put in charge of the overall budget including loss and profit, and are further moved to other subdivisions.

Some staff moves to the accounting or the finance department at the headquarters. In terms of the products handled by one employee, however, one division was the usual breadth of experience before being promoted to department managers at the headquarters.

It is commonly thought that regular rotation prevails in ordinary large Japanese firms, controlled by powerful personnel departments. The situation in the Japanese firm we studied is, however, somewhat different from the popular belief: the head of the accounting department of the division, not the personnel department, usually decides on moves within the division. To be more precise, the chiefs of the accounting groups of each factory present a list of candidates. Then, the head of the accounting department also prepares a list of the candidates in his or her division and makes – based on these lists – the final decision on the moves. However, a regular rotation occurs when employees stay in one position longer than four or five years; these employees are automatically enlisted for transfer. Posting and bidding or advertising procedures are used only at limited occasions, such as the launch into a new field of business, which has not yet been seen in the field of accounting.

3.3 Individual Careers

These general statements need to be compared with individual career information presented in figure 1, though the information pertaining to JA is limited to only seven cases. The horizontal axis indicates the breadth of career. The single-function type of career is divided in six categories ranging from very narrow to very broad "Very narrow" implies that a worker experienced only an important part of one sub-function; for example, such as either cost accounting or budget control within managerial accounting. "Fairly narrow" means that the employees work experience covers more than one important part within one sub-function, such as both of cost accounting and budget control within managerial accounting. "Small medium" implies experience covering one sub-function with a small part of another sub-function: for instance, managerial accounting plus a part of financial accounting. "Large medium" represents substantial experience with two out of all three sub-functions. "Fairly broad" implies experience in all three sub-functions. Finally, "very broad" is used to label those managers who supervise all fields of accounting, such as the head of an accounting department.

Yet, it is important to notice that all these descriptions are confined to employees' experience within the current firm, because there is not sufficient information available for incorporating external experience. The managers in accounting or marketing we interviewed did not know in any detail the work content of the external experience of individual employees.

Figure 1 indicates that the breadth of work experience is mostly either medium or broad for JA employees. This coincides with the general statement made earlier.

Figure 1: Breadth of Work Experience in the Accounting Department in the Japanese Casestudy

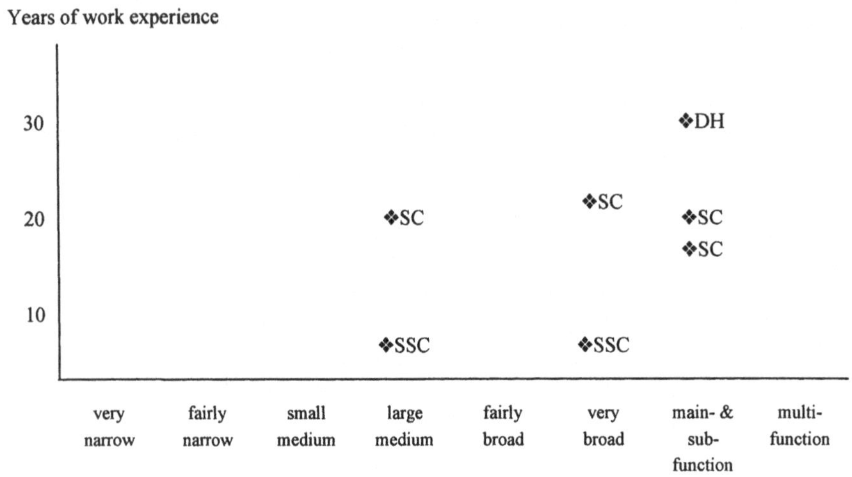

Notes: DH: department head; SC: section chief; SSC: sub-section chief.

4 Breadth of Career: British Cases

4.1 The Case of BA

4.1.1 Accounting in the Gas Division of BA

BA has slightly more than 45 thousand employees, most of whom work outside Britain, as is common for large British corporations. Nearly two-thirds of all these employees work in its major product division, industrial gas. The other three divisions utilize technologies derived from industrial gas. We focus on the industrial gas division.

Out of thirty thousand employees in the industrial gas division, only three thousand are located in Britain; they are engaged in manufacturing and selling the various kinds of industrial gases. The corporation has several hundred manufacturing facilities all over the world with only about 10% of them located in Britain. The industrial gas division consists of five subdivisions, each in charge of a geographical area of the world. The largest subdivision is in charge of Britain and Europe. It is this subdivision we studied.

The accounting department of the European subdivision consists of six sections. Three sections are in charge of different areas: Ireland, Britain, and the rest of Europe, respectively. The section handling Britain also handles financial management with a staff of more than 40. Two other sections manage budget control or financial analysis for different products. The last section studies computerization of the accounting system. It is the manager of this section who has been our primary interviewee. Our general information comes from both this manager and the director in charge of human resource management at both the headquarters and the industrial gas division.

Individual career information has been collected for eight employees including section and sub-section chiefs.

4.1.2 Transfer of Employees

According to the human resource director, it is company policy that new university graduates are the central source of recruits and, for most functions, only a small part of these recruits has external experience. His statement seems to express corporate policy rather than practice, however. Nearly half of those new university graduates recruited are engineers, a quarter for marketing, and a remaining quarter for accounting. Management trainees usually move among various jobs within one function for their initial two or three years. Thereafter, their careers proceed within one function. Although the firm is eager to enact cross-functional moves, such moves are actually very rare and mostly confined to very senior levels.

The experience for accounting employees is different. According to an accounting manager, two channels exist in recruiting for accounting: the new graduates and those who have acquired the qualification as accountants. Recently, more new graduates are hired because of the new possibilities of acquiring professional qualifications such as Cost and Management Accountant (CMA) or Certified Accountant (CACA) at night schools or by correspondence courses without serving in accounting firms. Increasingly these titles are valued as highly as the traditional Chartered Accountant (CA). At BA, although the position of head of accounting department has long been monopolized by those with CAs, the new head has a title of CMA. Once accounting employees acquire their qualification, job moves within the function are common either within a subdivision or between subdivisions. Inter-divisional moves are exceptional.

The procedures of moves varied with the distance and the level of moves. When the move is between two of the six sections within this subdivision, the head of this subdivision's accounting department selects the appropriate candidate from among his subordinates without any posting and bidding process. Only when no appropriate staff member can be identified within the department, notice of the vacancy is advertised in the accounting bulletin, which is circulated to the different subdivisions. It is the manager of the section in question, not the personnel department, who selects the candidate. For the senior level – directors and above – the story runs different. At this level management decides transfers without any advertising procedure.

4.1.3 Individual Careers

Individual career information is shown in figure 2, though the information pertaining to BA is limited to only six cases. It confirms the prevalence of the single function type. Out of seven section chiefs and assistant section managers, six have a single-function type of career. The only exception is the former head of the accounting department, who has been promoted to the position of general manager of an overseas subdivision belonging to the same division.

Figure 2: Breadth of Work Experience in the Accounting Department in the British Casestudy BA

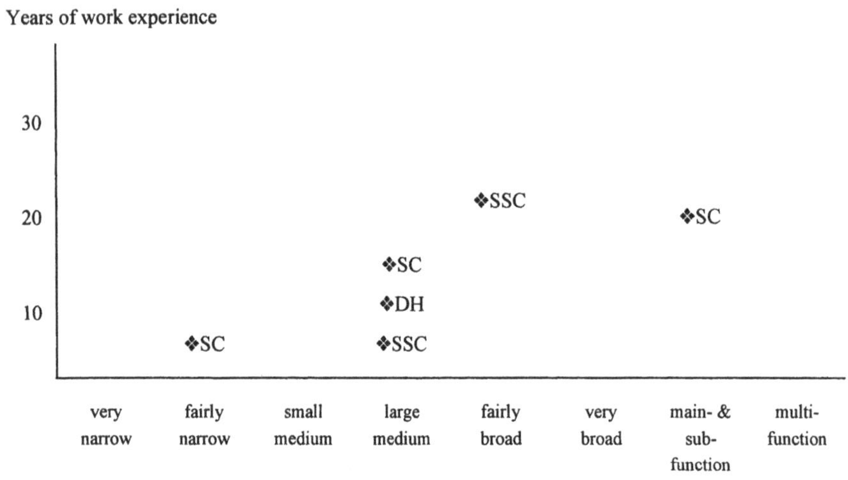

Notes: DH: department head; SC: section chief; SSC: sub-section chief.

The premise of most recruits being new university graduates is not supported, however. All seven employees whose careers are tracked have external experience, whether they acquired their CAs, or obtained other qualifications without service in accounting firms. Yet, all these external experiences are rather short-term, except for the current accounting director. Promotion from within prevails.

The breadth of skill formation is not narrow. Many employees move between subdivisions and have also experienced groundwork at the branch level.

Employees on fast track careers are broad in their work experience, though in a different way. Their careers are rather narrow in neither experiencing groundwork, nor various sections in the accounting department. They have been promoted too quickly to become broad at the low and middle levels of work. From the beginning, they are deployed to the demanding jobs in the most strategic section of the department. Yet, being promoted to positions of general manager or accounting department head broadens their careers. Here, a crucial difference between JA and BA can be observed: careers at BA vary, depending on whether the employees are fast track or not.

4.2 The Case of BB

4.2.1 Accounting in the Heavy Machinery Group of BB

BB employs 43,000 employees divided into two large groups: aircraft manufacturing and heavy machinery manufacturing. We focus on the heavy machinery group here, which has nearly 18,000 employees. Out of 18,000 employees, 11,000 are working in Britain, in ten divisions. Each division is in charge of a cluster of products, such as generators, switchboards, and control systems, most of which are non-mass production items.

The head of accounting department of a small division with only 350 employees is our primary interviewee. Nearly half of this division's employees are professionals and managers, reflecting the high technical level required in the manufacture of control systems of electric power plants or of train transportation. Most of this division's products are custom-made, taking as long as a year or so for completion. The manufacturing process requires a lot of software work and, therefore, many software engineers. Individual career information has been collected for only two employees, the head of the accounting department and the section chief of the accounting section within the accounting department.

According to the division's accounting department head, there are two channels of recruitment: one for individuals who have acquired qualifications and the other for new graduates without qualifications. The former channel is further divided into two: entry immediately after having obtained professional qualification and entry after a short external experience with qualifications. The latter channel admits employees to serve as trainees for an initial couple of years during which one has to acquire their qualification.

4.2.2 Transfer of Employees

Once they have acquired their qualifications, employees move within the accounting function, within the group, and even mostly within the area of north-east England, where many divisions are located. In other words, moves between divisions in the group are common. Employees at management level and above move across areas, even to overseas. Notably, accounting people are asked to experience both managerial accounting and financial accounting, while there are few moves between the computer section and the accounting section in the department.

Decisions on moves are mostly based on responses to advertising, or posting and bidding. When a vacancy occurs, the vacancy is advertised within the group. It is only when there is no appropriate candidate that the vacancy is externally advertised. Applicants usually consult with their current supervisors before applying for an opening, though there is no formal rule to do so. Normally the supervisors encourage the applicants in career development.

A steering committee, consisting of the accounting director of the group and the heads of the division's accounting departments, promote the moves between divisions. This kind of career development activity has been rare before this committee was established five years prior to our study.

4.2.3 Individual Careers

Individual career information is shown in figure 3. We explored seven individual careers out of ten staff members in this accounting section, although only three of them could be called professionals: the department head, the accounting section chief, and the assistant accountant. Since the assistant accountant had worked for only three years after having been recruited as a new graduate, only the other two are described in figure 3. Because this is too small a sample to reach any conclusions, the observations below include non-professional employees, underlining the characteristics of the professional careers.

The careers of these two professionals are rather broad. Moreover, it is confirmed by the example of the assistant accountant that new graduate recruiting is actually implemented. During and after finishing management traineeship, this employee experienced most jobs in the accounting section. Normally, promising people are given the chance to experience most jobs. Many, however, stay long on one job, having a rather narrow career. This is confirmed by individual career information of non-professional employees. In other words, this policy is not merely about appreciating a person because he or she has qualifications, but to strongly encourage those promising employees to acquire them.

Figure 3: Breadth of Work Experience in the Accounting Department in the British Casestudy BB

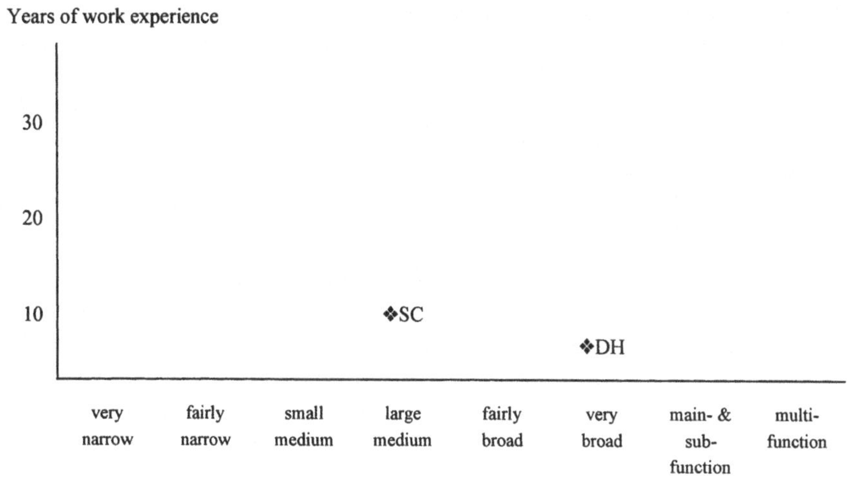

Notes: DH: department head; SC: section chief.

5 Reasons for Similarity and Difference

5.1 Necessary Components of Skills

In order to clarify the grounds for the features pointed above, the hypothesis is presented that a certain character of skills may lead to these features. This hypothesis is based mainly on the information obtained through the interviews with the accounting manager of JA.

It is safe to say that a typical job for college graduates with nearly ten years of accounting experience would be the budget control of a subdivision. This job has two main parts: compilation of the budget every six months and its administration afterwards. Controlling the administration of the budget demands higher skills than its compilation according to the statement of our interviewee. The difficulty lies in finding the causes of the gap between the budget and the monthly performance. If these causes can be correctly identified, the possibility of remedying the trouble is high and the next budget may thus become more efficient; if not, the prospect of making an efficient budget for the next term is unlikely.

Discovering the causes relies on a plethora of knowledge because there may be many diverse reasons for a gap between the budget and the monthly performance. Firstly, problems in the manufacturing process could be the reason. If the accounting staff is skillful in identifying such a cause and the problem can be solved accordingly, the next budget already becomes more accurate. Discovering where the problem lies, what kind of problem it is, whether it is likely to be frequently repeated, what measures are appropriate as a remedy, and how long a remedy will take to bear fruits, are the main items of problem solving. Thus, knowledge of the manufacturing process is one of the major skills necessary for accounting staff in charge of budget control.

Secondly, knowledge of the organization is indispensable. Trouble is not confined to machinery but can come out of the organization: miscommunication among the people who operate the machinery, for example, can cause the gap between the budget and actual performance. For identifying such a cause, staff needs knowledge of many factors, including what part of the organization suffers from miscommunication, what measures can be implemented for solving that trouble, and how they would affect the next budget.

Thirdly, factors outside the firm also need to be taken into account. Changes in demand, for example, heavily affect costs and therefore the gap between budget and actual performance. If an unexpected change in the demand for semiconductors, either quantitatively or qualitatively, occurs, many measures need to be taken, including transferring workers from one line to another so as to accommodate the required change in production. Such measures themselves increase costs and hence produce some gap, resulting in enormous differentials in efficiency. Forecasting changes in markets accurately is almost impossible for anyone; so uncertainty is a constant factor to deal with. In short, a lot of skills besides knowledge of accounting are required for the accounting staff to control the budget.

5.2 Acquiring Skills

Acquiring these skills requires OJT, beginning with cost control for one production line in a factory manufacturing semiconductors. This job consists of two parts: computing the standard manufacturing cost for each kind of semiconductor and analyzing the gap between the standard cost and the actual monthly cost. Similar to the problem of budget control is the analysis of the gap that demands higher skills. Again, for analyzing the gap knowledge of various factors is indispensable.

Thus, the skills needed to do a good job of cost control of one production line has a strong resemblance to those needed for budget control. The crucial difference is knowledge of a broader span of products, of the manufacturing process, and of the overall organization. Career development is structured to attain these skills through broadening experience.

After an initial year in charge of one manufacturing line, breadth of experience extends to the next line, to many lines at the same time, and even to another factory that manufactures different semiconductors. After experiences of six or seven years, accounting staff moves to one of the subdivisions in the semiconductor division. There, they control the budget of the manufacturing account first, then of the sales account, and finally of all the subdivision. Then, they move to another subdivision in the same division, and finally they take over budget control for the whole division. Thus, it can be understood how efficient this way of skill formation is. This is not meant that off-the-job-training (OffJT) is useless in teaching skills necessary to handle uncertainty. OffJT is definitely useful, in particular for supporting effective OJT and for acquiring basic knowledge of the profession. Yet, OffJT alone is not enough to provide all the skills needed.

5.3 Reasons for the Prevalence of Broad Single-Function Type of Career

While the statement above is a surmise based on the information obtained through the case of JA, this can explain why the broad single-function type of career prevails for all three cases. To analyze the causes of the gap between the budget and monthly performance, it is necessary to know a variety of factors. Even within the knowledge of accounting, the employee needs to acquire knowledge about several sub-fields; no cost accounting job could be well performed without knowing financial accounting, and no budget control of a subdivision is effectively conducted without knowing finance. One of the best ways to acquire these skills is to do the accounting in these sub-fields for a certain period.

At a glance, this reasoning may recommend broader span of experience than a single-function type of career. Since the budget control requires understanding many factors, as the manufacturing process, the organization, and the market, experience of various functions is likely to be needed. Marketing experience helps in reviewing sales forecasting, a vital component of the budget control, for instance. However, it is very costly to acquire sufficient skills in other functions. Therefore, a broad single-function type of career is a natural consequence as the most efficient career.

The importance of groundwork is also easy to understand. One of the most crucial factors in analyzing the causes of a gap in budget control is the knowledge of the manufacturing process in a subdivision. If the employee conducting this task has a very high aptitude, then simply asking veterans who know manufacturing well might be enough to gain understanding. But if many, not particular apt employees are required to conduct this budget control job – which is quite probable due to increasing uncertainty –, then cost-accounting work experience at the manufacturing sites would be the best training.

5.4 Differences in the Breadth of Work Experience

There are two major differences in the breadth of work experience between the three cases: the extent of external experience and the procedure for internal moves. External experience is discussed here only concerning the process of acquiring the qualification of accountants, since the ordinary work experience in other firms has not been disclosed so far.

Britain seems to be one of the countries in which professional qualifications prevail, and in particular in the accounting field the prestige of professional qualifications is still high. Yet, even the accounting qualifications are not of crucial importance. Although the most traditional, prestigious certification, the Chartered Accountant (CA) requires two or three years' work experience in accounting firms, other certifications such as the already mentioned Cost and Management Accountant (CAM) or the Certified Accountant (CACA) can be obtained without any experience in accounting firms. While working in ordinary firms, people can participate in night classes or correspondence courses to prepare for taking exams. Once the CA was far more prestigious and a precondition for the promotion to the position of a financial director in large corporations; recently, however, the other certifications are almost equally valued. Moreover, performance in the organization increasingly determines promotion. One of our primary interviewees, the department head at BB, said that she encourages her subordinates who are capable to acquire the qualification rather than merely crediting those who already have these qualifications. The know-how needed to conduct the daily tasks on the shop floor appropriately is mainly acquired through experience though.

The procedures of moves within an organization are also different. De facto regular rotation prevails at JA, although in a few cases posting and bidding is utilized. On the other hand, advertising or posting and bidding procedures are frequently adopted at BA and BB. For both cases however, posting and bidding is applied only to the level below department heads and to moves across department boundaries. Above the section chief, transfers are decided solely on the basis of succession planning or arrangement by the management. Moves within a department for British cases follow a different procedure. First, an appropriate candidate is sought within the department; when there is none, the vacancy is posted in the bulletin or in the firm's circular.

On these two procedures – posting and bidding and de facto rotation – our primary interviewee in marketing at BB makes the following comments: rotation is more effective for providing broad experience, but for fairness in the organization, posting and bidding is preferable. This clearly sums up the merits and demerits of the two systems.

There is another factor that cannot be overlooked. In any country, managers are naturally reluctant to let capable subordinates leave their groups. Thus rotation, that lets people move regularly whether they are capable or not, gives more employees a chance to develop broader experience. On the other hand, rotation usually fails to provide an opportunity for the workers to voice their own preference s.

6 Future Perspective

In assessing the future perspective, the vital issue is undoubtedly the breadth of career. The first step of examination is to analyze the interviewees' assessment of the current situation. To begin with JA, none of the interviewees prefers narrower careers; they all prefer slightly broader ones. The personnel manager prefers the broad single-function type of career. The interviewee in accounting appreciates a career that is broadened within a function. Moves between divisions in accounting even below the department-head level are needed, while moves at the higher levels already exist. It is also necessary to experience many sub-functions within accounting, because overseas activities require accounting people to handle finance in addition to managerial accounting and financial accounting.

The opinions of the interviewees in BA differ little from those of JA. The personnel director encourages more interfunctional moves for senior management, since most moves have so far been confined within a function. The BA accounting manager points out the increase of inter-divisional moves within a function, but does not mention inter-functional moves. He suggests that lack of groundwork (particularly for the people on fast track) is not crucial, since acquiring the necessary knowledge from shopfloor veterans can compensate for it – if the staff have exceptionally high aptitude. Almost the same story is told at BB.

In sum, all three firms intend to broaden the current single-function type of career slightly, and neither plan to go back to the narrow type nor move on to the multifunction type. The broad single-function type of career is common policy. This supports our hypothesis stated above.

References

The Japan Institute of Labour (1998), *Human Resource Development of Professional and Managerial Workers in Industry: An International Comparison*, Tokyo: The Japan Institute of Labour.

Koike, K. & Inoki, T. (1990), *Skill Formation in Japan and Southeast Asia*, Tokyo: Tokyo University Press.

Koike, K. (1988), *Understanding Industrial Relations in Modern Japan*, London: Macmillan.

Koike, K. (1997), *Human Resource Development*, Tokyo: Japan Institute of Labour.

Organisational Learning is Dead! Long Live Organisational Learning!

John B. Kidd

1 Global Forces

1.1 Demographics

Most of the developed countries have very low birth rates – lower than they need to sustain their current population. It has been argued that the globe has too many people, but it was never argued that the nations of the developed world should attempt to rapidly reduce their own population.

In the developed world we now see two connected issues – that of the percentage of the population able to work (productive population rate), and the dependency rate (the projected numbers of retired people against the numbers of workers) (Ness & Ciment 1999). Both are important figures – since those people at work create products and services, and in turn pay taxes from their salaries to support their nation in its many roles. One role is to maintain some form of Social Welfare – to pay for the health care of all ages, and to pay for the pension support of the elderly. Soon Italy, for instance, will have a dependency ratio of 0.7, which indicates there are too many retired people and too few workers. Thus there will be less than one working person to support each elderly person. It is not surprising under this scenario that firms look to populous lands to fill this gap in whatever way possible.

1.2 Global Supply Chain Management

Organisations, once stable for many years, have evolved into complex and highly integrated global sourcing, assembly, and distribution systems (Stock, Greis & Kasunda 1999). Through the 1920s – 1980s there was pressure only to mass-produce in more effective ways. Since then we have moved to a manufacturing regime which has to be *agile*, in which alliances are made (and dissolved) rapidly. This enables supply chains to flourish briefly to service a volatile market, then be reconstituted to serve another market even if customers probably only order one item with no repeats (Peppard 1996). Alliances become transient: yet, because there is mass customisation of nearly identical goods, there is a need to manage knowledge up and down-stream in the supply chain (Drew & Smith 1998).

One might consider that tiered supply systems are complex, but they are not unusual, for instance, the *big few* – GM, Ford, Toyota – in the automotive sector. Herein the final assembly of the vehicle is dependent on hundreds of suppliers working in concert, often to a just-in-time (JIT) regime activated by integrated information technology and communications (ITC) systems (Angeles 2000). In this system there may be a database freely available to all suppliers so, trusting one another, they can reduce the overall cycle time by forecasting downstream demand to initiate their own production before a formal order is placed by the higher tier in the system (Bhatnagar & Viswanathan 2000).

Ultimately in considering this global scene we must focus on the ability of individuals from different countries (having different beliefs and training) to trust each other, and who understand they have to share their knowledge with all others in the supply chain. For knowledge managers in multi-national enterprises (MNE) there are big issues in developing trust in (possibly) short-lived alliances amongst outsourced firms, and in developing and maintaining knowledge across the major facets of their core firms' competencies.

1.3 Financing Ventures

UNCTAD (United Nations Conference on Trade and Development) has tracked global FDI (foreign direct investment) for many years, noting how its flows are not predominantly between wealthy nation, but that the wealthy invest in poorer nations, and even the poor nations attempt some outward flows. The latter often have become NIEs (newly industrialised economies), and a few who are economically vigorous nations in Asia have been dubbed "tiger economies".

We note global FDI from 1997 to 1998 rose by almost 40% to $644 billion (UNCTAD 1999). The driving force behind the 1998 and 1999 FDI expansion was cross-border merger & acquisition (M&A), especially between firms in Japan, America and Europe, and to a degree embracing developing countries. The Asian financial crisis of 1997/98 affected the FDI in-flows into the Asian region which recorded a fall of 11% in 1998. However, preliminary estimates by UNCTAD suggest that FDI flows in 1999 to Asia increased by 1% over 1998 to $91 billion, contrary to the anticipated decline.

1.4 Transparency

Asians deploy opaque accounting practices and they also practice gift giving on a scale that seems to an American nothing short of bribery. To combat this effect the firms in America and elsewhere in the West press the eastern firms (many of whom may already be venture partners) to conform to GAAP (Generally Acceptable Accounting Principles), though it is not the only contender for a global standard – see the International Accounting Standards Committee (IASC)[1]. We must also think about the meaning of "generally acceptable" since it has been shown that accounting disclosure, at least historically, is strongly correlated with cultural measures (Gray & Vint 1995, Salter & Niswander 1995). All state that the Oriental cultures are biased towards secrecy and thus non-transparency. One may question if different regularity practices and more open markets in these regions will force firms to be more transparent (in a GAAP sense)? Perhaps it will just evince token gestures in the short-term given that many Asian countries have been unable for years to disentangle their opaque systems from those resting on bribery and extortion.

Further, research on the Oriental concept of probability and risk has shown those persons may be "fate-oriented" and less willing than westerners to take a probabilistic view of the world (Phillips & Wright 1977). This might suggest the need for sophisticated accounting is not perceived in Asia since "what will be – will be"; and while no subtle provisioning will hide poor performance, the collective spirit will carry an ailing firm without loss of face.

2 Anchoring the Old OL

2.1 Stable Traits

It is quite understandable that within one macro culture there will be fewer constraints upon the merging of firms than would be the case if they were originally from clearly different macro cultures – simply because we think we know and thus understand the others. Hofstede (1980, 1991), Trompenaars & Hampden-Turner (1997) have studied and measured *culture* over many years. Following the work of Hofstede, Kogut & Singh (1988) derived a measure representing cultural difference as a single number. It is based on the four original indices of culture created by Hofstede and gives quick insights into the potential for conflicts that may emerge in proposed joint ventures between firms of different nations.

1 The European Commission outlined on June 13th 2000 a strategy for financial reporting in the future in Europe. The strategy is designed to help eliminate remaining barriers to cross-border trading in securities, in particular by recommending that there be one set of accounting standards so that company accounts throughout the European Union become more transparent and can be more easily compared.

2.2 Process Modelling

We are the products of our early learning at home, at school, in universities and through our occupations. It is not surprising therefore that we find different embedded learning patterns around the world. Ben-Ari (1997) noted how very young Japanese children learn what later becomes for them very strong culture-bound mechanism; thus he linked the Hofstede Indices to the learning of Japanese children, and by implication to Japanese adults, some of whom will become managers in joint ventures or strategic alliances. It is almost a given that "if the going gets tough" we each revert to our early learning patterns (Siegel 1956:42). So whatever the desired working practices might be in strategic alliances, when the situation toughens we might assume there is growing pressure to work according to each parties' cultural norms. We give examples below of some national distinctions in process modelling:

Linstone (1984) describes an American viewpoint somewhat softer than that proposed by American operations researchers looking to hard-science and the derivation of algorithmic solutions. Here the T (technical) looks to the logic of problem solving and optimizing; the O (organizational) is action-focused on the group; and the P (personal) relates to the individual, accepting his/her limited ability to handle more than a few alternatives.

In the United Kingdom the Soft Systems Modelling (SSM) methodology has been promoted strongly and is now well accepted (Checkland 1981, Checkland & Holwell 1998). They advocate a resolute attempt be made to initiate and maintain discussions between the client and the consultant to be sure of jointly understanding the issues. In some ways this process is quintessentially British – it is pragmatic, it draws on such quantitative and qualitative techniques as needed during the evolution of the study, and it is multi-disciplinary.

The teachings of the Koran, from the Prophet Mohammed, suggest we should be modest in our behaviour: "The metaphor of the believers, in their mutual love and mercy, is that of the human body; if one organ is hurt, the whole body responds in pain." Thus an emergent Arabic process modelling system incorporates *Jassad* (quantitative modelling), *Aqel* (qualitative modelling) and *Rooh* (Action modelling). These draw together in a wholesome way the forces of nature.

In Japan we note a triadic relationship between "Humanity – Nature", "Body – Mind", and "Self – Other". It may be said that the ultimate reality for the Japanese lies in delicate transitional processes observable in visible and concrete matter rather than in eternal or abstract constructs (Nonaka 1994).

In ancient China the social situation was considered to comprise of two parts – *wu* (objective existence) and *shi* (human activities and their mechanisms). Both *wu* and *shi* have governing laws *li*, hence – *wuli* and *shili*. In following *shili* individuals develop a knowledge system about the laws of people's actions (Li &

Li 1998). Furthermore, a third factor – *renli* – concerns the socio-political patterns of interaction: thus it deals with the effects of the overlaps of different cultural and belief systems. When one is oriented towards *renli* one would ensure the designed systems support human needs as well as objective needs – thus the effectiveness of *wuli* and *shili* can only work when *renli* is recognised and undertaken. Some however will contend that in individual cases certain *li* are more crucial than others (Zhu 1998).

2.3 Organisational Culture

Given the different modelling process cited above it would be reasonable to assume that organisational cultures vary, country by country, as do perceptions of leadership style. For instance, we appreciate the tensions between firms of the east and west coasts of America; there were many political difficulties across the 11 time zones of old-Russia; and there are still conflicts between the 56 ethnic groups in the provinces of China.

2.4 Managerial and Leadership Models

Europe comprises many nation states with quite diverse histories and cultures. It is not surprising therefore that they have developed managerial styles which suit their indigenous populations (Calori & de Woot 1994). We accept that the recent removal of many trade and organisational barriers in the EU has increased the permeability of their national borders, yet there is inevitably a lag in the changes in personal and innovation processes which delays the convergence of European management styles.

Following the work of Lord & Maher (1991), a team of over 160 researchers have been co-opted into a global study under the aegis of (GLOBE) Global Leadership and Organisational Effectiveness Programme. Their interim result shows that leadership, as a concept, is culturally justifiable in Europe, notwithstanding its national diversity. They are likely to extend this finding across all its researched nations (Brodbeck et al. 2000). One interesting and, of course, tentative conclusion suggests that it is unlikely there will be a convergence of European cultures in the near future. It follows that the successful European managers' ability to build bridges in pan-European firms will enable this "euro-manager" to offer *global cross-cultural leadership* as a key competence.

2.5 Differences in Perceptions of Time and Context

Hall (1976) and Hall & Hall (1987) discuss how people deal with time and with the events taking place round them. Some persons are monochronic (M-time): they work as though time is linear. Others believe time is multi-stranded or polychronic (P-time): they work in a parallel-processing mode. And there are the "inbetweeners", who sometimes work in one mode or sometimes the other mode – epitomised by many French persons (Platt 1994).

Hall (1976) suggests that most of the world comprises "high context" (HC) persons. He recognised that high context (HC) messages are those in which most of the information is in the physical context or internalised in the person, while little is in the coded, explicitly transmitted part of the message. Thus an (HC) message is one in which most of the information the recipient already holds, so the message itself can be brief: it carries a highly condensed transmission. A "low context" (LC) message is more explicit, and in order to support the information invested in the message, has to be relatively verbose.

In conducting business we should note the Asians, Arabs, and Latin persons are HC, they *live, work and breath* in large networks with close personal relationships, often strongly linked through their families. They do not expect much background information in normal conversations since they *live* their contexts, and they keep themselves informed through their incessant network conversations. In contrast, Britain and American persons are LC (in general, so are most of the northern European people). LC persons compartmentalise their personal relationships, their work, and day-to-day life. As a consequence, they need to be much more verbose in their exchange of information. Thus there are difficult interactions – HC persons are impatient if given lots of information by LC persons; in turn, LC persons are at a loss when not told anything by the HC person. It follows that the hesitation of the LC person when out of context can be seen as obstructionist by an HC person. We may imagine the resulting (angry) silence that, in these circumstances, will decrease the trust between the individuals concerned.

3 Enabling the New OL

Business-modelling systems pursued by western multi-national managers are inwardly-looking and somewhat incompatible in their focus when merged with eastern views: compromise has to be made by each side on behalf of their firms. Importantly, managers of all the firms in a supply chain must deeply learn of the other's psychological processes to become more trusting and better able to criticize the merging of their business network processes. There has to be very sensitive practise along the reach of the global supply chain – since what is acceptable behaviour in one place is not so elsewhere, and some actions may even be unethical (Ralston, Egri, Stewart, Terpstra & Kiacheng 1999; Backman 1999). This is very important when cross-border alliances are undertaken. For example, McIvor, Humphries & Huang (2000) report on a group of business people, some from Hong Kong and some from southern mainland China. Those from Hong

Kong, having been exposed longer to western ways, acted as brokers, since they understood better the mores of the West. By their actions they instilled trust in each side of the partnership – for both the mainland Chinese and for the western managers.

Brandt (1990) found that for success in US-Japanese ventures it was vital to develop a high degree of trust early on. Madhok (1995) similarly urges a shift in focus from ownership issues to relational dynamics and social processes within the alliance culture. There is indeed a form of network culture at play here – but it is viewed more from a technical and business process aspect than from the person-to-person enterprise-wide process that might arguably be more appropriate.

On the other hand, again referring to Asian communities, we find that their networking mode is very important in developing and maintaining a sense of kinship. We have to consider the Asian process of *guanxi* which in China is universally practised: and the maintenance of which will involve gift giving (note the same word and social process is endemic in Japan). It is, however, instructive to note the (western-biased) observations of Collins (1997), who sees *guanxi* as a form of the old-boy network and other associations. She is not totally correct as it is difficult for an outsider to internalise the true meanings and roles of *guanxi* – although it is regarded as the special relationship between two persons in which long-term mutual benefits are more important than short-term gains. But it is not just a one-to-one relationship as there are reciprocities which may be developed between A, B and C. A may relate to B, and B relate to C – thus A may now relate to C through the common partner B. More widely still the networks that A, B and C have may all interrelate through their common agents. Lockett (1988) regards *guanxi* as one of the key features of Chinese society, but it is more than this – it is the mother of all relationships. We thus get to the notion of *guanxiwang* as the exchanges of goods and obligations within networks.

The exchanges of favour involving *guanxi* are not strictly commercial, they are also social – involving *renqing* (social or humanised obligation), and the giving of *mianzi* (the notion of "face") (Lou 1997, Yang 1994). Specifically, as China opened up, *guanxi* has become known as *social capital*. Taking a western view of this system, social capital is used to make tidy commercial contracts between corporations, leading the innocent westerner towards an over reliance on gift giving and banqueting as a means of conducting business. These activities are both normal facets of Chinese *guanxi*, but many western firms' operations go too far, causing western individuals to become known as "meat and wine friends". This defeats the object of true *guanxi* – which is the offering of favours during the development of a personal relationship naturally promoting business in China between Chinese business persons.

4 Shaping the New OL

4.1 Learning Processes

Some have described Organisational Learning as an oxymoron – saying that only people can learn and an organisation can not (Weike & Westley 1996). Easterby-Smith (1997) argues that OL may be studied within a wide spectrum of disciplines – psychology, organisational design, management science, strategy, production management, sociology and cultural anthropology.

4.1.1 A Western Approach

Huber (1991), whom Easterby-Smith classifies as analytic within the management science discipline, has identified several aspects of OL. Huber suggests that when some unit of an organisation acquires new knowledge, it is a sign of the existence of learning, but as long as the knowledge rests inside the unit, there is no chance of organisational learning. This represents a *simple* approach to learning predicated perhaps upon the characteristics noted by Hofstede, Hall, and others, who collectively suggest America is a nation composed of short-term, individualistic persons who do not network (in the same way as Asian persons). Other researchers present more complex learning models: embodied in forms of "action research" (Senge 1990, Eden, Jones & Sims 1983); or carried by "theories-in-use" (Agryris & Schon 1978); or the "double loop" learning approach (Argyris 1993).

Checkland (1981) treats this learning process differently – he suggests one has to get into the mind of the other in order to communicate meaning adroitly. There are worries over approaches which require groups of individuals to stay together long enough to benefit from the learning cycle because we see now rapid inter-firm personnel movement at managerial level in Europe and in America. These movements will inevitably break an individual's long-term group-focused learning cycle oriented to the cultural stance of a given organisation, although enriching at a personal level (again we may contrast this against the intra-firm exchanges of global staff deployment in the big Japanese firms).

4.1.2 An Eastern Approach

In knowledge based systems we have to grasp the issue of tacit knowledge – "that knowledge which we have, which we all feel we understand, but which ultimately defies clear enunciation." (Polanyi 1958) Given that mankind has basically the same needs we might assume that we solve our problems in similar ways – yet this does not occur. These processes are modified according to the peoples involved (for instance, according to their Hofstede differences with respect to hierarchy, to individualism, and to their long-term aims).

Nonaka and his co-researchers describe tacit knowledge as having two dimensions. First is the technical aspect – the "know-how" (Nonaka 1994, Nonaka & Takeuchi 1995, Nonaka & Konno 1998). The second is the cognitive – comprising the beliefs and mental models we all develop and carry over the years and whose schema are hard to change as we often take them for granted. They propose a model for change and learning having four quadrants:

- *Socialisation*: the sharing of knowledge between two persons.
- *Externalisation*: the expression of tacit knowledge through metaphor, analogies or narratives.
- *Combination*: the key processes are communication and diffusion of knowledge.
- *Internalisation*: the conversion of the explicit knowledge to the organisation's tacit knowledge by identifying the knowledge needed by oneself for working in the organisation.

4.2 Trust and Silence

Kao and Sek-Hong (1993) write on eastern and western attitudes characterising the eastern relationship as between individuals and organisations as "high trust"; and the western as "low trust and contract-oriented". However, they also point out that increasing individualism in Oriental societies is leading to a decrease in this (eastern) altruistic trust: perhaps they are *learning* from the West. Note earlier Graham & Sano (1984) described the stereotypical *John-Wayne-style* of American negotiating which emanates from a societal culture that centres the locus of action and decision making in the individual, yet extols a notion of fair play.

Graham & Sano (1984) also discuss underlying principles in the Japanese context. They noted *tate shakai*, a Confucian-influenced notion of a vertically graded social order that requires clear status markers; *amae*, referring to the emotion-laden reciprocal dependency; and *wa*, maintaining social harmony. Because of the once homogeneous nature of the Japanese people, there was no necessity for an explicit and coherent expression in speech. Rules of rhetoric and logic did not develop – instead, *sasshi* (empathy), *ishin denshin* (telepathy) became accepted aspects of a gesture-free body language considered to be characteristically Japanese; and their way of conducting *haragei* (silent discussion) is very disturbing to western businessmen (Matsumoto 1988). We note in Japanese literature it is not the precise term that is esteemed, but the *oku fukai* (deep and wide) and *ganchiku no aru* (suggestive) expression. These all defeat inter-cultural communication, and they stifle trust building. Supporting this argument, Lucier et al. (1992) identified features of Japanese organisations, which include emphasis on group orientation and identity, deferment of profits for long-term gain, and commitment to quality at every organisational level. They characterise American organisations, by contrast, as showing a lack of trust at all levels, a devotion to short-term profits, overspecialisation, complacency and arrogance.

Shih (1993), writing from a Taiwanese perspective, addresses a different element. He asserts that trust is a prerequisite for innovation and therefore has a central role in western business thinking. But he characterises the Chinese as especially prone to suspicion, and therefore less creative than they might otherwise be – though this is not a new observation (Smith 1894). And through their recent social history and from their personal observation of widespread dishonesty (Latourette 1972, Roberts et al. 2000) it is not surprising the Chinese might be *suspicious*, and therefore *silent* – especially when two in three persons in a group might be clandestine informers. However, theirs is internalised behaviour relating to Confucius' five cardinal relationships and their accompanying moral code. He proposed rules of engagement between the ruler-minister, father-son, husband-wife, elder and younger brother and friend-friend. Outsiders do not fit into the Confucian hierarchy; indeed, they represent a challenge to it. It is this missing sixth relationship that is of most concern to western business people, because in Asia they, the westerners, are the most extreme form of outsider (Li & Kidd 2000, Kidd & Li 2000). It is not surprising Confucius did not address this issue since, in his day, there would be very few *outsiders*. Now, to cover confusion, the Chinese may engage in silent behaviour, such as *fu go* – keeping words in the stomach before uttering them too soon. They have learned that "when a word has left the mouth, not even the swiftest horse can catch it" (Chinese proverb). So, lacking this sixth rule for *dealing with the outsider*, they prefer silence to making errors and losing face, or promoting the loss of face of the outsider. Many have written on "face" in Asian society (Bond 1994 on China, Holmes & Tangtongatavy 1997 on Thailand, and Backman 1999 on the darker side of Asian business where maintaining face leads to corruption) but have not raised the issue of the sixth dimension.

4.3 Discussion

Facts abound in organisations, and many firms now gather these into well categorised databases to make more explicit that which was explicit, but once only accessible by a few. Deep knowledge, however, is difficult to elicit. It takes time to gather the requisite persons together, to allow them to feel comfortable in the company of others and to let them judge the truth of the mission statement of the alliance within their own personal constructs and models. After that, they may begin the socialising process that moves them toward the exchange of mental models one with another. At that stage they begin to trust, as individuals. Later, as one person engages more deeply with more persons in the other's firm then organisational trust can flourish, and with this a translation of tacit knowledge to the explicit. Following this, the new explicit knowledge may become embedded and used in the alliance.

We note that "silence is golden" and that it may be better not to be a "chatter-box" since words may be valueless. Of course, in the vicinity of the Tower of Babel there was the cacophony of multiple languages – but herein we mean something deeper. It is about the problem of discerning value, or truths in the conversation, rather than simply accepting meaningless data exchange. The latter links to the adage of "garbage in, garbage out" – since poor data coming to one's mental model will lead inevitably to poor informating (in a Zuboff (1988) sense). However, if one's informant is silent we have another difficulty – one that carries the possibility of lying by omission, which may rupture any trust that has developed.

Thus we have to ask – why are people silent? Often the reasons reside in cross-cultural issues, and the lack of cultural literacy of the players (Merry 2001). In the culture-crossing situation, managers of the MNE must encourage cultural literacy so individuals from each side begin to trust, each in the other, thereby learning how to enhance their knowledge, and the organisation's learning (Edwards & Kidd 2000). We would accept the view of Richter (1999) – a smoother working of an alliance may be best guaranteed by the exchange of staff. But in fast and loose alliances, who should be exchanged with whom, since mixing management teams from different cultures carries risk? The risks also depend on the magnitude of the "cultural difference" as described by Kogut & Singh (1988). They may be unable to make the step-change to accept the other's cultural identity and thus ways of working. And equally problematic is their perception of leadership (Brodbeck et al. 2000).

Following this argument we suggest firms in the West might be advised to generate more conversations internally. Normally they would be operating as low context, low in (social) networking skills. But with the initiation of Q&A (question and answer) electronic databases they have the opportunity to engage in more complex conversations. Again we can liken this to the "informating" described by Zuboff (1988) wherein she describes how shop-floor workers, once they became supported by IT, could reformulate their personal models of the firms' operations and enjoin these with the models of other workers. Some knowledge managed firms of the West have their processes re-engineered and they decided to engage their newly freed workers (previously to be made redundant) in knowledge work – helping them mimic high context (Asian) networking (Snowden 2000).

5 Conclusions

OL takes time. It would seem that time nowadays is not freely available in the global alliance, nor even in local alliances. In these circumstances, new solutions in the new alliance are often old solutions from elsewhere, transshipped in the hope they will be accepted in the joint organisational framework. To address the promise of the future, alliances need time to translate their tacit knowledge into explicit knowledge and to open this to its corporate membership. Above all, the individuals concerned with this process have to learn to trust. The West and East interchange of understanding is a target but it is derived from a business need that may be untenable – as the western person is too short-term, noisy and dogmatically individualistic; and the eastern person is too acquiescent, and too opaque. But for understanding to occur we must ensure that there is some degree of trust between each nation/organisation – that is, individuals have to rise above their early learning and accept they don't know how the other will really behave, notwithstanding how they say they will behave. "Trust me" is not an issue, rather it is the development of the subtle process of accepting the unknown in the belief that both sides are honourable. Understanding the others' mental models is a case in point: we have to trust that others in using SSM, WSR or TOP have validity.

The implication for a multi-national organisation is that it is likely to be more effective to begin knowledge management initiatives on a national basis, even though at first this may appear to be reinforcing the barriers between the national groups. However, the importance of hierarchical links in the process of trust, and the need to "know oneself" before one knows the other justify this. The key role of communities of practice in knowledge management systems (as opposed to simply technological support) makes it essential that the local/national level is right first. Once this is on the way to being achieved, technical groups may then be used to make the first cross-national links and thus lead in to the development of organisational learning on a global platform. This requires the help of people who are "old and wise" in organisational terms.

References

Angeles, R. (2000), Revisiting the Role of Internet-EDI in the Current Electronic Commerce Scene, in: *Logistics Information Management* 13,1: 45-57.

Argyris, C. (1993), *Knowledge for Action: A guide to Overcoming Barriers to Organisational Change*, San Francisco: Jossey-Bass.

Argyris, C. & Schön, D. A. (1978) *Organisational Learning: A Theory of Action Perspective*, Reading, MA: Addison-Wesley.

Backman, M. (1999), *The Asian Eclipse: Exposing the Dark Side of Business in Asia*, Singapore: Wiley.

Ben-Ari, E. (1997) *Japanese Childcare: An Interpretative Study of Culture and Organisation*, London: Kegan Paul International.

Bhatnagar, R. & Viswanathan, S. (2000) Re-engineering Global Supply Chains: Alliances Between Manufacturing Firms and Global Logistics Services Providers, in: *International Journal of Distribution & Logistics*, 30,1: 13-34.

Bond, M. H. (1994), *Beyond the Chinese Face: Insights from Psychology*, Hong Kong: Oxford University Press.

Brandt, S. A. (1990), Perspectives on Joint Venturing with the Japanese in the United States, in: *Advanced Management Journal* 55,1: 34-36, 47-48.

Brodbeck, F. C. et al. (2000), Cultural Variation of Leadership Prototypes Across 22 European Countries, in: *Journal of Occupational and Organisational Psychology* 73: 1-29.

Calori, R., & de Woot, P. (1994), *A European Management Model: Beyond Diversity*, New York: Prentice Hall.

Checkland, P. (1981), *Systems Thinking, Systems Practice*, Chitchester: Wiley.

Checkland, P. & Holwell, S. (1998), *Information, Systems and Information Systems*, Chitchester: Wiley.

Collins, P. (1997), Postcard from China, in: *Management Services* 41,12: 36-38.

Drew, S. A. W. & Smith, P. A. C. (1998), The New Logistics Management: Transformation through organisational learning, in: *International Journal of Physical Distribution and Logistics Management* 28: 666-681.

Easterby-Smith, M. (1997), Disciplines of Organisational Learning: Contributions and Critiques, in: *Human Relations* 50: 1085–1113.

Eden, C., Jones, S. & Sims, S. (1983), *Messing About in Problems*, Oxford: Pergamon.

Edwards J. S. & Kidd J. B. (2000), "Trust Me! I'm a CKO": Multi-National Issues in Knowledge Management, in: In Dale R., Scarborough H. & Swan J. (eds.), *Knowledge Management: Concepts and Controversies*, BPRC Conference, Warwick University, UK, 10 – 11th February.

Graham J. L. & Sano Y. (1984), *Smart Barganing: Doing Business with the Japanese*, Cambridge, MA: Ballinger.

Gray S. J. & Vint H. M. (1995), The Impact of Culture on Accounting Disclosures: Some International Evidence, in: *Asia-Pacific Journal of Accounting* 2: 33-43.

Hall, E. T. (1976), *Beyond Culture*, New York: Doubleday.

Hall, E. T., & Hall, M. R. (1987), *Hidden Differences: Doing Business with the Japanese*, New York: Doublday.

Hofstede, G. (1980), *Culture's Consequences: International Differences in Work-Related Values*, London: Sage Publications.

Hofstede, G. (1991), *Cultures and Organisations: Software of the Mind*, London: McGraw-Hill.

Holmes, T. & Tangtongtavy, S. (1997), *Working with the Thais*, Bangkok: White Lotus.

Huber, G.P. (1991), Organisational Learning: The Contributing Processes and the Literature, in: *Organizational Science* 2: 88-115.

Kao, H.-S. & Sek-Hong, N. (1993), Organisational Commitment: From Trust to Altruism at Work, in: *Psychology and Developing Societies* 5,1, 43-60.

Kidd, J. B. & Li, X. (2000), Worse than the Tower of Babel – the Opacity of the Others' Concepts: a Note Upon Oriental and Occidental Paradigms, in: *Proceedings of the INROP IV Conference Paradoxes of Project Collaboration in the Global Economy: Interdependence, Complexity and Ambiguity*, Sydney January 10 – 12th, Sidney: University of Technology.

Kogut, B. & Singh, H. (1988), The Effect of National Culture on Choice of Entry Mode, in: *Journal of International Business Studies* 19: 411-432.

Latourette, K. S. (1972), *The Chinese – Their History and Culture*, London: Collins-Macmillan.

Li, X., & Kidd, J. B. (2000), The Realisation of Meanings: Understanding Expatriates' Needs in a Novel Environment, in: Haley, C. V. & Richter, F.-J. (eds), *Asian Post-Crises Management – Corporate and Governmental Strategies for Sustainable Competitive Advantage* (in press).

Li, Y., & Li, X. (1998), The Shili Process. Theory and the Evolution of Systems Methodology, in: Gu, J. (ed), *Systems Science and Systems Engineering*, Beijing: Kedya Press: 318-322.

Linstone, H. A. (1984), *Multiple Perspectives for Decision Making*, New York: North Holland.

Locket, M. (1988), Culture and the Problems of Chinese Management, in: *Organisational Studies* 9,4: 475-496.

Lord, R. & Maher, K. J. (1991), *Leadership and Information Processing: Linking Perceptions to Performance*, Boston, MA: Unwin Hyman.

Lucier, C., Boucher, M., White, J., Kowalski, C. & et al. (1992), Developing Organizational Trust Japanese Style: Reconciling Japanese and American Management Practices, in: *Organization Development Journal* 10,2: 49-56.

Madhok, A. (1995), Revisiting Multinational Firms' Tolerance for Joint Ventures: A Trust-Based Approach, in: *Journal of International Business Studies* 26: 117-137.

Matsumoto, M. (1988), *The Unspoken Way Haregei: Silence in Japanese Business and Society*, Tokyo: Kodansha International.

McIvor, R., Humphreys, P. & Huang, G. (2000), Electronic Commerce: Re-Engineering the Buyer-Supplier Interface, in: *Business Process Management Journal* 6: 122–138.

Merry, P. (2001), Cultural Literacy – its Links to Business Success in Asia-Pacific, in: Kidd, J. B., Li, X. & Richter, F.-J. (eds.), *Maximising Human Intelligence Deployment in Asia: the 6th Generation Project*, London & New York: Palgrave Press: Chapter 11. (forthcoming April)

Nonaka, I. (1994), A Dynamic Theory of Organizational Knowledge Creation, in: *Organizational Science* 5,1: 16-35.

Nonaka, I. & Konno, N. (1998), The Concept of "Ba": Building a Foundation for Knowledge Creation, in: *California Management Review* 40,3: 40-50.

Nonaka, I. & Takeuchi, H. (1995), *The Knowledge-Creating Company*, Oxford: Oxford University Press.

Ness, I. & Ciment, J. (1999), *Encyclopaedia of Global Population and Demographics*, Chicago: Fiztroy Dearbourn.

Peppard, J. (1996), Broadening Visions of Business Process Re-Engineering, in: *Omega* 24: 255-270.

Phillips, L. D. & Wright, C. N. (1977), Cultural Differences in Viewing Uncertainty and Assessing Probabilities, in: Jungermann, H. & de Zeeuw, G. (eds), *Decision Making and Change in Human Affairs*, Dordrecht: D. Reidel Publishing.

Platt, P. (1994), *French or Foe? Getting the Most out of Living and Working in France*, Brussels: Culture Crossings.

Polanyi, M. (1958), *Personal Knowledge*, Chicago: Chicago University Press.

Ralston, D. A., Egri, C. P., Stewart, S., Terpstra, R. H. & Kiacheng, Y. (1999), Doing Business in the 21st Century with the New Generation of Chinese Managers: A Study of the Generation Shifts of Work Values in China, in: *Journal of International Business Studies* 30 : 415-428.

Richter, F.-J. (1999), *Strategic Networks: The Art of Japanese Interfirm Co-operation*, Binghamton, NY: Haworth Press.

Roberts D., Balfour F., Magnusson P., Enguardio P. & Lee J. (2000), China's Pirates, in: *Business Week* June 5th: 26–29.

Salter, S. B. & Niswander, F. (1995), Cultural Influences on the Development of Accounting Systems Internationally, in: *Journal of International Business Studies* 26,2: 379-398.

Senge, P. (1990), *The Fifth Discipline: The Art and Practice of the Learning Organisation*, New York: Doubleday.

Shih, C. (1993), Trust is a Prerequisite for Innovation, in: *International Journal of Public Administration* 11: 1693-1698.

Siegel, S. (1956), *Non-Parametric Statistics for the Behavioural Sciences*, Tokyo: McGraw-Hill.

Smith, A. H. (1894), *Chinese Characteristics*, London: Revell.

Snowden, D. (2000), Cynefin, a Sense of Time and Place: an Ecological Approach to Sense Making and Learning in Formal and Informal Communities, in: *Proceedings of the KMAC 2000 Conference (July 16th - 19th:): Knowledge Management after the Hype*, Birmingham: Aston Business School.

Stock, G. N., Greis, N. P. & Kasunda, J. D. (1999), Logistics, Strategy and Structure: A conceptual Framework, in: *International Journal of Physical Distribution and Logistics* 29: 224–239.

Trompenaars, F. & Hampden-Turner, C. M. (1997), *Riding the Waves of Culture*, London: Nicholas Brealey.

UNCTAD (1999), *World Investment Report*, Geneva: United Nations Conference on Trade and Development.

Weike, K. E. & Westley, K. (1996), Organizational Learning: Affirming an Oxymoron, in: Clegg, S. R., Hardy, C. & Nord, W. R. (eds), *Handbook of Organisational Studies*, London: Sage Publications: 440-458.

Yang, M. (1994), *Gifts, Favours and Banquets: The Art of Social Relationships in China*, Ithaca, NY: Cornell University Press.

Zhu, Z. (1998), Confucianism in Action: Recent developments in Oriental Systems Methodology, in: *Systems Research and Behavioural Science* 15: 111-130

Zuboff, S. (1988), *In the Age of the Smart Machine: The Future of Work and Power*, Oxford: Heinemann.

Bridging the Gap of Uncertainty: A Fragmentary Case Study of Toyota's Prius

Enno Berndt & André Metzner

1 Introduction, Terms of Reference, Structure

1.1 Critique of the Hybrid

Hybrids do not have it easy: depreciatingly described as "neither fish nor flesh" they lack both flair and confidence to become a future success. Classical business strategy; i.e. profit maximisation and rational planning theory (Whittington 1994), labels hybrids as "lazy compromises". This school of thought distances itself from an "all-in-one" strategy by clearly defining operational objectives, limiting workable options, and finally selecting optimal variations (Beinhocker 1999). The main feature is the innovation's confrontation with risk: the entrepreneur, strategically aware, attempts to redesign the present in a goal-oriented, direct and fundamental way. Driven by a vision of leveraging the competitive balance in his favour, and of asserting himself against the stagnation of risk minimisation, he is oblivious to the costs arising from the destruction of mature competencies, resources and structures. His credo is one of strategic change. Therefore, a hybrid concept is deemed to be problematic; or the *sub-optimal* outcome of wavering, responsibility denial, blocking and wastefulness. In short: a non-strategic pseudo-business led by non-entrepreneurs.

Future development can be understood as a contradictory process; a collective search, parallel testing and the selection of feasible solutions under conditions of permanent uncertainty and change (Beinhocker 1999). In this way the hybrid appears in a totally different light; namely, as a material connection between the known and controllable *present*, and the uncertain, but soon approaching *tomorrow*. It represents then the provisional stage of tentative learning; a learning that communicates with the market in experimental loops, influencing market perceptions and creating the preconditions for further business on the long and unstable road to tomorrow (Weber et al. 1999).

By recombining existing structures and technologies into hybrids, collective competencies and resources are gradually rebundled. Through this, new product features are generated. Such an approach leaves the fundamental rules and routines of the organisation in a stable condition, albeit momentarily. It preserves maneuverability in important processes and decision-making phases, while not ruling out change completely (through ignorance), and while not freezing in fear of the unknown consequences of maintaining the status quo. This is because it frees up options, allows corrections, is adaptable and is – in the sense of a control circuit – tolerant of errors (Vester 1999). As a result, the hybrid is experiencing a high reputation in the pluralistic stream of evolutionary theories on business strategy (Whittington 1994). Its value can be likened to a flexible *pontoon bridge* spanning today and tomorrow.

Depending on which cultural and operational concept is applied, judgement on the hybrid differs. Namely, it relies on whether the view of the future is inductive or deductive, and whether future business is viewed as an incremental or as a radical innovation. When confronted by such polarisation in organisational strategy, E. Bernstein's view, in his discussion about the direction of German social democracy at the end of the 19th century, is perhaps poignant: "The movement is everything, the goal is nothing". Such kind of problem perception expressed as extreme polarisation, can always found in many places and situations. If the status quo threatens to extinguish itself; or rather, if the future is controlled by uncertainty; what can I (we) do?

1.2 Dealing with Uncertainty: Market or Organisation?

The need for an operational view is of course expedient when business processes and expensively-acquired business decisions covering resource allocation repeatedly occur; the consequences of which (may) have to be borne to a large extent by the non-decision makers.

The pressures of expectation and success are myriad when organisations have to face the decision of whether or not, and even how they should deal with new technologies. C.M. Christensen (1997) renews the debate voiced by M.L. Tushmann and Ph. Anderson (Anderson & Tushmann 1986) by asking why previously successful and mostly large organisations often fail in this area, and end up losing market leadership to smaller competitors. He searches economic history for the effects, consequences, and options such decisions have on the pre- and post-structures of single industries in specific market contexts. He then goes on to distinguish between "sustainable" and "disruptive" innovations. But these categorisations can be neither a simple distinguishing of present contrasts, i.e. *radical v incremental*, nor can they be easily equated with technology and innovation. This is because an *incrementally* developed technological core element is similarly capable of being a *disruptive* innovation. A *radical* technology can likewise form the basis for preserving innovation.

Christensen (1997) finally discovers the cause of this chronic failure of successful organisations to deal with disruptive innovation. This lies notably in their rationally planned decision-making structures and behavioural patterns; in abandoning their own (strategic) parameter tunnel they are looking *downwards*, instead of *upwards* in the linear tunnel.

Disruptive innovations manage to escape many sophisticated *strategy radars* not through any inherent invisibility, but by falling victim to the ignorance of rationalism. This is because innovations tend to appear in both established markets and organisations, and in most cases only in reaction to a technological or economic deterioration in performance. To exploit an innovation's revolutionary potential, the risk-taking entrepreneur needs to position himself in the *raw wind* of the marketplace, standing with his back to the wall, but at the same time with the support of an organisation which is small and agile enough to try out the impossible, to learn from its mistakes and to grow quickly in small steps (Christensen 1997).

In this way, a response to the innovation dilemma, in terms of business organisation, finally appears; that is, sandwiched between the paradigms of change and stability (Kühl 2000), in the innovative cauldron of the marketplace and the impetuous risk-taking of free enterprise.

In a later paper Christensen puts this idea into perspective (Christensen & Overdorf 2000) by identifying more precisely the abilities; or rather, the inabilities of organisations and divides their core components into three, namely: a) resource availability, b) processes: as formalised-routine decision-making, coordinating and operational flows, c) values: as internalised decision-making, operational, and evaluation criteria. Based on this framework, he develops specific operational alternatives for organisations to deal with disruptive technologies. The more the abilities of an organisation stem from its own processes and values, the more difficult it is to identify, and then to address, disruptive innovations. The reason is clear: an organisation's processes and values exist in order to reproduce visible, decision-making and operational patterns in a smooth and frictionless way. So, this raises once again the question: is the organisation in fact strategically and operationally incapable of dealing with innovation and uncertainty; that is, is it condemned to be *overtaken, without actually being caught up first*?

In viewing the hybrid, it is not the hybrid but the conceptual goal which prevails. The hybrid, as already argued, is a provisional stage; neither destination nor arrival. It is a bridge which must connect two banks and bear the transit between them. It is, therefore, its loading capacity which makes the hybrid of relevance; its distinction based on the specific way in which it selects and links its features. Is the problem made any clearer by determining the origin of hybrid products? If that is the case, then it would mean attempting to reconstruct a different ex-post (market dynamic) perspective. This would entail investigating historically-specific operational and behavioural patterns from individual organisations in their dealings with uncertainty, and mapping their strategic content; that is, the linkage and development models formed (Mintzberg et al. 1998). Generally, the *Zeitgeist* should be called much more into question in understanding how organisations relate to innovation and uncertainty, instead of only being concerned with exposure to market mechanisms. The degree of opportunity and ability of the organisation to change into a different form is, therefore, required.

This piece of work, in the form of a fragmentary case study, devotes itself to this issue by focussing on the first commercialised hybrid passenger car: Toyota's Prius. Committed to a multiple dialectic of global/regional, process/result, as well as evolution/revolution – (Waschke et al. 1999) this article looks at the implications, according to product and business strategy, of Prius's development in the competitive search by the car industry for future design options both before and after the millennium.

1.3 Editing of the Text

The following text consists of four chapters: the subsequent second chapter, based on the general situation of the Japanese car industry at the end of the 1990s, describes the meso-economic environment of the case study and its players; with renewed emphasis on the question *why* in the context of Prius. The third chapter concerns itself with the *how* of the product development and is split into five points. After that, the fourth chapter turns to the interpretation; that is, seeking again to address the *why* behind the strategic reasoning and development of Prius. Finally, the last chapter will return to the historical perspective of the general *theme* corridor (as mentioned in the first chapter). Here, the role of management is addressed; if innovation is to be developed in the typical organisational form while in the face of a change/stability paradox. The empirical basis consists of several secondary sources, covering the players' actions, which have been evaluated and continually observed as a part of a comprehensive (long-term) research project on "Strategy in the Field of Alternative Propulsion Systems".

2 The (Automobile) Problem: The End of Clarity

At the end of the 1980s the Japanese bubble economy was set for a period of sustained growth and Japan's car industry was celebrated as the global benchmark of efficient and flexible mass production with wide varieties. At the turn of the century, Japan's car industry finds itself in the middle of a problem which the car industries of the developed countries have been facing for long time ago, namely:

- an excess production capacity of ca. 30%-40%, stagnating purchasing power, suppressed prices, rising rate of expected capital return, and cost savings across the value chain; so, to ensure turnover in a saturated market, expenditure on marketing, advertising and service before, during and after vehicle purchase must rise;

- this is leading to an unremitting global struggle for customers; to develop, produce, and to sell new vehicles in constantly shorter product cycles; and the need to provide a wider portfolio of products and services while remaining close to the customer, staying competitive on price and cost, and riding the increasing volatility of the industry, overseas economies and social demands;
- the OEMs (Original Equipment Manufacturers) are now pressured to innovate from two sides; from internal industrial competition and from external social factors.

Within shorter product cycles, the car industry has to deliver a technological response to the ecological question it has set itself; plus to establish technological innovation not only as another selection and differentiation criteria but also as medium-term growth driver. Confronted by such contradictory *hybrid* expressions as "glocal", "cooption" and "mass customisation" (Kidd 1999, Kühl 2000), the imperative *either-or* must make way for the fragile *as well as* (Kidd 1999).

The degree of impact, the perceptive and operational ability as well as practical operations tend to vary in every single Japanese organisation (though may be not in the Japanese industry as the whole) according to focus, time and development in a wide range of value chain rationalisation and restructuring measures.

Meanwhile the map of corporate control (M&A) has recently transformed itself into an irresistible dynamic. Seemingly while only Toyota and Honda have remained independent, all other OEMs have either been taken over by Toyota (Daihatsu, Hino) or de-facto by foreign rivals (Mazda, Nissan, Mitsubishi, Isuzu); or have permitted strategic shares (Fuji Heavy, Suzuki, Yamaha) (see table 1).

Table 1: Important Shareholdings in the Japanese Car Industry (as of April 2000)

Share owner	Share ownership (in %)
Toyota	Daihatsu (51.2) Hino (33.8) Yamaha Motors (5.0)
Renault	Nissan Motor (36.8) Nissan Diesel (22.5)
DaimlerChrysler	Mitsubishi Motor (34.0)
General Motors	Isuzu Motor (49.0) Fuji Heavy (20.0) Suzuki Motor (10.0)
Ford Motor	Mazda (33.4)

Source: Nikkei Business, April 10th 2000: 18.

Nevertheless, the specific feature of the Japanese automobile industry is, that nearly all OEMs continue to support, besides traditional cost management, the high cost of development and speedy market entry of alternative engines as structure-securing strategies for progress (already embedded in the technology portfolio) (see table 2).

Table 2: R&D Competition in the Field of Propulsion Systems among Important OEMs (as of February 2000)

	Direct Injection (Gasoline)	Direct Injection (Diesel)	CVT	Hybrid	FCEV
Toyota	1996	1999	2000	1997	2004
Honda	-	from Isuzu	1995	1999	2003
Nissan	1997	1998	1992	2000	2005
MMC	1996	1999	2000	2000	2005
GM	2000	?	2001	2001	2004
Ford		?	2001	2002	2004
DC	2000	2000	2000	2002	2004
VW	from Toyota	1996	?	?	?
BMW		1999	-	-	2000
FIAT	from MMC?	1997	from Nissan	? *(2000)*	-
PSA	from MMC	1998	from MMC	?	-
Renault	2000	2002	from Nissan	2003	from Nissan

Note: Years in italics are added by the authors; BMW is not introducing a FCEV, but a Hydrogen Fuel Combustion Engine.

Source: Analysts report by Sugiura & Saito, Nomura Financial Research Institute, 2000/1/25, No. 00-24: 7.

2.1 The Idea of a Portfolio: When in a Hurry, Take a Detour

The difference between Japanese OEMs and their European counterparts (with focus on diesel direct injection) is striking. Most of the Japanese OEMs – with the exception of Honda – hold their entire innovation portfolio in their propulsion system related activities. This fact generally remains unchanged, even when the various programmes, focuses and competing alliances are highlighted, as the

Nikkei Business did in its article right after the Tokyo Motor Show 1999 (see figure 1).

Figure 1: Strategic Focuses of OEM-Alliances in the Field of Alternative Propulsion

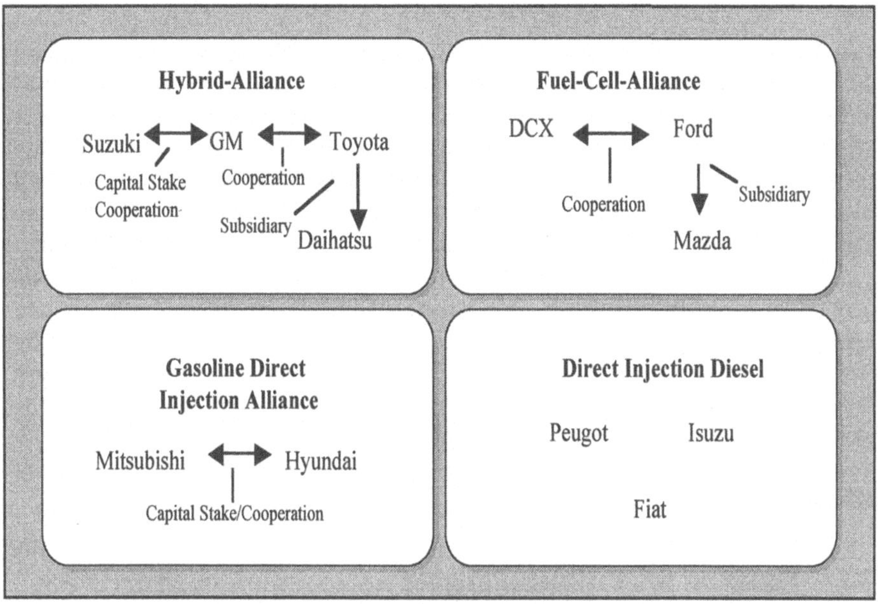

Source: Nikkei Business, November 8th 1999: 64.

Toyota's (and Honda's) wide scope of positioning may be based on its high exposure to the American, or rather the Californian market; coupled with its high ability and need for access to huge R&D resources. But, the same wide scope can be observed at those weaker OEM's, which have lost their corporate independence (as with Mazda/Nissan/ Mitsubishi Motor) due to continuing heavy losses and the corresponding accumulation of debt.

Why is that so? Business theory in fact states the opposite; namely, to apply the same concentration in times of resource scarcity when success relies on critical mass; that is, the first promises to achieve the last. In this way, the focus on engine related technology is clear, as the engine construction, next to that of the car body, is the R&D core competence of OEMs, also in Japan. This shows, furthermore, just how well previously successful strategies are recalled; in harking back to the cost efficient and flexible production processes of user-friendly compact cars which established the growth of Japanese car exports to America at the beginning of the 1980s which thus led to the strong position of the Japanese OEMs in the world market.

Here, all the tried and tested incremental operational models are now being rediscovered: The adaptation of specific product features to the changed environment using an existing product and production configuration framework; that is, taking the next feasible (small) step and building on this idea.

This *forward technology flight* therefore cannot possibly be resource-saving as during the development phase and market entry the alternative may not have pre-formed a new or sustainable trend, or may not be seem as emerging as one – a classic case of uncertainty. In this situation holding or maintaining a portfolio (as far as it can be built up during the good years) is rational as long as resources can be efficiently allocated (Beinhocker 1999). This is even more applicable when the elements of the portfolio do not cancel each other out, but complement each other and accumulate; that is, entering the next generation with a technological status quo. At the same time, however, each Japanese OEM, makes himself vulnerable to losing high technological brand image as well as customers to the competition by staying out of the race. This is because your competence is in doubt and your reputation destroyed, if – even calculated rationally and economically – the technological alternative or provisional model may be brought to the market with delay or its market launch entirely cancelled without delivering a groundbreaking alternative .

2.2 Focus on the Problem: Should a Champion be Worried about its Ridiculed Idea?

Table 2 and the technology portfolio of the Japanese OEMs show that Toyota had not only built up a full spread, but had also brought out a product for its brand series as a hybrid vehicle much earlier than its competitors. This is especially of note as it was in fact the hybrid segment, that was considered the dispensable provisional stage from classic fuel motor to electric-powered vehicle.

Several comparisons, undertaken by the Japanese Environmental Agency, show how the alternative engines are rated according to their emission and drive characteristics as well as to the estimated extent of their development in Japan. They do not indicate a clear advantage for the hybrid solution over the other alternatives.

Nevertheless, since 1994/95 Japan's biggest OEM has taken up and continued the development of a hybrid vehicle; the model 890 T (Prius) went into serial production in December 1997 and in the same month was launched onto the domestic market. Up until now (as of June 2000) around 39,400 vehicles of this type have been manufactured and supplied (see figure 2).

Figure 2: Trend of Sales (New Registrations) of the Prius

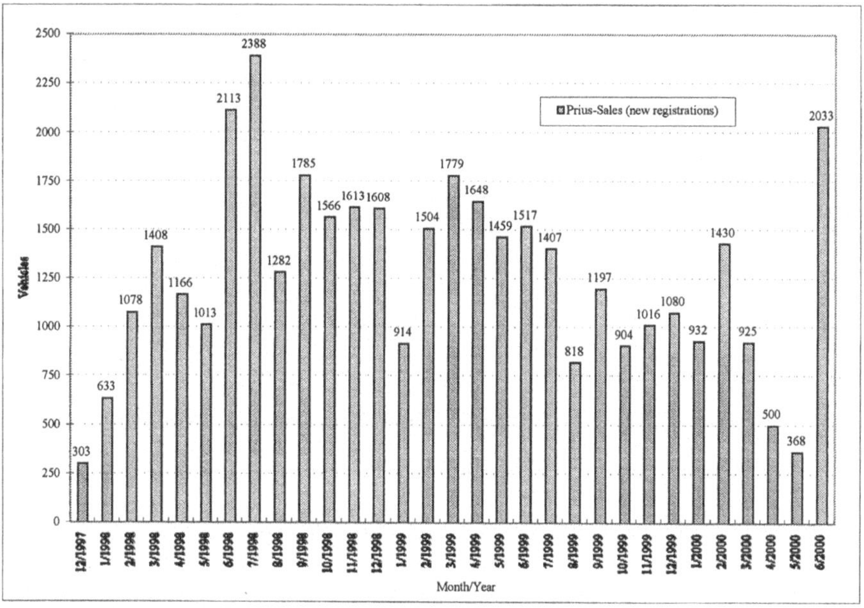

Note: Initially planned capacity: 1000 vehicles/month; planned capacity for 2000 (incl. export to US and Europe): 6000 vehicles/month; and total turnover until June 2000: 39387 vehicles.

Source: JAMA, Automobile Registration & Sales Data, monthly.

Just why and how did Toyota committed itself to the development and launch of a hybrid vehicle? A vehicle defiant of internal subsidisation; the Prius is not sold at a price covering its costs (see table 3); and similarly defiant of the fact that hybrid technology had been for a long time ridiculed and reproached by foreign competitors as being the deformed child of two sick parents – one the ecologically problematic combustion engine and the other the sizeable battery-dependent electric engine.

Table 3: Estimated Costs of the Prius (1998, First Model, in Thousand Yen)

Battery	E-Motor	Inverter	Car + Engine
500 (15%)	600 (18%)	600 (18%)	1600 (49%)

Note: Estimated costs of production per vehicle Y3.3 million; retail price (without taxes) for standard version: Y2.15 million.

Source: Financial Research Institute, Nomura Securities Co. Ltd.

3 Product Development: God Helps Those, Who Know How to Help Themselves

To present briefly a rejection and a thesis. The development process of the Prius does not correspond, as the PR department would have it, to the image of the ingenious and meticulously enacted battle plan; despite being created at the lofty intellectual level of the general staff and its strategists, and faithfully implemented by its obedient foot soldiers in the dogged battle with deceptive technological details. More realistically, the development is characterised by the search for practical solutions; being pushed from the outside (CARB), driven from above (the Board of Management), and being promoted and permanently problem- and experiment-driven (as well as reliant on chance). A critical success factor lies in the collective organisation of a results-oriented interest group and of a horizontal-virtual collaboration of various functions over and above the organisation's usual routines and rules.

The thesis follows the fragmentary chronology of events (lemura 1999, Ikari 1999, Katayama 1998). The connection of the events explaining in more depth the reasons for the behaviour of important players will be examined in chapter 4.

3.1 External Impulse: Obey What Comes in from Outside

It was first the news of CARB exhaust restrictions in 1989 which triggered off concentrated efforts at Toyota to develop low/zero emission vehicles (LEV/ZEV). Three years later, during the restructuring of central R&D, an electric vehicle (EV) department was set up to develop not only an engine line, but a completely electric-powered vehicle. The work reached its first peak at the beginning of 1996 with the launch of the RAV4L-EV, a small E-series vehicle intended as a swift reaction to CARB-ZEV regulations. The previous 1991 launch of the Town Ace

EV (van class) in Japan had failed in 1993 because of high costs (Y8 million), a long battery charge time as well as a restricted mileage. This failure, nevertheless, did not dampen project planning's desire to break into hybrid technology and to develop a hybrid coaster (minibus class); although resources were used for the benefit of the RAV4L-EV.

3.2 The Organisational Route: the Development of Critical Mass

The build-up of various activities; that is, the fusion of three independent impulses, namely: from *below* (manufacture), the *middle* (development) and from *above* (management) should ensure the hybrid idea becomes a material force.

Firstly, however, manufacturing technology departments and final assemblies of the major domestic production plants express concern about a development which would place an external body (e-motor) into the engine technology plant. This would consequently threaten its own technology core competencies in fuel motor and transmission manufacture with displacement. In 1993, they demand that external purchase of e-motors be ceased, and the development and production (of the next EV generation) be brought in-house. They support these demands by delegating ten engineers to technology development.

Secondly, in Autumn of 1993 the then chairman Eiichiro Toyoda issues the directive to set up a project group "Global 21" (G21). This should, in contrast to the usual unimaginative additions of secondary functions and features, outline the task of developing a future-oriented vehicle concept with a view to meeting the challenges of the next century. An experienced developer, from R&D's reorganisation (and horizontal collaboration), and a reliable department head, with support from the technology board, is to become leader of the project group. This settled once and for all the ecological issue as the central challenge, while not compromising on such hard-earned features as driver comfort and enjoyment. One proposal: to improve the fuel efficiency (miles per fuel unit) by 50% (by direct injection and a variable change-speed gear box) is rejected by the Board. Instead, the goal is to aim at a 100% efficiency improvement (i.e. halving fuel consumption per unit of distance); plus to have completion of the concept vehicle by Autumn 1995. This dual instruction (of composition and time) only left one option for the G21 team: to build a hybrid.

Thirdly, a project started in 1993 by the EV department concerning the evaluation of various hybrid forms concludes in Spring 1994 that the Parallel Series Hybrid (PSHV) should in fact be the technological forerunner. However, with its technological complexity and the enormous cost of electronic controls this alternative exceeds development capacity and is reclassified as a follow-up.

3.3 Project Organisation as Revolving Collaboration

The accumulated critical mass of problem awareness produced a kind *of air pressure* turning any internal problem into a problem of the whole organisation; that is, giving the hybrid project (G21) ist own special organisation within the organisation. This decision meant two things: firstly, that problems were recognised at varying levels of the organisation and the search for solutions institutionalised. Secondly, the *how* was thought of differently, instead of just instinctively feeding the task into the organisation's usual structures, rules and routines. One of two of the special groups consisting of project platforms would work as the centrifugal *turntable* for a project-guided exchange; that is, as if the experts, information and investment resources are scattered out from the rotating resource bundles.

In February 1995, a special group by the name of "Business Reform Vehicle Fuel Economy" (BRVFE) is founded within the EV department. Their task is to develop a hybrid engine line. (Shortly after this, the board of management *coincidentally* decides to launch a completely new vehicle by mid 1997 to prove just how seriously Toyota considers the ecological issue to be the pivotal issue facing the automobile industry as well as ist own product strategy). In February 1996, the G-21 project group is elevated to the position of sub-department by the name of "Zi" and takes responsibility for the continued development of the Prius and for corporate-wide coordination. Not until the important decisions (by the technology board) over the *what* and *who* are made will the announcement be given about the existence of the project in the organisation.

In May 1996, the biggest production plant Takaoka (producing 80,000 units per month) sends workers to the sub-department Zi, so sharing production costs and volume. Finally, because of company criticism of uncritical volumes, volume is built up from 200, to 300-500 and finally to 1,000 per month. This rules out mixed assembly on existing lines as most models are assembled in threefold volumes. A special final assembly, therefore, has to be set up: two previous assembly lines are re-utilized and the speed of cycle, a result of benchmarking by Kanto Motors (assembly of 60 luxury Century limousines) and Daihatsu (1,100 Midget II vehicles per month) is set at an extremely long 18 minutes (compared to the 30-90 seconds short cycle of Toyota assembly). BRFV begins a short time later to support the manufacturing technology department. All important electric-electronic components, especially the complicated control of the engine line, are to be developed in-house, optimised and the manufactured.

3.4 From Weakness to Strength, or the Art of Using the Energy of Others: Strategic Battery JV with Matsushita

The battery issue was from the start a sensitive one and for two reasons; firstly, the performance of the Prius, as well as all other developments linked to the project, depended on whether the electric battery's capacity, durability and weight could be simultaneously and substantially improved. Secondly, it was clear that Toyota was or is in a position neither to produce its own core components cost effectively nor (to square the circle) to develop the parameters required. The aim, to create the first and most independent series hybrid and to be in full control over all critical elements and processes of its development and manufacture, including dependence on the battery as core component, threatened to bring the whole venture crashing down.

BRVF first contacted Matsushita Battery, the domestic and world market leader of batteries, in March 1995. Toyota is one of the largest and most important customers for Matsushita; although Toyota does set high and seemingly unobtainable standards, Matsushita cannot afford to reject these out of hand. Furthermore, learning effects could be expected from close collaboration. For Toyota contracting out, in the sense of externalising problems according to the principle of "get it fixed or switch to another", was for cultural as well as for product strategy reasons never an option. Six months later both began work on battery development. The end of 1996 saw the first prototype promising to fulfil, provisionally at least, the most basic requirements. Subsequently, both drew up a joint venture in the form of Panasonic EV Energy (PEVE). This allowed Matsushita to develop and produce the battery cells, while Toyota supplied the control technology and took the battery system through final assembly. However, not until May 1997 was a battery prototype developed which could meet the needs of Prius.

So, Toyota solved the battery dilemma in as far as it undertook battery development and production early and in conjunction with the world's battery market leader Matsushita Battery. Through this joint venture Toyota was able to profit from being the first and biggest supplier of EV batteries, beating the competition on scale of component procurement and consolidating its position with further cost reductions. Each step forward by the competition in EV production, instead of posing a threat, was in fact a strengthening of Toyota's position (the judo principle). From 1999 arch rival Honda is buying PEVE batteries for its hybrid car Insight.

3.5 Unity of Content and Form: Purpose Design

Engine technology as such is not immediately comprehensible to the layman and, therefore, the final product must deliver a comprehensible message, which is carrying an effective differentiation criteria, visible to the customers: purpose design. This applies especially to the Prius, because this car was constructed under the principle of not burdening the driver with any off-putting, additional complexities in energy management (re-fuelling), usage and servicing; that is, to behave like a conventional fuel motor vehicle.

From the outset of the G-21 project an independent interior and exterior design concept was intended. Zi preferred a conservative three box sedan concept in the high volume compact class, smaller in size to the then Corolla, but more roomy than a Camry. The exterior was to transmit a feeling of the new hybrid engine line. Similarly, the interior was not only to guarantee a high seating position for better visibility, but also a more futuristic cockpit.

The tender is shared between the three Toyota design centres: California (CALTY), Brussels (EPOC) and Tokyo. This results in inherently-opposed conservative and progressive designs. The latter, a combination of egg form and three box sedan, submitted by CALTY, was applied, with minor adjustments, in January 1997. The interior, considerably influenced by the so called mid-centred-speedometer and mid-centred-cockpit-cluster, was confirmed in September 1996.

The interim result: although a new engine line was developed and promptly led into serial production, the process was unmistakably sensitive. The development and mass production of the Prius has, nevertheless, proven to be an example of the "new production development process" (Naschold et al. 1999); as the fundamental principles of integration, process-orientation and cross-functionality are so often repeated. In retrospect a system concept out of modularization and platform is attributable to the Prius which aids the reduction of development costs through the reuse of assembly systems. Notably, the Prius platform will be revived for the new Corolla (planned launch in September 2000), likewise the countless cockpit and interior elements are reused in other compact class models.

Functional overlaps, simultaneous design, product and production development in-house as well as with key suppliers all conspire to make short-term serial production and market launch possible. A virtual project structure (as with the rotating project turntable) helps ensure process competence and accountability, and raises co-ordination levels. Digital network process chains also improve data flow and interface management (Naschold et al. 1999).

4 Product Importance: Seeing Once is Better than Hearing a Hundred Times

When, as in the previous chapter, causes and effects in the chronology of product development have been defined, the field of interest should be removed from the process towards the impact of those effects that extend beyond immediate project realisation. According to K. Weick and H. Mintzberg this often occurs in the actions of organisations that are afterwards loaded with strategic importance in their sense of justified action (Mintzberg et al. 1998, Weick 1985); that is, even if these actions are not the precise execution of a straight-forward design or the reworking of a supposed known future, but a fragile tentative effort in experimentation, continual learning and compiled energy. Simply put, history is made, seen or accepted when written out, and replenished by the current ideas of the writer and the reader; that is to say, made understandable.

4.1 The First Proof of Being Different: a Sense for the Whole

In presenting the first thesis: The willingness to support Prius's existing organisational routines and rules beyond its resource-based decision-making criteria was born of the hope of solving future organisational problems. When the inflated volume of domestic market outlets began to contract, it became clear that the organisation could only grow against the competition if it was capable of offering a product which was attractive, unmistakable, and distinct in its message. The motto could no longer read: "ever more from the same amount", but "more individual". The decision to take the Prius into the serial production as quickly as possible had been made before it became finally clear that its development would run smoothly. And because the Prius – in the absence of other stable or differentiated alternatives – had been assigned the pivotal position in Toyota's *green branding* move. Not only had Toyota planned at great cost its so-called "eco-project" as the accompaniment to the market launch of various products out of its alternative engine technology portfolio, but also for the purpose of using identification with this idea as a role model for cultivating its image and brand value.

As an organisation its closed behaviour to the outside world engenders certain patterns of internal opinion-forming and co-ordination of action. Often observation of the organisation is only academic, while the tensions, efforts and victims of the last observation frequently remain politically coded and mostly unconsidered and disregarded. In his new year speech in 1997, the CEO Hiroshi Okuda quoted from the last year's corporate vision for 2005 "harmonious growth" and called on the workforce to develop new products, and to find new directions for production and sales. It was this message from *above* which was understood *below* as the acceptance by the management of the Prius (i.e. against opposition and doubt) and a challenge for everyone to support this project unquestioningly (i.e. no obstructing). This event is later found in a Toyota TV-commercial which, by Japanese standards, is surprisingly self-mocking: "The CEO gave us a good kick up the bum and out came ... the Prius." However, concerning the personnel-political dimensions of the project; the central figures involved at a middle management level are today on average one or two rungs higher up the ladder compared to their erstwhile colleagues.

Without the Prius project the eco-project would have long run out of steam. This is because all other products in alternative portfolios, as with direct injection or meagre-motor, had either already or simultaneously been offered by competitors, resulting in only limited possibility of differentiation. Conversely, Toyota, with the Prius, managed to seize the currently universal environmental message in a clear and sustainable way, so denying its competitors the environmental theme as core framework for their image identification and market communication. Worthy of note is the later ironic PR translation of "The Prius is not enough...".

Table 4: Ranking of Corporate Image (Survey of Non-Experts)

Theme	Year of Survey	Honda	Toyota
R&D	1995	7	12
	1996	11	11
	1997	8	5
	1998	5	4
International image	1995	10	7
	1996	12	10
	1997	9	3
	1998	5	4
Ecological sensitivity	1995	29	11
	1996	54	12
	1997	13	1
	1998	19	1

Source: Nihon Keizai Shimbun, "Corporate Image Survey", cited in: Nikkei Business, August 23rd 1999: 23.

At the same time Toyota, with the Prius, could have demonstrated its technological leadership; being in a position to positively influence the general perception of Toyota's competence, or corporate image, as well as raising the *moral* value of Toyota products, even where, in some cases, no material or technologically superiority existed (see table 4). Implicit myth generation and a certain perceptive manipulation conspired to distort reality, as in: "It's one of those products of the company, which made the Prius ..." The Prius has meanwhile come to represent, among public authorities and some private companies, an identification with environmental awareness.

Publicity for Toyota is maximised by the simultaneous launch of the Prius with the staging of the COP III conference in Kyoto. Within the first 45 days after its presentation 2,000 orders are registered, and within the first month of its release onto the market 3,500 orders are taken. MITI furthermore decides in its 1998 budget to support the Prius not only by reducing the sales tax by Y40,000, but by also additionally subsidising purchases for business as well as private use up to the sum of Y250,000.

4.2 From Head to Toe: the Dialectic of Product and Production

Strengths persistently give rise to weaknesses, and vice versa. The highly respected (but only partly understood) process efficiency of Toyota is the reason for, as well as the basis of, its product weakness. Product design has to submit to strict efficiency, evaluation measures and production standards. Swift obedience is a rational pattern of behaviour in the avoidance of conflict. This is in contrast to the arduously-won wisdom of reasoned compromises between various points of view and interests which can put a spanner in the works. The creation of a argumentation style, where one asserts one's own ideas, only fades away in the passive adoption of an ill-considered instead of a commonly-considered decision.

Here, the development and serial production of the Prius was likewise a practical case of a dialectic antithesis. In the beginning was...the product: Without simply turning back to the old logic (only with a change in its execution direction), and submitting production unconditionally to product requirements, R&D and production staff were working jointly. They were supporting and questioning each other in order to create a product with an exceptionally high future relevance for the corporation, realised and accepted by all those involved.

4.3 Continuity in Change: about the Lasting Value of Lasting Learning

Evident is that Prius' strategic advantage does not actually lie in the product or technology itself. Every competitor was or is now capable of developing a similar product; as Audi already by 1995 and Honda 1999 with the Insight have demonstrated, and the many public hybrid studies since then have substantiated this. Moreover, there exists doubt – in view of high vehicle weight and actual consumption under real user conditions – about net technological effectiveness in terms of reducing energy use and harmful emissions. And we of course know that the environmental problem is not instantly curable purely by product technology alone, but rather through systematic social change (Vester 1995).

Prius' sustainable advantage then has much more to do with the reciprocal influence on the thinking and behaviour of the actors involved at the various levels of product, production, organisation and its environment. Hypotheses and antitheses are tested in a practical way and further developed into active learning. In this way, the need for change is experienced and then made. Put another way, a long-lasting advantage lies in the experience, the make-up of product technology, production and the market environment, jointly created and adapted under the restraint of time, and where the quality of the relationship and patterns of behaviour are questioned and changed.

Figure 3: Innovation of Automobile Propulsion Systems in Small Steps and Detours

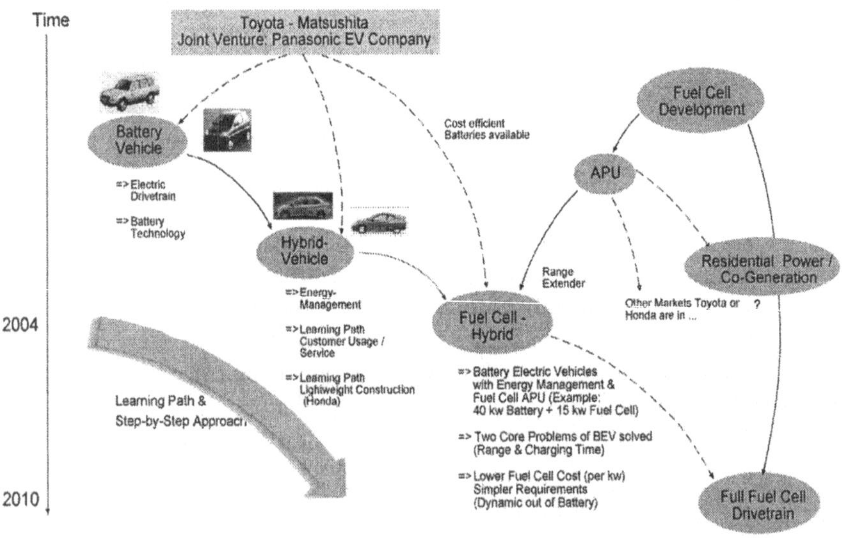

Moreover, the *course of events* only seems to raise the value of the hybrid option. The justified, historic mission of the hybrid vehicle is seen to be, on the one side, the growing fragility of the diesel option and, on the other, the unexpected lengthy time and high cost of fuel cell engine development as automotive application.

Both factors conspire to make an interim, better, more timely and efficient bridging option more significant (see figure 3). If this is really so, then the whole idea of holding a portfolio can be seen not only from the angle of learning, but also from the original motivation of risk-spreading. Not to mention the positive image effect as perceived by the outside world and which leads often to a view, that the matter was already planned and carefully carried out.

This conjures two different images. One of pole vaulting, making great leaps, but ultimately endangering life and limb with the motto "all or nothing". And the other, the more laborious, but less dangerous, progress of hopping entailing smaller steps (Weber et al. 1999:34,64). Figure 4 sketches out four routes in the commercial conflict areas of differing product qualities. The Prius would accordingly be a tip logic product, setting continuity as its point of departure, and thereby generating as a result of the process a new quality standard.

Figure 4: Continuity and Discontinuity between Old and New Quality

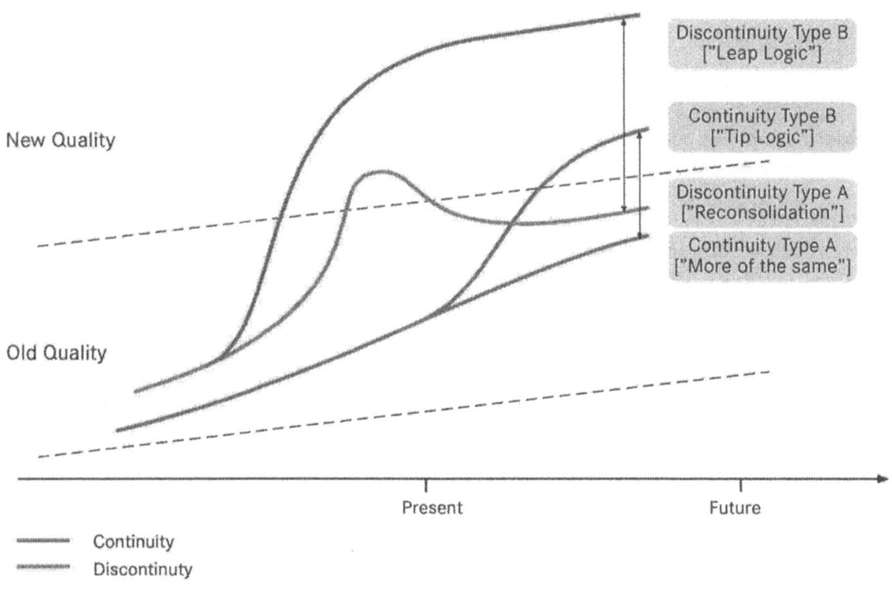

5 Strategic Action and Innovation-Support as a Management Role

Whatever concept of strategy may be taken as a basis for interpreting collective action: The prerequisite for action is the careful perception of itself and of its environment. Fujimoto addresses Toyota's characteristic behavioural quality (the quality of its relationships to the environment) as *kokorogamae* (being prepared) (Fujimoto 1997).

This position – taking seriously surrounding developments – is not only the point of departure for the Prius. It also forms the initial basis for other current and strategically important Toyota projects: The establishing of an alternative (interdisciplinary) organisational unit for comprehensive design concepts "Virtual Venture Company" (VCC), the implementation of the platform project "New Basic Car" (NBC) with a broad model offensive (Vitz/Yaris, Fun-Car-Go/Yaris Verso, bB, WiLL Vi), of the internet portal GAZOO, of the bundling of the sales network, and the launching of the marketing-lifestyle-concept WiLL.

This stance or attitude is, in a fluid environment, a central precondition for collective action and corporate behaviour. This is because it brings light into problem situations, making operational demands as well as the uncertainties and vagueness linked to operational conditions recognisable. This enables risk-management to be pursued by developing options, and by outlining corresponding guidelines not as simple adjustments between target and present state, but as a guide for open action.

It goes without saying that resources have to be allocated (options naturally have their costs, and under certain circumstances, values and prices too). To retain or to apply a relative resource surplus in the building up, development and selection of such options meanwhile, in the age of *lean management*, *re-focusing* and short-term profit, is in no uncertain terms an uncontroversial or merely micro-political matter. Learning not for learning's sake, but as an awareness of risk, feeling and exploring options for a future design is, moreover, neither the work of individuals nor an exact calculable science. It must, though, be organised within the organisation.

Time and other burdens on resources, the fragile matter (moreover, the problem) and its connections to other areas and levels (and to their problems, too), the implicit risk involved in the temporary or final breakdown of a learning process, and the courage to make corrections during the process all demand from the top management an especially normative support for innovation – not leaving this to market forces or competitors, but having design and implementation built into its own organisation.

Firstly, the task is to organise the productive power of collaboration in the learning process in such a way that it is not crushed or overwhelmed by the organisational gravitational force of existing rules, routines and vested interests. Management should be more instrumental in creating this process so that it is accepted as having the highest level of interest, and is able to offer a distinct opportunity for independent business development.

However, instead of deciding the concrete agendas of organisational formats (consortium, matrix, virtual project and so forth) and their operational guidelines, what is called for is the networking and support of self-interested collaborative coalitions. J. Beckert defines these conditions as being the necessary dual certainties for each innovator; on the one side, the innovator must judge the established rules, routines and players in respect to their reaction to his destructive violation and venture against them; that is, judging the benefit of his offensive action; and on the other, management must be able to establish and to formulate this violation, in view of its success, as a new rule and routine (Beckert 1999).

Secondly, the task is to build up, transfer and set a majority ruling in transparent measures for the strategic evaluation and selection of options and learning outcomes as well as for corresponding worker-political guidelines. This is to be able to deal with the company-wide option portfolio consistently and environmentally-sensitively, and without undermining the morale of those dealing with of one or more options which may have an uncertain outcome.

And thirdly, the task is to justify, and to implement such an action and operational design as a long-term, qualitative, expanded, core reproduction of the organisation not only within the organisation, but also externally set against other primary stakeholders. And lastly, to take responsibility for all results.

6 Postscript

After the Japanese competitors launch their first HEV models onto the market, Honda in November 1999 with the Insight and Nissan in March 2000 with the HEV-Tino, Toyota released the second Prius model (minor change) in May 2000. The first HEV van (based on the Estima model) is expected (at the earliest) in November 2000. Ford and General Motors plan to begin their HEV serial production in 2003 or 2004.

References

Anderson, Ph. & Tushman, M. L. (1986), Technological Discontinuities and Organisational Environments, in: *Administrative Science Quarterly* 31: 439-465.

Beckert, J. (1999), Agency, Entrepreneurs, and Institutional Change – The Role of Strategic Choice and Institutionalised Practices in Organisations, in: *Organisation Studies* 20,5: 777-799.

Beinhocker, E. D. (1999), Robust Adaptive Strategies, in: *Sloan Management Review* 40,3: 95-106.

Christensen, C. M. (1997), *The Innovator's Dilemma – When New Technologies Cause Great Firms to Fail*, Boston: Harvard Business School Press.

Christensen, C. M. & Overdorf, M. (2000), Meeting the Challenge of Disruptive Change, in: *Harvard Business Review*, March-April: 66-76.

Fujimoto, T. (1997), *Seisan shisutemu no shinkaron* [Theory of Evolution of Production Systems], Tokyo: Yuhikaku.

Iemura, H. (1999), *Prius toiu Yume* [A Dream Named Prius], Tokyo: Futaba Corp.

Ikari, Y. (1999), *Haiburiddoka no Jidai* [The Era of Hybridisation], Tokyo: Kojinsha.

Katayama, O. (1998), *Toyota no Hôshiki* [The Toyota System], Tokyo: Shogakukan.

Kidd, P. T. (1999), *Revolutionising New Product Development – A Blueprint for Success in the Global Automotive Industry*, London: FT Management Report.

Kühl, S. (2000), *Das Regenmacher-Phänomen – Widersprüche und Aberglaube im Konzept der lernenden Organisation*, Frankfurt, New York: Campus.

Mintzberg, H. et al. (1998), *Strategy Safari - A Guided Tour Through The Wilds of Strategic Management*, New York: Free Press.

Naschold, F. et al. (1999), *Vom Chandlerischen Unternehmensmodell zum Wintelismus?*, Veröffentlichungsreihe papers Wissenschaftszentrum Berlin für Sozialforschung, FS II 99-204.

Nihon Keizai Shimbun (1999), *Toyota – "Okudaisumu" no Chôsen* [Toyota: The Challenge of the "Okudaismus"], Tokyo: Nihon Keizai Shimbunsha.

Vester, F. (1995), *Crashtest Mobilität – Die Zukunft des Verkehrs*, München: Heyne.

Vester, F. (1999), *Die Kunst vernetzt zu denken – Ideen und Werkzeuge für einen neuen Umgang mit Komplexität*, Stuttgart: DVA.

Waschke, Th. et al. (1999), Perspectives of Mobility in Future Societies, in: *Zero or Near Zero Emissions? Congress Proceeedings*, 2-3 September 1999, Graz: 87-101.

Weber, M. et al. (1999), *Experimenting with Sustainable Transport Innovations – A Workbook for Strategic Niche Management*, Seville, Entschede: Institute for Prospective Technological Studies.

Weick, K. (1985), *Sense Making in Organisations*, London: Routledge.

Whittington, R. (1994), *What is Strategy and Does it Matter?*, London: Routledge.

The Society: Towards Pluralism?

Japan's General Elections of June 2000: Revolution or Ripple?

J.A.A. Stockwin

1 Introduction

A leading British newspaper recently commented on the Mexican presidential elections that ended the dominance of the PRI – a political party that had ruled Mexico continuously since the era of silent films:

> Corruption feeds on political monopoly, but then eats away at governments' legitimacy, (...). Corruption led in 1993 to a momentary defeat of Japan's Liberal Democratic Party; it was a factor in the downfall of India's Congress Party in 1996; and it is a source of something close to outrage in China. (...) The one-party state was one of the salient features of the 20th century; the 21st should, with luck, see its disappearance. (Financial Times, 4th July 2000)

Perhaps the greatest puzzle about the politics of Japan is continuity of rule by a single political party over four and a half decades, in a political system where free elections are institutionalised. The Liberal Democratic Party (LDP) – a party of broadly conservative persuasion – was founded in November 1955, and has formed every national government since then, except for the period between August 1993 and June 1994, when it was out of office. This is not as long as the PRI in Mexico, but still, an exceptionally long period. It ruled on its own, as a single-party administration, for all of the period between 1955 and 1993, except that, between 1983 and 1986, it was in coalition with a tiny splinter group called the New Liberal Club. The NLC had defected from the LDP in 1976 following the Lockheed aircraft purchase scandal, and in 1986 returned to the LDP fold. In any case, the LDP/NLC coalition was not strictly speaking necessary for the LDP to preserve its grip on government.

Other indicators of its phenomenal success are that the LDP held an absolute majority in the House of Representatives between 1955 and July 1993, and again between September 1997 and June 2000. Even in those periods where it lacked a Lower House majority, it was overwhelmingly the largest party in terms of its representation in the House of Representatives. And that is true even of the nine-month period in 1993-1994 when it was out of office entirely. With only one exception, every President of the LDP since its foundation has become Prime Minister. The exception was Kôno Yôhei between 1993 and 1995. During the first few months of Kôno's LDP presidency, his party was out of office, and in the second few months, the LDP had allowed a Socialist to become Prime Minister as the price of forming a coalition with the Socialists and one other small party. But from January 1996, when Hashimoto Ryûtarô took over the prime ministership, this post has once again become an LDP monopoly. To these indicators should be added the fact that local administrations have been (with the partial exception of the 1970s) overwhelmingly in the hands of local politicians who are either members of, or favourable to, the LDP. Moreover, and crucially, the LDP is linked in with powerful interest groups and government ministries through a spider's web of networks that no other political party can remotely match.

Despite such a formidable record, however, the last decade has been a difficult one for the LDP. This is partly for reasons of electoral politics, but also because of much broader issues of economic stagnation, international pressure and popular reaction against corrupt practice.

A much-underestimated cause of difficulty for the LDP is that it has ceased to enjoy an absolute majority in the House of Councillors in the Upper House elections of July 1989, and has never regained a majority since. Even though the Upper House has powers much inferior to those of the House of Representatives, it is able to block bills sent to it from the Lower House, which requires a two-thirds majority to overturn the Upper House veto. It is true that the budget, treaties and designation of a prime minister are exempt from these provisions, but in matters requiring ordinary legislation, the House of Councillors has been able to cause considerable embarrassment to the LDP. That party has then been forced to seek agreements – or actual coalition arrangements – with other parties in order to keep its legislative programme on track.

The proximate cause of the fall from office of the LDP in 1993 was not so much an electoral reaction against it as the defection of two separate groups, which soon formed the *Shinseitô* and *Sakigake* parties respectively. Both these parties participated in the non-LDP coalition government of seven parties (and one Upper House grouping), led by the popular but untried Prime Minister Hosokawa Morihiro in August 1993. The Hosokawa Government did not last long, its achievements did not live up to expectations, but it established an agenda of reform – both in political and economic areas – that was to be used as a benchmark by the governments that succeeded it. Japanese politics since the fall of Hosokawa can be interpreted in retrospect as a process whereby the LDP has gradually clawed its way back to political dominance. This has been achieved through a series of coalition, quasi-coalition and patron-client arrangements in which other parties and interest groups (including, incidentally, many labour unions) have taken on the character of semi-dependence on largesse dispensed by the LDP. Indeed, while Japan's ruling party has always been a "broad church", in the recent period more and more previous outsiders have been welcomed into association with it.

This has been essentially a traditional LDP method of coping with difficulties and with opposition. If opposition cannot be marginalised, then it must be bought off. There is no doubt that the LDP has achieved notable successes with such a time-honoured approach. Since the early 1990s, however, a key advantage underlying LDP electoral successes to that point has been in virtual abeyance. Until then, the party could point to the spectacular successes of the Japanese economy to persuade electors that the economy was safe in its hands. It could argue convincingly that the "Japanese model" of managing the economy was superior to those overseas models based on the primacy of free competitive markets and small government. Since the early 1990s it has become more difficult to make this case. The lustre of the Japanese model has been tarnished by slow or negative growth, special treatment for failing enterprises, poor control of the banking sector, further government indebtedness fueled by successive stimulation packages, and all-too-evident corruption. Thus the reputation for efficiency and effectiveness of governments headed by the LDP has also tended to fade.

What is indeed surprising in these circumstances is that the LDP has continued to hold its own – more or less – in successive elections. Part of the explanation for this may no doubt be found in the effectiveness of LDP networking, with its clientelist overtones, and part also in the innate conservatism of the electorate. But it is difficult to imagine a European country where, if a government dominated by a particular political party had for ten years so badly mismanaged the economy as the government of Japan since the late 1980s, that party would be returned to office.

Why then has this happened? We may best understand it, perhaps, if we focus our attention on successive attempts to form viable parties of opposition. These attempts, so far, have enjoyed surprising lack of success. In the years of single-party dominance from 1955 until the late 1980s, the principal party of Opposition was the Japan Socialist Party. This party, however, after making substantial progress up to the early 1960s, became prisoner of obsolescent ideologies, and allowed itself to become overly dependent on narrowly based labour union organisations. By the 1970s it was widely regarded as a party uninterested in government, preferring the relative luxury of opposing the LDP and satisfying its faithful followers. Then in 1986, by chance it elected a charismatic woman, Doi Takako, as its leader, and profiting from LDP corruption scandals and unpopular policies, unexpectedly won the 1989 elections for half the seats in the House of Councillors, depriving the LDP of its majority in that House. For a short while, the JSP seemed to be the wave of the future, but since it had not sufficiently reformed itself, its star soon faded, and it split disastrously in 1996.

The next attempt to form a viable opposition party capable of replacing the LDP in office occurred in December 1994, with the formation of the *Shinshintô* (New Frontier Party) out of most of the parties that had participated in the Hosokawa coalition government of 1993-1994. The prime mover in its formation was the right-of-centre reformist politician Ozawa Ichirô. For a while, the enterprise looked as if it might succeed, but eventually it proved unable to overcome its numerous internal contradictions, and disbanded in December 1997.

The most recent attempt – still continuing – is the *Minshutô* (Democratic Party), founded in September 1996 and much expanded in the early months of 1998 following the collapse of the *Shinshintô*. Its core consists of the former right-of-centre factions of the pre-1996 JSP, but it also contains a variety of conservative elements. It attacks LDP corruption, wishes to reform the political system and embark on substantial measures of economic deregulation. But it has faced substantial difficulties over leadership, and has shown a good deal of uncertainty about how far it ought to oppose the LDP government, and how far to cooperate with it.

As we can see from these principal attempts to form a viable opposition (Johnson 2000), success has so far been limited, and there appear to be structural reasons for this. Not the least of these is the power of the LDP-centred structure of networks, with their tendency to buy off and absorb potentially or actually challenging elements. Having lost power in 1993, the LDP was able to form a coalition government less than a year later with its former political enemy the JSP and the small *Sakigake* party. Some time after both those coalition partners had suffered grievously at the 1996 general elections, the LDP decided to change allies. It took on board first Ozawa's Liberal Party (late 1998) and then the *Kômeitô* (late 1999) to form a grand coalition. Surveying these developments, and with perhaps a little exaggeration, we may compare the LDP-Government structure to a plantation of pine trees that do not permit the growth of other vegetation below their branches.

2 The General Elections of 25th June 2000

Elections for the House of Representatives in June 2000 were preceded by a change of prime minister. Obuchi Keizô, who had taken over from Hashimoto after a poor LDP showing in Upper House elections in July 1998, suffered a severe stroke in April, and died a few weeks later. His prime ministership was noted for modest measures of deregulation and for successive stimulation packages, whereby massive quantities of public money were pumped into the economy in order to stimulate growth (or stem decline). His successor was Mori Yoshirô, a faction leader with little charisma and an aptitude for making off-the-cuff remarks that would cause adverse reactions from articulate opinion. In particular, his statement that Japan was "a country of the gods (*kami no kuni*),[1]

[1] "Country of the gods" is a much more appropriate translation than "divine country", favoured by most of the foreign English-language press.

centred on the *tennô*" stirred a hornets nest, both nationally and overseas, though this and other "reactionary" statements may well have been carefully calculated to appeal to the core LDP constituency outside the big cities.

The general elections held on 25th June 2000 for the House of Representatives were only the second such elections to be held under the new system instituted in 1994. Electoral reform was in effect the only major substantive achievement of the Hosokawa coalition Government in 1993-1994, and even that was only finalised some months after it had fallen from office. [2] The first election under the new system had been held in October 1996, and resulted in some improvement in the position of the LDP, though it was still short of an absolute majority. Defections, however, from other parties into LDP ranks had gradually improved the LDP position, so that by the time of the June 2000 elections it controlled 271 out of a total of 500 seats. The total number of seats, however, had now been reduced from 500 to 480, so that a party winning 241 seats would hold an absolute majority.

The LDP went into the election campaign heading a three party coalition government, including the *Kômeitô* (a party backed by the lay Buddhist organisation *Sôka Gakkai*) and the Conservative Party (*Hoshutô*). The latter were a group of parliamentarians who had previously belonged to Ozawa's Liberal Party (*Jiyûtô*), but wishing to remain in the coalition, had split from the Liberal Party when that party left the coalition early in 2000. A matter for concern among (principally urban) sections of the electorate was that the three parties of coalition together commanded a greater than two-thirds majority in the Lower House, and close to that in the Upper House. During the parliamentary session held in the summer of 1999, several highly contentious bills, which tenacious opposition

---

2 The House of Representatives electoral system since 1994 (with modifications):

1. There are 300 single-member, first-past-the-post seats, and 180 (previously 200) seats allocated by the D'Hondt system of proportional representation in 11 regional blocs.
2. Each elector has two votes, one for the local single-member district, and one for the local regional bloc of which it is a part.
3. Candidates may contest a regional bloc only as part of a party list.
4. Candidates may, if they wish, stand (run) for election in both types of constituency.
5. Parties may order their lists for a PR regional bloc either by sequential numbering (1,2,3,4,5...), by equal numbering (1,1,1,1,1....) or by a combination of the two (e.g. 1,2,3,4,4,4,4,4,....).
6. Where a candidate fails to be elected in a single-member district, and is part of a party list that is equally numbered (see 5) in the relevant regional bloc, the result is determined on the principle of *sekihairitsu* (margin of defeat). Thus if a candidate polls 90,000 votes in a single-member district where the winning candidate polls 100,000 votes, that candidate will be elected in the regional bloc ahead of a candidate in another single-member district polling 80,000 votes against 100,000 for the winning candidate. In the first case the *sekihairitsu* is 90% and in the second case 80%. The regional blocs are a "second chance" for candidates standing in both types of constituency.

forces would previously have blocked, were passed with ease, using the Government's massive majority.[3] It did not escape the attention of critics that a two-thirds majority of each House of Parliament is required (as well as a simple majority in a referendum of the people) in order to revise the 1946 Constitution.[4]

The results of the 2000 elections are given in Table 1.

Table 1: Results of Elections for the House of Representatives, 25th June 2000

Party	Pre-election	June 2000 election
Liberal Democrat (LDP)*	271	233
Democratic Party (DPJ)	95	127
Kômeitô (KP)*	42	31
Liberal Party (LP)	18	22
Japan Communist Party (JCP)	26	20
Social Democratic Party (SDP – former JSP)	14	19
Conservative Party (CP)*	18	7
Reform Club	5	0
Sakigake	1	0
Independent**	9	21
Vacancy	1	-
Total	500	480
Coalition Total	331	271

* Coalition members
**includes Independent Group, Liberal League and Independents

Source: Asahi Shinbun, June 26th 2000.

Several aspects of the electoral results deserve comment. First of all, the LDP was reduced from a comfortable majority to a position where it was seven seats short of an absolute majority. This was a blow to the party's pride, but hardly a disaster, since there would, on previous form, be a number of Independents who could be tempted to side with the party or formally join its ranks. Its coalition partners, however, had done badly, the *Kômeitô* losing 11 seats out of 42 and the

3 This was a few weeks before the *Kômeitô* formally entered the coalition government, but the Obuchi Government could already count on its parliamentary support for most purposes.

4 For a view highly critical of this situation, see Yamaguchi (1999).

Conservative Party losing 11 seats out of a previous total of 18. At the declaration of the final results, therefore, the total number of seats controlled by the coalition was 271, or the same as the LDP alone had controlled on the eve of the elections.

The biggest victor in the elections was the Democratic Party (*Minshutô*), which gained a 25 per cent increase in its representation. This party had campaigned on a platform of deregulation and reform of the political system, but since many of its candidates had previously belonged to parties of the moderate left, it could hardly be identified as a party of radical free market economics. Moreover, the reputation of the party had suffered from disputes over its leadership, and the current leader, Hatoyama Yukio, was a politician who appeared to lack the acuity of political judgement needed for top political office. What the Democratic Party had in fact achieved was a proportion of the total seats in the Lower House approximately equal to that won the former JSP – a "perpetual" opposition party – for much of the postwar period. Considering the inability over a long period of successive LDP-led cabinets to restore the economy to health or bring about effective reform of the politico-economic system, it is surprising, not that the Democratic Party did so well, but that it did not perform a great deal better.

Two other parties somewhat improved their position, though from a low base. One was the Liberal Party, created by Ozawa as a right-of-centre party of small government, after the break-up of the New Frontier Party (*Shinshintô*) at the end of 1997. It joined the Obuchi Government late in 1998, but pulled out early in 2000, in dispute with the Government over the slow pace of implementing its reform agenda. As a result, it lost about half of its parliamentary representatives, who wished to stay with the coalition government, and formed the Conservative Party. The fact that the Liberals gained a few seats, whereas the Conservatives lost most of theirs, suggests that support for Ozawa's brand of deregulatory reform commanded significant, and perhaps growing, support.

More surprising, perhaps, was the fact that the Social Democratic Party (SDP), led by Ms Doi Takako, also gained a few seats. This party, heir to the left wing factions of the former JSP, campaigned on a clear and unambiguous platform of pacifism and feminism. The modest success of these two very different parties may be seen as indicating that in a political landscape where the major parties had become difficult to distinguish from each other in policy terms, there was a market for parties that appeared to present clear alternative visions of Japan's future.

Finally, two parties – *Kômeitô* and the JCP – did surprisingly badly in the elections, possibly for reasons not entirely dissimilar. By comparison with all other parties, these two have always been by far the most centrally and tightly organised, with an extensive core of highly committed followers and ample funding, controlled from the party centre. Both of them are careful to suppress, or drive underground, the factional divisions that affect nearly all other parties. Both until the 1990s had depended on electoral clienteles that, though significantly different, felt disadvantaged and were critical of current government policies. In the case of the *Kômeitô,* electoral pacts in its favour by the LDP in a number of constituencies had not worked well.[5] There may well have also been an electoral reaction against it since it had abandoned its role of government critic in favour of entry into government. In the case of the JCP, indications of a more compromising stance towards government in the months preceding the elections seem to have alienated some electors.

2.1 Regional Blocs

Some light may be thrown on the election if we break down the results according to regional bloc (see Table 2). This of course only relates to results in the 11 regional blocs, where candidates are elected by proportional representation. It is not relevant for votes cast in single-member districts.

Two points emerge clearly from this table. The first is that the Democratic Party actually polled more votes than the LDP in four of the 11 regional blocs: Hokkaidô, Tokyo, Minami Kantô (centred on Yokohama) and Tôkai (centred on Nagoya), and was close to parity with the LDP in one: Kinki (centred on Osaka). These (with the exception of Hokkaidô, where unusual circumstances prevailed)[6] were the metropolitan areas, where population was most heavily concentrated. In Tokyo, the most urban of all the 11 blocs, the Democrats had a 9.5 per cent margin over the LDP. By contrast in regions with strong rural traditions and interests, the LDP was well ahead. The average percentage advantage of the LDP over the DPJ in Tôhoku, Hokuriku-Shinetsu, Chûgoku, Shikoku and Kyûshû was 12.2 per cent. The LDP had a much smaller advantage in Kita Kantô, which combines rural areas in its northern part with a highly urbanised sector bordering Tokyo. Thus, the electoral results appeared to show a sharp – indeed sharpened – divide between urban/metropolitan parts of the country and those based on rural and small town areas that had been the most significant beneficiaries of government subsidies and protection.

5 Yamaguchi (1999:31) argues that the prospect of forming electoral pacts with the LDP was a principal reason why the *Kômeitô* entered into a coalition government with the LDP.

6 In Hokkaidô the Democratic Party had inherited virtually the whole of the JSP/SDP organisational machine when that party split in 1996. Hokkaidô, in any case, partly because of the historical strength of the mining industry there, had a longstanding left wing tradition.

Table 2: Percentage of the Total Vote by Party, in the 11 Regional Blocs

Name of bloc	LDP	DPJ	KP	LP	JCP	SDP	Others
Hokkaidô	25.6	31.2	12.8	8.2	12.7	8.9	0.6
Tôhoku	32.0	21.2	9.8	16.3	8.1	10.7	2.0
Kita Kantô	30.6	24.7	12.6	12.4	10.7	8.3	0.6
Tokyo	19.5	29.0	12.7	13.6	14.3	6.6	4.2
Minami Kantô	24.7	27.7	12.4	12.0	11.5	9.6	2.1
Hokuriku Shin-etsu	35.0	25.3	8.8	11.1	9.2	10.4	0.3
Tôkai	28.6	30.6	11.7	9.7	10.0	7.4	2.0
Kinki	23.7	23.3	16.1	9.5	15.8	9.1	2.5
Chûgoku	35.6	21.7	15.3	8.9	8.9	9.2	0.4
Shikoku	36.0	20.7	13.7	8.4	11.0	10.1	0.3
Kyûshû	31.4	20.3	14.4	9.3	8.2	13.2	3.2
Average	29.3	25.1	12.7	10.8	10.9	9.4	1.6

Source: Asahi Shinbun, June 26th 2000.

The other point is that a remarkably high proportion of the vote in the regional blocs was tied up in votes for the four "minor" parties: *Kômeitô*, Liberal Party, JCP and SDP. Across the country, no less than 43.8 per cent of the electorate had cast its vote in the regional blocs for one of these four parties. Indeed, in the Kinki region the figure was a clear majority of 50.5 per cent, forcing down each of the two "major" parties into the region of 23-24 per cent. Here it is important to remember that the regional blocs only accounted for 180 out of a total of 480 seats. Nevertheless, the multi-party character of Japanese politics has become strikingly apparent, and with it the necessity for coalition formation.

2.2 Women in Politics

The number of female parliamentarians is some indication of political change in Japan, where politics has traditionally been a male bastion.

Table 3: Number and Percentage of Women in the House of Representatives, in August 1999, and following the General Election of 25 June 2000

	Single member		PR blocs		Overall	
Party	Aug 99	June 00	Aug 99	June 00	Aug 99	June 00
LDP	3	4	2	3	5	7
DPJ	0	3	3	3	3	6
KP	1	0	2	3	3	3
LP	1	0	1	1	2	1
JCP	0	0	5	4	5	4
SDP	1	3	3	7	4	10
CP	0	1	0	0	0	1
Kaikaku	0	0	1	0	1	0
Independent	1	2	0	0	1	2
Total	7	13	17	21	24	34

Source: Nihon Seikei Shinbunsha (1999), *Kokkai Binran* [Parliamentary Handbook] 102nd edition, Asahi Shinbun, June 26th 2000.

From Table 3 we may observe a modest increase in the proportion of women who are members of the House of Representatives. Whereas in August 1999, the number was 24, following the elections of June 2000, that had increased to 34, or 7.1 per cent of the total. This indicates the continuation of a rising trend, but is still far below the proportion of women in many European legislatures. It was particularly striking that the Social Democrats had now overtaken the Communists as the most female-friendly of the political parties. Consistent with the markedly feminist SDP agenda, women now actually formed a majority (10 out of 19) of its Lower House representation. At the other end of the power spectrum, the number of women who were LDP MHRs had indeed increased, but remained a pathetic 3.0 per cent of the party's total. The Democrats were not much better with 4.7 per cent, even though they now had twice as many women as before. For the most part, therefore, women in the House of Representatives remain a minority-party phenomenon, with little access to power.

2.3 Tokyo University Graduates

The prevalence of graduates of Tokyo University among Japanese parliamentarians has often been regarded as an indicator of elite bias in representation, much like the dominance of "Oxbridge" graduates in the British

House of Commons.[7] Whatever the rights and wrongs of it, our statistics indicate that this phenomenon is alive and well in Japan.

Table 4: Tokyo University Graduates in HR, June 2000 General Election

Single member	total seats	PR blocs	total seats	Total	Percentage
68	300	30	180	98	20.4%

Source: Calculated from Asahi Shinbun, June 26th 2000.

Table 5: Tokyo University Graduates, by Party, June 2000 General Election

Party	Seats	% of Tokyo U. graduates
LDP	54	55.1
DPJ	21	21.4
KP	3	3.1
LP	4	4.1
JCP	5	5.1
SDP	1	1.0
CP	2	2.0
Independent	8	8.2
Total/Average	98	20.4

Source: Calculated from Asahi Shinbun, June 26th 2000.

As shown in Tables 4 and 5, a fifth of those elected to the House of Representatives in June 2000 had graduated from this single tertiary institution, with its long traditions of patronage by the State. Of those, more than half (55.1 per cent) were affiliated with the LDP, and a little over a fifth (21.4 per cent) with the DPJ. Very few of them belonged to the smaller parties, though several were Independents.

In the next table, we give a breakdown of the universities from which MHRs graduated from in selected prefectures (single member districts only).

---

7 With poetic license, Karel van Wolferen (1989:432) concluded that the abolition of Tokyo University would be the most positive step towards reforming the Japanese political system.

Table 6: University (and other Educational) Background of Members Elected from Single-member Districts in Selected Prefectures, June 2000 General Election

(a) Hokkaidô

University	Number having graduated
Tokyo University	5
Waseda University (Tokyo)	2
Keiô University (Tokyo)	1
Chûô University (Tokyo)	1
Nihon University (Tokyo)	1
Hokkaidô University	1
Takasaki Economics University	1
Rakunô Gakuen University (Hokkaidô)	1

(b) Tokyo

University	Number having graduated
Waseda University (Tokyo)	7
Tokyo University	3
Keiô University (Tokyo)	3
Meiji University (Tokyo)	1
Chûô University (Tokyo)	1
Nihon University (Tokyo)	1
Jôchi (Sophia) University (Tokyo)	1
Hôsei University (Tokyo)	1
Tokyo University of Engineering	1
Tokyo University of Education	1
Ritsumeikan University (Kyôto)	1
Utsunomiya University	1
Princeton University	1
George Washington University	1
High school	1

(c) Osaka

University	Number having graduated
Kansai University (Osaka)	2
Kyôto University	2
Osaka University	1
Dôshisha University (Kyôto)	1
Osaka Prefectural University	1
Hiroshima University	1
Fukui University	1
Waseda University (Tokyo)	1
Chûô University (Tokyo)	1
Nihon University (Tokyo)	1
Keiô University (Tokyo)	1
Sôka University	1
Gakushûin short course University`	1
George Washington University	1
Osaka Higher Medical School	1

(d) Shikoku (four prefectures)

University	Number having graduated
Tokyo University	6
Keiô University (Tokyo)	2
Jôchi (Sophia) University (Tokyo)	1
Chûô University (Tokyo)	1
Aoyama Gakuin University (Tokyo)	1
Waseda University (Tokyo)	1
Defence University (Tokyo)	1

Source: Calculated from Asahi Shinbun, June 26th 2000.

What appears to be indicated here (though a fuller analysis is needed to establish it conclusively), is that the predominance of Tokyo University graduates is much higher in the remoter prefectures than in the metropolitan areas. In the four prefectures of Shikoku, not only did Tokyo University dominate, but also universities within Tokyo were almost in a monopoly position. The same was true to a slightly lesser extent in Hokkaidô, where even the prestigious Hokkaidô University was very poorly represented. By contrast, in Osaka, MHRs had attended a wide range of universities, some local and some outside the area, but there was not a single graduate of Tokyo University, and only four from other major Tokyo Universities. Even in Tokyo itself, there were more than twice as many Waseda University graduates as graduates of Tokyo University, though the large majority of Tokyo parliamentarians had attended one or other local university. We may tentatively conclude from this that the dominance of Tokyo University is connected, not only with the dominance of the LDP, but also with the rural and small town regions of the country, where the system of LDP-centred kickbacks and subsidies is concentrated.

2.4 Party Breakdown in Single-Member Districts

Again taking a selection of regions and prefectures, we examine party breakdown among those elected from single-member districts.

Table 7: Party Breakdown in Selected Regions, Single-member Districts only, House of Representatives, following the June 2000 General Election

(a) Hokuriku-Shinetsu (Niigata, Toyama, Ishikawa, Fukui and Nagano prefectures)

Party	Number of MPs in single-member districts
LDP	16
DPJ	3
Independent	1

(b) Kyûshû (Fukuoka, Saga, Nagasaki, Kumamoto, Oita, Miyazaki, Kagoshima and Okinawa prefectures)

Party	Number of MPs in single-member districts
LDP	25
DPJ	5
KP	1
SDP	2
Independent	4

(c) Tokyo

Party	Number of MPs in single-member districts
LDP	9
DPJ	13
Independent	3

(d) Aichi Prefecture (includes City of Nagoya)

Party	Number of MPs in single-member districts
LDP	5
DPJ	9
CP	1

(e) Osaka Prefecture

Party	Number of MPs in single-member districts
LDP	8
DPJ	5
KP	4
SDP	1
CP	1

Source: Calculated from Asahi Shinbun, June 26th 2000.

The purpose of the exercise involved in constructing this table is to elucidate the prospects for development of a two-party system, broadly along rural/urban lines of division. One of the most formidable obstacles to the formation of a two-party system having the possibility of some alternation in office has been the fact that in most electoral districts the LDP has enjoyed a built-in majority. Under the electoral system that operated up to 1994 other parties were able to obtain representation since each district elected several members (typically three, four or five) without any vote transferability. That electoral arrangement was able to sustain what has been called a "one-and-a-half party system" for many years, though it was tending to become a system based on one government party and several parties of opposition.[8] Under the new arrangements, as we have seen, the 11 regional blocs from which candidates are elected by proportional representation saw a challenging performance by the DPJ, and by four minor parties. The 300 single-member constituencies, however, strongly favour LDP candidates, with their indomitable personal support machines, practically eliminate the minor parties, and generally disfavour the DPJ.

The question is, how far might this situation change with increasing polarisation between big cities and non-metropolitan areas. In table 6 we have selected two broadly rural/smaller city and town regions (Hokuriku-Shinetsu and Kyûshû), and three urban/metropolitan prefectures (Tokyo, Aichi and Osaka), and provided a breakdown of seats won by the various parties in each. Predictably, in the former, the LDP was overwhelmingly successful. In Tokyo and in Aichi, the DPJ was comfortably ahead of the LDP, while in Osaka the LDP was ahead of the DPJ on its own, but behind a combination of all other parties (though the coalition had a clear majority). One conclusion that may be drawn from this is that the DPJ may need itself to enter into electoral pacts – and thus potentially into coalition arrangements – with other parties in order to come within sight of a joint majority in the House of Representatives. It seems clear that the prospects for winning an election based principally on urban/metropolitan votes alone are rather slim.

2.5 The Matsushita School of Politics and Management

The *Matsushita Seikei Juku* (Matsushita School of Politics and Management) – henceforth MSKJ – was inaugurated in the 1980s by the founder of Panasonic, the late Matsushita Kônosuke, as a tertiary educational establishment to train politicians and managers, promoting reformist ideas. Its graduates were numerous and active in Hosokawa's Japan New Party, started in 1992 and central to his reformist administration in 1993-1994. The success of its graduates in successive elections, therefore, is a significant indicator of the progress of a reformist mind-set within Japanese politics.

In the June 2000 elections graduates of the MSKJ election to the Lower House of Parliament increased from 15 to 20, that increase being entirely accounted for by an additional five elected on the DPJ ticket. An additional 12 MSKJ graduates stood for election unsuccessfully, making an overall success rate of 62.5 per cent. It is also worth noting that 15 of the 20 successful candidates were elected from districts that may be considered as urban/metropolitan. Of the 32 MSKJ graduates running for election, only one (unsuccessful) candidate stood for a party (the Liberal Party) other than the LDP and DPJ, though two stood as Independents.

---

8 The "one party" was of course the LDP, the "half party" was the JSP/SDP, while inroads into the constituency of the latter (and, to a lesser extent, the former) were made by a number of minor parties.

Table 8: Members of the House of Representatives Who are Graduates of the Matsushita School of Politics and Management (MSKJ)

	As of August 1999	Following June 2000 election
DPJ	8	13
LDP	6	6
Independent	1	1
Other parties	0	0
Average age	39	40
Year first elected: 1986	1	1
Year first elected: 1990	0	0
Year first elected: 1993	10	9
Year first elected: 1996	3	2
Year first elected: 1997*	1	0
Year first elected: 2000	-	8
Not re-elected, 2000	-	3
Total	15	20

* By-election.

Source: Nihon Seikei Shinbunsha, *Kokkai Binran* [Parliamentary Handbook], various editions. For the June 2000 elections, personal communication from the MSKJ.

We thus have a picture of body of relatively young, highly motivated, politicians or political aspirants largely cultivating urban or metropolitan districts. They are almost exclusively affiliated with the two major parties (especially the major party of opposition), trained according to an intensive common programme likely to incline them towards political reform, and enjoy a high electoral success rate. Known originally for their formative role in Hosokawa's Japan New Party in the early 1990s, they continue to constitute a dynamic and potentially reformist force in Japanese politics.

3 Conclusions

The high hopes for reform of the political system raised by the events of the early 1990s have been slow to come to fruition. A substantial reform of the government administration is due to be implemented at the beginning of 2001, and the financial system is also undergoing substantial changes. Nevertheless, the spider's web of special interests centred on the LDP and linking in the government bureaucracy, local authorities and a plethora of interest groups remains more or less intact. We may speculate that had the LDP been excluded from office for substantially longer than the nine months it was left floundering in the political wilderness in 1993-1994, it would have atrophied to the point of no return. In the event, however, it was able to claw its way back to power via a series of opportunistic coalition arrangements with other parties only too willing to be "bought" in return for some access to central power.

Rather than a model of two-party alternation in power (or the variants on this, involving alternative groups of parties, that may be found in Europe), Japanese party politics bears resemblance to a model contrasting "mainstream" with "periphery". To vary the metaphor, the system is akin to the solar system, in which some planets are close to the sun and warmed by it, while others are very distant and remain cold. The general elections of June 2000 recorded a modest advance in the direction of a more balanced system, with the notable advances made by the Democratic Party. That party, however, has merely reached a level of success obtained at various stages in its history by the former Japan Socialist party, which was regarded as a party of perpetual opposition.

The LDP is weaker than it was – and suffered a clear though limited reverse in these elections – in that it no longer controls the Upper House, and needs to form coalitions with other parties in order to stay fully in control of the legislative agenda. But it is still remarkably skilful in making sure that the principal levers of power remain largely in its own hands.

One thing that has been changing is the axes of division in party politics.[9] The old Japanese-style division between a conservative, somewhat nationalist, right wing, and a pacifist-inclined left wing is not entirely dead, but is less salient than it used to be. To a very considerable extent it has come to be replaced by a division between traditionalists and modernisers. To vary the terms somewhat, we may describe these two schools as consisting of those who wish to retain a system protecting myriad vested interests and those who favour reform. The latter want deregulation, reduction in the power of the government bureaucracy and reduction in restrictions on market forces. It may be remarked that the merits of the arguments do not necessarily lie entirely with the modernist camp. For instance, a strong case may be made for increased regulation of a certain kind, in areas such as protection of the environment. Nevertheless, the long period of economic stagnation since the early 1990s – and the feeble attempts by government to reverse it – strongly suggest that a more open economy would be beneficial.

The division between traditionalists and modernisers is not simply a division between different political parties. There are traditionalists and modernisers in nearly all the parties, including the LDP. To some extent, though not entirely, the

---

9 For a most insightful analysis, see Otake (1999).

distinction between these two schools coincides with differences of interest and outlook between generations. In the June 2000 general elections, the traditionalists have done rather badly in the cities, but their strategies have largely succeeded outside the main metropolitan areas. Thus the traditionalist-moderniser split is increasingly coincident with a rural-urban division, though there have been elements of this in evidence for a long time.

The party system remains fluid, with a number of minor parties able to dispute the aspirations of the major parties to control the political world altogether. Electoral arithmetic makes coalition government a necessity for the LDP, and the only real chance for the DPJ to come to power seems likely to be through some sort of coalition arrangement. We should not assume, however, that the present party political landscape is immutable. The Democratic Party is of recent origin and cannot be said to have entirely established its credentials as a permanent part of the political landscape. Certainly, its performance in these elections will have given a boost to its confidence. As for the LDP, it is, as ever, divided between various distinct groupings, some based on personal support (*habatsu*) and some on policy interest (*zoku*). It is, as we have emphasised, at the centre of a vast network of special interests stretching throughout the economy and throughout the administration.

If an earthquake is to strike the Japanese political system and lay the way open to genuine modernising reshaping of that system, that earthquake may well need to take the form of a split in the LDP. Such a split would need to be, not the kind of splintering at the edges that took place in 1976 and in 1993. It should be a split down the middle, between modernists and traditionalists, urban-based and rural based, younger dynamic politicians and older ones mired in the corruption of the existing system. It would be foolhardy to attempt to assess the chances of such a development in the next few years, but without something as radical as this, it will be difficult indeed for the Japanese system to lift itself out of the quagmire into which it has become embedded.

Japan's millennial election has produced more of a ripple than a revolution, but chaos theory teaches us that the flapping of a butterfly's wing in one continent may produce a hurricane in another. Small events may create big events, and an accumulation of ripples may eventually create revolution. It is the pattern of these ripples that we should be following in the months and years to come.

References

Johnson, S. (2000), Opposition politics In Japan: Strategies under a One-Party Dominant Regime, London & New York: Routledge.

Otake, H. (1999), *Nihon Seiji no Tairitsu Jiku* [The Axes of Division in Japanese Politics], Tokyo: Chûkô Shinsho.

van Wolferen, K. (1989), *The Enigma of Japanese Powe: People and Politics in a Stateless Nation*, London: Macmillan.

Yamaguchi, J. (1999), *Kiki no Nihon seiji* (Japanese Politics in Crisis). Tokyo: Iwanami Shoten.

Samurai and *Sarariiman*: The Discourse on Masculinity in Modern Japan

Annette Schad-Seifert

1 New Men's Studies

Historically orientated women's and gender studies have recently become a firmly established field of research in the social science sector of Japanese studies. This corresponds to the generally strong position that gender studies have acquired in the human and social sciences today. Women's and gender studies have proliferated in academic circles, since the question of gender is today viewed as both a socially and a culturally constructed phenomenon. Suddenly, all kinds of scholars, including those who either because of their age or because of their attitude formerly did not show any interest in the claims of feminist women's studies during and after the 1970s, are borrowing heavily from the problems and methods generally pursued by gender studies for their own research. Thus feminist women's studies have to a certain extent been replaced by gender studies, even though the latter is looked at with scepticism by the representatives of the so-called "old" women's liberation movement. Feministically orientated women's studies usually have their roots in the political call for liberating women and for overcoming the traditional patriarchal structure of academic life. These scholars are now confronted with the fact that their topics of research are being occupied by various other academic disciplines. Thus, these topics are gradually losing their political relevance (Mies 1997:60-61).

However, we cannot deny that the dismissal of the utopian social ideals of the women's liberation movement has made it possible for social science research to treat some theoretical premises of feminist women's studies more critically than previously. One disputed point of criticism is the question whether patriarchy is universal (Butler 1991:19). In women's studies *men* were mainly seen as representing and enforcing the system of patriarchy. This led to the assumption that it would be easier for them to learn and adopt a male gender role, since they used to play the more powerful part in gender relations.

Another controversial point is the obvious fact that, both as objects and as subjects of research, women are overrepresented in women's studies. It goes without saying that this was necessary at first in order to develop an autonomous position outside the traditional academic discourse, which was in the past and still today is very much dominated by men. But the fact that chiefly women are involved in women's and gender studies shows that the mechanism of exclusion works in much the same way there as it does in male-dominated academic circles.

However, there have recently been approaches in gender studies in which man as a "gendered being" is discussed, and various scholars have started to study male identities from the viewpoint usually taken for women in women's studies. Similarly, a *men's lib* was developed in the days of *women's lib* and has been in existence since. It evinces solidarity with the utopian social ideals of the women's movement in its battle against patriarchy. One of the central positions of the women's movement originally maintained that "neither of the sexes can liberate itself without liberating the other." In the 1970s the social sciences had a strong foothold in psychoanalysis and this led to a new sociology of patriarchy. Also, historical studies of the origin of patriarchy became very popular (e.g. Pilgrim 1977, Bornemannn 1979). In the US, therapeutically orientated studies of the "new man" emerged (Goldberg 1976). The majority of people participating in the men's movement aimed at self-imposed "emasculation" or rather at getting rid of traditional male gender roles. Yet, it was not entirely appreciated by the feminist women's movement. Putting aside a traditional male identity can not be realized by simply imitating female behavior. It could only be attained by figuring out other ways of "being different" (Blazek 1999:233).

Strong support of the men's lib movement is emerging from *gay communities* and *gay studies* in the US, which are able to postulate specific ways of being different more clearly because of their representatives' particular gender identity as homosexuals. The homosexuals' movement has certainly contributed a lot to the emergence of *men's studies* in America since the late 1980s and even more so during the 1990s. This type of research is now gaining popularity in other countries in various fields of study as well.

Although men's studies are proliferating in a number of fields, they are nevertheless very closely linked with gender studies, which means that men's studies and gender studies more or less share the same theoretical principles.

In order to define more clearly the field of knowledge in which problems related to men's gender identity are studied, a distinction has been made between *new men's studies* and *old men's studies*. The latter category contains fields of study that treat adult man as a representative of universal humanity.

New men's studies are not yet well established in American research and are even critized for mainly dealing with 20th century North-American man and his way of life. It has to be said that in historical studies and in studies concerning non-Western cultures attention to the construction of masculinity can hardly be found.

In the field of Japanese studies there have already been some reflections on masculinity and on the subject of men's studies in Japan in a variety of contexts. Some scholars draw attention to areas with a more or less *purely* male culture, such as for example the army, criminal organizations (Kersten 1997), the Yakuza

(Raz 1990), and nationalistic all-male associations (so-called *Männerbünde*) (Stanzel 1990). Others are reconsidering the concept of patriarchy in Japanese social history (Neuss-Kaneko 1997) or take a look at discourses on fatherhood in Japanese modern history (Fuess 1997, 1998). A look at American research reveals that the aforementioned rise of gay studies in the social sciences has influenced Japanese studies in that area. Studies on homosexuality in Japan have lately begun to boom (Leupp 1995, Pflugfelder 1999, Treat 1999). Among them, both Leupp's and Pflugfelder's works contain very important discussions of the cultural history of homosexuality in pre-modern Japan.

2 The Samurai as an Ideal of Manliness in Modern Japan

In recent sociological research on the concept of masculinity from the perspective of gender studies, the question of what exactly makes a man behave as a man is a much-debated issue (Connell 1995). In discussing this, the production and interpretation of cultural images of masculinity are often taken into consideration. But what specifically is understood by "masculinity" and what is at issue if it is used as a scientific concept?

Certainly, masculinity is both a cultural and a social construct, and therefore is not exclusively linked to those whose biological sex is male. When considering masculinity, we usually refer to cultural images, fictions, ideals and performances, and in so doing try to understand how these images are linked with social practice. For example, we could study masculinity of women by analyzing what makes a woman performing a man appear mannish. In her *queer studies*[1] of English literature Sedgwick (1997:354-55) therefore maintains that women as well as men can contribute to the production of both masculinity and femininity. In the Japanese context the male roles (*otokoyaku*) performed by women in the all-female Takarazuka Theatrical Revue can be cited to illustrate this phenomenon (Robertson 1998:93).

Thus, we have to be careful if we want to connect cultural images with social life. As it has been suggested above, models of masculinity are not only produced by men but by society as a whole. For the individual man, complete subjugation to male models is not always desirable, and this explains why many men do not consistently adapt themselves to such models and even abandon them. There are several possible causes for this, and particularly in current Japanese society

---

1 *Queer* originally was a pejorative expression for homosexuals. However, its sense has changed in gender studies. *Queer studies* reject the binary concept of the two sexes, which forces deviant types of sexual behavior to align with notions of sexual dualism and thus start out from the assumption that gender is basically unstable.

traditional male role models seem to be becoming less and less valid for the younger generation.

But in the Japanese case, what exactly do we understand by the traditional male role model?

In the history of ideas, the concept of masculinity is usually referred to as manliness, a term used to define a brave and resolute man. In the modern discourse on Japanese culture the concept of manliness is sometimes linked to the ideal of the samurai. One of the pre-eminent studies of Japan's samurai culture is Nitobe's *Bushidô – The Soul of Japan* (1987), originally written in 1899.

By referring to the code of conduct of the aristocratic warrior class in feudal Japan, Nitobe was obviously trying to correct an international opinion that despised Japan. The German physician Erwin Bälz, who stayed in Japan from 1876 to 1905 as a physician-in-waiting to the imperial household and as professor at the Tokyo University Medical School, wrote in 1904 that in a book awarded by the National Academy of France the Japanese were described as "an essentially feminine people" (Bälz 1936:14). The French attempt to ascribe the feminine gender to the Japanese nation may be seen as one of the reasons why Nitobe – in a number of works published in English and explicitly addressed to the "reader of English everywhere" – tried to elucidate the unwritten code of laws governing the lives and conduct of the Japanese people calling it *bushidô*. Nitobe explained *bushidô* as the Japanese version of chivalry, which for him was a pure masculine virtue[2], Nitobe's need to link Japan's national power with the idea of masculinity is clearly the reason why he extends the militaristic ethos to the whole nation. For him, *bushidô* emanates from the warrior class, but as it was "filtered down from the social class where it originated, and acted as leaven among the masses," it also furnished "a moral standard for the whole people." (Nitobe 1969:163) As the "precepts of knighthood" became an ethical ambition for the whole nation the "*Yamato Damashii*, the Soul of Japan, ultimately came to express the *Volksgeist* [national or ethnic spirit] of the Island Realm." (Nitobe 1969:164)

The construction of *bushidô* as the Japanese national spirit has clearly to be understood as a case of invention of tradition by Nitobe. For example, Bälz expressed his doubts about Nitobe's argument that the way of the warrior which contains certain elements of Buddhism and Confucianism is essentially a concept of Shintoism. In this way, Nitobe intended to indicate that *bushidô* was of Japanese origin. Contrary to Nitobe, Bälz argued that "martial spirit and scorn of death" was also to be found in other warrior cultures, such as for example the classical Greek (Bälz 1936:18).

While Nitobe's description of the warrior code of behavior could easily be understood as a glorification of feudal values, it is quite clear why *bushidô* also

2 In fact, it was not exclusively male. Samurai women could participate in the warrior spirit, too, although their participation always seems marginal and paradoxical.

qualified as a cultural model of manliness and hence as an ideological support for Japanese militarism during the pre-war and wartime years. However, it is important to point out that among liberal and anti-reactionary thinkers the samurai ethos also served as a model for rebellious action against the state. This explains why for example Saigo Takamori's revolt against the Meiji government became legendary among those intellectuals who usually did not favor the ethical code of the feudal regime.[3]

The ambivalent character of the manly samurai can also be detected in prevalent images of masculinity in Japanese popular culture. The samurai roles commonly performed in the popular warrior dramas (*jidaigeki*) on TV generally exemplify the *rônin* type. The *rônin* is a masterless vassal who has outlived his service as a warrior. He lives an unsettled life as a social outcast, but still follows the ethical code of a nobleman. In the popular movie "The seven Samurai" (*Shichinin no samurai*) the famous Japanese actor Toshiro Mifune fights for the rights of the underprivileged. In this role he clearly exemplifies the image of a heroic rebel.

Although the samurai has obviously gained popularity and attractiveness as a historical figure among members of various ideological camps, we should not forget that the samurai as a model of manliness is just one among many existing images of masculinity. If we consider types of everyday male gender identities we have to realize that masculinity does not follow a single role model but consists of a variety of pluralistic, contradictory and ambivalent social meanings.

3 Middle Class Masculinity

The late nineteenth century in Japan was characterized by the appearance of enlightenment and of social and economic writings which helped to circulate the image of a bourgeois middle class culture and the social ideal of its specific gender relations. However, reading about the middle class family did not immediately prompt the Japanese to imitate this model because the image of a middle class imposed quite contradictory rules of behavior onto its members. The private sphere of the household was characterized by human relations of intimacy (Mihashi 1999:182-184). Bonds of love and affection between married partners as well as between parents and children were supposed to foster the unity of the family. Yet, a counterworld to the family circle was formed by the free market as a model of society where individuals competed with each other.

3 The preminent intellectual historian of postwar Japan, Maruyama Masao, gives an excellent example of this argument in his study "Chûsei to hangyaku [Loyalty and Rebellion]". In: Maruyama (1992:3-109).

In Japan liberal-minded intellectuals strongly favored the middle class model of family and society, which resulted in propaganda for the improvement of women's status. The practice of polygamy was especially treated with hostility by an increasing number of male intellectuals. Until that time it had been a legal privilege of male members of the aristocratic class to keep one or several mistresses, either as secondary wives (*mekake*) in the same household or as part-time lovers living separately.

The inferior position of women and the culture of "one husband keeping many wives" was a point of criticism, particularly in the debates of Mori Arinori and Fukuzawa Yukichi, who were members of the first all-male group of enlightened Japanese intellectuals, founded in 1873 and called "Meirokusha". Fukuzawa held that taking more than one wife violates the laws of nature, since the number of men and women in the world is roughly equal, and maintained that even a lofty mansion is no more than a beast's hut if it is a house of one father and many mothers. He even argued against those who insisted that a man should be allowed to take a concubine for securing an heir and thus fulfilling the prime duty of a filial son according to Mencius (Fukuzawa 1969:49-55). Therefore, he did not hesitate to blame Japanese government officials for having the habit of keeping mistresses, since this would bring discredit on Japan as a future civilized member of the international community.[4]

In 1898, Fukuzawa wrote in his "Autobiography":

> As long as I remain in private life, I can watch and laugh. But joining the government would draw me into the practice of those ridiculous pretensions which I cannot allow myself to do.
>
> The second reason, which cannot but be distasteful for me to go into, is the low moral standard of the average officials. They live in large houses, dress well, and are often very generous. They may show a splendid spirit in their political activities, clean and courageous. But in private life they have the sad habit of affecting the offhand manners of Chinese "heroes", disregarding the restraint that is a part of a man's moral duty. They keep concubines in their houses and outside, committing the crime of polygamy, but they seem to feel no shame about it; they do not even endeavour to hide it. I must say that these men are promoting the new civilization on the one hand and practicing the debased customs of the old on the other. (Fukuzawa 1981:309-10)

What is at issue here in Fukuzawa's argument is not so much immediate support for women's rights but rather a claim for self-imposed renunciation of male sexual supremacy in family life, which was indirectly supposed to help gaining international respect for Japan.

---

4 Until 1889 the male household head could officially register a secondary wife in his household. The newly established Civil Code abolished this rule and mistresses were no longer regarded as family members. This process reduced the legal status of secondary wives and their children (Neuss-Kaneko 1990:62, 153).

Fukuzawa and Mori, who propagated the middle class model of the caring type of husband, were made a laughing stock by others, for example Katô Hiroyuki, who maintained that the system of near equality between husband and wife in modern Europe had in fact created a situation where husbands were becoming the slaves of their wives. Katô as well as the majority of Meirokusha members did not postulate equal rights for women, because they thought this would definitely involve the risk of reducing men's rights and privileges (Braisted 1976:376-379).

The abolition of the traditional feudal male gender roles required the creation of a new male identity. This explains why the propagation of a man's duties as husband and father was directly linked to the strengthening of the paternal character of the household head. The patriarchal image mainly presented by the scholars of the Japanese enlightenment movement was visibly expressed through photographs showing men with short hair and a long beard, and it was utilized as a counter-identity to the traditional model of feudal masculinity.

The nineteenth century social dynamics of middle class masculinity were further complicated by the fact that a professional career as well as participation in public societies became more important in a man's social life. In this regard the Japanese modernization process had much in common with Western civil societies. In the latter the communal spirit of clubs is generally utilized to compensate for the fierce competition of the business world, as well as to support men's specific gender privileges. Therefore, public life and club activities were generally pursued under the exclusion of women both in Japan and the West.

Middle class masculinity has taken on various forms in modern Japan, and if we wish to understand the direction of its evolution it is important to examine more thoroughly the correlation of traditional male bonding and human relationships in modern organizational structures. Clearly, the communal spirit of all-male peer groups did and still does have an impact on the interdependence of masculinity and gender identity in modern Japanese society.

Ethnological studies of Japanese village communities by Kreiner (1990) have vividly shown that bachelor or all-male peer groups had an important function in traditional village communities. According to Kreiner the characteristics of the Japanese traditional peer group system can today be observed in the social structure of urban industrial society if human relations among employees of modern industrial corporations are analyzed.

> In Japanese schools there is an association system of male peers (*dôkisei*: pupils or students of the same year) on the one hand and a rigid structure of groups into predecessors, persons of the same age and late-comers (*sempai-kôhai*-system) on the other, which gives the older ones the right to bully or order about the younger ones and assigns the duty to the younger ones to serve and attend. This system is directly continued in the organization of large corporations and their employees (salarymen). (Kreiner 1990:214 [*English translation by ASS*])

I refer to Kreiner because the sociologist Kersten, in his comparative study of male violence in Australia and Japan, quite erroneously compares the Japanese stereotype of the modern middle class man, the *sarariiman*[5], with the manly virtue of the military samurai thereby confusing a cultural ideal with a social model.

> From Japanese as well as Western perspective the traditional ethos of the samurai is generally linked to Japanese culture and also to the economic-financial position of the Japanese nation in the world. Therefore the formative influence of the bushi-culture, the samurai, is related to the Japanese context of gender relations, masculinity and violence. (Kersten 1997:151 [*English translation by ASS*]).

4 The Institution of the *Sarariiman* and the New Type of Man

A *sarariiman* was without doubt one of the most appreciated members of society in postwar Japan, because the status of an office worker usually guaranteed a moderate but secure income. During the period of Japan's high economic growth in the 1960s and 1970s the desire to achieve the status of *sarariiman* was partly the result of the Japanese model of personnel management with life-long employment, a wage system based on seniority and a spirit of commitment to one's company (Lebra 1993:31). Others have stressed the similarity between the Japanese employment system and the dutiful and self-sacrificing spirit of militaristic organizations in the Second World War, in order to point out the inhumane aspect of the employment policy (Ueno 1995:216). Probably the same logic is at issue in Kersten's argument, when he compares the loyal spirit of the *sarariiman* with the code of conduct endorsed by the samurai culture. However, important as the *sarariiman* may be as a model followed by a whole generation of postwar Japanese men, it nonetheless is hardly regarded as a particularly manly virtue to become an office worker in a large renowned Japanese company. On the contrary, the *sarariiman* type of man is considered rather unmanly and submissive, as it has been illustrated by western readings of Japanese popular culture (Buruma 1984). In the early 1960s the dutiful and self-sacrificing image of the office worker was made fun of by a parody of the so called "irresponsible man" (*musekinin otoko*). This was a paradoxical image propagated by music and TV programs, showing a type of man who indulges in his hedonistic inclinations (Kôdansha 1997:6-8).

5 The Japanese term for "salaryman" originated in the 1920s and has today various meanings. In the narrow sense of the word it is a male, white-collar worker, who is a university graduate and a core employee of a large Japanese corporation (Matanle 1999:37). The Japanese word *sarariiman* is still widely used today.

The image of the salaryman as the hegemonic symbol of masculinity in Japan has been challenged by a number of recent publications, including works by Kondo (1990) and Ogasawara (1998). Today a *sarariiman* is considered to be a man of one's father's generation, an old man, a so called *oyaji*. He represents a model role which most of today's Japanese young people would rather not like to adhere to. A considerable proportion of Japanese men in their thirties and forties who have graduated from prestigious universities find it more and more difficult to fit into the role of a loyal and well-disciplined employee. In a series of articles published in the September issue of the year 1997, the Japanese weekly journal AERA tried to fathom the motives of "boys in their thirties who cannot become adult (*otona ni narenai 30dai booizu*)." Statements such as "I don't want to have a career (*shusse wa iranai*)", "I'm fed up with competition (*kyôsô wa iya da*)" and "I want to get away (*nigetai*)" vividly express their escapism (AERA 1997). Although all the interview partners are employees of well-established and renowned large companies or publishing houses, they do not regard it as the aim of their life to sacrifice themselves for their employer. Much in contrary to the post-war generation of baby-boomers (those born at the end of the 1940s and now in their fifties), the "boys in their thirties" have significantly reduced their commitment to the corporations' interests. Moreover, the last census of the year 1995 showed that 37% of the thirty to thirty-four-year-old men, 23% of the thirty-five to thirty-nine-year-old men and 16% of the forty-year-old men were unmarried. These figures represent an increase of 9% in comparison to the census ten years ago in all three of these age-groups. The tendency both to remain single and to confess to having escapist views provides some sociologists with sufficient argument to call this group "the halfway generation" (*chûto-hanpa no sedai*).

Although the number of unmarried young and middle aged men in Japan is steadily increasing, they cannot afford to ignore marriage completely. Many of them are compelled by parents and relatives to leave the status of a bachelor and find a suitable partner for marriage. According to AERA, most of the bachelors seem completely satisfied with living a "halfway"-existence. Unless they are pestered by their relatives to marry or unless they fear being unprovided-for in case of illness or in old age, they would prefer to remain single. Nonetheless, only a minority is still resolute enough to abandon marriage, because, as Ueno has argued, in Japan a man who remains single is not seen as a *real* adult (Ueno 1995:8).

Ten years ago, men of the so called "new type" trying to avoid becoming an *oyaji* type of man usually refused to commit themselves to a professional career in order to have more free time for taking on household responsibilities. Today's men in their thirties and forties, however, regard both their professional work and having a family as a burden they would rather not submit to. The new "new type" of man seems to have grown up with a lot more individualistic and hedonistic values than the members of the first postwar generation. Iwao (1993:61) has suggested that the current generation of young adults is a product of consumer culture: “Unlike their seniors, they do not so much work for work’s sake than to be able to play.”

According to Ueno (1995) the increasing proportion of unmarried middle aged men in Japanese society can be put down to the fact that young women have changed their attitude towards marriage. They no longer regard getting married as the only way of getting economically provided-for; they rather think of marriage as a kind of luxury they will choose when they want. Young women no longer look upon the wedded state as their lot in life, and they are prepared to remain single if they can get along on their own. According to Iwao this attitude is a further reason why men have more and more difficulties in finding marriage partners (Iwao 1993:63).

For Ueno the growing number of bachelors in Japanese society does not quite prove the fact that patriarchy has come to an end, but confessions such as “I don’t want to become like my father anymore (*mô otôsan no yô ni naritakunai*)” give at least rise to the hope that the traditional male gender roles are on their way to being fundamentally rejected (Ueno 1995:8-9).

However, it is difficult to be sure whether an actual change of mind has already taken place. Surveys made by Japanese marriage bureaus such as OMMJ or TSUBAI on the motives of male applicants who are looking for a partner have revealed that these men want to live together with a mate for unmistakably conventional reasons.

To the question: “What is the situation in which you would most like to be married?”, the most frequent answers given in May 1996 were:

1) “When an illness confines me to bed.” (60% 32-34 years-old; 73% 35-37 years-old)

2) “When I return home to my dark and quiet apartment.” (55%, 64%)

3) “When I want to eat home-cooked meals.” (57%, 53%)

With regard to this survey it seems that men in Japan still tend to be rather unimaginative, at least as far as their vision of what they expect from a wife is concerned. Some sociologists express their disappointment about men’s inadequate appreciation of the changes in women’s attitudes and warn that Japanese gender relations will not improve unless men alter their attitudes and behavior (Iwao 1993:67).

5 Concluding Remarks

It goes without saying that by using masculinity as the basis for a theory, the changing structure of gender relations and gender identity in Japan cannot be examined in all its aspects.

However, from the above the conclusion can be drawn that traditional male role models are going to be less powerful than before. The fact that both alliances in all-male peer-group organizations and the companionship between the sexes are no longer stable reflects on the ongoing fundamental transition of gender roles in Japanese society.

Recently, men who have failed in their professional career created their own network called the "Association of Outcasts (*dame-ren*)". Its aim is to take the offensive against contempt by their social environment because they do not fit into the model of the reliable adult man (Dame-ren 1999). Opposition to hegemonic symbols of masculinity is created and sustained in this type of network.

I suggest that more attention should be given to this kind of new social movement in social science research, in order to challenge the still rather biased descriptions of middle class men and their institutional context in Japan.

References

AERA (1997), Otona ni narenai 30dai booizu, in: *AERA* 1997.9.29: 6-14.

Bälz, E. (1936), *Über die Todesverachtung der Japaner*, Stuttgart: J. Engelshorn Nachfahren.

Blazek, H. (1999), *Männerbünde – Eine Geschichte von Faszination und Macht*, Berlin: Ch. Links Verlag.

Borneman, E. (1979), *Das Patriarchat. Ursprung und Zukunft unseres Gesellschaftssystems*, Frankfurt a.M.: Fischer.

Braisted, W. R. (1976), *Meiroku zasshi - Journal of the Japanese Enlightenment*, Tokyo: Tokyo University Press.

Buruma, I. (1984), *A Japanese Mirror: Heroes and Villains of Japanese Culture*, London: Jonathan Cape.

Butler, J. (1991), *Das Unbehagen der Geschlechter* [Gender Trouble - Feminism and the Subversion of Identity], Frankfurt a.M.: Suhrkamp.

Connell, R. W. (1995), *Masculinities*, Berkeley: University of California Press.

Dame-ren (1999), *Dame-ren sengen* [Dame-ren Manifest], Tokyo: Sakuhinsha.

Fuess, H. (1997), A Golden Age of Fatherhood? Parent-Child Relations in Japanese Historiography, in: *Monumenta Nipponica* 52.3: 381-397.

Fuess, H. (1998), Home, The School and The Middle Class: Paternal Narratives of Child Rearing in Fujin no tomo, 1908-1926, in: Wöhr, U., Hamill-Sato, B. & Suzuki S. (eds.), *Gender and Modernity - Rereading Japanese Womens's Magazines*, Kyôtô: International Research Center for Japanese Studies: 69-83.

Fukuzawa Y. (1981), *The Autobiography of Fukuzawa Yukichi: with Preface to the Collected works of Fukuzawa*, Tokyo: Hokuseido Press.

Goldberg, H. (1976), *The Hazards of Being Male – Surviving the myth of Masculinity*, New York: Nash Publishers.

Iwao, S. (1993), *The Japanese Woman - Traditional Image and Changing Reality*, New York et al.: Free Press.

Kersten, J. (1997), *Gut und (Ge)schlecht – Männlichkeit, Kultur und Kriminalität*, Berlin, New York: de Gruyter.

Kôdansha (1997), *Kôdansha Nichiroku Nijû Seiki, 1962, Shôwa 37 nen* [Kôdansha 1962 year book of the Twentieth Century], Tokyo: Kôdansha.

Kondo, D. (1990), *Crafting Selves: Power, Gender and Discourses of Identity in a Japanese Workplace*, Chicago: University of Chicago Press.

Kreiner, J. (1990), Altersklassenordnung, Burschengruppen und Kultbünde in Japan, in: Völger, G. & v. Welck, K. (eds.), *Männerbande, Männerbünde. Zur Rolle des Mannes im Kulturvergleich* Vol. 2, Köln: Rautenstrauch-Joest-Museum: 205-214.

Lebra, T. S. (1993), *Japanese Patterns of Behavior* 8. print (1976), Honolulu: University of Hawaii Press.

Leupp, G. P. (1995), *Male Colors - The Construction of Homosexuality in Tokugawa Japan*, Berkeley: University of California Press.

Maruyama M. (1992), *Chûsei to hangyaku - Tenkeiki Nihon no seishinshiteki isô* [Loyalty and Rebellion - Phases in the history of ideas of changing Japan], Tokyo: Chikuma Shobô.

Matanle, P. (1999), The Salaryman and Japan's Modernity, in: *Social Science Japan.* 15: 36-39.

Mies, M. (1997), Die Methodischen Postulate zur Frauenforschung: Ein Rückblick nach zwanzig Jahren, in: Völger, G. (ed.), *Sie und Er. Frauenmacht und Männerherrschaft im Kulturvergleich* Vol. 1. Köln: Rautenstrauch-Joest-Museum: 55-62.

Mihashi O. (1999), *Meiji no sekushuariti - Sabetsu no shinseishi* [The Sexuality of Meiji - A History of Mentality of Discrimination], Tokyo: Nihon Editaa Skuuru Shuppanbu.

Neuss-Kaneko, M. (1990), *Familie und Gesellschaft in Japan. Von der Feudalzeit bis in die Gegenwart*, München: Beck.

Neuss-Kaneko, M. (1997), "Patriarchat" in Japan. Anmerkungen zu einer Diskussion, in: *Nachrichten der Gesellschaft für Natur- und Völkerkunde Ostasiens e.V.* No.161-162: 41-59.

Nitobe I. (1987), *Bushido: the Soul of Japan, an Exposition of Japanese Thought*, (New York, London 1905), 10. print, Rutland, Vt., Tokyo: Tuttle.

Ogasawara, Y. (1998), *Office Ladies and Salaried Men: Power, Gender, and Work in Japanese Companies*, Berkeley: University of California Press.

Pilgrim, V. E. (1977), *Der Untergang des Mannes*, München: Goldmann.

Pflugfelder, G. M. (1999), *Cartographies of Desire: Male-Male Sexuality in Japanese Discourse, 1600-1950*, Berkeley: University of California Press.

Robertson, J. (1998), *Takarazuka - Sexual Politics and Popular Culture in Modern Japan*, Berkeley: University of California Press.

Raz, J. (1990), Yakuza – die kriminelle Geheimgesellschaft Japans, in: Völger, G. & v. Welck, K. (eds.), *Männerbande, Männerbünde. Zur Rolle des Mannes im Kulturvergleich* Vol. 1. Köln: Rautenstrauch-Joest-Museum: 127-133.

Sedgwick, E. K. (1997), Mensch, Boy George, du bist dir deiner Männlichkeit ja unglaublich sicher!, in: Erhart, W. & Herrmann, B. (eds.), *Wann ist der Mann ein Mann? Zur Geschichte der Männlichkeit*, Stuttgart: J.B. Metzler: 349-362.

Stanzel, V. (1990), Mishima und seine "Schildgemeinschaft", in: Völger, G. & v. Welck, K. (eds.), *Männerbande, Männerbünde. Zur Rolle des Mannes im Kulturvergleich.* Vol. 1. Köln: Rautenstrauch-Joest-Museum: 121-126.

Treat, J. W. (1999), *Great Mirrors Shattered - Homosexuality, Orientalism, and Japan*, Oxford, New York: Oxford University Press.

Ueno C. (1995), "Oyaji" ni naritakunai kimi no tame no menzu ribu no susume [An Encouragement of Men's Lib for you who don't want to turn into an 'Oyaji'], in: Inoue T., Ehara Y. & Ueno C. (eds.), *Danseigaku* [Men's Studies], Tokyo: Iwanami Shoten: 1-37.

Technology and Gender in Japan

Ilse Lenz

1 Technology and Gender

For a long time, technology was assumed to be a socially neutral as well as a gender neutral force of historical development. However, research on social impact of new technologies, especially on biotechnology and computertechnology, brought new insights: It was realised that in-depth technological innovations bring special power potentials to some groups of society and tend to marginalize others. It was further recognized that this is not only a problem of social class but also of gender.

It is difficult, however, to proceed from observing male technological predominance to an understanding of the causes. One leading approach has been that differential access of men and women to new technologies results from essential gender differences: biological differences and different gender roles or gendered socialization; men and women are assumed as different and thus as relating in different ways to technology. This way of arguing has been called the "difference assumption" (Wetterer 1992).

Yet, the trap of stereoptyping looms largely here. People jump easily to stereotypes about women, men and technology which sometimes subconsciously repeat old cliches about women's deficits towards technology. Further this assumption promotes reductionist views as it reduces women to their gender role and renders the diversity in aspirations and skills of women today invisible.

Thus, my following approach does not see essential gender difference as constitutive for a gender different relationship to technology. On the contrary, I rather want to propose that gender is used to create and legitimise differences in the approach to technology in the first place which also can be used to legitimise hierarchies. This approach has been called the "hierarchy assumption" (Wetterer 1992, 1995). I will therefore inquire how gender is ingrained into work organization by structuring social relations around technology in such ways that hierarchical gender relations emerge. We may also ask whether gender norms are created and reproduced this way.

Therefore I concentrate on technology and its impact on work organisation. Until now, the impact of microelectronic technology has been mainly researched on the following level: How will employment quantitatively and qualitatively be changed? Key questions were new patterns of skill and new lines of segmentation of the workforce. But I consider the impact of technological innovation on gender relations in employment following the "hierarchy assumption" which has been mainly focussed on cultural-symbolical or institutional effects in a rather general way up to now. Authors have elaborated how specific images of "feminity" have shaped work chances of women and how institutional regulations have tended to marginalize them.

As an attempt to proceed from this general perspective to a more concrete analysis I integrate the aspect of technology into the discussion of gendered labour market segmentation. The underlying assumption is that technological change is assimilated in new forms of work organization. These new "paradigms" are not determined by technology, however, but result from complex processes of social bargaining between management, different groups of employees and their organizations. Therefore on the other hand, the social interpretation (*soziale Auslegung*) of technology is mediated partially by the basic mechanisms of gendered labour market segmentation. The old and new paradigms intersect, leading to unexpected results as well as to the reproduction of established forms of gender inequality.

Chapter 2 summarizes a model of gendered labour market segmentation which has been designed for international comparisons (i.a. Japan and Germany). In chapter 3, I compare the impact of microelectronic (ME) innovation in two branches of industry in the 1980s: electronic mass production (audio and TV) and data processing. Chapter 4 winds up by providing some conclusive remarks.

2 Technology and Gendered Labour Market Segregation

The discussion on gendered labour market segmentation may be characterized by two trends: the focus on actors or on the supply-side (as in the human ressource approach) and the concentration on social structure and organization. The following model relies rather on the social-structure-approach as it sees the emerging of structures as a results of "gendered social negotiation" between groups of management and employees in the specific field of the labor market and enterprise organization.

In studies on women and work a family-centered or dual system theory is still common. It is based on the assumption that women are disadvantaged because of the unequal division of labour at home. Whereas this indeed is an important element in labour market segregation, it does not give a sufficient or comprehensive explanation. It is not very useful in many forms of indirect discrimination or in the case of already employed women with high or professional qualifications.

Research on such cases has made clear that factors related to internal labour markets and to the rules of enterprise organizations play an important role.

Therefore I propose to distinguish between key external factors and key internal factors in gender labour market segmentation and to follow the interplay of these factors.

2.1 External Factors

Important external factors are located in *material* or sociopolitical relations such as gender division of labour at home or the policy regime on public care, taxes, labour and social policy. They are also based on cultural-symbolic relations such as gender norms and ideology, gender-specific socialization and subjective consciousness. I would like to follow this broad grouping of factors.

2.1.1 Socio-political Relations

2.1.1.1 The Domestic Division of Labour

The division of labour at home can be neopatriarchal, leaving most or all of unpaid work to women, or it can be more egalitarian. In Germany the domestic division of labour has somewhat shifted to the latter. But there is a remarkable gap between attitudes and actions of men: A majority of men wish a self reliant female partner who has her own job, but only a minority is really prepared to share housework and childcare in an egalitarian way. Childcare and the lion's share of housework is done by women.

In Japan in the last twenty years, we can also observe a pluralisation of attitudes towards gender roles. Up to the 1970s the *classical* division of labour was dominant; married women, espially mothers, were therefore supposed to withdraw from the labour market and concentrate on their children[1]. But today, about one third of men and women (37%) now wants a "cooperative family" with men playing their father role more actively. 17% would even like to be independent from their partner. (Lenz 1997:194)

2.1.1.2 The Provision of Public "Care-Work"

Though the majority of mothers in Japan as well as in Germany has a paid job, public childcare is still based on the model of "housewife and mother first". Public childcare in Germany mostly starts at the age of three and is predominantly limited to the morning. In Japan public childcare is more widespread. However,

---

1 Let me mention in passing that this domestic division of labout in the nuclear family is a thoroughly *modern* phenomenon reaching its peak in the 1970s whereas premodern peasant households emphasized the productive role of women in agriculture and family business.

time regulations are also not adapted to fulltime work but allow women only to work parttime.

Regarding care for the elderly, Osawa (1993) has demonstrated that social policy in Japan relies heavily on the availability of "housewives" as primary and unpaid care workers for the elderly. In Germany, too, care for the elderly is mostly the burden of the family, i.e. women. Born et. al. (1996) could show that a "combination of obligations" (Verpflichtungsverbund) as careworker for children and elderly relatives has been shown as the main cause for women's irregular access to the labour market.

2.1.1.3 Social Policies, Tax Policies and Labour Policies

Often their wordings are gender neutral, but their outcome is gendered: In Japan married couples have a free-tax benefit for a second income up to a certain sum; this has proved a an incentive for parttime work (and an indirect discouragement of fulltime work) for women as the low parttime wages are in some way compensated by the tax break. In Germany the clause on "spouse-splitting" in tax law also is considered as an indirect subvention for maintaining the *classical* division of labour at home.

2.1.2 Cultural-Symbolic Relations

2.1.2.1 The Social Gender Ideology

In the last twenty years, gender roles have been changing in Japan. Although the roel of men as "breadwinner" is still common, women's roles have diversified: they can choose the *classical* housewife role or they can combine job and family responsibilities. Interestingly, combining job and family is seen as a strictly female problem. In Germany we can witness a parallel process of a modernized female image as "superwoman" who has children, a job and a glamorous appearance – on parttime employment. These gender norms and images are shared by most men (and many women); they are translated into gender stereotypes which influence attitudes and behaviour of individual actors or groups in enterprise organization as well.

One further important element of gender ideology is the ascription of technical competence for men and boys as opposed to girls. Technological superiority of men is a key component of gender ideology. It implies the cultural norm of women's technological distance and female competence in assistant or subordinate positions. The male superiority in technology superiority fits perfectly with the ideology of the male "breadwinner".

2.1.2.2 Gendered Socialization

During education at school there is a strong emphasis on science and technical education for boys on the one hand and on languages and humanities for girls on the other hand. At college and university level this cleavage is somewhat relaxed. We can distinguish between purely male connotated technical fields as engineering and more *mixed* fields as natural sciences (mathematics, chemistry and biology). Furthermore, in Japan the gender composition of former *male* disciplines has changed over years: 1960 the share of women university students[2] in mathematics was 11.8%, in 1985 already 18.5% and in 1995 23.6%; in engineering it remained constantly lower (1960: 0.5%; 1985: 3.9%; 1995: 7.7%). Humanities have been more or less changing from *male* to *female* disciplines: Women made up 34.1% in 1965 and 67% in 1995 (Sorifu 1995:55). Therefore we can observe 1) a pattern of gendered socialization up to university education with a strong male connotation of natural science and 2) that this gender connotation of disciplines is slowly changing but the basic pattern of genderisation of disciplines is still recognizable.

Yet, there is a active minority of women who have gained independent competence in technical fields. In Japan in the 1980s the share of female university graduates who graduated in engineering has risen from 4% in 1980 to 14.7% in 1990; in 1996, it dropped again to 8.3%[3].

2.2 Internal Factors

Internal factors refer to internal labour market regulations. The term "regulation" here means formal and informal rules structuring labour market processes which are durable and somewhat consistent (Jürgens 1984). They may be legal or conventional. One example for rules based on conventions is the importance of accumulation of enterprise skills by on-the-job-training (OJT) in Japan or the privileged position of Facharbeiter skills in Germany.

The majority of rules is formally gender neutral, but is based on a *model* of skilled male employees. Thus in Japan the regularly long-term (male) employee in big firms is considered as "the Japanese employee" even if this group constitutes a continually declining minority of 20% to 25% of the workforce. In Germany, too, the skilled (male) "normal workers" (Normalarbeiter) in fulltime employment is regarded as the norm even if he possibly never formed the majority of the workforce. Therefore these regulations can be called androcentric. The aim of this section is to identify key factors on a meta-level beyond the specific national contexts in order to compare their similar or different impacts. Central rules have developped around the following factors[4]:

---

2 University refers to the four year university (*daigaku*) where women were a minorty of 13.7% in 1960 and still of 32.7% in 1995; junior college refers to the two year colleges which are *feminized* with 67.5% of women in 1960 and 91.4% in 1995 (Sorifu 1995:51).

3 The corresponding share of male university graduates was 24.8% in 1980, 30.6% in 1990 and 25.9% in 1996 (Rôdôshô 1996:51).

4 For pragmatic reasons some of these factors are discussed together.

- skill,
- comprehensive use of human resources,
- work time and
- flexibilization of employment.

2.2.1 Skill Formation

The Japanese management system is characterized by a linkage of long-term membership in one enterprise and employer's investment in the skill formation of long-term employees (Koike 1988). In Japanese industries, skill formation by OJT and forms of rotation was designed for the core workers. Female workers were in general excluded from OJT after the first short introductory training up to the 1980s. Management assumed that investment in women's skill would not pay off as women would leave the firm on marriage and childbirth – a practice that was strongly encourage by the firm. Another argument for the exclusion of women from in-house training programs is the belief that women are not able to lead male colleagues (Kanbayashi 1994). Both assumptions are recently challenged by the increasing seniority of women and their experience in leading management positions.

Yet, many firms are still reluctant to give women access to OJT or Off-the-Job-Training. OJT and Off-the-Job-Traning is increasingly integrated into enterprise career paths[5]. Whereas in 1995 in about one half of the respondent firms all careers paths are open to women and men in the administration, only 37% of firms have gender-open career paths in engineering jobs (Rôdôshô 1996:66). Segmentation in engineering and technical fields thus is especially deeprooted.

These training strategies reflect the above described gender ideology. However, the assumption that women have no leadership potential vis-à-vis men is not related to their housewife role but to a pervasive patriarchal norm of the enterprise labour market. This is a striking illustration of the relation of external and internal factors in gender ideology, leading to cumulative discrimination.

---

5 This was a reaction of management to the first Equal Opportunity Law 1986 which prohibited gender discrimination in recruitment and training; enterprises devised two or three separated career paths: 1) the integrated career (*sôgôshoku*) with continual training aiming at comprehensive skill and promotion into management with increasing experience (about 95% male); 2) the routine career (*ippanshoku*) with routine or assistant jobs (about 95% female); thus gender discrimination has been merely reorganized (Lenz 1997:197).

2.2.2 Comprehensive Use of Human Resources

Employer's investment in employee's skills is motivated by a long-term, intensive and comprehensive utilization of this core male workforce. The enterprises sets a premium on long-term membership as expressed by the seniority based wage and promotion system and by high job security. The Japanese long-term employment and seniority rules for wages and promotion can be seen as an enterprise centered compromise between management and the core male workforce. But this compromise is gendered and women are marginalized. Women are regarded as short-term "peripheral" workforce. Until the Equal Opportunity Law 1986, many firms set rules that forced women to resign at marriage or after the first child.

2.2.3 Work Time

Time regulations are a prominent factor in gender segmentation of the labour market. As mentioned above, in Germany the "normal worker" is considered a fulltime worker. In Japan, not only fulltime work, but also large overtime is expected from the (male) core workers. The prohibition of night work for women in both countries has been ambivalent results in protecting their health, but also reducing their chances in the labour market. In Germany this prohibition has been abolished, in Japan it has been relaxed by the Equal Opportunity Law.

External factors like the unequal domestic division of labour and the lack of adequate social childcare cause women to opt for employment with short workhours. In Germany, about 90% of all parttime workers are women In Japan, parttime work is also *feminized* today; whereas only 42.8% of parttime workers were women in 1960, in 1996 around 70% are women (Rôdôshô 1996:79). Most women who had to resign because of marriage or childcare obligations return into the labour market as parttime workers.

Parttime work in Japan must be considered as a special form of irregular employment which is excluded from the reciprocal relationship of regular core workers and their firm. About 20% of parttime workers have working hours similar to fulltime employees; they are called "pseudo-parttimers" (Osawa 1993:82). The parttime status is not reversible because the women cannot switch over to fulltime even if some of them look for regular employment (Rôdôshô 1996:86).

2.2.4 Flexibilization of Employment

In Japan as well as in Germany, a significant minority of workers is switched to irregular or precarious forms of employment such as dispatched work, registered work, dependent self employment as a subcontractor and so forth. In Japan flexible employment has mushroomed since the 1980s with a marked female majority creating new forms of employment like dispatched work, contract or registered work or work at home; they already make up 20% of all employees[6]. Flexibilization increasingly reaches out to young or elder male workers as well. Some young men prefer irregular work as a "free worker" to escape the constraints of company control. Elder male employees may suddenly find themselves as dispatched workers in subcontracting firms or as parttimers after pension age. Yet, feminization of flexibilization is still a dominant trend.

We can observe a marked gendered differentiation of employment forms and corresponding levels of social security. One emerging pattern is a strong polarization between a group of regular employees on the one hand and a reservoir of flexible employees without employment protection rights (like parttimers) on the other hand; between these two groups, there is a continuum of groups of employees with differentiated and stratified status. A parallel trend is the flexibilization of different kinds of skilled women's work: Female specialists in data processing are increasingly hired in flexible forms. This is a management strategy to reduce labour costs for specialists and to avoid long-term commitment and labour protection clauses (Rôdôshô 1996). Management can easily externalize such commitment on the assumption that women are part of the social security net through their husbands. It has not been recognized that more women want rights of their own or prefer a single life, rendering this concept of "family social security" obsolete.

2.3 Direct Forms of Gender Discrimination

We mainly commented on formally gender-neutral regulations which proved to be gendered in reality. Only some particular rules refer explicitly to women, such as protective laws concerning women and motherhood protection. Often they form a basis for discrimination. Thus one can point out two forms of gender discrimination: The direct form which refers to women as women and the indirect form which lower women career chances relative to men due to androcentric rules of recruiting, training and mobility. The direct forms includes cases of hiring women only before marriage or of assigning them to unskilled or semiskilled work without any other argument than they are women. The indirect forms are more intricate as they are constituted in a complex interplay of different interconnected factors. In Germany as in Japan after the Equal Opportunity Law 1986, the indirect forms of discrimination are highly relevant.

6 In 1995 irregular workers (parttime work included) numbered 10.43 million persons; 7.7 millions are female; they made up 39.8% of all female employees (Rôdôshô 1996:37).

2.4 Summary

As key internal factors of gender segmentation in Japan, the following has been highlighted: The rules of training, promotion and wage assessment are designed to benefit regular long-term firm membership which is usually accessible only to male core workers.

Internal labour market rules interact with external factors in a cumulative vicious circle: In Germany and Japan, firms often give female workers no career chances because they suppose they will concentrate on housework and children. The internal factors also reinforce each other: The widespread exclusion of women from integrated careers, their marginalization in OJT and off-the-job-training and their assignment to routine and assistant jobs contribute to making female wage work less attractive and lead to high fluctuation and lower seniority of women. The vicious circle can be broken, however, by special constellations. I will try to explain this in more detail in the context of technical innovation.

3 Two Case Studies: ME Innovation in the 1980s and the Software Industry

I would now like to use the model of chapter 2 for analysing two different developments in technological innovation: the case of ME innovation in the electronic industry in the 1980s and the integration of women into the software industry.

3.1 The Case of ME Innovation in the Electronic Industry in the 1980s

ME innovation is contextualized in different societies with their prevalent patterns of technological innovations and their specific industrial relations. The condition for ME-innovation were quite favourable in Japan (Lenz 1988). ME-innovation in Japan thus proceeded extremely rapidly. The first robot was imported into Japan in 1967 by an US firm, but in the early 1990s Japan had the highest amount of robots in the world. The "robot monarchy" has come to the small and medium enterprises as well. Therefore, CNC machines and CAD/CAM techniques have become rather universal in all sectors of Japanese industries. Since 1985, Japanese industry has entered the stage of system rationalization linking production processes into informatized automated networks (FMS/CIM). Japan held the first demonstration models of unmanned (sic!) factories. (Lenz 1988)

Whereas in Germany ME-innovation started with office automation in the late 1970s and then entered the factory, in Japan office automation was carried out simultaneously or somewhat later than production automation.

The employment effects of ME innovation can be seen in three dimensions:

- quantitative employment,
- new skills and skill formation patterns and
- new patterns of rigidity and flexibility of the workforce.

During ME-innovation in the 1980s in the electronic industry, we were witness to a reorganisation of the workforce along the lines of gender, age and work status: Young men became the new core workforce handling new ME machinery. This can be illustrated with an example of my field research: In one factory an assembly line of television sets with 200 female workers was replaced by an automatic line of six young men.[7] They are trained in programming, easy maintenance and on the spot re-programming. Gender ideology promoted the belief that men are competent at new technologies; and the internal labour market rules with the exclusion of women from qualified on-the-job-training hindered the promotion of competent women from the production floor.

In the electric industry, we thus observe a reshaping of labour market segments with a shift towards higher and technical skills, an increase of white collar workers and a concurring decline of blue collar workers, especially women and elder male workers. From 1982 to 1988 the number of female blue collar workers decreased by 18.3% in the electric industry whereas engineers and technicians increased by 44.8%. There is also a simultaneous shift towards irregular employment such as parttime or contract work which increases by 9.7% (Denki Rôren 1989: 84).

The barreers to upgrading female workers in ME-relevant skills seemed formidable. The first Denki Rôren study of 1983 (Denki Rôren 1983) indicated that 60% of enterprises did not allow women to work at ME-machines. A survey of five big enterprises in 1989 showed similar results: Only 32.6% of female workers, but 54.9% of male workers had access to ME-machinery. Moreover, there is a certain gender gap in the type of machinery: Male workers worked with fixed sequence or programable robots (14.4% and 13.1%), with CAD (12.8%) and NC-machinery (12.7); female workers with automatic control devices (37.2%), CAD (18.6%) and automatic insert machines (Denki Rôren 1989:148). This gender gap is related to the prevalent patterns of division of labour: women are

---

7 Of course the example cited is only an illustration for a trend which has been empirically proved mainly by representative studies (Denki Rôren 1983, 1989). See also Tokunaga et al. (1991) with similar results and Moldaschl (1991) for analogous processes in German electronic industry around 1986-1991.

primarily allocated to bonding and repetetive work and men to processing and to maintenance.

The dominant form of training for men was OJT (27.5%), in-house training (15.4%) and self-study (8.4%) whereas 41.7% of male workers did not receive any special training. The latter group is much larger in the case of female workers (65.2%) which corresponds to the fact that only one third has access to ME technology anyway (Denki Rôren 1989:156-157).

Female workers were naturally unsatisfied with their situation; they criticized the assistant, simple and monotonous nature of their jobs. In 1985, female workers complained mostly that their wages were low and that they were assigned assistant work in 1985; in 1990 monotonous work ranged third in the list of most often voiced grievances (after low wages and understaffing) (Denki Rôren 1991). Nearly one third of female production workers and a majority of technicians (65.3%), researchers (76.3%) or software programers (63.9%) would "level up" their recent job by specialization. It thus is plausible to conclude that the present job organisation is not accepted by many women.

There is a strong tendency towards integration of tasks in the hand of young male core workers: In 1988, in about 60-65% of firms, some part of progamming, machine control and maintenance was performed by the same person who in general can be supposed to be young and male (Denki Rôren 1989). This trend has increased since the first study of 1983. Apparently, a new type of multiskilled male core worker with general informaitonal skills is formed.

Who has been replaced? First and foremost unskilled or semiskilled female workers. Another target for redundancies is the group of elder male workers, who had previously enjoyed rather stable but slow promotion. According to the study of five companies by Denki Rôren in 1989, employer's expectation that workers over 40 years can handle ME-machinery is low (around 20%) but it is high concerning workers under 30 years (Denki Rôren 1989). Therefore, elder workers tend to lose their former positions; nonetheless the promise of permanent employment holds in general, although in a rather attenuated form.

However, trade union policy was oriented basically positively towards ME-innovation in order to participate in industrial modernization. But unions demanded prior consultation and protection of certain groups, especially elder male workers. The employment guarantee for elder workers was mostly deliverd in "soft" ways of employment transfers such as dispatch of workers. The protection for women workers in ME-innovation did not highly rank in the agenda of trade unions. This corresponds to the subordinate position of women in Japansese unions in the 1980s who were represented in the enterprise union executive comittee – if at all – as the head of the rather unimportant women's (sometimes women's and youth) department. In spite of some positive changes, this situation has basically not changed until today.

To conclude, I want to point out two aspects: Whereas a small share of women slowly gains access to management positions in banks or trading companies, women in large electronic firms are still uniformly seen as semiskilled or assistant workers. There is a marked age and gender bias in favor of young male workers. But many blue collar tasks have not been eliminated from the industry but have rather been transferred to the small and medium-sized suppliers.

3.2 The Software Industry – Skilled Work for Women?

A contrasting trend is the entry of women in skilled professions, especially in data processing. The main impetus came from the new aspirations of women, i.e. from the supply side.

Software has emerged in the context of ME-innovation. In the 1980s women managed to advance into specialized high-skill jobs in data processing. They had a share of 30% in all branches of data processing, but about 20% in programming, 30% in administrative data processing and 10% in research. Therefore the software industry has "opened a window of oppurtunity" towards less gender-stereotyping, even if new segregation lines along job positions emerge. It is a sharp contrast to the trend of gendered exclusion and marginalization of women outlined in the above discussion about the impact of ME-innovation.

The software industry has been creating a rapidly expanding, high-skill labour market from the 1970s on. The Denki Rôren study (1985:23) reports that 54.9% of male and 36.6% of female software workers graduated from university. A recent survey says that 51.6% of software workers are university graduates in 1995 (Jôhô Sangyô Rôdô Kumiai Rengôkai 1995:14). It thus seems reasonable to assume that the extraordinary high qualification level was maintained in the software expansion.

The entry of women in skilled jobs in data processing can not only be attributed to a dramatic increase of labour demand; changes on the supply side has to be put in consideration, too: Rising numbers of female students in general and more female students in mathematics and natural sciences (chemistry, physics etc.) in particular have been conducive for a career in this new industry. One condition is the recognition of the high educational and professional aspirations of women which has not matched by equivalent chances in the general labour market yet.

Another important factor is the predominance of flexible work organisation in project teams in the software industry. According to one study, 71.5% of the software industry's technical staff were organized in project teams and only 24.5% of employees were assigned to task groups along the conventional lines of departments (Totsuka 1990:49ff.). The main management method is indirect control by the team leader which enhances flexibility. Small firms with less than 30 workers had mostly no specialised office for personal management (Totsuka

1990:47); OJT was rather unsystematic and had to be developed in shifting teams. In small and medium data processing firms women were included in the OJT-schemes.

Larger firms with more than 100 workers, influenced by the Japanese personnel management style, foster, howver, long-term employment, OJT and low mobility (Totsuka 1990:150ff.) Nevertheless, even in these large firms flexibility in project teams is prevalent and women tend to be included in OJT-schemes on the programing level. I propose the hypothesis that in less stereotpyed and more flexible work organizations the chance for individual contributions – of women as well – to be recognized is greater.

Software firms also developed rather generous schemes of flexible work time for mothers, for parent leave or service at home with full employment status. The main rationale behind this is to make a long-term and effective use of the skills of female employees in which the firms had invested possible. As women are increasingly considered as valuable and effective employees, creative management strategies for combing work, partnership and especially care for children have implemented.

This development can be hypothetically linked to the model of gendered labour market. Three important internal factors on the labour market can be named. Firstly, the shortage of skilled labour in the software industry created a massive demand; therefore investments into female human capital became rational and thus new personnel strategies for combining work, partnership and childcare had to be devised because investments in skill formation would be lost otherwise.

The second factor is the experimental and interdisciplinary character of skill formation in the software industry which kept the concept of skill "open" without strong formal or gendered demarcation. Due to this emerging "open" concept of skill, women could gain qualified meaningful work relying on their high achievements in general education.

Thirdly the value of general education as well as a female advance in natural sciences counteracted the gender ideology of a male monopoly on technical competence.

4 Conclusion

My final conclusion may sound contradictory: Whereas stereotyping of women as victims in technological change is generally not adequate, complex gender relations are working towards differentiation in a more diverse way and towards indirect discrimination. We need more studies in which the relevant context should be considered in depth and detail. This paper suggested the importance of technological innovation and the resulting work organization. It analyzed the aspects of skill formation, labour market demand and changes of social values. Two further crucial factors can be surmised: the level of social consciousness which has changed considerably in Japan and the forms of organisation and social bargaining for more equal participation.

References

Born, C. et al. (1996), *Der unentdeckte Wandel. Annäherung an das Verhältnis von Struktur und Norm im weiblichen Lebenslauf*, Berlin: deGruyter.

Cook, A. & Hayashi H. (1980), *Working Women in Japan. Discrimination, Resistance and Reform*, Ithaca: Cornell University Press.

Denki Rôren (1983), *Maikuruerekutoronikusu Eikyô Chôsa Hôkoku* [Research Report on the Impact of ME], Tokyo: Denki Rôren.

Denki Rôren (1989), *ME Gijutsu ga Koyô to Rôdô ni Ataeru Eikyô ni Kansuru Dai Niji Chôsa* [The Second Research on the Impacts of ME-Technology on Employment and Labour], Tokyo: Denki Rôren.

Denki Rôren (1991), *Josei Kumiai-in Ishiki Chôsa Kekka* [Research Results on Female Union Members], Tokyo: Denki Rôren.

Dieth, R. (1995), *Die Frauenpolitik des japanischen Gewerkschaftsdachverbandes Rengo*, Soziale und Wirtschaftliche Studien über Japan/Ostasien No. 109, FU Berlin.

Japan Institute of Labour (1984), *Microelectronics and the Response of Labor Unions, Results of a Questionnaire Survey of Labor Unions*, Tokyo: JIL.

Japan Institute of Labour (1985), *Technological Innovation and Industrial Relations* (Japanese Industrial Relations Series 13), Tokyo: JIL.

Jürgens, U. (1984), Die Entwicklung von Macht, Herrschaft und Kontrolle im Betrieb als politischer Prozeß - Eine Problemskizze zur Arbeitspolitik, in: Jürgens, U. & Naschold, H. (eds.), *Arbeitspolitik*, Opladen: Leske+Budrich: 58-91.

Jôhô Sangyô Rôdô Kumiai Rengôkai (1995), *Sofutowea Gijutsusha no Hatarakikata to Ishiki ni Kansuru Ankêto* [A Survey on Software Engineers], Tokyo: Jôhô Sangyô Rôdô Kumiai Rengôkai.

Kanbayashi, C. (1994), Die betriebliche Karriere von Frauen: Eine Analyse unter besonderer Berücksichtigung der Charakteristika des japanischen Managementsystems, in: Demes, H. & Georg, W. (eds.), *Gelernte Karriere. Bildung und Berufsverlauf in Japan*, München: iudicium Verlag: 441-470.

Koike, K. (1988), *Understanding Industrial Relations in Modern Japan*, Houndmills: CK Press.

Lenz, I. (1988), *Geschlechtlich gespaltener Arbeitsmarkt und Perspektiven der mikroelektronischen Rationalisierung: Aspekte der japanischen Entwicklung*, Habilitationsschrift am FB 6 Sozialwissenschaften der Westfälischen Wilhelmsuniversität Münster 1988.

Lenz, I. (1989), Die unsichtbare weibliche Seite des japanischen Aufstiegs: Das Verhältnis von geschlechtlicher Arbeitsteilung und kapitalistischer Entwicklung, in: Menzel, U. (ed.), *Im Schatten des Siegers: Japan Vol. 3: Ökonomie und Politik*, Frankfurt: Suhrkamp: 227-271.

Lenz, I. (1997), Neue Wege, alte Barrieren? Veränderungen für Frauen in der japanischen Betriebsgesellschaft, in: Lenz, I. & Mae, M. (eds.), *Getrennte Welten, gemeinsame Moderne? Geschlechterverhältnisse in Japan*, Opladen: Leske+Budrich: 179-210.

Moldaschl, M. (1991), *Frauenarbeit oder Facharbeit? Montagerationalisierung in der Elektroindustrie*, Frankfurt: Suhrkamp.

Osawa, M. (1993), *Kigyô Chûshin Shakai o Koete. Gendai Nihon o "Jendâ" de Yomu* [Beyond the Enterprise Centered Society. A Gender Analysis of Contemporary Japan] Toyko: Jiji Tsûshinsha.

Osawa, M. (1997), Abschied von der Betriebsgesellschaft? Die Herausbildung der betriebszentrierten Gesellschaft und der vergeschlechtlichten Sozialpolitik in Japan. in: Lenz, I. & Mae, M. (eds.), *Getrennte Welten, gemeinsame Moderne? Geschlechterverhältnisse in Japan*, Opladen: Leske+Budrich: 271-316.

Rôdôshô (annual), *Hataraku Josei no Jitsujô* [The Situation of Working Women], Tokyo: Rôdôshô.

Sôrifu (1993, 1994), *Josei no Genjô to Shisaku* [The Situation of Women and Measures], Tokyo: Sôrifu.

Tokunaga, S. et al. (1991), *Japanisches Personalmanagement - ein anderer Weg? Montagerationalisierung in der Elektroindustrie III* (Forschungsberichte aus dem Institut für Sozialwissenschaftliche Forschung e.V., ISF München), Frankfurt, New York: Campus Verlag.

Totsuka, H. (1990), *Nihon no Sofutowea Sangyo* [Japan's Software Industry], Tokyo: Nihon Keizai Shimbunsha.

Wetterer, A. (1992), Theoretische Ansätze zur Analyse der Marginalität von Frauen in hochqualifizierten Berufen, in: Wetterer, A. (ed.), *Profession und Geschlecht. Über die Marginalität von Frauen in hochqualifizierten Berufen*, Frankfurt, New York: Campus: 13-41.

Wetterer, A. (ed.) (1995), *Die soziale Konstruktion von Geschlecht in Professionalisierungsprozessen*, Frankfurt, New York: Campus.

"Heartful Guidance": Fighting Juvenile Deviancy in a Japanese Community

Gesine Foljanty-Jost

1 Introduction

One of the most distinctive characteristics of Japanese youth is its diligence and obedience. American scientists have especially praised the secondary qualifications of Japanese students, which have prepared them to become a highly motivated and well integrated workforce. Yet in the 1990s the efficiency of the Japanese educational system with regard to the social integration of youth has been profoundly questioned. The problem has been described by the term of *gakkyû hôkai* (disruption of classrooms), indicating the breakdown of discipline in Japanese schools, the end of school culture and loss of control on the side of adults.

This article deals with strategies of the adults' world to regain control. I will argue that the increase of problem behavior of Japanese juveniles in the 1990s indicates that previous strategies of fighting deviancy have failed. Nonetheless, the analysis of recent activities in the Japanese community of Niigata, where our field work has been done, demonstrates that patterns of control remain mostly unchanged. On the other hand, the local communities follow the guidelines of the Ministry of Education in shaping their control: They have established a dense network of public and semi-public institutions to control juvenile problem behavior. But whereas during the 1980s controlling implied strengthening of rules and punishment, today the concept of control follows the idea of "heartful guidance".

2 Deviancy and Control: The Postwar Experience

Problem behavior by adolescents in Japan is not a new problem at all. There are various proposals to define periods with typical juvenile problems (Tokuoka 1992, Mori 1999:32, for an overview see Metzler 1999). We can distinguish at least four waves since 1945.

During the first wave, which began in the late 1940s, the term "juvenile problem behavior" was mainly related to juvenile delinquency and crime. It has been argued that post-war poverty and war-related broken families were the reasons for high incidences of theft, violence and robbery. Those who became delinquent were young adults and older adolescents. Reactions mainly concentrated on the enforcement of legal control. As one of the most important steps, in 1954 the institution of youth police (*shônen keisatsu*) was established.

The second wave of problem behavior appeared during the period of high economic growth, lasting till the early 1970s. According to Matsumoto (1967) from the 1960s, juvenile delinquency was no longer related to pressures like low social status of parents and economic poverty, because equality in terms of socio-economic status had been realized for all children. The age of delinquent juveniles became younger. Delinquency became related to the phenomena of *ochikobore* (failure at school). Japanese schools experienced a first wave of school refusal and violence. The reaction of the Japanese Ministry of Education was to fight student delinquency by strengthening legal control. In 1963 the so-called *gakkeiren* (*gakkô keisatsu renraku kyôgikai*: coordination committees of schools and local police stations) were established, binding schools and police together in preventing delinquency. Till 1970 more than 90% of Japanese schools were affiliated to a school-police coordination committee. Schools were asked to cooperate closely with the family courts and provide them with detailed reports about students. As Tokuoka (1992) put it, schools became part of the legal institutions of formal social control.

The third wave of delinquency was reported from the 1970s. Going along with the educational expansion of the 1970s with more than 90% of junior high school graduates entering senior high school, juvenile delinquency became now clearly a school problem: More than 70% of all juveniles becoming delinquent were students, mostly of junior high schools. Schools became the place where delinquency occured. The patterns of reactions changed according to the change in the characteristics of delinquency: the number of formal interventions by police decreased, while the number of cases which were re-defined as problem behavior – instead of delinquent behavior – increased, making the schools the most important agent of control (Mori 1999:34). This is said to be the beginning of the so-called *kanri kyôiku* (regulated education), with the school taking over the function of family and community in teaching and educating children.

The first peak of the third wave was reached in the early 1980s with violence against teachers and classmates, followed by a second peak in 1985 with bullying. According to the analysis of Hirota (1998) the reaction of schools, administration and the Ministry of Education was characterized by even stricter formal and informal control of students' behavior. Informal control of students' appearance (hair style, uniform), school backpacks' contents, and manners became stricter. Teachers who were ready to employ corporal punishment were put in charge of classes with problem behavior. Even though legally forbidden, corporal punishment became part of teachers' educational practices. The cooperation of schools with local police became closer again. Schools became partners of the police (Tokuoka 1999).

Till the 1990s these methods of counteracting deviancy seem to have brought positive results: the number of reported cases of delinquency decreased for some years. But what was remarkable was the simultaneous re-appearance of problem behavior in a different form. When violence at school appeared in the 1980s, control was strengthened. In the following years the number of cases of violence at schools decreased. But a new type of violence, namely bullying, appeared. And again control was improved, combined with new counseling services for the victims of bullying and their parents. And again the number of bullying cases decreased for some years. Yet, being successful in controlling bullying, a new problem came into focus: the increasing number of students who refuse to attend school. Tokuoka (1992) has argued that non-school-attendance is a result of the strategy of suppressing delinquency by control without solving its real reasons. While bullying can be seen as a *hidden* form of violence, practized mostly after *open* violence had been successfully suppressed, non-school-attendance symbolizes resignation in the face of overwhelming control to prevent bullying.

As table 1 shows, in the mid-1990s old problems returned. In 1996, cases of violence against teachers reached the numbers of 1982, as well as the 1986 numbers of bullying were reached in 1996. Juvenile crime has been increasing since 1996. But unlike during the 1980s, the increase is accompanied by an increase in non-school-attendance, the dropping-out of senior high school students, and reports on sexual misconduct of young women (*enjo kôsai*). Drug misuse is increasing, and the number of girls becoming delinquent is rising, too. Many young students no longer follow school regulations concerning dressing and hair fashion: They are dying their hair yellow and shortening their school uniform skirts to an absolute minimum. Deviancy is no longer limited to school but is taking place outside schools as well.

What therefore is new in the development of problem behavior of Japanese students in the 1990s is that:

- All known types of delinquency increase at the same time.
- They are accompanied by the rise of so-called anti social and "immoral" forms of behavior.
- Differences between urban and rural regions diminish.
- The scope of those who become deviant becomes broader with regard to gender and age: No longer only junior high school students but also elementary and senior high school students and not only boys but a rising number of girls as well become deviant.

Table 1: Problem Behavior of Students in Japanese Public Schools (Percentage of Deviant Students Referring to All Students of the Given Type of School)

	1985	1990	1997
Inner-school-violence at senior high schools[a]	0.021	0.041	0.146
Inner-school-violence at junior high schools[a]	0.087	0.091	0.364
Inner-school-violence at elementary schools [a]	–	–	0.01
Non-school-attendance[b] of junior high school students	0.483	0.784	1.690
Non-school-attendance[b] of elementary school students	0.037	0.085	0.209
Dropouts [c]	2.2	2.2	2.6
Senior high school students arrested by police	1.215	1.055	1.571
Junior high school students arrested by police	1.999	1.376	1.419

Notes: (a) Since 1997 numbers include violence outside of schools.
(b) More than 50 days per year.
(c) Senior high school students only.

Sources: Monbu-shô (1998), *Seito Shidô ue no Sho-mondai no Genjô to Monbu-shô no Shisaku ni tsuite* [Concerning the Actual State of Problems in Students' Guidance and the Policies of the Ministry of Education], Tokyo: Ôkura-shô Insatsu-kyoku. Monbu-shô (1998), *Monbu Tôkei Yôran Heisei 10 Nenban* [Educational Statistics 1998], Tokyo: Ôkura-shô Insatsu-kyoku: 51,57. Sômu-chô (1999), *Seishônen Hakusho* [White Paper on Juveniles], Tokyo: Ôkura-shô Insatsu-kyoku: 15-17. Hômu-shô (1998), *Hanzai Hakusho* [White Paper on Crime], Tokyo: Ôkura-shô Insatsu-kyoku: 203.

Since nearly all of those who become delinquent are students, the new wave of delinquency in the midst of the 1990s remains a problem of the schools (Foljanty-Jost 1999).

It is this diffusion of the phenomenon of deviancy in the 1990s that has provoked Japanese colleagues to talk about *ippan-ka* (generalization) of deviancy. Even though the numbers are not higher than in any western society – rather lower –, the public debate on education, family and the role of the local community demonstrates a high sensitivity towards juvenile behavior, because the wide range of problem behavior demonstrates the failure of previous strategies of ensuring conformity among young students by strengthening control further.

The challenge Japan is facing now is how to reorganize the mechanism of social control in a way that will ensure conformity and the re-integration of young students into society.

3 Regaining Control: The Strategy of the Ministry of Education

For the Ministry of Education the new wave of problem behavior is part of the overall crisis in Japanese society in bringing up the next generation. The Ministry regards families' and communities' inability to educate their children as one of the main reasons for juvenile problem behavior (Monbu-shô 1998). Parents are regarded as being unable to communicate with their children and to educate what the Ministry calls "sound minds" in children. The strategy of the Ministry is therefore complex: Since former strategies for prevention (namely the enforcement of control) are no longer sufficient, the task for the 1990s is to encourage and support parents in educating their children. Controlling is therefore supplemented by the promotion of various counseling systems. One is directed to juveniles to compensate for the lack of communication opportunities in their social environment. Another is a counseling system for parents to "help to enrich home discipline" (Monbu-shô 1998: point 3.2). By carrying out national campaigns like "Let's communicate with our children" (*kodomo to hanasou*) the Ministry intends "to educate people" (Monbu-shô 1998: point 3.2). It is in line with this sceptical approach to the educational competence of the nation's parents that the Ministry heavily relies on the local community for the implementation of its prevention policies.

"It is necessary to build a broad cooperative relationship between schools, families and communities." (Monbu-shô 1997: point 3) The institutions of the local community like PTA (parents-teachers-associations), serving as the link between family and school, *minsei i'in* (volunteers for public welfare), serving as the link between the community and the local administration, and the neighborhood associations (*chônai-kai* or *jichi-kai*) represent members of the locality who have experience in communal engagement.

"In each community, we will promote the tightening of schools' links with related institutions, including child welfare facilities, (...) and police, with related organizations such as PTAs and juveniles' organizations, and with residents." (Monbu-shô 1997) That means that besides the civil organizations of the local community, the police is also regarded as an integral part of the local educational network. In its notice to the prefectural boards of education in 1997, the Ministry stresses that the establishment of the police-school-coordination committees in 1963 has been an important step in fighting delinquency and encourages the communities for a strong engagement in school-police cooperation (Monbu-shô 1997). The coordination committees are considered as part of local networks for prevention. The Ministry is calling for the improvement of joint controlling and counseling activities by the local institutions, including a complete exchange of information concerning general behavior, attendance at classes and so forth of students who could be expected to show problem behavior in the future (Monbu-shô 1997). This reflects the recommendations of the Central Council for Education, the most influential advisory council of the Ministry, which has recommended that schools should firmly cooperate with the police and child guidance centers in dealing with problem behavior (Central Council for Education 1998).

To summarize: the response of the Ministry of Education to juvenile problem behavior is two-fold. On the one side the words are *soft*, suggesting a pro-social approach of re-integration towards parents and students with problem behavior. On the other side the strategy of securing conformity by reactivating all local agents of social control has remained the same *hard* approach of suppression.

4 Implementation of Prevention by the Local Educational Network

With the policies of the Ministry of Education in mind, the question arises how the reactivation of the local community for the recovery of social control of children's behavior is implemented. In our research, we are focussing on the activities of the city of Niigata, the capital of Niigata prefecture in north-east Japan, with 500,000 inhabitants. Situated in a rural area with lower rates of entrance to senior high school than the national average, the number of juvenile offenses in 1997 was higher than the national average, but number, development and type of juvenile problem behavior like violence at schools and sexual misconduct of girls handled by police is in line with the national average. Nevertheless, because of the increasing rate of non-school-attendance and a case of juvenile suicide due to bullying in Niigata prefecture, problem awareness among schools and related institutions can be expected to be high.

We have obtained our data from field studies in Niigata between 1998 and 2000 by doing semi-structured interviews at three junior high schools and with representatives of local and prefectural institutions, and some private groups, all of which are engaged in dealing with deviancy education and children's welfare.

We have supplemented the data with the analysis of documents, internal papers and materials provided by the institutions.[1]

With regard to their influence on children's behavior, we would have expected a pyramid-shaped structure of the prevention institutions with schools forming the basis, followed by the local community and finally the local police and the family court as the agents of formal control, but in fact it is more appropriate to talk about a local network of prevention, which is cooperating and sharing actions with each other. The network consists of public institutions like the local police, the board of education, and the schools and semi-public local organizations like juvenile supporters and juvenile guardians, intertwined by various coordination committees and joint conferences.

4.1 The Board of Education

The board of education is serving as a link between the national educational administration and the local schools. It is expected to implement the guidelines and regulations of the Ministry of Education. It is coordinating local policies and local agents of education. Corresponding to the two-fold policies of the Ministry of Education we can basically distinguish two types of dealing with problem behavior. What we call *indirect* measures are those, which provide informations on the problem and recommendations, while *direct* measures are defined as those which are addressed to the problem child or his or her parents.

As indirect measures, the Niigata board of education is eager to provide parents, teachers and the general public with informations and training by providing publications, handbills, or posters. It collects data concerning problem behavior at schools, and organizes meetings of the institutions concerned for mutual information exchange. These measures attempt to define the values of the community and desirable forms of behavior and are directed to all students and teachers.

Direct intervention mainly consists of the implementation of controlling and counseling. Therefore, the board heavily relies on semi-volunteers, thereby responding to the Ministry's demand for mobilizing the local community for prevention activities. It employs so-called students' carekeepers (*seitô shidô-in*) and juvenile guardians (*gaitô hodô-in*), both of whom are engaged in street patrols in residential areas as well as at places of special concern like the central station,

1 The field research has been part of a research project sponsored by the Volkswagen Foundation between 1998 and 2001 on juvenile delinquency and its prevention in Japan. Members of the research team under the superintendence of the author are Dr. Manuel Metzler, Annette Erbe, and Anne Metzler. Preliminary results of the project are published in the series of the Institute of Japanese Studies, Martin-Luther-University of Halle: Materialien zu Jugend und Devianz in Japan: Occasional Papers. Dr. Manuel Metzler has provided some of the material used for the article.

game-centers, and shopping malls. They are mainly elder women and men in their sixties, who want to get involved in shaping the community and the future generation. What the city expects them to do is precisely defined in the handbook for juvenile guardians. Section 4 reads:

> Juvenile guidance conducted by the guardians is 'an appeal of love' (*ai no yobikake*). Therefore situations should be avoided which may even run a risk for the health. (Niigata-shi 1998:6)

This means that street guardians are asked to refrain from provoking the juveniles, since the guardians are not provided with any statutory rights. They should not even ask the juveniles' names but only talk to them, asking for instance why they smoke or where the money for the expensive handbag is from. Their status can be described as an engaged *neighbor*, who has the moral legitimacy to care for his or her community.

For counseling, the board provides the schools with professional school counselors and additional local staff for offering communication opportunities to students at school. It aims at friendly guidance with terms like "heartful counseling" or "*kokoro no kyôshitsu*" (classroom for the heart), indicating that the basic approach is to support those who deal with the problematic juveniles and to provide space for student-centered communication. In the case of school counseling professionals are frequent, but in the case of counseling outside school, the board engages volunteers as counselors. Through its center for educational counseling, the city offers telephone counseling, general educational counseling and since 1994 counseling for students who refuse to attend classes. The care for children who refuse to attend classes is entrusted to volunteers. The only qualification asked for is that these volunteers have experience and time. Typically, they are former teachers who are ready to spend their time with visiting children at home for support and counseling, trying to persuade them to attend the so-called *tekiô shidô kyôshitsu* (the class room for adaptation). Their engagement is high, as demonstrated by an interview with a volunteer home visitor:

> I visited his house six years or so [a boy, who refused to attend school *G.F.-J.*], but I never met him. (...) Many of us thought that we should stop visiting him. But I continued my visits. (...) Finally one day, I saw him strolling with his dog through the paddy-fields. I called him but he totally ignored me. Today he is attending senior high school, and likes it. And he is playing baseball in the school's team. That's why I think whatever happens we never should give up. (Interview with Mr. Sekine, home visiting counselor of the center of educational counseling, board of education, city of Niigata, May 23rd 2000)

Volunteers supplement home visiting activities of other institutions. Since they are usually not members of the neighborhood, they can offer more privacy than the members of the neighborhood association.

4.2 The Local Community

The local community is the intermediary level with close ties to school, family and administration as well. It is structured according to neighborhoods with neighborhood associations (*chônai-kai* or *jichi-kai*) as the smallest institutional unit. The local social environment is regarded as an integral part of the process of socialization. In the perception of parents as well as in the self-definition of local neighborhood associations, the community functions as a partner of the family in bringing up children (Hayo 2000:153-171).

Members of the neighborhood associations organize street patrols in their community, directly appealing to students who show problem behavior. They provide the households belonging to the association with informations and cooperate closely with the *minsei'in*, people from the neighborhood who are officially entrusted by the city with serving as a link between the administration and the people, paying special attention for securing social well-being in the community. They organize meetings of related groups, like mothers and teachers, support the local police by controlling students in the locality, and ask local shopkeepers for cooperation in their activities for improving social environments of the juveniles. The influence of the activists derives from their status as well-known people in the community with good reputations, living there for years and knowing everybody. In their activities they therefore mainly rely on personal contacts with parents and children of their neighborhood.

4.3 The Police

The police in Niigata is divided into 5 stations, all of which have been heavily involved in controlling young people. Following the intensification of prevention of delinquency, only recently juvenile control has been delegated to the so-called juvenile support center of the police, which is mainly responsible for street patrols, but which offers telephone counseling as well.

> We do not especially take care of delinquency, but of immoral behavior. For instance when students spend their time in public places instead of at school, or when drop-outs gather at particular places in the town, smoking or even drinking, we talk to them. (Interview with Ms. Takahashi, chief of the section for life security, juvenile division, West-Police Station, Niigata city, May 5th 1999)

As this remark of a young female police officer demonstrates, the police perceives itself not only as an institution which has to prevent and control delinquency, but extends its responsibilities to the control of young people who show the slightest forms of non-conformist behavior. The idea behind this approach is not to exert pressure on the students, but talk to them as friends. "It is better for us not to wear uniform but approach the students like a normal 'aunty', not as a severe policewoman." (Interview with Ms. Takahashi, chief of the section for life security, juvenile division, West-Police Station, Niigata city, May 5th 1999)

Even in the case of the police, which should be the very institution authorized for street patrols, volunteers are asked for support. For instance, they were called for help in the case of two junior high school students who did not show up at school or at home any more, but spent their time at the shopping center. In this case police asked the people in the neighborhood for support because the police are not allowed to visit homes on preventive purposes only.

In those cases when students repeatedly attract police attention, the school is contacted. Especially at weekends and during holidays police ask teachers to join them in their patrols to places where their students spend their leisure time. Usually one teacher per school attends such patrols even when they take place during night, in order to obtain information about their students' behavior. But even if no special problems have occurred, the coordination committee of school and police forms an institutionalized forum for information exchange. During the meetings the police provides the school with information about general trends of delinquency and special problems in the school district and presents information and recommendations on how to deal with problem behavior. The police supports, controls and guides, but it refrains from intervening into problem behavior at schools unless requested.

5 Conclusion: Fighting Deviancy by "Heartful" Controlling and Counseling

Even though the institutions involved in prevention mentioned above vary in terms of legal status, institutional goals and structure, they share a basic approach towards social control of children. Thereby all of them basically follow the recommendations of the Ministry of Education. The result is an impressing density of counseling services and control activities. While controlling is the traditional way of dealing with deviant juveniles, counseling is a new approach, which started in the 1980s during the first wave of violence at schools.

Counseling at school is offered by professionals, psychologists and teachers, constituting a hierarchy with regard to the distance from the student. Yet, for preventive control and intensive communication with their students, teachers mostly feel too busy. Thus, the board of education has introduced the system of the "heartful counselor" (*heartful kaunserâ*)[2] who is not a professional, but an experienced person from outside, offering communication to all students. The

2 "Heartful" in this case is not a translation from Japanese, but it is the original expression used in official documents in Japanese.

"heartful" as the Japanese call him or her does not belong to the school staff, but is expected to gain the trust of the students as somebody from "outside". In cases of deep concern and severe problems, schools may receive a psychologist as a school counselor, funded by the Ministry of Education for two years.

Counseling at school is also supplemented by counseling services provided by the police, by the welfare-center of the prefecture, by the board of education, and even by the teachers' union and volunteer groups. Counseling services are dense, seldom by psychologists, but offered by regular staff or engaged citizens with some experience in bringing up children. They supplement each other, showing no distinct differences in their programs.

Unlike counseling, controlling is – with the exception of the police – mainly under the responsibility of volunteers. Since all institutions of the prevention network engage volunteers, the net of street patrols is impressively dense, and even though the volunteers belong to different institutions as demonstrated in table 2 their way of acting is similar. In 1998 2000 patrols were done with more than 6000 juveniles addressed by the juvenile guardians of the board of education alone. In places which are regarded as especially problematic, such as game-centers, the guardians prefer to keep in close contact with shop-owners, visiting and informing them about problems in the district. They collect information on the location and number of vending machines with pornographic comics, cigarettes and alcohol and contact the owners asking them to refrain from selling harmful products to juveniles.

Table 2: Prevention by Street Patrols / City of Niigata (as by 2000)

	affiliation	members' profile	number	number of patrols
juvenile guardians (*gaitô hodô in*)*	Niigata-city: board of education	volunteers, citizens with educational experience	880*	5692 (1997)
children's care-keepers (*shûnin jidô in*)	Niigata-city	volunteers nomi-nated by the Ministry of Health		
juvenile supporters (*shônen hodô in*)	police	volunteers, people with experience	760 (prefect.)	2 times per month
juvenile carekeepers (*shônen shidô in*)	police	staff of the police	120	8 per day
students' care-keepers (*seitô shidô in*)	Niigata-city board of education	people with experience	338	4 per day

* including the so-called play leader, who are engaged to arrange games and sports activities in the communities and juvenile carekeepers (*seishônen ikusei in*).

The approach is traditional and reactivates the responsibility of the local community for their children, for security and order. All of those who are on street patrols share the view that they should approach the students in a mild and friendly way. The term "appeal of love" (*ai no yobikake*) expresses the new approach, which is perceived to be less of guidance (*hodô*), but more of "bringing up" (*ikusei*) children. As one female juvenile guardian, who is especially concerned with smoking, put it:

> We should not only concentrate on the behavior, but when we reflect the spirit and the motive behind the way of behavior, we will understand the feeling of the child and will listen to it. I think this is the best weapon against smoking. I think that this is the reason why already everywhere the concept of guidance has changed to become that of bringing up. (Interview with Mrs. Ôzawa, board of education, city of Niigata, May 25th 2000)

To summarize our findings:

- The self definition and legal status of the institutions involved in social control vary, but their strategies do not, consisting of informing, controlling and counseling.
- The overlapping of activities ensures a high density of counseling opportunities and tight control of places which are regarded to be harmful for students.
- The system relies heavily on volunteers, and the boundaries between public and private control become therefore unclear.
- The prevention of juvenile problem behavior in the 1990s resembles the traditional approach of activating members of the local community as mediators between administration and police on the one hand and the people in the community on the other.
- By employing older members of the local community to serve as juvenile guardians, public agents choose a pseudo-personal form of intervention, aiming to create personal linkages between young people, local adults and the public institutions of police, school and city administration.
- By the engagement of volunteers control receives a soft and mild image. The adult world presents itself as friendly, refraining from punishment and other sanctions, but relying on moral suasion.

References

Central Council for Education (1998), *To Cultivate Children's Sound Minds that Develop a New Era – A Crisis of Losing Confidence in Bringing up Next Generation*, http://www.monbu.go.jp/series-en/00000013/.

Foljanty-Jost, G. (1999), Randale an Japans Schulen: Ursachen und bildungspolitische Antworten, in: Pohl, M. (ed.), *Japan 1998/99, Politik und Wirtschaft*, Hamburg: Institut für Asienkunde: 245-261.

Hayo, M. (2000), *Gakkô to Chiiki no Kizuna. Chiiku Kyôiku o Hiraku* [The Bonds Between School and Community. For an Opening of the Local Education], Tokyo: Kyôiku shuppan.

Hirota, T. (1998), Kodomo no Genzai o dô Miru ka [How to Look at the Future of Children?], in: *Kyôiku Shakaigaku Kenkyû* 63: 5-22.

Kobayashi, M. (1999), *Protokoll einer Problemklasse, übersetzt und kommentiert von M. Metzler*, Materialien zu Jugend und Devianz in Japan, Occasional Papers, Vol. 9, Halle: Universität Halle.

Matsui, I. (ed.) (1997), *Chihô Kyôiku Gyôsei no Kenkyû* [Local Educational Administration], Tokyo: Taga Shuppan.

Matsumoto, Y. (1967), Kyôiku no Bunka to Hikô Hassei [Differential Educational Attainment and Adolescent Delinquency], in: *Kyôiku Shakaigaku Kenkyû* 22: 111-125.

Metzler, A. (1999), *Jugenddelinquenz und Jugenddevianz*, Materialien zu Jugend und Devianz in Japan, Occasional Papers, Vol.5, Halle: Universität Halle.

Monbu-shô (1997), *Program for Educational Reform*, http://www.monbu.go.jp/ series-en/00000004.

Monbu-shô (1998), *"Kodomo to Hanasou" Zenkoku Kyanpeen* [The National Campaign "Let's Talk to the children"], http://www.monbu.go.jp/kodomo/ kodomo.html.

Mori, T. (1999), *Die Krisentheorie. Ein Erlärungsmodell für delinquentes Verhalten Jugendlicher, übersetzt und ausgewählt von A. und M. Metzler*, Materialien zu Jugend und Devianz in Japan, Occasional Papers, Vol.6, Halle: Universität Halle.

Niigata-shi, Kyôiku Iinkai Seishônen-ka (1999), *Niigata- shi Shônen Ikusei'in Techô* [Handbook for Juvenile Guardians in Niigata City], Niigata.

Tanaka, M. (1986), *Kore kara no Chônai-kai. Jichi-kai* [Local Communities of the Future), Tokyo: Jichi-kai Kenkyû-sha.

Tokuoka, H. (1992), Seishônen Mondai to Kyôiku Byôri [Juvenile Problems and the Educational Pathology], in: *Kyôiku Shakaigaku Kenkyû* 50: 146-163.

Tokuoka, H. (1999), *Seishônen Taisaku to Seishônen Mondai no Henshitsu* [Juvenile Policy and the Change of Juvenile Problems], unpublished manuscript.

PART TWO: THE EXTERNAL PREPARATIONS

FOREIGN RELATIONS: ASIAN OR GLOBAL LEADERSHIP?

The "New Asianism"

Peter Duus

1 The Old Pan-Asianism

"Is Japan really part of Asia?" The question has agitated Japanese intellectuals, politicians and pundits for more than a century. As the Japanese embarked on the road to modernity in the late nineteenth century they found that geography and culture no longer matched. A widening cultural gap with their neighbors on the continent raised the question of just where Japan belonged: with the countries immediately across the sea or with the more distant "civilized" societies it sought as models and mentors?

In his 1885 essay "On Departing from Asia" (*Datsu-A Ron*) Fukuzawa Yukichi offered one answer to this question. Writing after a pro-Japanese reform coup had failed in Korea and China had suffered yet another defeat at the hands of a European power, he urged his countrymen to cut loose from Asia and cast their lot with the "civilized" nations of the West. Japan might be located at the tip of the Asian continent, he wrote, but in spirit its people had sloughed off Asian backwardness. The Chinese and the Koreans, on the other hand, remained in the thrall of ancient ways and ancient customs and had failed to defend themselves against the outside world. It made no sense for Japan to join them in resisting Western encroachments. "People who associate with bad friends must share their bad reputation," he concluded. "In spirit we must decline to associate with our bad friends in the eastern part of Asia." (Fukuzawa 1885)

A few years later Okakura Kakuzô offered a different answer. He sought to re-embrace Asia as a source of Japan's own culture and as a marker of Japan's national identity. In his *The Ideals of the East*, first published in English at the turn of the century, he not only saw Japan as part of Asia but proclaimed it to be a museum of Asian thought and culture. "It is in Japan alone that the historical wealth of Asiatic culture can be consecutively studied through its treasured specimens," he wrote (Okakura 1903:6). Like the other "Asiatic races", the Japanese shared the "broad expanse of love for the Ultimate and Universal" that was their "common thought-inheritance" and that set them apart from the peoples of the West, who loved "to dwell on the Particular, and to search out the means, not the end of life." (Okakura 1903:1)

The famous proclamation that opens his book – "Asia in One" – was a classic statement of the Pan-Asianist solidarity that Fukuzawa had rejected. The Asians were not "bad friends" but people who had lost confidence in themselves. In Okakura's view the Japanese victory over China in 1895 placed a responsibility on Japan as the first Asian power to resuscitate that confidence. "Not only to return to our own past ideals, but also to feel and revivify the dormant life of the old Asiatic unity, becomes our mission." (Okakura 1903:223) While Okakura never made clear what he meant in concrete terms, his notion of "mission" was cultural not political. What he had in mind was a reassertion of the value and validity of the Asian "thought-inheritance" over and against Western "civilization".

The concept of *Asia* was, of course, a Western construct. The word itself, as Martin Lewis and Karen Wigen have reminded us recently, was an invention of the Greeks, who first divided the world into three parts: Asia, Europe and Africa. From the outset the concept of *Asia* was deployed to delineate cultural differences as well as a geographical region. Aristotle, for example, saw the nations of Asia as "intelligent and skillful" but lacking in spirit while those of Europe were "full of spirit but somewhat deficient in intelligence and skill". The Greeks, he happily concluded, were both "spirited and intelligent" since they were positioned exactly between Europe and Asia (quoted in: Lewis & Wigen 1997:214).

By the 19th century *Asia* had become a stable category in Western Orientalist discourse. On the one hand, this discourse contrasted a backward, stagnant and despotic Asia with a progressive, dynamic, and liberal West; on the other, it contrasted a spiritual, idealistic, mystical Asia with a materialistic, instrumental and practical West.[1] Fukuzawa dovetailed the two dichotomies to explain why there was a vast economic, material, and technological gap between the two regions: Asia was backward and stagnant precisely because it was idealistic and mystical. But Okakura stood Fukuzawa on his head by arguing that the "materialistic" West could benefit by learning from the "spiritual" Asia. Although in fundamental disagreement over Japan's relationship to Asia, both men operated within the same discursive space.

During the early twentieth century Japanese intellectuals, public and private, navigated back and forth between the extremes of rejecting Asia or embracing it. Some saw Japan as the West's representative in Asia, some saw it as Asia's protector against Western intrusions into Asia, and some saw it as a cultural mediator between the two. By the 1930s and 1940s, however, cultural pan-Asianism was eclipsed by a politicized version. The expansion of the Japanese empire beyond the original colonies into China, then into Southeast Asia, summoned up new visions of a Japan at the center of a new "Asia for the Asians". The visions varied in name – "East Asian Community", "New Order in East Asia", "East Asian Federation", "Greater East Asia Coprosperity Sphere", and so forth – but they shared a common goal: that Japan should create a new regional

1 One of the most eloquent statements of these dichotomies can be found in Alcock (1863:329-376).

system based on political, economic and cultural cooperation and solidarity among the nations of Asia (Hashikawa 1996).

Wartime pan-Asianism demanded "departing from the West", whose materialism was now construed as a sign of moral and cultural weakness rather than racial or cultural superiority. The new regional system to be constructed in Asia was displace the global political, economic and cultural hegemony of the Anglo-American powers. But beneath the surface some intellectuals harbored doubts. None wrestled with them more energetically than Miki Kiyoshi, who resuscitated the Orientalist dichotomies to build a rationale for a new "East Asian culture" but realized that the diversity of Asia was more obvious than its unity, that claims of Japan's "uniqueness" were difficult to reconcile with Japan's "Asian-ness" and that Japan's ability to shape a new order in Asia was ultimately indebted to borrowed Western technology and institutional models (Miki 1941).

2 The Postwar Retreat from Pan-Asianism

With the collapse of the empire in 1945, the pan-Asianist position receded from public discourse. If the Japanese did not completely "depart from Asia" they certainly kept it at a distance during the early postwar era. Except for Takeuchi Yoshimi and a few others, intellectuals rarely raised the issue of Japan's Asian identity or debated its character as an Asian country. This was not entirely a matter of choice. The wartime attempt to build a new "East Asian community" left deep-rooted hostility toward Japan in most parts of Asia. Even after the resumption of normal relations with the outside world at the American Occupation, their neighbors did not receive the Japanese with open arms. Until 1965 Japan had no official diplomatic ties with either part of Korea nor with the People's Republic of China until 1973. Even in those countries of Asia where Japan resumed diplomatic relations Japanese businessmen and other travelers kept a low profile. Under these circumstances it was difficult for most Japanese to sustain a sense of connection with the rest of Asia.

As a result of Japan's *reorientation* under the American Occupation, Japanese political and intellectual elites found it easy to turn once again toward the West, and particularly the United States, as mentor and model. But Japan's incorporation into the Western camp in the Cold War as the main American ally in East Asia and the Western Pacific shifted the terms in the discourse over identity. With Asia divided between a Communist bloc (PRC, North Korea, and North Vietnam) and a non-Communist bloc (Japan, South Korea, Indonesia, Philippines, Malaysia, Thailand), the old slogan "Asia is One" made no sense. The debate over national identity revolved around a new axis: the new ideological confrontation between a "free" West and a "totalitarian" East. Identification with Asia was framed in the 1950s and 1960s in global strategic and ideological terms not cultural ones. If intellectuals sought to identify Japan with Asia, as many on the left did, it was either to urge alignment with the Bandung bloc of "neutral" Asian-African nations or with the PRC against American monopoly capitalism.

Outside the left, and particularly during the period of rapid economic growth, identification with Asia made less sense. For example, in an influential and controversial essay in 1957, Umesao Tadao made a new argument for identifying with the West. He divided the societies on the Eurasian landmass into a "primary zone" (including Japan and the Western European countries on the continental littorals) and a "secondary zone" (including the PRC and the USSR in the center). The division was based not on culture, spirit or ideals but on material lifestyle and historical development. Umesao noted parallels between Japanese and European history not to be found in the histories of the other Asian countries, and he underlined the economic similarities shared by societies in the "primary zone". He made no value judgements or value claims about the superiority of the "primary zone", however, but simply sought to overcome heavily ideological conceptions of "Asian solidarity" and "Western superiority" by demolishing the Asia-Europe dichotomy on which both were based (Umesao 1957).

In the 1970s and 1980s the *Nihonjinron* boom overwhelmed the discourse on cultural identity. The issue was no longer whether Japan belonged to *Asia* or the *West* but what made it uniquely different from both. The rapid growth of its economy made Japan much more affluent than its Asian neighbors, and its economic resilience allowed Japan to flourish when the Western economies lagged. This remarkable economic success required an explanation that many intellectuals found in the "unique features" of Japanese society and culture. It was no longer necessary for Japan to look outside itself for models; it had become a model itself, not only for its Asian neighbors but for the advanced Western countries. The question of *Asian* cultural identity was irrelevant. What counted was defining the "uniqueness" that made the Japanese model appropriate for export.

3 The Return of Pan-Asianism

In the early 1990s, however, a new brand of pan-Asianism – what some called the "new Asianism" – made its appearance.[2] A number of intellectuals and pundits tried to reconnect with Asia by suggesting that Japan had more in common with its continental neighbors than with the societies of the West, including the United States. Why this renewed interest in Asia? In part the "new Asianism" was a response to the end of the Cold War. The collapse of the Soviet bloc provoked a general rethinking of Japan's role in world politics. During the Cold War it had

---

2 For a brief general discussion of the "new Asianism" see McCormack (1996: Ch. 4).

been easy and comfortable to follow the lead of American Asian policy but the end of Cold War certainties made possible new choices. It was no longer necessary to side with the *West* or to keep *Asia* at arm's length.

The end of the Cold War coincided with other developments that encouraged the emergence of a "new Asianism". One was a sense of growing estrangement from the United States over chronic trade friction and (to a lesser extent) defense issues. The maddeningly steady growth of a trade deficit with Japan provoked the American government to demand that the Japanese "level the playing field" and/or give up its "free ride" on defense. Animated in part by envy, in part by resentment, and in part by a sense of fair play, American pressure on Japan was bipartisan, pursued by the Clinton administration as eagerly as by the Bush administration. Not surprisingly, many Japanese commentators read American pressure as *Japan-bashing.* Washington also seemed increasingly eager to cultivate closer ties with Beijing and the rapidly growing China market. Some Japanese observers saw this as a zero-sum game since historically US-Japan relations had always deteriorated when US-Chinese relations improved. Many Japanese felt that the United States was abandoning them after more than a generation of faithful clientship. Finding or cultivating firm new friends in Asia seemed a logical, indeed an urgent alternative to the US-Japan alliance.

Growing economic ties between Japan and other countries in the Asian region also encouraged the "new Asianism". As the yen appreciated in value after the 1985 Plaza Accord, Japanese investment in Asia, particularly in Southeast Asia, experienced a sudden surge. Large manufacturing firms began to build offshore manufacturing or assembly facilities in Asia, and more and more *Japanese* products were being made in Taiwan, Malaysia or Korea by local workers under the supervision of Japanese managers. Trade with Asian economies grew rapidly as well. By the early 1990s its total volume surpassed that of trade with the United States. And where Japanese trade went Japanese pop culture, from *karaoke* bars to idol singers, soon followed.

In effect a *de facto* new Asian economic region centering on Japan seemed to be taking shape in the early 1990s. The "new Asianism" focussed on the need to consolidate or institutionalize this de facto regionalism in response to the creation of new economic regions such as NAFTA and the European Community. (A few even spoke of the return of the Greater East Asia Co-Prosperity Sphere, a chillingly impolitic rhetorical move that unsettled some outside observers.) At first, however, the main initiative for institutionalizing an Asian economic region came not from the Japanese government but from Prime Minister Mahathir of Malaysia, who proposed the formation of an "East Asian Economic Caucus" in preparation for an intra-Asian economic union in which Japan would play a leading role – and from which the United States would be excluded. Many "new Asianists" quickly seized on the proposal to countervail American proposals for an Asian-Pacific Economic Council. Others called for economic strategies such as increased ODA, technical cooperation, or educational exchange programs to tie Japan closer to its Asian neighbors.

Many advocates of the "new Asianism" also proposed regional security arrangements paralleling NATO in Europe. The Cold War had not come to an end in Asia as decisively as it had in Europe. The continued separation of the PRC and Taiwan, the division of Korea into north and south, and signs of a new Chinese irredentism over offshore islands claimed by several parties remained sources of strategic anxiety in the region. It is interesting to note that much of the "new Asian" rhetoric focussed on Japan's relations with the Southeast Asian countries and elided the presence of China in the region. Proposals for a new regional security system centered on ties between Japan and the ASEAN countries, who appeared uneasy about the enormous potential military strength of China. Kitaoka Shin'ichi, for example, suggested convening of an Asian version of the Conference on Security and Cooperation in Europe to guarantee a collective commitment to status quo of national borders in the region and to ban the export of weapons to "rogue nations" (Kitaoka 1995:99).

Perhaps the most ardent and persistent advocate of the "new Asianism" was Ôgura Kazuo, a high-ranking Foreign Ministry official. In a 1993 article that attracted much attention he called for a "restoration of Asia" – the real Asia not the social imaginary manufactured by the West. The rapid economic and political development of the Asian countries constituted a challenge to claims for the universality of Western values, he argued. Taking cues from Mahathir and Lee Kuan Yew, Ôgura called for a reassertion of an "Asian spirit" and the propagation of "Asian values" such as discipline and hard work, family and social solidarity, rejection of material desire, and harmony with the environment to the rest of the world. Like Okakura he criticized the failures of a Western "mechanical civilization grounded in the limitless pursuit of individual desires and untiring self-assertion" (Ôgura 1993:62). But most of all he wanted to overcome the mindset of Asian intellectuals who like Fukuzawa had "departed from Asia" in a cultural sense. The tone of Ôgura's arguments became more modulated as economic slowdown in Japan and elsewhere in Asia tarnished the luster of the *Asian Economic Model* in the late 1990s but he continued to insist that Asia should make its voice heard in the international arena.

The "new Asianists", unlike prewar pan-Asianists, assumed that Japan and Asia were embedded in a rapidly globalizing world, and they took account of the historical transformation of the region under the impact of modernization. They did not propose to secede from the global community as the advocates of the Greater East Asia Co-Prosperity Sphere had but rather to rally the Asian countries as a countervailing force to Western, and particularly American hegemony. In a sense calling for the "restoration of Asia" was a way of calling attention to the special needs, interests and conditions of the Asian region. But by insisting on Japan's "Asian identity" the "new Asianists" also sought to bring to an end

Japan's long postwar neglect of Asia and its overwhelming economic and political orientation toward the United States.

The problem with the "new Asianism" was that *Asia* was no longer a stable or uncontested concept it had been in Fukuzawa's and Okakura's day. Given the explosion of economic growth in the Asian countries, the old dichotomy between a "dynamic" West and a "stagnant" Asia obviously no longer held true. And as any casual observer walking through the shopping sections of Tokyo, Shanghai, Bangkok or any other major Asian metropolis could testify, neither did the dichotomy between a "spiritual" Asia and a "materialist" West. Asians were as hell bent on the pleasures of material affluence and consumerism as anyone in the *West*, and the Asian economies enjoyed no better record on maintenance of harmony with nature than did other industrial economies. In cultural or "civilizational" terms, it did not make any sense to speak of Asia as a distinctive regional unit any more. Nor did the question of "Asian identity" seem to be of much concern to ordinary Japanese whose identification with the world was much more complex than the formulas of "new Asianism" suggested.

4 Public Opinion and the "New Asianism"[3]

As the discourse on "new Asianism" was gathering momentum, in July 1994 the Asahi Shimbun polled 2316 national voters about their views on Asia and its relations with Japan (Asahi Shimbun 7/20/1994, JPOLL). The poll offered a revealing snapshot of a Japanese public either indifferent to or uneasy about its relations with Asia. To be sure, a majority of the respondents (55%) felt a personal connection with Asian countries and Asian people but a perhaps surprising one third (33%) did not. It was also striking that very few of the respondents thought that Asia was likely to emerge as the world's most important region in the future or that Japan would become the most influential country in Asia. Nearly 60% disagreed that Asia would overtake the West in the 21st century. Only 16% thought Japan would be the most influential country in Asia, and most respondents thought that either China (44%) or the United States (30%) would. Indeed, a perusal of other public opinion polls from the early 1990s

3 The data utilized in the following section were originally collected by the Prime Minister's Office (5/1/1996 & 5/1/1997), Asahi Shimbun (7/10/1994, 6/28/1995, 9/16/1996, 9/19/1996 & 3/17/1999), Yomiuri Shimbun (2/1/1995, 10/26/1997 & 10/20/1998), Nihon Keizai Shimbun (4/27/1997), NHK (3/1/1993, 7/1/1993, 5/1/1994 & 12/1/1994), Jiji Press (3/30/1993) and USIA (5/23/1990, 6/12/1991, 11/6/1991 & 10/18/1993). All data were obtained from the Japan Public Opinion Location Library (hereafter JPOLL), Roper Center for Public Opinion Research, University of Connecticut. Neither the original collectors of the data nor the Roper Center bear any responsibility for the analyses and interpretations presented below.

suggest that few Japanese thought that leadership in Asia was as important as Japan's relationships with the United States and Europe (USIA 5/23/1990, JPOLL; USIA 6/12/1991, JPOLL; USIA 11/6/1991, JPOLL).

The 1994 Asahi poll showed that when most Japanese thought of Asia, they thought of East Asia first, Southeast Asia second, and South Asia (India and Pakistan) hardly at all. When asked which three Asian countries most interested them, the respondents put China (58%), North Korea (45%) and South Korea (41%) at the top of the list. With the exception of Hong Kong (12%), all the other Asian countries from Taiwan and Cambodia (9%) to Mongolia (2%) and Laos (1%) were only of marginal interest. Other polls taken during the 1990s show that interest or curiosity about other Asian countries dropped off in direct relation to their distance from Japan (Prime Minister's Office 5/1/1996, JPOLL). In such a climate of opinion, building a strong sense of "Asian unity" – except at an amorphous and abstract level of "Asian values" – was bound to face difficulties.

Oddly enough, even though a majority felt some connection with Asia nearly equal majorities in the 1994 Asahi poll thought that other Asians neither liked nor trusted the Japanese: 56% felt that Asian people disliked that Japanese people and 53% also thought that Asian countries did not trust Japan.[4] The principal reason, according to these respondents, was that Japan had not provided enough compensation to Asian countries for the losses caused by the Second World War. Even though many intellectuals and politicians wanted to reconnect with Asia it was clear to ordinary Japanese that "problems of the past" constituted a formidable barrier to comfortable relations with their Asian neighbors, especially the Koreans and the Chinese (NHK 7/1/1993, JPOLL; Nihon Keizai Shimbun 4/27/1997, JPOLL).

Ironically, the "new Asianism" emerged at peculiar moment in the formation of public memory in Japan. While the notion that the Japanese people themselves were victims of the war had gained ground in the postwar period, the emergence of the *comfort women* issue in the early 1990s reminded the Japanese public how much suffering Japanese armies had inflicted on the areas they occupied. So did the fiftieth anniversary of the war's end in 1995. Despite convoluted, grudging and fumbling efforts of the politicians to shape a plausible public apology to the world, and to the Asian countries in particular, the general public quite clearly understood that words were not enough. What is particularly striking is how consistently large majorities of the respondents to public opinion polls expressed the view that the Japanese government had not addressed these issues nor compensated wartime victims adequately.[5] In the 1994 Asahi poll, for example,

4 A 1996 Asahi poll showed that 61% thought that other Asians disliked the Japanese (Asahi Shimbun 9/19/1996, JPOLL).

5 As early as 1993 a Jiji Press poll indicated that a strong majority of respondents thought that if the Heisei emperor were to visit China or South Korea he should apologize explicitly (20%), apologize subtly (33%), or declare Japan a pacifist nation

72% said that Japanese had not given enough compensation to the countries it occupied before and during the Second World War, and other polls showed strong support for direct monetary compensation from the national budget to former comfort women (NHK 12/1/1994, JPOLL; Asahi Shimbun 6/28/1995, JPOLL). Behind this support for compensation undoubtedly lay concern that failure to address the historical residue of prewar and wartime imperialism would continue to poison the atmosphere and undermine the emergence of Japan as a regional leader.

The deeper one probes into Japanese views as reflected in public opinion polls, however, the clearer it becomes that many Japanese felt as uncomfortable with Asia and Asians as they thought the Asians were with Japan. It was a sad commentary on Japan's relations with its neighbors during the 1960s and 1970s that when asked which countries they disliked the most, respondents consistently ranked Japan's four immediate neighbors in Asia (the two Koreas, the PRC and the USSR) at the top of the list. By contrast, one or another of the Western countries (usually the United States or Switzerland) ranked at the top of the "most liked" countries (NHK 1982:182-183).

During the 1990s, however, the overall trend in polling results was toward more positive views of China and Korea. Renewal of diplomatic and economic relations with China accounted for changing assessments of China, whose negative rating dropped noticeably during the decade. A USIA poll in 1991 found that 50% of the respondents had an unfavorable impression of China but that figure dropped to 31% in a similar poll just two years (USIA 6/12/1991, JPOLL; USIA 10/18/1993, JPOLL). Indeed, a 1993 NHK poll found for the first time China ranked among the top ten favorite countries, in fifth place on a list that otherwise contained only European or North American countries (NHK 3/1/1993, JPOLL). Undoubtedly the opening of the China market and increased trade with China explain this trend. Impressions of South Korea also seemed to have improved after the overthrow of military rule in the late 1980s but North Korea remained a bogeyman. While a 50% majority in a 1995 Yomiuri poll had a good impression of South Korea only 10% had a similar view of the North (Yomiuri Shimbun 2/1/1995, JPOLL).

Nevertheless it appears that on a personal level many Japanese feel much more comfortable with non-Asian foreigners than with Asians. In several polls, when asked whether or not they would resist the idea of renting a foreigner a room in their home for a year, respondents were more likely to do so toward a Southeast Asian, a Chinese, or a Korean than to toward an American or European (NHK 5/1/1994, JPOLL). In some substantial way, it appears that many Japanese have "departed from Asia" psychologically. Economic relations stand as what they feel they have most in common with other Asians. In the 1994 Asahi poll over a third

(23%) – only 14% said that there was not need for him to apologize or mention the war (Jiji Press 3/30/1993, JPOLL).

of the respondents identified "industry and economy" as their main interest in Asia; 28% mentioned "culture and life", and only 10% mentioned "history" or "politics." Otherwise the lure of identity with the West remains strong. In a 1993 NHK poll 47% of the respondents, echoing Umesao a generation earlier, felt Japan belonged to the "group of advanced countries in North America and Europe"; only 31% felt it belonged to the "group of Asian countries" (NHK 3/1/1993, JPOLL; NHK 7/1/1993, JPOLL). And when the 31% were asked why they felt Japan was closer to Asia, a majority mentioned geography (44%) or skin color (17%) rather than culture, spirit or values (NHK 7/1/1993, JPOLL). In other words, "Asian-ness" seems to be defined as a physical or racial quality rather than a cultural one.

In the 1990s most Japanese seem comfortable with a split identification with the outside world. While the 1994 Asahi poll indicated the proportion of those who thought relations with Asia were more important (28%) to Japan's future than relations with the West (6%), the overwhelming majority thought relations with both (60%) were equally important. Clearly most Japanese felt that they belong as much to a larger global community of advanced industrial nations as they do to a regional community with their neighbors. Polls continued to show that while many believe that Japan should exercise a leadership role in Asia they give higher priority to "global leadership". Membership in the Big Seven (or Eight) conveyed greater status than leadership in Asia. For that reason polls show that the Japanese public prefer participation in a regional organization that is Asian-Pacific or Pacific Rim in structure rather than in a purely "Asian" one that would exclude "non-Asian" Pacific neighbors in the Western Hemisphere and Russia (NHK 7/1/1993, JPOLL; Prime Minister's Office 5/1/1997, JPOLL).

In the midst of calls for a "new Asianism" a sense of connection with the United States remained strong. Respondents to a 1994 Asahi poll indicated that more than two-thirds (67%) thought that postwar American influence on the ideas and life style of the Japanese people was a good thing (Asahi Shimbun 9/16/1996, JPOLL), and other polls showed that majorities continued to think that in the future the United States would be more important to Japan than China (Yomiuri Shimbun 10/20/1998, JPOLL; Asahi Shimbun 3/17/1999, JPOLL). Support for continued military ties with the United States also remained strong despite the public disgust at the rape of an Okinawan school girl in 1995 or the disputes over the use of land on Okinawa for American bases. The American presence was seen as a stabilizing rather than disruptive force, and given the fact that the Japanese public sees the Asian region as "dynamic" but "unstable" (Asahi Shimbun 9/16/1996, JPOLL) the America presence is reassuring. During the postwar period, most Japanese feared its immediate neighbors as the main source of security threats, and that seemed to remain true in the1990s. A Yomiuri poll in late 1997 showed that 69% thought the Korean peninsula constituted such a threat, 32% thought China did, and 23 % thought Russia did. Only 15% had similar fears about the United States – the same percentage that thought the

Middle East did (Yomiuri Shimbun 10/26/1997, JPOLL). And a 1999 Asahi poll showed that two greatest threats to the peace of Japan were thought to be conflict on the Korean peninsula (75%) and conflict between China and Taiwan (27%) (Asahi Shimbun 3/17/1999, JPOLL).

In sum, the "new Asianist" desire to reconnect with Asia as a strategy for the post-Cold War world order found little support among the Japanese public. Evidence from opinion polls makes clear that the majority saw no particular advantage or interest in pursuing such a strategy. Nor did they feel any need to choose between "departing from Asia" or "embracing Asia." If there was a mainstream view on Japan's position in the international order, it was that Japan could belong to both *Asia* and the *West* – and that in fact it already did. Certainly in an era when Shakey's Pizza offers the cheapest lunch in Tokyo and my California supermarket carries *sushi bento* lunches, that seems a reasonable position.

5 Conclusion

The globalization of the world economy may not have eroded national identity very considerably but it does appear to be undermining the *regional* or *civilizational* identities that were *common sense* in the nineteenth and early twentieth centuries. As cultural and economic landscapes become more and more jumbled, the old metageographies no longer fit the global order. Contemporary cultural geography requires a new vocabulary. We should probably think of the world not as a map of bounded and contiguous physical spaces but as a diagram of overlapping economic and cultural networks. "Instead of assuming contiguity," suggest Lewis and Wigen, "we need a way to visualize discontinuous 'regions' that might take the spatial form of lattices, archipelagos, hollow rings, or patchworks" (Lewis & Wigen 1997:200). On such a map distant places can have deeper and more lasting connections than places close to one another, and Japan can be part of the *West* as easily as it can be part of *Asia*. Under these circumstances the very notion of *Asia* gradually loses its significance either as a marker of identity or a basis for cultural connections, and during the coming decades it may become obsolete for the Japanese as well as for the rest of the world.

References

Alcock, R. (1863), *The Capital of the Tycoon. A Narrative of Three Years' Residence* Vol. 2, New York: Harper.

Fukuzawa Y. (1885), Datsu-A Ron [On Departing from Asia], in: *Jiji Shimpô*, 3/16/1885, quoted in Takeuchi Y. (ed.), *Gendai Nihon Shisô Taikei: Ajiashugi* [The Structure of Mind in Contemporary Japan: Asianism] Vol. 8, Tokyo: Chikuma Shobô, 1963: 38-40.

Hashikawa B. (1996), Dai To-A Kyôeiken no Rinen to Genjitsu [Ideology and Reality of the Greater East Asia Coprosperity Sphere], in: Iwanami (ed.), *Iwanami Kôza: Nihon Rekishi* [Iwanami Lectures: Japan's History] Vol. 21, Tokyo: Iwanami Shoten: 265-319.

Kitaoka S. (1995), Putting Old Diplomatic Principles in New Bottles, in: *Japan Echo*, Special Issue 1995: 99.

Lewis, M. W. & and Wigen, K. E. (1997), *The Myth of Continents: A Critique of Metageography*, Berkeley: University of California Press.

McCormack, G. (1996), *The Emptiness of Japanese Affluence*, Armonk & New York: M.E. Sharpe.

Miki K. (1941), The History of the Sino-Japanese Cultural Relations, in: Miki, K. & Hosokawa, K. (ed.), *Introductory Studies on the Sino-Japanese Conflict*, Tokyo: Japanese Council, Institute of Pacific Relations: 1-19.

NHK (1982), *Zusetsu Sengo Seronshi* [The History of Public Opinion in Post-war Japan, explained in Graphics], Tokyo: NHK Bukkusu.

Ôgura K. (1993), Ajia no Fukken no tame ni [For the Restoration of Asia], in: *Chûô Kôron*, 7/1993: 60-73.

Okakura K. (1903), *The Ideals of the East: With Special Reference to the Art of Japan*, London: John Murray.

Umesao T. (1957), Bunmei no Seitaishikan Josetsu [An Introduction to a Static Historical View on Culture], in: *Chûô Kôron*, 2/1957: 32-49.

Japan's Eurasian Diplomacy: Hard-Nosed Power Politics, Resource Diplomacy, or Romanticism?

Reinhard Drifte

1 Introduction

The global changes since the end of the Cold War in 1989, in particular the end of the Soviet Union in 1991, faced Japan with the need but also the opportunity to adjust and broaden the diplomatic as well as geographic scope of its relations with the states on the Eurasian continent. The heavy western support for the economic transition of Russia and the Eastern European countries recast the environment in which Japan had been pursuing its revisionist goal of regaining the so-called Northern Territories. The rise of the five Central Asian republics as well as the three South Caucasian republics[1] from the ashes of the Soviet Union demanded an adjustment of Japan's diplomacy to Russia, China, Central Asia and Europe while providing it with an opportunity to use its economic might and strengthen its standing as an Asian power. This recast of the Eurasian political-strategic map is also influencing Japan's options in the Middle East from where it receives over 80 per cent of its crude oil supply.

Japan's response to these political and economic challenges and opportunities has been rather slow. In 1997 the Japanese government seemed to have waken up to it when Prime Minister Hashimoto declared in July 1997 his so-called Eurasian Diplomacy which was mainly aimed at recasting Japan's approach to Russia. Part of this Eurasian Diplomacy involves strengthening political and economic relations with the new republics in Central Asia and the South Caucasus, a policy referred to as Silk Road Diplomacy (SRD).

In this contribution I want to examine the following issues which arise from the Eurasian Diplomacy, focusing on the relations with the new Central Asian republics:

---

1 The five Central Asian countries are Kazakhstan, Uzbekistan, Turkmenistan, Kyrgystan, and Tajikistan (referred to as CACs), and the three republics in the South Caucasus are Georgia, Armenia and Azerbaijan (SCCs). Together they are here referred to as Silk Road countries (SRCs).

- How did Japan perceive the changes to its Eurasian environment after the end of the East-West conflict?
- Who were the actors and what were their motives?
- What has this Eurasian Diplomacy meant for Japan's relations with the eight countries along the historic Silk Road?
- What role are Japan's economic power and interests playing in the implementation of the Eurasian Diplomacy? Is Japan on the way to become a major player in the rush for energy and raw material resources in the Silk Road region?
- What does Japan's new role in the Silk Road region mean for Japan-EU co-operation?

Providing answers to these five questions gives us also a deeper insight into Japan's self perception as an Asian country with a western political and economic system, highlights the possibilities of influence of a few well-placed high-ranking officials of the Japanese government in the policymaking towards a peripheral area, and contrasts Japan's use of ODA with that of other western countries.

2 Facing a New Strategic Environment

Most of the changes related to the end of the East-West conflict in 1989 occurred in the Euro-Atlantic region while they were much less spectacular in Asia. But the emerging security architecture in Europe and the growing political and economic relationship between western Europe and Russia and the successor states of the former Soviet Union gave Japan a feeling of being left out, raising the fear of losing diplomatic but also economic opportunities and leverage.

The eastward expansion of NATO since 1990 is having a major lasting impact on Japan's strategic environment, notably what concerns its relations with Russia and China, but initially Japan was deprived of any shaping influence on this emerging Eurasian security structure. In addition to membership expansion, NATO established in December 1991 a North Atlantic Co-operation Council (NACC, to become in 1997 the Euro-Atlantic Partnership Council, EAPC) for regular meetings with the former members of the Warsaw Pact. In 1994 NATO established the open Partnership for Peace (PfP) structure. Today all successor states of the Soviet Union are member of the EAPC and almost all are also member of the PfP (except Tajikistan). These structures have become very active in promoting political dialogue at all levels, and are now an essential part of preventive diplomacy and crisis management on the Eurasian continent.

These developments initiated by the western side of the Eurasian continent had several direct and indirect influences on Japan's diplomatic position and options. The initial pro-EU and pro-US thrust of Russian diplomacy, notably under Foreign Minister Andrei Kozyrev, widened the gap between Japan and Russia. While Europe and America – for reasons of geographic proximity and nuclear arms control concerns respectively – tried to support Russia politically and economically to guarantee the safe transition to a peaceful Russia, Japan initially used its political and economic potential as a lever to achieve the return of the Northern Territories from a weakened Russia. But this policy backfired and moreover isolated Japan among its western partners.

While America and the EU were eager to give Russia the benefit of the doubt concerning its transition from an autocratic state with a planned economy to one with democratic structures and an open market economy, the Japanese side, government as well as private sector, were much more skeptical about the chances of Russia's rehabilitation. Japan made it very clear from 1991 onwards that Russia could not expect any economic aid beyond humanitarian aid until it had returned the disputed Kurile islands. It also blocked Russia's admission to the G-7 until 1997.

The impact of NATO's eastward expansion on China also affected Japan. China is opposed to NATO as a military alliance and even more fears that its expansion will further strengthen America and its western allies. After the Gulf War 1991 China had hoped that the world would move towards multipolarity. To countersteer western moves, China and Russia are now moving closer together with implications for their diplomatic position against the Euro-Atlantic eastward expansion as well as for the strength of China's military. Signs for a closer relationship are the frequent summit meetings between the leaders of both countries and the use of the expression of "strategic relationship" since President Boris Yeltsin's April 1994 visit to China. Despite all the limitations of the scope of a Sino-Russian rapprochement and its questionable future, notably in the economic sphere, there are many in Japan who are concerned about NATO's expansion pushing both countries together into an uneasy alliance with negative implications for the Eurasian security environment. Particularly worrying for Japan have been Russian arms sales to China at the rate of about $1 billion per year.

3 Adjusting to the New Realities

The European and American use of the expressions "from Vancouver to Vladivostok" and "Euro-Atlantic Community" convinced Japan at the beginning of the 1990s that it had to become internationally more active and overcome the bottleneck of the territorial conflict with Russia in order to avoid isolation. Japan therefore took several measures to strengthen its links with Europe, change its initially negative attitude towards the CSCE/OSCE, and dilute the western focus on Eastern Europe/Russia by taking initiatives towards Central Asia.

Japan has shown great interest in being more closely associated with European institutions. The Joint Declaration between the European Community and Japan ("The Hague Declaration of July 18th 1991") led to an annual Summit Meeting and established the framework for political dialogue between the European Union and Japan. Since 1996 Japan has observer status in the Council of Europe and in December of the same year Japan acquired the status of Partner for Co-operation (next to South Korea the only Asian country) in the Organization for Security and Co-operation in Europe (OSCE). Japan's economic power facilitated its admission to the OSCE and consequent involvement in the rehabilitation of Eastern Europe, Russia and the SRCs. Japan as the second largest economic power and with its status as the world's top ODA donor was seen as an important partner by the CSCE/OSCE, its role being appreciated by the EU as a *soft-security provider* in the OSCE region (Ueta:387,393).

Greater emphasis on the rehabilitation of the Central Asian republics became a means for Japan's policymakers to countersteer the European and American focus on Russia and Eastern Europe at the expense of other developing countries, particularly those in Asia, where Tokyo's greatest political and economic interests are at stake. Already in 1992 the Japanese press reported statements emanating from the Gaimushô (Ministry of Foreign Affairs) which stressed that although aid to Russia was important, Japan as an Asian nation would prefer to support more the new Asian republics. It was also made clear that focusing on the new Asian republics and on the East Asian part of Russia would provide a better political climate for a return of the disputed Northern Territories (Japan Times October 29th 1992 & October 30th 1992).

Japan extended diplomatic recognition to all SRCs soon after they gained independence. Already in March 1992 the Japanese government began planning aid for these countries. It took the lead in getting the five Central Asian countries (CACs) on the Development Assistance Committee (DAC) list in November 1992 (valid from January 1993), against French and American opposition, in order to legitimize Japanese ODA to these countries (Yasutomo:90).

Japan was also a leader in getting the CACs accepted in international development banks. Today all eight SRCs are member of the World Bank, the International Monetary Fund and the European Bank for Reconstruction and Development (EBRD). In addition, thanks to Japan's efforts, the CACs became also (with the exception of Turkmenistan) member of the Asian Development Bank (ADB) in Manila for which Japan customarily provides the president and the greatest amount of funds. Normally no country can be member in more than one regional bank.

After gaining independence Japan's officials as well as the private sector had high expectations in the SRCs and a great number of delegations went out to visit them (Muto:54). Foreign Minister Watanabe Michio visited as the first Japanese cabinet minister the region (Kazakhstan and Kyrgystan) in May 1992. A high-level delegation from the Ministry of Finance under the leadership of vice minister Chino Tadao went in October 1992 to Uzbekistan, Kyrgystan and Kazakhstan.

4 The Role of Personal Preferences and National Interests

It was the influence of several well-placed individual bureaucrats that in the end galvanized various interests groups to create a consensus for what became in 1997 Japan's Eurasian Diplomacy and resulted in considerable attention to the CACs.

Two high-level bureaucrats soon emerged as the main promoters of Japan's relations with some of the Central Asian countries. One was the diplomat Magosaki Ukeru, who in 1993 became Japan's ambassador to Uzbekistan where he stayed until 1996. He had studied at Harvard University and had become one of the top diplomats of the Ministry of Foreign Affairs. As a Russian speaker with experience at the embassy in Moscow he was able to relate more easily to the Silk Road region and integrate it into a Japanese strategy.

The other bureaucrat was Chino Tadao who as Vice Minister of the Ministry of Finance not only visited the region as early as in May 1992, but who was also involved the G-7 discussion for support to the Commonwealth of Independent States (CIS) members in the same year, meeting many representatives of these new countries.

Chino's fascination with Central Asia and particularly Kyrgystan was certainly helped by the success of the personal chemistry with local leaders and the affinity with an Asian culture, but there were also wider institutional interests. These new republics with their background of Soviet style planned economies were willing to listen to another Asian country which not only came along in a less messianic way than other western countries, but which had proved by its own economic success that an economic development model putting less emphasis on free market principles and allowing a much greater role of the state was very promising. It was the heyday of Japan's economic success and the country had begun a campaign to promote the *Japanese model* with developing countries. This was extended to the Soviet Union and its successor states after former Soviet President Mikhail Gorbachev visited Japan in April 1991. As a result Japan initiated a boom of economic policy-related training programmes (Terry:5-6). The Ministry of Finance as well as other ministries were eager to enhance their clout by joining in the creation of such training programmes.

Direct economic interests in the SRCs played a modest role because it became soon clear that the socio-economic conditions for doing business were not in place yet, and Japanese business has always been known for being rather risk-adverse. Although the SRC cover an area of 4.2 million square kilometres, the total population is only 70 million. Only in the long-term, business viewed the opening of the Eurasian heartland as a new opportunity in terms of markets, new sources for raw materials and fuels. Clearly, the potential of the SRCs for oil and gas and as transit corridors for these energy sources was recognized.

In the first instance, as an enlightened Russianist and strategist, Magosaki realized that Japan had manoevered itself into a *cul de sac* with its policy of using aid as a leverage to gain points in the quest for the return of the Northern Territories from Russia. The Silk Road Diplomacy therefore became a tool to win the old Russian School in the Gaimushô over to a new Russian policy. This paved the way for the summit meeting between Boris Yeltsin and Hashimoto in Krasnojarsk in July 1997 as well as the Kawana agreement in April 1998 which led Japan to take a more long-term perspective towards the solution of its territorial claims (Interview with Professor Yamauchi Masayuki, May 10th 2000).

Another consideration was the importance of the SRCs in relation to the stability of the Middle East. Given the political instabilities in the SRCs countries with their activist Islamic fundamentalists, Japan's policymakers understood very soon that this situation could destabilize the Middle East and thus affect the oil supply from the Middle East and the Gulf area (Internation Herald Tribune December 16th 1992).

The impact of the CACs on China's regional policies could also not fail to impress Japan's policymakers. In the most immediate future, stabilizing the CACs would prevent China from having to use force against its own Muslim minority (notably Uighurs) and against its Central Asian neighbours, thus reducing the need for military strength. In the long run, however, a stabilized Central Asia might provide a *soft containment* of China and help to integrate it into the region while strengthening Japan's hand in the regional competition with China.

Finally, involvement in the SRCs was seen as enhancing Japan's desire to expand the global reach of its diplomacy and to reduce the effects of American unilateralism in the post-Cold War era. After the US-led war against Iraq in 1991 Japan became concerned about a growing American unilateralism in international relations which was nurtured by the disappearance of the Soviet Union, the eastward expansion of NATO, and successful American leadership in the post-Cold War era, particularly in conjunction with Europe. At the same time, being seen as a global actor enhanced Japan's legitimacy to request a permanent UN Security Council seat. Helping the SRC's also was potentially useful in garnering some more votes in favour of this quest.

5 The Cultural Affinity Attraction

In Japan's public discourse, strategic arguments are usually not playing a prominent role because of Japan's pacifist orientation or, in the case of China, negative diplomatic reactions. Direct economic interests were understood as long-term. Instead we find in the discussion of Japan's evolving relationship with the SRCs a strong emphasis on Japan's cultural and racial affinity with these new republics. Japanese visitors to the region could not fail to be taken in by the cultural and racial similarities which was generously exploited by the leadership of the visited countries. The resulting emotional affinity has not only become part of official speeches but is quite genuine and can be found with liberal as well as realist thinkers and policymakers. The 1990s saw a boom in everything related to the Silk Road. For many Japanese their Buddhist origins are to be found here which applies also to many Chinese sites along the Silk Road. The irony is that the Central Asian Silk Road countries today are Islamic and view the Buddhist archaeological remnants more as means to promote their national identity building after the long years as part of the Soviet Union or to gain foreign currency through tourism. Moreover, the *affinity* perspective is rather artificial in view of Japan's much higher living standard, western and democratic orientation and so forth.

In response to this attraction and to help these countries with their nation building, the Japanese government has paid particular importance to cultural diplomacy and is giving considerable cultural grants (Enoki:48-53). In addition to serving as a starter for closer relations with the CACs, the cultural and racial affinity argument catered for the needs of various policy constituencies such as those looking for strengthening Japan's identity as an Asian nation, establishing Japan as a bridge between East and West, or reinforcing Japan's legitimacy as an Asian leader.

The cultural and racial attraction of Central Asia was a very important vehicle in attracting Japanese visitors to Central Asia and to forge very close personal relationships with the political leadership of most of the countries. In the case of Uzbekistan it is Magosaki's strong personal involvement as well as Chino's support which accounts for the fact that the number of Japanese visitors to Uzbekistan (1998: 1,686) is so much above that of Japanese visitors to Kazakhstan (1998: 666) and that most visitors were from the Japanese bureaucracy, notably the Ministry of Finance. (Magosaki:68)

The personal relationships of leading figures like Magosaki and Chino explains also partially Japan's special focus on Uzbekistan and Kyrgystan. The prominent place of Kyrgystan in Japan's Silk Road Diplomacy was supported by Edamura Sumio who was ambassador in Moscow until 1993 and who took a special liking to this Central Asian country. While attention to Uzbekistan may be understandable in view of it having with 24 million the biggest population of all SRCs, personal factors have played an undeniable role, and this has been even more the case with Kyrgystan which has only a population of 4.6 million, few natural resources and is very isolated in terms of trade routes to the outside.

Economically, Uzbekistan has initially done best among all the other countries which in Japanese eyes was due to the strong guidance by the government and its dislike for the structural policies of the World Bank and the IMF as regards foreign exchange policy, privatization and deregulation. Magosaki describes very openly how he and his colleagues agreed with the Uzbeki government's opposition to the IMF's alleged attitude that transition to a free market economy had even to be done at the sacrifice of social stability. (Magosaki:68)

While Japan has become Uzbekistan's most important bilateral ODA provider, it does not rank among Uzbekistan's top three trading partners. In terms of Foreign Direct Investment Japan ranks 5th after Britain, Malaysia, Turkey and America with a share of 9.7 per cent. But since most of the ODA is distributed by the Ministry of Foreign Affairs and the Ministry of Finance, individuals like Magosaki and Chino could sustain Uzbekistan's high ODA ranking.

The element of personal preference is also obvious in the case of Kyrgystan. Thanks to Chino's personal links to Kyrgystan (he visited first in 1992) and the role of Japanese economists like Professor Kaneda Tatsuo (he was the President's advisor for four years), Kyrgystan has been shown much greater attention than its size, political or economic weight would warrant. In this case its much greater adherence to IMF policies did not hurt. While Japan is Kyrgystan's biggest individual ODA donor since 1994 when it overtook America, Japan ranks very low in terms of trade and investment.

6 The Launch of the Eurasian Diplomacy in 1997

It took until summer 1997 before small steps and individual efforts to come to terms with the changes on the Eurasian continent were integrated into an official policy. This happened under the administration of Prime Minister Hashimoto Ryutaro who had become prime minister in January 1996. Having put Japanese-American security relations on a new footing after the disappearance of the Soviet threat, Hashimoto moved on to adapt Japan's Russia policy correspondingly. In a speech on July 24th 1997 to the Keizai Doyukai (Japan Committee on Economic Development), he explained his new policy towards Russia and the whole Eurasian continent. This speech can be considered as the first conceptualization of Japan's Eurasian Diplomacy and its subsidiary policy, the Silk Road Diplomacy.

The background of most of the policymakers involved in drafting the speech indicates the centrality of Japan's relations with Russia to which the largest part of the speech is devoted. The developments on the Eurasian strategic chessboard had by 1997 highlighted the need for a new Russia policy which would not further erode Japan's leverage to advance its quest for a solution of the Northern Territories and drive Russia into the arms of China. The negative impact of NATO's Eastward expansion was strengthened by American policies towards Central Asia: in September 1997, America flew 500 soldiers more than 12,000 km from Fort Brag to Uzbekistan to a parachute drop over Uzbekistan as part of the Centrazbat 97 manouevers. The exercise was expanded in 1998 and was to be repeated in September 2000. Turkey took also part in 1997 and 1998. Although this was a US-sponsored event, it was reported in the Chinese and Russian press as a NATO operation (Bhatty & Bronson:132-135). In 1999 Central Asia was included in the area of responsibiltiy of the Central Command of the US armed forces. NATO secretary-general C. Solana as well as the permanent American representative to NATO, R. Hunter, visited Central Asia in 1997, and the new NATO secretary-general Robertson did so in July 2000.

Moreover, the weight of China on the Eurasian continent had further increased. It was expanding its relationship with Iran for economic and political reasons (Iranian energy exports to China, Chinese arms exports to Iran) which has negative implications for regional stability, the global control of weapons of mass destruction and their delivery vehicles, and for Iran-America relations. It became an active commercial actor in Central Asia that is co-operating notably with Kazakhstan in exploring and exporting oil and gas.

The first part of Hashimoto's speech reflects therefore concern about Japan's relative sidelining on the Eurasian continent and the narrowing of its options in the new post-Cold War world. Hashimoto proposed to contrast the new security order developing from the Atlantic Ocean across Europe to Russia, reaching even the Pacific Ocean, with a Eurasian diplomacy "viewed from the Pacific Ocean", and spanning Russia, China and the Silk Road countries.

Addressing relations with Russia and the solution of the territorial issue, Hashimoto proposed having the bilateral relationship guided by the principles of trust, mutual benefit and a long-term perspective. To attract Russian interest, he made detailed proposals for economic co-operation. Since this speech, Japan's new Russia policy has basically consisted of providing Russia more material and political incentives in the hope of getting more Russian flexibility on the territorial issue, while Japan would accept a step-by-step solution. Japan started to give more economic support to Russia and supported Russia's admission into the Asia Pacific Economic Co-operation (APEC) in 1998. Politically, meetings between Prime Minister Hashimoto and President Yeltsin increased. As a result Russia considers Japan part of its plan to create a multi-polar world without dominant centres of power. (Panov:28) It is this part of the Eurasian Diplomacy which has been implemented most thoroughly, and which was sustained by Hashimoto's successors.

Only in the third part of his speech, after touching Japanese-Chinese relations and mentioning in particular co-operation in the environmental and energy sector, did

Hashimoto briefly deal with the SRCs and his new Silk Road Diplomacy as part of his Eurasian Diplomacy. He proposed to develop relations with the region into three directions:

- promotion of political dialogue to deepen mutual trust and understanding,
- co-operation for economic growth and for natural resources development and
- political co-operation to secure peace and stability through nuclear non-proliferation, democratization and the fostering of stability.

In order to give substance to the SRD, the government proposed an Action Plan to promote the exchange of high level official visits, to open further Japanese embassies in the Silk Road region and to refocus ODA to meet Japan's strategic goals.

In 1997, two major Japanese delegations had already gone to the region, one headed by House of Representatives member Obuchi Keizo, followed by a visit of Director-General Aso Taro of the Economic Planning Agency. After Hashimoto's speech, the first state leader visiting Tokyo was in February 1998 Azerbaijani President Geidar Aliyev, followed by the visit of President Askar Akaev of Kyrgyzstan in October 1998, Georgian President Shevardnadze in March 1999, Uzbekistan Prime Minister Utkir Sultanov in March 1999, and Kazakh President Narzabaev in December 1999.

However, Japan failed to make any progress on raising its diplomatic profile in the SRCs beyond the embassies in Tashkent and Alma Maty (followed in May 2000 by an embassy in Baku). In comparison to Japan's three embassies in the Silk Road region, Britain has embassies in all SRCs, except Kyrgystan and Tajikistan. Germany has embassies in all countries except Tajikistan. The reason for Japan's lack of diplomatic representations are mostly structural: Since the government is very strict about expanding its bureaucracy in order to cope with the budgetary deficit, the Gaimushô has to make cuts in order to create new posts.

7 Japan's Use of ODA

By far the most sustained efforts in implementing Hashimoto's Silk Road Diplomacy have been made in the achievement of the goal of extending ODA which has eventually become the main pillar of Japan's SRD. ODA as a policy tool does not exist for Russia since Japan does not give any bilateral ODA to that country. Japan's economic incentives towards Russia are un-tied loans ($1.5 billion by Japan's Ex-Im Bank, together with the World Bank) and humanitarian aid.

Japan's "Medium-Term Policy on ODA 1999" speaks of the SRCs' geopolitical significance and the importance of access to their energy resources. Japan's ODA is therefore to "aim at support for establishing a foundation for self-reliant economic development, support the process of democratization and transition to market economies, and alleviate social problems and dealing with the negative legacy of the Soviet past" (Ministry of Foreign Affairs 2000a).

On a cumulative basis, the most important donors to the SRCs have been the individual EU member states, America and Japan (see table 1). In 1997, Japan's total ODA to all eight SRCs was $157.0 million, that of America $116.0 million and of the individual EU member states $102.7 million (Ministry of Foreign Affairs 2000b: 288-294). This was a rather strong increase of Japanese ODA to the SRCs from only $2.57 million in 1993.

A special feature of Japan's bilateral aid to Uzbekistan, Kyrgystan and Kazakhstan is the very high share of yen loans which was 85.6% in 1998 (see table 2). This compares with a global average of only 42.5% in Japan's ODA. In contrast to Japan, the largest portion of the EU's aid to the SRCs is technical aid. Japan's share of technical aid is very low with 6.5%, compared with Japan's global average of 32.3%. The top recipients of technical aid were Uzbekistan, Kazakhstan and Kyrgystan which received about equal shares. One reason for the high share of yen loans is Japan's support for transport and communication infrastructure. Another reason for the low amount of technical aid is Japan's focus on receiving trainees from these countries as the main part of Japan's technical aid, rather than sending experts. Preventing more technical aid from Japan is also the fact that these countries are using Russian which does not help with Japan's policy of aid on request.

Table 1: Top Five ODA Donors to Silk Road Countries (in Million Dollars)

Country	Donors				
	1	2	3	4	5
Kazakhstan					
1995	FRG (11)	USA (8)	Japan	UK	France
1996	USA (63)	FRG (13)	Japan	UK	France
1997	Japan (43)	USA (37)	Germany	UK	France
Kyrgystan					
1995	Japan (46)	USA (19)	FRG	CH	NL
1996	Japan (44)	USA (28)	FRG	NL	Denmark
1997	Japan (18)	FRG (9)	CH	USA	Denmark
Tajikistan					
1995	USA (18)	NL (9)	FRG	UK	Sweden
1996	USA (21)	UK (8)	FRG	NL	Finland
1997	USA (13)	NL (6)	CH	FRG	UK
Turkmenist.					
1995	USA (16)	Japan (1)	FRG	UK	Sweden
1996	USA (12)	Japan (1)	UK	France	FRG
1997	Japan (1)	UK (1)	FRG	France	Finland
Uzbekistan					
1995	FRG (47)	Japan (16)	USA	France	UK
1996	FRG (30)	Japan (25)	USA	France	UK
1997	Japan (83)	FRG (21)	USA	France	Italy
Armenia					
1995	USA (60)	NL (13)	FRG	Italy	Sweden
1996	USA (88)	NL (8)	FRG	France	Sweden
1997	USA (22)	NL (5)	France	Japan	FRG
Azerbaijan					
1995	USA (11)	FRG (6)	NL	CH	UK
1996	USA (9)	NL (4)	FRG	UK	Sweden
1997	FRG (4)	Japan (3)	Norway	USA	UK
Georgia					
1995	USA (52)	FRG (10)	NL	UK	Norway
1996	USA (55)	FRG (34)	NL	Italy	UK
1997	USA (32)	FRG (15)	NL	Japan	CH

Source: Ministry of Foreign Affairs (2000), *ODA Annual Report 1999*, Tokyo.

Table 2: Japan's ODA Disbursements to the Silk Raod Countries 1994-1998 (in Million Dollars)

Country	Loan Aid (net)	Grant Aid	Technical Aid
Kazakhstan	109.1	8.4	33.7
Kyrgystan	115.4	38.8	26.4
Tajikistan	–	0.2	1.4
Turkmenistan	–	4.3	2.4
Uzbekistan	154.3	49.5	27
Armenia	–	8.8	1.2
Azerbaijan	0	5.3	1.4
Georgia	–	8	1.2

Source: Ministry of Foreign Affairs (2000), *ODA Annual Report 1999*, Tokyo.

8 Japan's Economic Involvement in the SRCs

In contrast to the ODA picture, Japan's private economic sector's involvement in the SRCs has been very slow to take shape. Since 1997, trade and investment between Japan and the SRCs has not shown any remarkable development, particularly if viewed in comparison with other G-7 countries and South Korea. In Kazakhstan Japan ranked at the end of 1998 6th (in cumulative terms) after Indonesia, but was in 1998 the second highest investor with $227 million, after America with $397 million (Kazakhstan 1999: 14-15) In Uzbekistan Japan was in 1997 the 5th largest investor. In Georgia Japan was in 1998 9th largest investor, led by Sumitomo (Georgia 1999:13).

Trade between the SRCs and Japan is also very low. According to the Japan Export Trade Organization (JETRO) in 1999 trade between Japan and the five Central Asian countries amounted to a total of $331.5 million. Trade with the three South Caucasian republics totaled $44.9 million in 1999, up from $30 million dollars the previous year. In 1998 the total share of the eight countries in Japan's total exports was 0.04%, and in Japan's imports 0.06%. The most important trade partner in 1999 was Kazakhstan, followed by Uzbekistan and Azerbaijan. (See table 3)

Table 3: Japanese Trade with the Silk Road Countries (in Million Dollars)

Country	1997		1998		1999	
	Export	Import	Export	Import	Export	Import
Kazakhstan	331.2	196	52	119	57	85
Kyrgystan	2.4	1.2	1.1	0.5	6.5	0.6
Tajikistan	1.8	1.2	5.6	0.1	3.1	0.1
Turkmenistan	3.8	3	7.6	0	14.7	0.3
Uzbekistan	55.6	36.1	66.5	41	83.5	33
Armenia	0.3	0.1	1.8	5.7	1.1	0.7
Azerbaijan	20	2.3	18	0.2	34.6	0.1
Georgia	1.6	1.1	3.2	0.6	6.8	1.5

Source: Japan Export Trade Organization, Tokyo.

The low level of investment and trade between the SRCs and Japan is not only due to the difficult economic conditions of these countries, but is also related to Japanese business practice of avoiding risk, particularly at a time of an economic slump at home which has reduced funding available for investment.

Judging from Japan's investment in Kazkhstan and Azerbaijan, it is evident that Japan's long-term economic interest is the oil and gas potential of the Silk Road region. Next to the region's geopolitical importance, it is this interest which is mentioned in official Japanese statements when referring to the rationale of the SRD. There are considerable oil and gas resources mainly in the Caspian Sea Basin which includes Kazakhstan, Azerbaijan and Turkmenistan. Even those SRCs which don't have these resources play an important role as potential transit corridors for transporting the oil and gas, either via road or pipeline. Japan has a continuing interest in diversifying its energy supply and reducing its dependence on the Gulf and the Middle East.

The gas reserves of the region are also of great interest to Japan because of its shift to natural gas as a source of primary energy for environmental and economic reasons. In 1973, Japan's reliance on natural gas for primary energy was only 1.5% but since then it had increased by 1999 to 11.4%. In order to develop these energy resources on the Eurasian continent substantial Japanese investment in exploration, development and transport would be necessary.

However, the Caspian Sea is at the centre of international interest for new oil and gas production with Japanese companies having only very limited stakes in the ongoing exploration and development of these new energy sources. Apart from the reasons mentioned before in the context of Japan's low trade and investment in the SRCs in general, the risks of exploiting oil and gas resources are especially high because of the ownership problems among Russia, Azerbaijan, Kazakhstan and Turkmenistan.

Yet, the biggest problem for the export of oil and gas from the SRCs remains the lack of transport and the great distances to the major markets. Russia still has a strong grip on the export networks of all energy producing SRCs and naturally favours the products of its own oil and gas fields. Moreover, the transport capacity of its pipeline system is limited. However, apart from practical problems, consumers in Europe and East Asia want to diversify their supply sources and often prefer SRCs where they could gain greater influence due to their economic and technological advance.

9 The Japanese-European Dimension

Japan and Europe basically share an interest in the stability and successful transition of the former Soviet republics to prosperity and democracy and both value the contribution of the other for this goal. With the next enlargement of the EU, the Union will share borders with Ukraine, Belarus and Moldova. It thus has a strong interest in stabilizing these new border regions in addition to helping Russia to become a responsible political and economic power.

As a result of this shared interest, Japan-EU co-operation has developed in several – although very limited – sectors. We have already mentioned the growing political co-operation and consultation within the OSCE and other fora. In the field of ODA, one has to mention the European Bank for Reconstruction and Development (EBRD). Japan is a founding member of this 1991 established bank in which it has a share of 8.5%, equivalent to that of Britain, Germany, France and Italy (America: 10%). Through the Japan-Europe Co-operation Fund (JECF) of the EBRD, it contributed 124 million euro to the Bank's Technical Co-operation Funds Programme (TCFP) on an untied basis. Although the JECF initially reached all of the 26 countries belonging to the EBRD's operations, the fund has increasingly focused on projects in Central Asia.

Apart from the EBRD framework, there is otherwise little co-operation in the field of development between Japan and the EU. However, in view of the many political and economic issues involved in helping the development of the SRCs, more co-operation will have to be undertaken between the EU and Japan since neither on their own can succeed.

One shared interest of Japan and EU is a better transport infrastructure spanning the Eurasian continent. In 1993 the EU established TRACECA (Transport Corridor Europe-Caucasus-Asia). TRACECA's basic aim is to improve rail transport links to the West (although it was extended to include Mongolia), in particular through the Caucasian corridor, and it therefore may be of less interest to the Japanese government. But although there is no coordination, Japanese support for infrastructure projects in Georgia (port of Poti) and in Uzbekistan and Kazakhstan (rolling stock for rail transport) ultimately helps TRACECA. Other Japanese assistance to the infrastructure of the SRCs is given in the forms of financing by the Japanese government and private sector investment. Moreover, Japan is indirectly extending help to improve the transport infrastructure of the SRCs through its membership in the EBRD which provides loans to the region.

In order to facilitate private sector activities in the exploitation and transport of oil and gas, better governance and institution building is required in the SRCs. One way to address these problems is the EU-initiated 1994 Energy Charter Treaty. It attempts to create a better political, economic and legal framework for the planned energy projects involving the Eurasian countries. Japan signed the Treaty on 16 June 1995 but has not yet ratified it. It seems that Japan is still waiting for the ratification of the Treaty by Russia, and business does not seem to be very enthusiastic.

10 Conclusions

Japan's Eurasian Diplomacy seemed to have gone off to a good start in 1997. Japanese-Russian relations improved considerably but without the return of the Northern Territories to Japan having come any closer.

Looking at the genesis of the Eurasian Diplomacy and particularly the SRD, we have seen the crucial role played by a few high ranking bureaucrats from the Ministry of Foreign Affairs and the Ministry of Finance. This strong personal involvement and the invocation of cultural-racial affinities not only explain the relatively high attention to a rather peripheral region and the favouring of certain SRCs, but also the prominence of Japan's ODA as the main sustaining pillar of the SRD in the absence of any substantial business commitment.

A close examination of the private sector involvement in the SRCs has clearly shown that while there may be interest, this does not lead to any substantial trade or investment. Trade and investment is focusing on the countries with energy sources, supported by targeted ODA projects. However, there are no conspicuous projects like South Korea's Daewoo automobile assembly in Uzbekistan or Canada's gold mining investment in Kyrgystan. Even in Azerbaijan, Japanese involvement in exploration and development of energy sources is marginal, overshadowed by many other countries with smaller national economies. While all foreign countries suffer from the political and economic shortcomings of the

SRCs, Japan's private sector is also hampered by its economic crisis at home which further reduces its already low readiness to take risks.

While at least for the moment Japan's ODA programme is expanding, the political pillar of the SRD is weakening. Japanese visits to SRCs have declined although the region's heads of states still like to visit Japan. Official references to the Eurasian Diplomacy and the Silk Road Diplomacy have almost disappeared. The killing of a Japanese professor during an UN mission in Tajikistan in 1998 and the abduction of Japanese geologists in the Kyrgystan/Tajikistan border area in 1999 have further cooled Japan's enthusiasm, exposing the vulnerability of a diplomacy relying so much on personal and emotional foundations. The focus of Japanese attention has now shifted to some extent to Azerbaijan and the Caspian Sea because of the increasing international competition for oil and gas there, the heavy American involvement aiming at excluding Russia and Iran as transport corridors, and the regional importance of the adjacent Middle East. But Japan's economic and political role will be only marginal since no one wants to get involved in the great disputes which surround the planning of energy transport routes.

Against this background, it would appear that closer political and economic coordination and co-operation with Europe could help Japan in balancing its political and economic interests on the Eurasian continent.

At present, Japan is wary of hurting its relations with Russia because of its territorial demands and the fear of a closer Russian-Chinese relationship. This is demonstrated by Japan's abstention from criticizing Russia's military policies in Chechnya and its unfettered open credit lines to Russia in contrast to the EU and America. Japan therefore will only be a reluctant partner in economic projects which may be seen by Russia as inimical to its economic and political interests, such as the routing of transport infrastructure away from Russia. The question is how the Japanese government will react when it has to face the reality that its political and economic concessions to Russia have failed in bringing the country any further to a solution of the territorial dispute.

Japan-EU co-operation on ODA is complicated by differences in aid strategies (e.g. the role of the state, emphasis on structural adjustment), the sheer complexities of the EU aid bureaucracy and by the EU's political aims. The EU is much more than Japan involved in helping the SRCs with the establishment of political and governmental institutions, writing laws, and similar governance issues. The EU has inserted political and human rights conditionalities into the Partnership and Co-operation Agreements signed with the successor states of the former Soviet Union (McFarlane:12).

In contrast, Japan has fewer inhibitions in working together with authoritarian regimes than the EU and America because it considers the role of economic rehabilitation more instrumental to stability than the emphasis on human rights and democracy. As a result, some CACs politically use Japan in times when there has been yet again a negative statement by the EU on human rights.

As a result Japan's role in the Silk Road region is most conspicuous as a development aid provider that makes an important contribution to the stabilization of the SRCs, but hardly as a political or economic competitor or facilitator. While there may be opportunities for Japanese-European co-operation in the SRCs, different interests, structures and aid philosophies severely limit them.

References

Bhatty, R. & Bronson, R. (2000), NATO's Mixed Signals in the Caucasus and Central Asia, in: *Survival* 42,3: 129-145.

Enoki, Y. (2000), Hito wa Pan Nomi ni Ikiru ni Orazu [Man Cannot Live on Bread Alone], in: *Gaikô Forum* 140: 48-53.

Georgia (1999), *Country Profile*, prepared for Business Forum London April 1999.

Kazakhstan (1999), *Country Profile*, prepared for Business Forum London April 1999.

Magosaki, U. (1995), Gaikôryoku Kyôka ni Mazu Nihon no Kankeisha to no Kyôryoku Kankei [The Key to a Stronger Japanese Diplomacy: Closer Ties with Non- Diplomatic Circles], in: *Gaikô Forum* 83: 66-73.

McFarlane, N. (1999), *Central Asian and Caucasian Prospects: Western Engagement in the Caucasus and Central Asia*, London: Royal Institute of International Affairs.

Ministry of Foreign Affairs (2000a), *Japan's Medium-Term Policy on ODA 1999*, Tokyo: MOFA.

Ministry of Foreign Affairs (2000b), *ODA Annual Report 1999*, Tokyo: MOFA.

Muto, K. (1995), Ima Hatasu-beki Nihon no Keizai teki Yakuwari [Japan's Economic Role] *Gaikô Forum* 83: 46-55.

Panov, A. N. (1999), Russia and Japan at a New Stage of Relations, in: *Asia-Pacific Review* 124: 25-34.

Terry, E. (1995), *How Asia Got Rich: World Bank vs. Japanese Industrial Policy*, Japan Policy Research Institute Working Paper no. 10.

Ueta, T. (1998), Japan and the OSCE, in: *OSCE Yearbook 1997*, Baden-Baden: Nomos Verlagsgesellschaft: 387-395.

Yasutomo, D. T. (1995), *The New Multilateralism in Japan's Foreign Policy*, Houndmills: Macmillan.

New Networks of Foreign Aid: Cross National Comparisons of Multilateral Development Assistance

Paul Kevenhörster

1 Introduction: The Role of Multilateral Development Assistance

The theory of international regimes integrates national and international levels of politics into a new perspective of international *co-operation (*Haggard & Simmons 1987). By a process of integration, international organizations formulate and strengthen an institutional policy. The international system can be characterized by one trend towards *diversification* and another one towards *globalization.* In order to cope with these trends, the international management of globalization and interdependence requires effective international organizations and stable networks of multilateral co-operation.

Global problems are confronting national political actors with increasing requirements of policy coordination: environmental pollution, migration, crime and drugs, to name the most important issues. Because the donors of bilateral development aid cannot cope with these problems effectively within the traditional framework of bilateral technical and financial assistance for various reasons (i.e. insufficient infrastructure, budget restrictions, economic and foreign policy constraints), networks of multilateral co-operation have become increasingly important. Therefore donor countries have to ask themselves whether multilateral development assistance makes sense and how effectively the international institutions of multilateral aid actually operate. This question is quite sensitive as the multilateral institutions have come, for various reasons, under close scrutiny by politicians, journalists and development experts. Among many bureaucrats and politicians "multilateralism" has been rather unpopular for a long time because it is much more difficult for national development administrations to implement their policy preferences in the complex structure of international organizations. The role of multilateral development aid must, therefore, be discussed within the domestic and international policy framework (Inoguchi 1991:103-124).

The role of multilateral development assistance can be interpreted by three hypotheses:

1) Multilateral development assistance supports a foreign policy of interdependence.
2) Multilateral development policy is a result of complex structures of interest aggregation, by which government respond to internal and external pressures.
3) In a world of multilateralism traditional patron-client relationships will play, in the long term, a less important role for development assistance.

To what extent do contributions to networks of multilateral aid in fact correspond with the prevailing philosophy of development strategy on one side (i.e. basic human needs promotion, self-help-promotion, human development) and internal and external pressure, based on economic interests, strategic considerations and national foreign policy imperatives on the other? To answer this question, an assessment of the structure and profile of multilateral development assistance is necessary.

Multilateral development assistance offers several *comparative advantages* to the prevailing patterns of bilateral aid: a global scope of development co-operation, higher degree of coordination and integration into development strategies, better access to know-how, better presence *sur place* and, finally, a stronger dedication to genuine development oriented policy goals as compared with foreign economic and strategic interests (Klingebiel 1993:25). There are issues that multilateral agencies can handle more effectively than individual donors, because available resources are much greater, and multilateral agencies can draw in contributions and know-how from the full range of members (Chalker 1990:355).

2 The New Global Context

In 1995, disbursements of Official Development Assistance (ODA) decreased by 9 per cent in comparison with 1994; the American ODA fell by more than a quarter, Italian ODA by over a half, and also French ODA underwent significant reductions (OECD 1997:63). During the last years, bilateral disbursements have contracted more sharply than multilateral disbursements, not due to a shift in favor of multilateral aid but to the timing of DAC members' financial contributions to multilateral development institutions. It is an effect of the replenishment cycles for these institutions that pressures on the total volume of development aid have a much stronger impact on bilateral programs on a year-to-year basis. The rapid expansion of European commission programs since 1990 has considerably affected the bilateral budgets of several members of the EU. For that reason, multi-year commitments are becoming increasingly unpopular (OECD 1997:71). Consequently, the share of the World Bank and the United Nations in total ODA has been falling while the EU's has expanded. The regional development banks' share has been relatively stable.

For multilateral development institutions strong pressures for change come from three directions (OECD 1997:107):

1) the need to re-examine the overall role of public sector multilateral institutions in global development financing,
2) extensive reviews of the achievements of these institutions and
3) a general tightening of ODA budgets of all members of the Development Assitance Committee (DAC) by limiting the number of partnership countries and narrowing the scope of their development co-operation activities.

These tendencies have recently been demonstrated by the 11th replenishment of the International Development Association (IDA) and the 7th replenishment of the African Development Fund. Multilateral development assistance still counts for about one third of all ODA mainly provided by OECD-members via the World Bank, UN-organizations, regional development banks and the EU. The European multilateral development assistance is, however, blamed by its critics, as a sort of "collective bilateralism" (Nuscheler 1995:459), due to the real existing structure and priorities of its financial flows and technical aid.

Perspectives and priorities of the Bretton Woods institutions and the OECD donor community are very much shaped by the G7-World Summits in general, the G5 (USA, Japan, France, Britain, and Germany) and the G3 (USA, Japan, Germany) in particular. These groups are usually preparing an informal foreign economic and development policy consensus on the basis of G7 and World Bank meetings. Such informal networks of co-operation between the leading donors are the more important, the greater the number of UN-organizations in charge of a large multitude of development policy aspects is (at present about 50 organizations).

How important and influential these networks are, can be seen in the case of the United Nations Development Plan (UNDP) and the United Nations Conference on Trade and Development (UNCTAD). While the UNDP strictly followed the course of broad and solid consensus building among its members, thus effectively integrating the OECD-members in charge of about 90% of the resources, and by this approach could stabilize its position within the United Nations, UNCTAD followed the rule of majority-decisions giving OECD-members lesser weight and, in addition, destabilizing its own existence. The actual financial weight of OECD-members corresponds to a much higher degree with the World Bank structure and to lesser degree with majorities of UN institutions. At the same time, the World Bank also exerts a tremendous influence on perceptions and perspectives of the development policy-orientations in all donor and recipient countries by its strategic guidelines and its policy papers.

The institutions of multilateral development assistance suffer, at present, from large budget deficits. In march 1997 America owed the United Nations $1.2 billion (three quarters of what is owed on the regular budget): $40 million to the World Health Organization, $95 million to the Food and Agriculture Organization and $200 million to the International Development Association (Mathews 1997:8). Being already $160 million behind the Global Environment Facility, the American Government owes, in addition, $200 million in pledges to each of the Asian and Latin American development banks and $66 million to the African development bank. In the long term, this does not only mean a loss of influence but also a shifting, more complex structure of influence exercised by the big donors on the system of multilateral institutions, which depend on observed obligations, i.e. paying assessed dues according to international agreement and not by unilateral decisions. Therefore, in accordance with a recommendation by the United Nations Association, it has already been suggested that dues should be owed quarterly, and interests should be charged on overdue bills.

3 The Role of Multilateral Institutions

To the ODA regime multilateral institutions have become increasingly central: multilateral aid very often meets recipients need more effectively than bilateral aid which is regularly more "political" and more directed to donor self-interests (Hook 1996:24).The international ODA regime is based on some mechanisms for the formulation, negotiation, and implementation of norms and principles. The dominant role of OECD's DAC has been, however, more successfully illustrated by establishing target norms (e.g. 0.7% of GNP for ODA) than by guaranteeing compliance with them. Even its annual reviews of individual donor policies and ministerial meeting have proven to be unable to induce such a compliance.

During the last years, the flow of private capital to developing countries has considerably increased ($173 billion in 1994), but 80% of this flow is concentrated on just ten countries. Therefore, most developing countries do depend on multilateral finance institutions, especially on multilateral development banks (MDB). In these five banks, almost all developed nations are represented, each of the developing countries generally at least in two of these finance institutions. This system is, for are foreseeable future, indispensable. On the other side, regional development banks are currently coming under stronger pressure to reassess their performance and to adapt their organizational structure to new requirements of aid effectiveness (Wapenhans 1996:185).

After the end of the Cold War an increased emphasis on multilateral aid programs of European donors has been, to a large extent, supported by a growing recognition of transnational interdependence (Hook 1996:98). The "collective bilateralism" of the European development assistance can be seen by the incorporation of important elements of French colonial philosophy of "associationism" into the Treaty of Rome (against Dutch and German objections), thus integrating twenty-two former colonies of Belgium, France, and Italy into an European free trade area. In 1973, when Britain joined the European Community, its former colonies, forty-six African, Caribean and Pacific countries were associated within the framework of the Generalized System of Preferences.

From the very beginning, this "European associationism" has been a defensive strategy in order to avoid the negative effects of de-colonization (on the supply of industrial raw materials) and to retain political influence. The institutional arrangements between donors and recipients of European development assistance are administered in accordance with the principle of parity. European aid remain relatively free of explicit commercial ties (Hook 1996:100). In the 1990's members of the EU as Britain, the Netherlands, and Germany insist on explicit conditions being attached to aid commitments in close coordination with the World Bank and the IMF in order to implement the concept of *sustainable development.*

Within the wide scope of multilateral development institutions the World Bank has strengthened its position, being the most influential development institution while the UN-organizations suffer from lacks of coordination and identification on the side of big donor countries. As markets become increasingly globalized, the World Bank concentrates its efforts on building a strategic framework pursuing the following objectives:

1) help borrowers to create a capacity within their national administrations to identify critical needs for technical co-operation,
2) create a capacity to administer, monitor, and evaluate technical co-operation and
3) familiarize recipients with various sources of technical co-operation (Raphaeli 1996:235).

4 Policy of Leading Donors

An increasing number of demands for ODA in its various forms is directed, at present, to Japan as the leading economic power in Asia and to Germany as an economically strong member of the EU (Gaimushô 1994:54). At the same time both countries are asked by their partners, especially by America, to adopt a more active foreign policy within the international framework of United Nations, OECD, NATO, and APEC. However, it is still doubtful whether both countries can fulfill these rising expectations as "Global Civilian Powers", thus concentrating their efforts of increased international co-operation on foreign economic policy, development assistance and cultural exchange while evading requests for a broader participation in the military sphere of integrated *Peace Keeping Operations.*

In the fiscal year 1995 Japan contributed $150 million to UNDP, $121 million to the United Nations High Commissioner for Refugees (UNHCR), and $71 million to the United Nations Population Fund (UNFPA). In the first two cases Japan has been, besides the U.S., the second largest contributor, in the case of UNFPA the largest contributor in the world. In spite of considerable decrease of ODA in 1996 (24% compared with the previous year), Japan kept its position as leading donor country, still following its five-year ODA plan from 1993[1]. In the past, the government even increased the ODA budget when it has been freezing other budget items (Nikkei Weekly, April 14th 1997:1).

As far as the IMF is concerned, Japans and Germany's shares (5.65%) are the second greatest following the USA (18.9 %). Similar is the ranking of capital shares in the World Bank: USA 17.9%, Japan 7.43%, Germany 5.74%, Britain 5.5% (Ôkurashô 1995). The corresponding shares in the IDA are 25.9% (USA), 21% (Japan), 11.97% (Germany) and 8.4% (Great Britain). In the meantime Japan has also joined the European Bank for Reconstruction and Development (EBRD) at the same rank (8.5%) with Germany, Great Britain, France, and Italy. In addition, Japan finances a "Co-operation Fund Japan-Europe", even if the Japanese government hesitates to get involved in Eastern Europe and Russia on a broader scale.

By expanding its development assistance and by extending its international commitments Japan intends to keep the spending of its ODA in close connection with its foreign investments and to implement a balanced and integrated system of bi- and multilateral aid (Gaimushô 1994:201), a perspective also basically shared by the German government. Both governments want to use respective strengths of bilateral and multilateral aid and maintain a balance between the two types of development assistance. Through an interactive linkage of bilateral and multilateral aid they plan to make development co-operation more effective by broader and more intensive co-operation between donor countries and multilateral organizations (Ministry of Foreign Affairs, Japan 1996:151).

Also on the country level (Bhutan, Myanmar, Kiribati, Nepal, Cambodia, Vietnam) exists a rapidly growing partnership between Japan and the UNDP, the United Nations' largest provider of grant funding for development and the main institution for coordinating UN-development assistance (UNDP 1997). With Japan being a leading contributor to the UNDP, Japan and the UNDP are closely associated at the level of multilateral policy. Referred to as *multi-bi co-operation*, this approach combines bilateral and multilateral assistance to the advantage of recipient countries, because coordination of aid is an important precondition for its effectiveness. Therefore, *multi-bi co-operation* is not only an effective instrument of aid coordination, but also a method of increasing influence of leading bilateral

---

1 In the budget year 1996/97 Japans multilateral development assistance increased by 6% compared with the previous year (contributions to UN organizations by 6.3%, contributions to international finance organizations by 5.5%) (Gaimushô 1996:49).

donors on institutions of multilateral development assistance. Functioning not only as a way of cost-sharing and parallel financing *multi-bi arrangements* between Japan and UNDP can make an important contribution to a dynamic development process and to systematic and institutional change by combining UNDP's capacity and know-how with Japan's financial and technical strengths as a leading donor. Japanese experts in addition, favor an even stronger coordination of bilateral development assistance by the UNDP, an approach, in spite of DAC-recommendations not very much supported by other bilateral donors.

The official development assistance of leading donor countries is undergoing major transitions, which will have far reaching impacts on the global network of development co-operation (OECD 1996:7). ODA has become an important instrument of their foreign policy, especially their commitment among the members of the DAC. While Germany has formulated a concept of policy dialogue in the early 1980s, Japan, too, is expanding its "software" type aid in human resources development and institution building. In line with this trend, both governments have begun to play more than before an active role in several areas of international policy coordination (OECD 1996:10), as it can be seen in the case of the Tokyo International Conference on African Development, the Mongolian Assistance Group Meeting, the International Committee on Rehabilitation and Reconstruction of Cambodia, and the Comprehensive Forum on Indochina. Furthermore, Japan and Germany advocate increased South-South-co-operation in order to transform North-South confrontations of the past into constructive partnerships.

In the donor community the share of ODA for multilateral aid is slightly decreasing. While DAC-members in the first half of the 1980s spent about one third of their Official Development Assistance for multilateral aid, in the first half of the 1990s the percentage of bilateral aid increased at the expense of multilateral assistance (71.5% to 28.5%). Comparing the percentage of multilateral development assistance and the flow of total aid to low-income countries, among all main donors, Japan's position is almost the same as the position of Germany and America and not too distant from France, Australia, Switzerland and Austria (see figure 1). Besides Britain, only small donors like Denmark, Ireland, Belgium, Finland and Norway are spending a relatively high share for multilateral aid, while Japan and especially America and France are largely concentrating their development assistance on bilateral aid in particular regions of political and economic interest (Japan: Asia, Pacific; USA: Latin America, Middle East, Africa; France: francophone Africa). Even if the share of Japanese multilateral aid slightly increased since 1990 from 22.8% to 28.8% in 1993 (Gaimushô 1994:196), in the case of Germany's development aid a continuing decrease from a rather high level of 34% is expected in the coming years.

If one assesses this tendency by the criteria of *sustainability* and *effectiveness*, one has to take into account that just 20.4% of bilateral aid of all donors, but 41% of all multilateral aid is spent for development projects and programs in Least

Developed Countries (LLDCs). In the case of Japan only 14.7% of bilateral aids is flowing to LLDCs (Gaimushô 1994:120). This means that as far as genuine criteria of basic needs of development policy are concerned, multilateral aid is reaching the poorest countries to a higher degree than bilateral aid. For the improvement of basic human needs, multilateral assistance is considerably more effective, as demonstrated by comparative international survey (Cusack & Kaufmann 1994:5,12). Bilateral aid seems to follow traditions and routines of foreign policy, as well as foreign economic and strategic interests to a higher degree than multilateral assistance.

Figure 1: Shares of Multilateral Aid and of ODA to Low-Income Countries

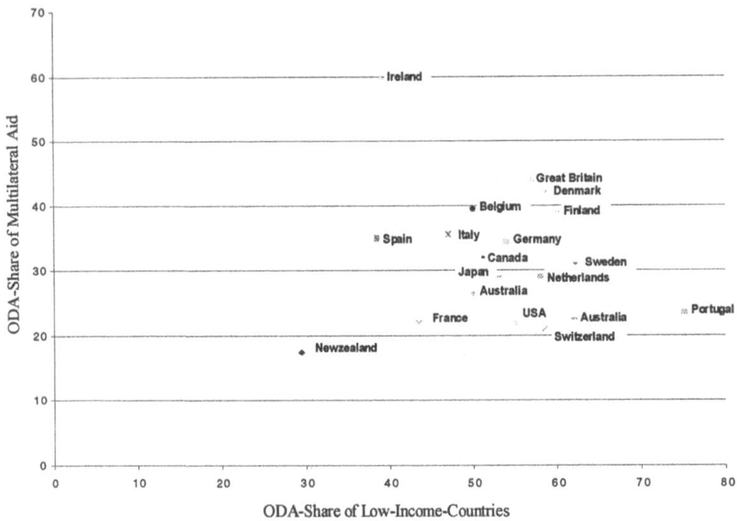

Source: OECD (1994), *DAC Report 1993*, Paris: OECD:91.

While development assistance has been a primary tool of Japan's foreign policy during the last decades and, therefore, enjoyed a privileged status in the budgetary process, leading policymakers within the Liberal Democratic Party now want to shift aid emphasis from quantity to quality (Nikkei Weekly, June 9th 1997:2). Therefore, the *Prime Minister's Conference on Fiscal Structural Reform* has decided in June 1997 that ODA should be cut back by 10% in the 1998 budget and not increase later. In this context, an increased emphasis is placed on direct aid, which bypasses multilateral organizations. It seems to be that in the political decision making process within the Japanese government the predominantly multilateral approach of the Foreign Ministry will become less important than the more bilateral approach, traditionally favored by the Ministries of Finance (MOF) and of International Trade and Industry (MITI) (Foerster 1994). With an accumulated public debt which is close to its gross national product Japan cannot continually increase development assistance with a general leveling of the budget.

In Europe, on the other side, since the beginning of development co-operation, Nordic states are strong multilateralists and support international organizations very intensively in order to promote equity in a world of power-politics. Quite above the DAC-average of 24% Denmark, Finland, Norway, and Sweden collectively transfer about 30% of their ODA through multilateral institutions. These countries prefer UN-organizations to the World Bank and regional development banks (Hook 1996:117), and therefore UN-organizations get the largest share of Nordic multilateral assistance. The reason for this aid-pattern is that these institutions allow LDCs to participate in decision making and try to insulate their aid-activities from political and commercial pressure.

The multilateral development assistance commitment of Germany is, at present, closely scrutinized by the Bundestag (Federal Parliament). Vis-à-vis its critics within parliament, who criticize the ineffectiveness of international organizations, the Federal Ministry for Economic Co-operation and Development sticks to its multilateral commitment, thus preventing parliament from tying German contributions to specific conditions which would contradict basic functional requirements of effective work on the side of international development organizations (Bundesministerium für wirtschaftliche Zusammenarbeit und Entwicklung 1993:6).

On the side of European donors, there is a broad consensus for a share of 30% ODA for multilateral institutions, on the other side, however, an increasing scepticism towards the effectiveness of European and UN-development assistance. The *European Court of Audit*, in the meantime, has uncovered tremendous shortcomings of effective planning structures in the field of development policy and development co-operation. Therefore, German policy planners are pursuing a policy perspective which could be characterized as: *As much bilateral assistance as possible, as much multilateral assistance as necessary*. An increasing multilateral engagement on the side of the German government can, for this reason, not be expected. With respect to UN-development assistance, Japan and Germany, at least, do not intend to compensate short-comings of American contributions. While, however, the Japanese government is increasingly formulating its own perspectives of international co-operation, the position of the German government is, with respect to multilateral development policy, increasingly mediated by European perspectives and European institutions.

5 Perspectives of Multilateral Development Policy

Development assistance provided by multilateral organizations still possesses various advantages compared with the patterns of bilateral aid: the provision of aid through a global network, the expert knowledge and professional experience of the particular organizations, and the more effective co-ordinations of aid across multiple countries and regions (Ministry of Foreign Affairs, Japan 1997:132).

Beside the quantitative impact of multilateral development assistance there are also more subtle, qualitative influences on the structure of policy orientation of international organizations. This can be illustrated by conflicting views on "targeted loans" and the role of government intervention, as seen by the World Bank and the Japanese government. In this discussion on appropriate development strategies of developing countries and regional development banks the World Bank favors a more market-orientated approach, while the Japanese government supports a more active role of industrial policy as performed by its own Ministry of International Trade and Industry (MITI). By such discussions, the influence of Japanese development policy orientations on programs of multilateral development organizations will rather increase in the near future (Rohde 1997).

European policy coordination in the field of development assistance has been broadly diversified in the past. At present European development aid is still concentrated too much on former French and British colonies (Köhler 1996:29). Even if multilateral funds are financed directly through national budgets, national parliaments have little chance to control the use of these funds. Compared with bilateral financial and technical co-operation, European development co-operation is ineffective and inflexible. EU's development policy and the bilateral development policies of EU member states should, therefore, be better coordinated. In the meantime, the European Commission insists on working out stabilization and structural adjustment programs for individual EU-partner states in Africa, the Caribean and the Pacific in close co-operation with the World Bank and the IMF. Still, however, the European Parliament is excluded from the decision-making process.

Within the new framework of multilateralism and multilateral development assistance in particular governments can develop and implement a pattern of foreign policy which corresponds to the interdependence of the international system and to the necessity to create and support effective international regimes. Japanese experts, therefore, speak in this respect of *taigai seisaku* (policy of interdependence) instead of *gaikô seisaku* (national foreign policy) (Satô 1989:5), German experts speak of "global responsibility" and "global partnership" in the age of multilateralism and regionalization. As it can be seen in the case of the United Nations Industrial Development Organization (UNIDO), leading donors can exert a considerable influence on the perspectives and even the very existence of particular UN-organizations.

For both leading international donors an expansion of their multilateral commitments is compatible with the above mentioned tendencies and based on an internal, stable policy consensus. Japan and Germany in particular should – beyond their commitment to Peace Keeping Operations (PKO) of the United Nations, NATO or the West European Union (WEU) – follow an approach of a stronger engagement within the United Nations, the World Bank and the IDA, the APEC, Nato and the EU in the direction of "Pacific Globalization" and "Atlantic Globalism" respectively based on a solid partnership with America (Funabashi 1993, Funabashi 1994).

Networks of multilateral development assistance do depend on effective bilateral relations. This indispensable basis has been demonstrated in several cases: the co-operation among Japan, America and Europe for the reform of the United Nations and the operation of the WTO; the joint effects of Japan, America and the Republic of Korea in dealing with the issue of nuclear weapons development in North Korea; the co-operation of countries in Asia-Pacific in the APEC; the increasing intensity of bilateral co-operation between leading donors like Japan and Germany (Ministry of Foreign Affairs, Japan 1996:5). Beyond these networks of co-operation, there exists an increasing level of exchange and co-operation across regions (e.g. co-operation of the EU in the problem of nuclear weapons development in North Korea, Japan's participation in the reconstruction of the former Yugoslavia, and the first Asia-Europe Meeting (ASEM).

Consensus-building within the UN-system in particular rests on bargaining procedures among and within groups of member states. While formally, this process is based on compromises *between* these groups, consensus-finding *within* groups is not less important. Intra-group-decision-making and consensus-finding seems, in this respect, even more important for development policy planners (Bohnert 1995:21). Policy preferences and policy perspectives are, therefore, from the very beginning of the entire bargaining process, less transparent. This structure is a considerable disadvantage for the implementation of re-distributive policy goals, as required by the development approach of the UN-system.

Relating these conclusions to the debate on the theory of international relations, they seem to be highly compatible with a *structural functional perspective*: International interdependence leads to functional integration, i.e. to increased international co-operation, to growing integration and multilateralism (Haas 1990, Alexander 1985). For these reasons, co-operation within the United Nations, the World Bank, the OECD and regional organizations has shaped an evolving multilateralism as an essential complementary factor in achievements of development co-operation: green revolution, fall in birth rates and reduced poverty (OECD 1996:1). Still, efforts have to be undertaken to finance multilateral development co-operation programs which are effective and sustainable. Therefore, bi- and multilateral donors have to work for better coordination of the international aid system with partner countries. This is at the same time a fundamental requirement of all perspectives of *Global Governance*. In addition, the co-operation between state and non-governmental organizations has to be strengthened from the local up to the international level. International regimes can, in this context, function as intermediaries and build a link between the different levels of international co-operation.

In any case the roles and mandates of specialized UN-agencies and commissions should be urgently reviewed, as strongly recommended by the G7-communiqué of Lyon in 1996, in order to eliminate overlap, improve effectiveness, and integrate development functions. The process of coordination and reform should be implemented by the Administrative Committee on Co-ordinations (ACC) and by the Economic and Social Council (ECOSOC). The result should be a more efficiently and rationally structured UN-system that effectively, at Headquarters and at field-level, encompasses funds, programs, and development activities of specialized agencies. This will require especially harmonized standards for program and project design, common rules for decentralization of authority, common budget processes, common programming and joint sessions of the Executive Boards of Funds and Programs with the ECOSOC. Multilateral institutions should concentrate their resources in the poorest countries, shape their programs in a way that addresses the most important sectoral and cross-sectoral challenges, and build up their own expertise on the basis of comparative advantage (Chalker 1990:357).

Compared with the bilateral aid multilateral development assistance fulfills several specific functions: It compensates the regional concentration of bilateral assistance to a certain degree, internationalizes "bad risks", supports national development institutions vis-à-vis national finance ministries and other dominating institutions, especially by training and dialogue programs which are too expensive for single projects of bilateral technical assistance, and it offers developing countries by its organizational structure and institutional network new chances of effective political articulation (Betz 1976).

Within the broad spectrum of organizational reform of UN-organizations the implementation structure of development assistance has been increasingly criticized. Development assistance of UN-institutions should follow clear priorities and be devoted to specific global problems. Within this framework *Public Private Partnership* (PPP) and *client orientation* should be more promoted In order to make development assistance operations more effective, the *Resident Coordinator (RC)*-system should be strengthened, e.g. by the appointment of country program-managers. In addition, the RC-system should be more effectively coordinated with the United Nations Secretariat, while *Inter-Agency Task Forces* and joint country offices ("country desks") should more effectively co-ordinate UN-funds and -programs. These funds and programs must integrate their activities into common conceptual frameworks of specific priorities and programs. The United Nations Development Program (UNDP) should play a leading role in this restructuring process.

6 Concluding Remarks

In the meantime, the United Nations Secretary General has decided that the activities of the Secretariat in the economic and social areas will be integrated and that the functions of the Department of Policy Coordination and Sustainable Development, the Department for Economic and Social Information and Policy Analysis, and the Department of Development Support and Management Services will be merged into a single Department (United Nations 1997:1). In addition, the Secretary General has strengthened the position of the UNDP Resident Coordinator as his designated representative for development co-operation and requested that all UN-funds and programs in charge of development activities at the country level join together in a common UN-development assistance framework. Furthermore, a Policy Coordination Group, composed of the heads of Departments and Offices of the Secretariat and the heads of UNDP, UNICEF and UNFPA has been established under the chairmanship of the Secretary General. These steps are very much in accordance with the EU's "Proposals for Reform" of the UN-system (European Union 1996). As James Speth, head of UNDP, has put it: A genuine reform of the United Nations must "include both streamlining and strengthening" and must make the institution "more accountable, efficient, and transparent".

References

Alexander, J. C. (1985), *Neofunctionalism*, Beverly Hills.

Betz, J. (1976), Funktionen der Multilateralisierung von Entwicklungshilfe, in: *Politische Vierteljahresschrift* 17,3: 344-368.

Bohnert, M. (1995), Normen in Institutionen des Nordens und bei Nord-Süd-Verhandlungen, in: Deutscher, E. (ed.), *Welche bewußten oder unbewußten Normen des Nordens prägen die Nord-Süd-Beziehungen?*, Bonn: 18-22.

Bundesministerium für wirtschaftliche Zusammenarbeit und Entwicklung (1993), *Parlamentarische Kontrolle der multilateralen Entwicklungsinstitutionen*, Informationsvermerk für den Bundestagsausschuß für wirtschaftliche Zusammenarbeit, Bonn.

Chalker, L. (1990), Britain's Role in the Multilateral Aid Agencies, in: *Development Policy Review* 8,4: 355-363.

Cusack, T. R. & Kaufmann, J. P. (1994), *The Evolution of Western Foreign Aid Programs*, 16. IPSA-World Congress, Berlin.

European Union (1996), *Proposals of the European Union for Reform of the United Nations System in the Economic and Social Areas*, Brussels.

Foerster, A. (1994), *Japans Zusammenarbeit mit der Dritten Welt zwischen Entwicklungsorientierung und außenwirtschaftlichen Prioritäten*, Deutsches Institut für Entwicklungspolitik, Berlin.

Funabashi, Y. (1993), *Nihon no Taigai Kôsô Reisengo no Bijon o Kaku* [Japan's International Perspective: A Vision for the Post-Cold-War-Era], Tokyo.

Funabashi, Y. (1994), *Japan's International Agenda*, New York & London .

Gaimushô (Ministry of Foreign Affairs, Japan) (1994), *ODA Hakusho 1994* [ODA Whitebook 1994], Tokyo.

Gaimushô (Ministry of Foreign Affairs, Japan) (1996), *ODA Hakusho 1996* [ODA Whitebook 1996], Tokyo.

Haas, E. B. (1990), *When Knowledge Is Power: Three Models of Change in International Organizations*, Berkeley.

Haggard, S. & Simmons, B. A. (1987), Theories of International Regimes, in: *International Organizations* 41,3: 491-517.

Hook, S. W. (ed.) (1996), *Foreign Aid Toward the Millenium*, Boulder & London.

Inoguchi, T. (1991), *Japans International Relations*, London.

Kevenhörster, P. (1993), *Japan. Außenpolitik im Aufbruch*, Opladen.

Klingebiel, S. (1993), Multilaterale Entwicklungspolitik, in: *Aus Politik und Zeitgeschichte*, 12-13: 22-28.

Köhler, V. (1996), *Consequences of the Maastricht Treaty for European Development Policy*, Bonn.

Mathews, J. (1997), Play the Common Rules and Pay Those UN-Dues, in: *International Herald Tribune*, March 11th, 1997: 8.

Ministry of Foreign Affairs, Japan (1996), *Diplomatic Bluebook 1996*, Tokyo.

Ministry of Foreign Affairs, Japan (1997), *Diplomatic Bluebook 1997*, Tokyo.

Nikkei Weekly (1997), Japan Ponders Foreign-aid-priorities, in: *Nikkei Weekly*, April 14th, 1997: 1.

Nikkei Weekly (1997), New Breed Seeks Quality in Foreign Aid, Not Quantity, in: *Nikkei Weekly*, June 9th, 1997: 2.

Nuscheler, F. (1995), *Lern- und Arbeitsbuch Entwicklungspolitik*, 4th ed., Bonn.

OECD (1994), *DAC Report 1993*, Paris.

OECD (1996), *Shaping the 21st Century: The Contribution of Development Co-operation*, Paris.

OECD (1997), *DAC Report 1996*, Paris.

Ôkurashô (Ministry of Finance) (1995), *Heisei 7nendo Yosan oyobi Zaiseitôyûshi Keikaku no Setsumei* [Comments to the 1995 Budget and Fiscal Investmaent and Loan Program], Tokyo.

Raphaeli, N. (1996), Technical Cooperation and the World Bank, in: *The International Journal of Technical Cooperation* 2,2: 224-235.

Rohde, M. (1997), Japan in der UNO, in: *Japan – Politik, Wirtschaft, Gesellschaft*, April 1997: 256-261.

Satô, H. (1989), *Taigai Seisaku. Gendai Seijigaku Sôshô* [Foreign Policy. Modern Political Science Publications], Tokyo.

UNDP (1997), *Japan and UNDP – A Partnership in Development*, New York.

United Nations (1997), *Executive Summary of the Measure Outlined in the Letter Dated 17 March 1997 from the Secretary General Addresses to the President of the General Assembly*, New York.

Wapenhans, W. A. (1996), Multilaterale Entwicklungsbanken, in: *Entwicklung und Zusammenarbeit* 37: 183-185.

Japan's Image of Europe and Strategy Towards It

András Hernádi

1 Introduction

Japan in the latter half of the 1990s, despite a decelerating growth rate, can be considered the second most important economy in the world. This has served as the basis for Japan's international prestige, and for its self-esteem. Not unexpectedly after the end of the Cold-War period and some crucial changes in Japan's domestic politics (an end to 38 years of Liberal Democratic domination), Japan's view of the world and foreign-policy approach have become more varied.

Practically all Japanese declarations about its foreign policy continue to assume that relations with the United States form the cornerstone. However, the role Japan plays in Asia, or more specifically the Asia-Pacific region, has entered the foreground, probably reflecting the increase in the region's global economic importance. The enhanced importance being attached to the Asia-Pacific region is apparent in the momentum behind the APEC scheme, and in the way Japanese investment is turning towards Asia again. This has even been interpreted as a reversal of the slogan behind the Meiji restoration of 1868: "Let us leave Asia and join the West." (Business Week April 10th 1995:36)

Moreover the Japanese, for economic considerations again, have been placing greater emphasis on their European contacts during the 1990s. The changes in the world have favored the view that countries should rely on multi-partite relations. Moreover, the European Union has been gaining importance, and its processes of deepening and enlargement have aroused considerable attention in Japan. (Although there has been an increase in Japanese activity in some CEE countries, it must be said at the outset that the region is still seen as a residual sphere by the Japanese government and business community.) Japan in the 1990s, with its global interests and aspirations to manifest these interests at international forums, can hardly afford not to stress its policy and strategy towards Europe.

Before outlining the main constituents of this policy and strategy, and illustrating them mainly through recent opinions and analyses, it is worth going back to the roots of the Japanese-European relationship. These roots are still viable and visible today, due to the distinctive emphasis that Japan places on tradition.

2 The Roots of the Japanese-European Relationship

Endymion Wilkinson's 1983 book *Japan versus Europe* presents a treasury of information about the value judgements that still permeate the Japanese-European relationship. At the heart of these lies the fact that the Japanese have always sought to learn from the outside world, while finding themselves on the periphery of great cultural powers, such as China, Europe, and most recently the United States. This strong wish to learn has often led to an idealization of the areas observed, even though the practical experience gained of them has not always corresponded with the prior information gathered about them.

Japan's imitation of Europe reached its climax in the decades of modernization in the 1870s and 1880s. Adoption covered not only industrial inventions and innovations, but a wide range of European institutional and judicial models. Wilkinson remarks that in those days "it was the Japanese who complained of sudden influxes of European goods disrupting domestic industries (...) [and] the Japanese regarded Europe as a disciplined, group-oriented society possessing the secrets of efficient industrial production." (Wilkinson 1983:32)

During the 250 years of isolation preceding the Meiji restoration of 1868, the Japanese had looked suspiciously on influences from abroad. The Confucian scholar Seishisai Aizawa in 1825 looked disapprovingly on the Dutch studies popular mainly among Japanese who served as interpreters in Nagasaki:

> These students, who make a living by passing on whatever they hear, have been taken in by the vaunted theories of the Western foreigners. They enthusiastically extol these theories, and some going so far as to publish books about them in the hope of transforming our civilized way of life into that of the barbarians. (quoted in Wilkinson 1983:103)

Some forty years later, Yukichi Fukuzawa's book *Seiyo jijo* (Conditions in the West) sold 250,000 copies in 1866, its year of publication.

The initial enthusiasm gave way to *disillusionment*, due largely to the first-hand reports of Japanese travelling in Europe after the First World War and in the years of the great depression. Hajime Kawakami wrote in his study *Tales of Poverty*, published as early as 1917,

> Although England, America, Germany and France and many others are rich countries, their people are very poor. It is surprising that in these civilized countries there are so many people who are poor. (quoted in Wilkinson 1983:119)

The protagonist of Saneatsu Mushanokoji's novel *Love and Death*, published in 1939, writes in a letter:

> Wherever one goes one sees only Occidentals (...) somehow I have the feeling that we are looked down upon. (...) A solitary Japanese among a group of Occidentals is hardly an imposing figure. This is due to a large extent to our not being suited to Western style clothes, but even if we try to make something of the color of our skin

> and our physique, we still have very little to boast about. Nevertheless, I am confident that from the standpoint of spiritual power and intelligence we are not in the least inferior. The majority of Europeans love pleasure too much. Few of them have any faith in a future life. For the most part they live idly from day to day. (quoted in Wilkinson 1983:120)

After the Second World War, the hitherto vacillating attitude towards Europe gave way increasingly to a competitive relationship, mainly due to Japan's fast economic development. Meanwhile European criticism of Japan became increasingly strident. The criticism was fuelled by protectionist sentiments, joined in the 1970s by envy of Japan's smaller defense burden and alleged compliance towards economic demands from America.

There are three main factors pertinent to Japan's attitude towards Europe at this time.

1) Japan received no moral support from Europe at the time of the Nixon shocks in 1971 (the sudden rapprochement with China and the 15% import surcharge levied on Japanese products).
2) After the oil-price explosion of 1973–4, Europe's role in the world economy began to decline.
3) The debates among Japan and the countries of Europe never reached the level of a bilateral relationship between Japan and the EC.

As Wilkinson eloquently puts it, "As there was no united EC policy towards Japan, and so long as the Community lacked an effective industrial policy, it was too weak to do little more than cry 'wolf' to Japanese exports. In doing so, it seemed to many Japanese, the Commission did more to stimulate fears of protectionism than it did to calm them." (Wilkinson 1983:219).

By the second half of the 1970s, both sides seemed to have accepted realities and begun a mutual re-evaluation of each other, perhaps partly in order to improve their positions in relation to America. It appeared, a decade and a half after Prime Minister Ikeda had floated the idea of trilateralism, during a visit to Western Europe in 1962, that the time had become ripe for it at last. From 1977 onwards, almost all heads of state or premiers from the member countries of the EC paid visits to Tokyo, and their trips were duly reciprocated. In 1979, following a rather awkward incident,[1] even the summit meeting of the world's great economic powers was held in Tokyo. The second oil-price explosion helped both sides to realize their community of interest in three respects:

1) Both were political allies of America.
2) Both lived by global trading.

---

1 In a leaked *secret* document, Sir Roy Denman, Director of External Relations of the EC, described the Japanese as workaholics and their houses as rabbit hutches.

3) Both their economies were reliant on imported energy.[2]

As Drifte (1986:102) has pointed out, the Japanese also provoked Western criticism by emphasizing that they were different, if not unique. Their widely pursued, quasi-scientific activity known as *nihonjinron* (study of Japanese character) has long been seeking arguments to prove how hard it is for outsiders to understand the Japanese, a unique group of mankind. The inference is that their problems with foreigners, and foreigners' problems with them, are largely based on incomprehension. Japanese politicians, of course, are happy to cash in on this line of argument. The Japanese Foreign Ministry even sent out complimentary copies to European opinion leaders of Wilkinson's book, which was poignantly subtitled *A History of Misunderstanding.*

3 Official Ideas and Views

The official Japanese view on how to upgrade the Japanese-European relationship characteristically entails handling it within a framework of trilateral cooperation among America, Japan and Europe. This gives at least the appearance of even-handedness between the country's relations with the United States and Europe.

In a speech to the Royal Institute of International Relations, at the Egmont Palace in Brussels on October 18th 1994, Hiroshi Fukuda, then Deputy Minister of Foreign Affairs, pointed out that the importance of Europe in the world is rising, both economically and politically. He noted that it plays a significant role in liquidating the remnants of the Cold War, mentioning in particular the Organization for European Security and Cooperation, as a rising symbol of basic values such as freedom, democracy, legality, human rights and a market economy. Concerning the common responsibilities of Japan and Europe, Fukuda emphasized that it was not satisfactory for the two parties simply to aim at harmonizing their economic interests and improving their bilateral relations. They should also coordinate the responses they give to outside economic and political challenges, for instance by promoting reform in the CIS countries, preventing and resolving regional conflicts, and settling various problems of a transnational character. The foundation for such a partnership, in his view, had been established by a Japanese initiative, expressed in the Japan-EC Common Declaration of July 1991.

Fukuda went on to mention the fears expressed by several EU countries that the Japanese-US trade negotiations might go against the interests of the EU, since bilateral agreements can be discriminative against third countries. He underlined that former Japanese agreements with America had been favorable not only to

2 These three elements were first mentioned together by Daniels (1986:10).

America. Japan was going to adhere to the main concept that all their bilateral agreements should apply to third countries as well.

On political and security issues, Fukuda talked of the great importance attached to deepening the dialogue with NATO and the CSCE/OSCE. Although not formally a member of the latter, Japan was actively cooperating with it, and had acquired special status in it since 1992, even taking part in its meetings. (Studia Diplomatica 1994:4-13)

An attempt to clarify some of the frequently debated issues was made in a book published under the name of Yohei Kono, Foreign Minister in the Murayama Government. Examining whether Japan's trade surplus can be considered a cause of unemployment in America and the EU countries, the book said:

> Generally any casual relationship between a country's trade surplus and unemployment in its trading partners is not recognized. (e.g. the EU's trade account in 1993 changed into surplus from deficit, while its jobless rate climbed from 9.3% to 10.8%.) It is possible that an increase in imports to certain sectors will temporarily reduce production or employment in the country concerned. However, if structural reform is made promptly, production and employment in industries with comparative advantage will increase, and as a result, overall employment in that country will not be affected. However, employment could be adversely affected if labor transfer to industries with comparative advantage is hampered by the rigid labor market and other structural problems. As for the current account, in the case of countries with current account deficits, it is also necessary to consider their capital accounts. That is, capital inflows from abroad, such as direct investment, help create jobs at home. Free trade promotes the development of the world economy through the effective allocation of resources and thereby contributes to job creation. It is therefore important to maintain and strengthen the multilateral free trading system through international cooperation. (Kono 1995:56)

On Japan's position on moves toward economic regional integration and cooperation, Kono (1995) called for "open regional cooperation", explaining as follows:

> Economic regional integration and cooperation tend to lack transparency in relations with countries outside the region. In particular, institutional arrangements for regional integration, such as customs union and a free trade area, will inevitably lead to discrimination against countries outside the region. Japan has maintained that regional integration and cooperation should conform to the following three principles: a) Exclusive or discriminatory moves that may lead to the formation of an economic bloc should be avoided in order to keep the integration and cooperation open to countries outside the region as well. b) Such regional moves could be consistent with the multilateral free trade system and conducive to maintaining and strengthening it. c) Full consideration should be given to the trade and investment interests of third countries. (Kono 1995:66)

In the Joint Declaration issued after the 4th Japan-EU Summit Meeting in Paris on June 19th 1995, there are some clear statements that echo the official Japanese views expressed above:

- The Japanese side welcomes European integration and the fact that a strong EU plays a stabilizing role in the region and wishes to maintain constructive relationships with other regions. (Paragraph 4).
- The Japanese side welcomes the positive measures taken by the European side, which are to promote efforts by the European private sector to export to Japan. (Paragraph 9)
- Regional economic integration is going on in parallel with the increasing worldwide interdependency, and may contribute to the welfare of the world. It must [therefore] be in harmony with the further multilateral liberalization of trade, while regional agreements have strictly to meet WTO stipulations, among others Article XXIV. of the 1994 GATT and Article V of GATT. (Paragraph 15)
- The idea raised by the EU to hold a Japan-Europe Cooperation Conference where representatives of governments, universities and the private sector would take part was met by interest' from both sides. (Paragraph 20)

4 Some Authoritative Views

Masaru Yoshitomi, an internationally renowned economist who has long been a leading researcher at the Economic Planning Agency of Japan, called the Europe 1992 program

> in part a reaction to the declining competitiveness of European firms vis-à-vis the American and especially the Japanese in high-technology industries. The commission attempts to coordinate trade, competition, and technology policies so as to reduce Japanese dominance in so-called strategic industries. Furthermore, the allegedly predatory exports and closed domestic market of Japan have often been used to justify European protectionist policies. (...) The external implications of Europe 1992 for Japan are essentially twofold. One is that Europe 1992 may intensify discriminatory actions against not only imports of Japanese high-technology products but also Japanese multinationals. The other is that Europe 1992 highlights fierce competition not only among different nationalities of multinational companies but also among different production and management systems and industrial organizations unique to each nation. (Yoshitomi 1991:70-71)

A reference book published in 1993 by the research institute of Mitsubishi commented on the chances of a federal Europe:

> As the economies of the member states are not on the same level, they will proceed in two groups. Germany, France and the Benelux countries are likely to be in the sub-group of the 'advanced', who wish to switch to the ECU by January 1997 or 1999 at the latest. (...) Great Britain, attributing more importance to her national sovereignty, would, together with other countries, enter the same road somewhat later. (...) The way towards a larger European union is not without problems and division, and will certainly take longer than the deadlines cited nowadays would suggest. All these European steps will, no doubt, stimulate the process of unification both in North-America and in Asia. (...) The move towards a larger European unity is taking place by a wider front, *i.e.*, with the participation of the twelve EC members, the EFTA countries, the Baltic and the East-European states. (...) Among the compromises arrived at one could witness the acceptance of German and French standpoints on monetary union and the British one on political union. It is still uncertain, however, whether all these will occur according to present-day scenarios. One of the problems is that the participating countries cannot enjoy the advantages of a bigger market on an equal scale. For the time being, they do not even deal with the issue of European technological development, lagging far behind that of Japan or the United States. (Makino 1993)

The Policy Council of the Japan Forum on International Relations, consisting of politicians, business people and directors of research institutes, accepted recommendations at its meeting on September 16th 1993, on the subject of "Political Cooperation with Europe: Japan's Agenda for 21st Century". The document also emphasized the need for closer cooperation among the highly developed countries in reforming the post-Cold War international order. Participants welcomed the Joint Japan-EC Declaration of July 18th 1991, as having augmented the two-tier system of relations with a new, political dimension as well. (From then onwards, political and diplomatic relations also began to be organized in a multilateral way.) Apart from advocating the maintenance of such high-level contacts, it was also recommended that there should be cooperation with European and pan-European organizations such as the CSCE and NATO. With the former, it was suggested that Japan take an increasing role in peace-keeping negotiations and exchange of information on conflicts in Eastern Europe and the former Soviet Union. As regards NATO and the North Atlantic Cooperation Council, the call was for a more intensive dialogue on political and foreign policy issues. Strengthening of the G7 framework and promotion of Japanese-European dialogue in the UN were also mentioned. G7 was considered a field where multilateral (Japanese and European) cooperation with America could be pursued, manifesting the global roles of both sides. Within the UN, a Japanese-European dialogue on reforming the organization and its Security Council was recommended. Other proposals by the Policy Council included Japanese-European cooperation in the non-proliferation of nuclear and conventional weapons, the coordination between Japan and Europe in policies toward Russia and a Japanese-European cooperation in regional issues in the Middle East and Africa. With regard to Asia, it was pointed out that Japan, as a major developed country within Asia, can efficiently support Europe's interests.[3]

Stronger direct, bilateral economic ties were called for in the recommendations, because the authors agreed that in a world that preaches globalization but pursues regional and national interests, Japan and Europe should build their relations within a cooperative framework. In order to be able to do so, however, the perception gap between them has to be bridged. Therefore, personal and cultural exchanges should be more frequent in all fields of life. Efforts resembling traditional Japan-US exchanges could promote such development. The establishment of a Japan-Europe Foundation was proposed.

5 Researchers' Opinions

Nobuo Noda, professor of Kyoto University, expressed his views on the relationship with Europe in an indirect way, yet his almost philosophical approach certainly deserves attention. Although in the context of the Japan-US relationship, he says that now the Cold War is over and "the bonds that hold the Western camp together have begun to loosen," Japan and many other countries have to reconsider whether they "really fit the Western democratic model". He adds, "In Japan's case the alternative is membership in the community of Asian nations" and "to make use of stronger bonds with its neighbors to break free of its subordination to America." At the same time, as if placing the European card in the pack, he warns of the danger that a "rising tide of Asianism" could flow in an anti-American direction. (Noda 1995)

The concept of the Japanese *vis-à-vis* Europe is conveyed also in an indirect way in a study by Volker Fuhrt, a researcher at the Institute of the German Society for Foreign Affairs, in Bonn. In his view, reports by and debates in the Japanese media on Europe in the 1990s have been concentrating on two issues: the move towards a unified internal market, and the political changes in Eastern Europe. Regarding the former, he says that fears, in the main, have been worded about the formation of a *fortress Europe*. With Eastern Europe a joyful registration of the collapse of communism has often been coupled by remarks from Japanese experts that similar, not necessarily crisis-free, developments in their own region (e.g. in China and Korea) would not be definitely welcome. (Fuhrt 1993)

3 Makino (1993); Japan Forum (1993). Japan has been trying for many years to become a standing member of the Security Council. Its economic potential offers justification for such status. Assurances of Japan's good intentions include Article 9 of the country's constitution, the small proportion of GDP spent on defense, and the country's contributions to UN peace-keeping activities.

Based on three articles in the Japanese monthly Chuo Koron in 1990, Fuhrt (1993) says that the Japanese do not possess enough information to judge bilateral relationship. They think that the tensions stem from their being different and the Europeans being chauvinistic. Regarding the lessons Japan could draw from the example of Europe, mention is most often made of the quality of life, the welfare state, the policy towards foreigners, and the model of management. According to Fuhrt (1993), such views are motivated by a certain type of neo-nationalism and/or a minority complex. To illustrate the fluctuation in Japanese self-confidence, Fuhrt (1993) cites some opinion-poll findings. The share of those who saw Japan as more developed than foreign countries rose from 52% to 71% between 1963 and 1983, but fell back to 62% by 1988. In 1973, 70% of the sample thought Japan could learn a lot from abroad. By 1988 the opinion was held by 76% (Kreiner 1984:84-115, NHK 1991:101).

An article by Michihiko Kunihiro (1989) gives surprisingly early expression to Japanese fears about Europe's intentions with the Single European Market. The author sees behind the scheme a major attempt to carry out crucial structural adjustments. Although these would be supported by Japan, there are concurrent doubts about whether the system of free trade will remain sustainable on a global scale. The article then discusses specific fields of greatest concern to Japan:

- Concerning the quantitative restrictions on Japanese imports applied by most EC countries, the author mentions Japan's concern about the discriminatory measures that distort EC relations with Japan.
- With direct investment in Europe, the rules on 'European content' cause concern, as many Japanese firms have trouble finding components of the right quality locally.
- With reciprocity, there are frequent cases where *quid pro quo* benefits cannot be exchanged because of differences in the legal and social systems.
- There is the possibility of the EC making use of unilateral measures concerning intellectual property rights, for protectionist purposes. (Kunihiro 1989)

The title of an important paper by Professor Kensei Hiwaki of Tokyo International University already refers to "asymmetry" in the European-Japanese relationship. In the introduction he states,

> As far as political interests are concerned, there have not been many quarrels between [the EC and Japan]. (...) In the sphere strictly of economic relations, especially in that of bilateral trade, however, Japan and the EC have long harbored animosity against each other. This is perhaps due to their differing standpoints and conflicting interests, to say nothing of the disparate entities of the negotiating parties (a nation-state versus a supranational organization). (...) Japan has long tended to perceive the [European] Commission and some of the member states as being protectionist and discriminatory.' [This led the Japanese to voice] suspicion

> that the EC is tacitly classifying its imports into three general categories for discriminatory treatments, first from Japan, second from the other external members, and third from the non-GATT members. [During the integration process, Japan has repeatedly feared] that the current unfair discrimination of Japanese imports by the individual member states would be mostly reinstituted at the EC supranational level. (...) Any compromise policy [regarding the 'Japan problem'] might very well accommodate the strong voices of the weaker and/or protectionist economies among the member states, and of the weaker and/or sensitive sectors among their industries. (Hiwaki 1992)

Hiwaki (1992) is also of the opinion that international developments in the early 1980s "offered momentous opportunities to start an official Japan-EC dialogue, also resulting in positive mutual relations and regular conferences of the foreign ministers." The same period was characterized by a change from "confrontation and friction" to "dialogue and cooperation", according to Kazuyoki Odaira, a Japanese career diplomat (quoted in Nippon Kokusai 1990, Chapter 5). The second breakthrough in the relationship was able to take place after the fall of the Berlin Wall. This political leap forward, however, could not resolve the mainly trade-related inhibitions, behind which there were also emotional reflexes, by then, on the EC side, while the Japanese, after the Single European Act, were nervous about the prospect of a *fortress Europe*.[4]

At the international conference on "A New European Order and Japan-Europe Relations", held in Tokyo by Chuo University in December 1995, Hungarian delegates were surprised to find that hardly any Japanese speaker attempted a comprehensive approach to the subject. One refreshing exception was Professor Toshiro Kuroda of Niigata Women's College, whose ideas deserve quoting in detail:

> What is to be the basis for order in post-Cold War Europe? Six years after the fall of Berlin Wall, the answer to this question is still unclear. The visions of a 'return to Europe', a Europe 'free and whole', and a 'European peace order' have not been fulfilled. The bipolar structure of Cold War Europe has given way to a unified system of democratic states, but rather to a system with regional differences. It is possible to identify four broad regions, which have similar constellations of political and economic patterns: Western Europe, East-Central Europe, the Balkans, and the European states of the former Soviet Union. It is an open question whether the very different polities and societies in these regions can be brought together into an effective common political framework. Post-Cold War Europe has also

[4] Hirohide Narusawa mentions three factors that may contribute to a *fortress Europe*: (i) The existing North-South problems within the EC and the coexistence of strong and weak industries (and firms) may cause the EC authorities to protect the weaker. (ii) The question of local content, and the unsettled definitions and criteria regarding product origins, Community firms, and so on., may give rise to unfair discrimination against outsiders. (iii) Owing to the Community's different historical, political and economic relations with each, Japan may receive discriminatory treatments compared with America. (quoted in Hiwaki 1992)

> considerable diversity of patterns of governance within each region. Although they no longer take an ideological form, they are again coming to influence patterns of conflict and cooperation. How far will these differences inhibit the development of a common political framework? Will the drive toward economic and political integration in Western Europe contribute to the building of such a European political architecture?
>
> Western European societies have very high levels of interdependence, created by their trading links, cross-border investment and common institutions through multiple integration processes. Together with the sense of community that has developed out of shared cultural and political values, these links have created both an economic community and a pluralistic security community. (...) With the changes introduced by the Single Act and by the Maastricht Treaty, it seems to be certain that there are features of the EU that go far beyond any other international regime and we are facing a mixture of intergovernmental and federal organizations. European integration has been a very original attempt at pooling or blending sovereign powers, and it also created central authorities that could exert powers transferred to them by the states in a number of important areas: agriculture, external trade, competition policies, and so on. The decision in principle taken at Maastricht in December 1991, to move towards a common currency, a common foreign policy and possibly an ultimate defense policy identity, signified both a step towards political integration and an attempt to strengthen the system of West European cooperation. The resulting structure did not immediately alter the nature of the West European polity. Nation-states remained in charge. Nevertheless, the Maastricht Treaty gave the impression that a major step from national to supranational governance was taking place. (Kuroda 1995)

6 Eastern European Aspects

Kuroda (1995) must also be commended for his thoughtful discussion of several Eastern European aspects of the new European order.

> The most important challenge to a European new order may be the place of ethnic minorities in Central and East European states – difficulties in relations between minority and majority communities. Given the prevailing climate of nationalism, demands for secession, for new states, or for greater states bringing together dispersed groups, have been powerful. The problem combines with the dubious legitimacy of new state boundaries and opens the issue of redrawing frontiers.
>
> Perhaps even more notably lacking in the Maastricht process is an underlying common value set on a European scale. This is why the EU could not effectively prevent the breaking up of multi-ethnic societies in the Balkans. Western European integration has been implemented on the assumption that one can distinguish the nation from the European state whose powers are now shared with the EU. The distinction points, indeed, to a European state, but one without a European nation, since there are still no European mass media, parties, interest groups (except in business), or public. The establishment at Maastricht of a common European

> citizenship is only a formal first step. Without such a European nation, many feel, so to speak, denuded, for the national state is losing power, but the European would-be state, uncomfortably straddling nations with diverse traditions and interests, seems incapable of defining a common policy in matters as vital as defence and diplomacy, as the failure of Yugoslavia shows. (Kuroda 1995)

Finally, it is worth considering a surprising link made by Professor Akira Kudo of the University of Tokyo, when considering changes in the economic relations between Japan and Europe. He writes:

> The collapse of the Japanese political regime of 1955 (...) may be seen as part of the chain reaction to the European upheaval. (...) [On the other hand] the Japanese economy has grown too large to be neglected in explaining the present socio-economic upheaval in Europe. On the contrary, Japan's economic power has been one of the important factors responsible for triggering the upheaval. In fact, European efforts to unify the European Community market by the end of 1992 might be said to have been undertaken primarily as a European response to the economic challenge posed by Japan. One might also say that the collapse of the socialist systems of the former Soviet Union and Eastern Europe was prompted, to a large extent, by the weakening of their economies under the overwhelming impact of the rapidly growing economies of East and Southeast Asia with their close links with Japan's economy and private firms. (Kudo 1995)

References

Daniels, G. (1986), Foreword, in: Daniels, G. & Drifte, R. (eds.), *Europe and Japan: Changing Relationships since 1945*, Woodchurch, Ashford, Kent: Paul Norbury.

Drifte, R. (1986), Euro-Japanese Relations: Realities and Prospects, in: Daniels, G. & Drifte, R. (eds.), *Europe and Japan: Changing Relationships since 1945*, Woodchurch, Ashford, Kent: Paul Norbury: 97-123.

Fuhrt, V. (1993), Perzeptionen und Perzeptionsdefizite: Die gegenseitigen Wahrnehmungen Europas und Japans, in: Maull, H. W. (ed.), *Japan und Europe: Getrennte Welten?*, Frankfurt/New York: Campus Verlag: 283–304

Hanabusa, M. (1979), *Trade Problems between Japan and Western Europe*, London: Royal Institute of International Affairs

Hiwaki, K. (1992), View from Japan: Asymmetries in the Evolving European-Japanese Dialogue, in: Hummel, R. (ed.), *Toward Political Union: Planning a Common Foreign and Security Policy in the European Community*, New York: Westview Press: Chapter 14.

Japan Forum (1993), *Political Cooperation with Europe: Japan's Agenda for the 21st Century*, JF-PR-10-E, Tokyo: Japan Forum on International Relations Inc.

Kono, Y. (1995), *Japanese Viewpoints*, Tokyo: The Japan Times Publishers.

Kreiner, J. (1984), Das Deutschland-Bild der Japaner und das deutsche Japan-Bild, in: Kracht, K., Lewin, B. & Müller, K. (eds.), *Japan und Deutschland im 20. Jahrhundert*, Wiesbaden: Gabler Verlag: 84-115.

Kudo, A. (1995), *A Partnership of Imbalance: Changes in the Japan-European Relations*, Occasional Papers in Capitalist Economies and International Relations No. 9, Tokyo: University of Tokyo, Institute of Social Science.

Kunihiro, M. (1989), The External Implications of 1992. A Japanese View, in: *The World Today*, February.

Kuroda, T. (1995), Preliminary Notes on the Changing Nature of a New European Order, mimeo.

Nippon Kokusai (1990), *Kokusai Nenpo 1983–1984* [Annual International Report], Tokyo: Nippon Kokusai: Chapter 5.

NHK (1991), *Gendai Nihonjin no Ishiki Kozo* [The Structure of Consciousness of the Japanese Today], Tokyo: NHK.

Noda, N. (1995), The Dangerous Rise of Asianism, in: *Japan Echo* 22,1: 6–11

Makino, N. (ed.) (1993), *Total Forecast,* Cassell's Asia Pacific Business Reference Japan 1990s series, Tokyo: Mitsubishi Research Institute.

Shirakawa, I. (1989), Sainen Suru Hogoshugi [The Resurgence of Protectionism], in: Shirakawa, I. (ed.), *Beika Jiyuboeki-Kyotei - EC Togo Wo Miru* [Observations on the US-Canada Free Trade Agreement and European Integration], Tokyo: Toyo Keizai Shimpo-sha: 34–37.

Studia Diplomatica (1994), *Studia Diplomatica* Vol. XLVII, 6: 4–13.

Wilkinson, E. (1983), *Japan versus Europe: A History of Misunderstanding*, Harmondsworth: Penguin.

Yoshitomi, M. (1991), External Trade Implications of Europe 1992 for Japan, in: Barfield & Perlman (eds.), *Capital Markets and Trade: The US Faces a United Europe,* AEI Studies No.52.

GLOBAL MARKETS: THE NEW PARADIGM

From Scarcity to Insatiability: Globalization, Lost Variety and the Levelling of Cultural Differences

Galen Amstutz

1 Silk from Wild Cocoons: An Anecdote about Ethical Integration

Here is a probably unfamiliar "economics and ethics" or "business ethics" anecdote which is derived from the Tokugawa-period history of Jôdoshin Buddhism, the largest of the traditional Buddhist organizations in Japan.

In Tokugawa Japan, the managed production of silk (sericulture) became a major industry, often encouraged by governments of the regional domains in order to produce a profitable commodity for the national market. In the ordinary method, silkworms were raised artifically inside buildings, and then the silk was obtained by boiling the unhatched cocoons and unraveling the fiber. This procedure resulted in mass killings of the worms. However, in certain areas of Japan such as Aki province, members of devout Shin Buddhist communities, who objected to the mass killings of the insects in this manner to obtain a product which was not strictly necessary, devised ways to obtain silk from the discarded cocoons of wild silkworms. Such cocoons were left on the floors of woodlands after the worms had already matured and broken out. The discarded cocoons could be collected and with the right technique turned into a another kind of cruder silk fiber (pongee) which was still strong and useful. (Arimoto 1997:84-87)

Now, this anecdote is not entirely typical of Tokugawa Japan, and it was not even true of all the Shin Buddhist communities in spite of their general aversion to killing. However, it was a reflection of one moment in the history of a sophisticated traditional pre-industrial society in which people had learned to cope with existence in a manner which integrated several dimensions of their experience: ecological, economic, psychological, and religious. This traditional Buddhist society was not a sentimental or utopian one: the practice of making silk from wild cocoons was related to an almost punishing rigor in the alignment of practical possibilities and a deep ethical perspective. But again, the result was a kind of moral integration, which linked material minimalism, scarcity, compassion, a philosophical theory of the mind, and a form of early modern market life.

In stable societies of the past, such a degree of integration was sometimes possible and points towards certain human potentials which can, at least at some times, exist. Of course such anecdotes and forms of integration may belong only to the past and have no direct bearing on life at the beginning of the 21st century. The 20th century has certainly not been integrated. It is a truism that the past century has been a human episode of enormous disintegration and confusion on many levels, moral and social and environmental.

Some would argue, despite the end of the cold war, and the immense new transfer of information being made possible by the new technologies, that the current processes of globalization are but a continuation of such disintegration and confusion. Yet one can be more optimistic: there are indications of considerable movement back towards a unified reconsideration of an integration of ethics and economics and society. Indeed, one of the byproducts of "globalization" is that certain kinds of intellectual and moral problematics become more universalized than ever before.

2 Some Ethical Ideas That Are Already Being Well Integrated into Mainstream Business Discourse

It goes without saying that there is now, for almost any subject, an unmanagable quantity of detailed research available, which may tax the powers of even the experts and specialists and undermine attempts of ordinary laymen to get any synthetic overviews! Nevertheless, for the sake of discussion, I would like to generally suggest that since the end of the cold war some specific kinds of movement towards ethical integration can be identified.

First, agreement on the superiority of mixed economies, under democratic political regimes, which join market forces and government regulation. Although many of the conflicts between left and right that emerged in the 19th century are more or less ritually recycled (at least in American journalism) for the most part the issues of 20th century totalitarianism are past. In a broad manner there is consensus, which we might loosely call "liberal," that modern societies work best with "mixed economies" i.e. with one or another of a variety of regimes which make some combination of private, free market activity and public governmental regulation. This is not to say that we lack significant remaining controversy about the types of mixtures which should be made, or disagreements among leading nations about the details. Whenever an American comes to Europe, for example, he or she can still be surprised by the relatively higher degree of social welfare and social protection, and the difference in decisions made about trade-offs in terms of employment, growth, and so on. But in their diverse forms, mixed economies are the future.

Second, a growing body of thought about a more universalistic corporate ethics. One can refer, for example, to several items from the statement of "core beliefs" which originates with the Caux Round Table, an organization of business leaders from Japan, the EU and the United States.

> Corporations must be increasingly responsive to issues affecting the physical, social and economic environments not only because of their impact on business performance but also out of a pro-active sense of responsibilities to all constituencies served.
>
> Corporations need to consider the balance between the short-term interests of shareholders and the longer-term interests of the enterprise and its stakeholders.
>
> Corporations should lead by example through business practices that are ethical and transparent, and that reflect a commitment to human dignity, political and economic freedoms, and preservation of the planet.
>
> Corporations cannot act alone but should seek to address key global issues through cooperative efforts with governments, other institutions and local communities. (Caux Round Table 2000a)

Caux leaders are also concerned about global unemployment dilemmas, the gap between the haves and the have-nots, and trust and transparency in business dealings.

In an Asian studies context, it is notable that Caux literature has been marked by references to Japanese ideas of kyôsei ("living and working for the common good"). According to Ryuzaburo Kaku, chairman of Canon Corporation, four stages of kyôsei are envisioned: a) capitalism, with owners and managers keeping all profits of enterprise; b) profit-sharing, where the company recognizes the contribution of all workers and shares profits with them; c) stakeholder recognition, in which the company enlarges its definition of stakeholders to include not only shareholders and employees but also customers, suppliers and the local community where it operates; and d) global consciousness, in which the company thinks and acts globally, including not only geography but going beyond to a concern for the interrelated good of all humanity, regardless of national borders. (Caux Round Table 2000b)

With the recent advent of the world wide web, a mass of information about the social role of business is being collected and displayed on the internet. An important example is the organization Business for Social Responsibility (Business for Social Responsibility 2000). BSR thought tends to argue that practices of corporate social responsibility actually boost the economic performance of business, in terms of improved finances, reduced operating costs, enhanced brand image, increased customer loyalty, improved quality, more stable employment, and reduced regulatory oversight. (Business for Social Responsibility 2000)

The third and final movement is the growing recognition of environmental limits, and the problem of sustainability. This requires little comment. With issues such as global warming and ozone depletion so widely known, the environment has penetrated virtually everywhere as a global problematic.

Obviously the practical implementation of any such consensus on movements to mixed economies, corporate ethics, or environmental sustainability still has far to go. However, it seems that the 21st century is going to provide abundant resources for a extensive and accessible discourse about business and labor ethics along such lines, a discourse relatively unpolarized by the the right vs. left politics of much of the 20th century.

3 Some Other Ideas That Are Not Being so Well Integrated into Mainstream Business Discourse

Yet the above movements toward an integrated perspective, however edifying and progressive, also have important intellectual flaws. Much of the consensus is based on modern neo-classical economic principles of (individual) rational advantage. However, when addressing real human possibilities, consensus on such a limited neo-classical basis – whether concerned with the mixed economy, corporate ethics, or sustainability – can be accused of being romantic, utopian, and indeed from certain scientific points of view quite softheaded.

Therefore, three other points about ethics and business will be examined, which also may be essential to an integrative understanding but which are rarely adequately brought into the mainstream discussion. It will be suggested that any emergent, integrative consensus built only around the ideas of mixed economy, corporate ethics and sustainability, and not taking these other sorts of knowledge into consideration, may not be enough to solve our challenges.

The first point is the relativity of conditions of "consumption" which produce human happiness and well-being.

It should be clarified that we are not talking about the world of extreme scarcity of the weakest countries, the world which gives rise to the discourse of developmentalism. Sometimes, a "relative poverty" argument has been used to undercut the justice claims of the poorer countries. As the economist Amartya Sen has long noted, there has to be some kind of material "bottom line" or floor in considerations of scarcity and poverty.[1]

---

[1] Sen (1983) has been associated with arguments about how relative and absolute features have been mixed up in definitions of poverty, yet an important practical role must be played by certain types of absolute definition which he calls the capabilities approach.

However, if we go beyond the sphere of extreme poverty and basic developmentalism, the question of relativity of perception becomes quite prominent.

Of course the idea of relativity in material satisfaction is an ancient one. From religious studies we know that there are a multiplicity of ways to create complex existential maps of experience, with a diversity of ideas about "consumption." From a more strictly modern perspective, by drawing upon anthropology, we know that human culture is highly adaptable, flexible, and – if the productivity of the environment is not too extremely low – even under low-tech circumstances, culture is not necessarily closely causally determined by the environment.[2]

And, although postwar neoclassical economists long tended to ignore the topic of consumption, it turns out recently that as critical thinkers have made approaches to the problem, they have a great deal of trouble finding "reasonable" consumption standards and even clear definitions of "consumption." Essays in a recent survey volume, for example, reveal that conceptions of acceptable consumption (like definitions of poverty, or "the good" in classic philosophical speculation) are enormously situational, and subject to complex, multidimensional definitional arguments without clear consensus (Crocker & Linden 1998:1-18).

The second, more positive point is that the conditions which really make a difference to human well-being are principally "psychological" factors, such as social relations, which are not strongly dependent on high levels of wealth.

It hardly needs to be noted that the conservative moral messages of mainstream religious traditions are skeptical of markets and consumption. However, there also exists a highly developed moral-aesthetic secular critique of "consumer society." Material insatiability is almost a positive moral creed in some parts of the societies of advanced countries, yet a tradition of American commentary concerned with consumer society in the "successful" USA often describes a pervasive inner malaise, emotional poverty, uneasiness and melancholy (Rosenblatt 1999). In this familiar rhetoric, material appetite is not about some playful and joyful exploration of the world. Rather, it has to do with inner anxiety and imbalance; it is based in fantasy;[3] it leads to moral discontinuity and incoherence; it leads to addictive behavior; it leads to social fragmentation, loss of cohesion, or mis-focused individualism; and it can lead to social cruelty to the weak even under conditions of general abundance.

---

2 Although his work is largely concerned with development Amartya Sen's thought is also full of sophisticated relativistic elements (Sen 2000).

3 Market thinkers suggest that environmentalists and religionists are guilty of naivete and romanticism and utopianism about the "simple life," but there is plenty of evidence that market-theorists are guilty of equal naivete and romanticism and utopianism about the effects of markets and unregulated hypercompetitive economic motivations.

Many of these skeptical perspectives on consumerism have been developed and popularized in the environmental movement, which has many parallels with the suspicions about insatibility that are embedded in historical religious traditions.

Literary or quasi-religious ecological treatments may make it seem that this kind of criticism is about social and moral "aesthetics," i.e. seemingly arbitrary choices about social "flavor" and "quality." However, the key point can be understood quite scientifically. Empirical psychologists have repeatedly judged that the conditions which really make a difference to human well-being are social relations, quality of work, and availability of leisure, none of which are strongly dependent on high levels of wealth per se. (Argyle 1987). Empirically, social support is the primary condition of human happiness, yet the conditions of market society tend to erode social support and (among other things) to increase the incidence of clinical depression in countries with advanced market economies (Lane 1998: 218-248). There is a weak statistical relationship between well-being and money; more important instead is the importance of "inconspicuous consumption" (leisure, freedom from stress, family life) (Frank 1999:64-93). A very rich synthesis of these arguments has recently been published by the American political scientist Robert Lane (2000).

Finally the third point, perhaps deserving of most emphasis, concerns the dangerous role – perhaps biologically driven – of unregulated status competition in key areas of human life, including economic consumption.

Of course as a topic of political science theory egalitarianism has been the subject of a huge discourse. That is not the topic here, nor is the concern with the leftist aspect of the critical consumer-studies literature, which takes the position that consumerism is created by corporate manipulation of the public. I adopt an alternate view, in which the problem is not markets per se – markets do largely perform as advertised by economists – but rather the underlying psychological motivations, especially irrational status competion, which fuel activity in markets among the participants.

A scientific perspective on the problem has been reflected in the work of the American scholars Fred Hirsch and Robert H. Frank. Both place a skepticism about unregulated status competition on a rationalist basis free of moral sentimentality. [4]

Thus Hirsh (1976) argued that when an economy satisfies the needs of a population for basic biological needs, the concept of economic growth becomes much more compelx and ambiguous. As the level of consumption rises, it takes on more and more of a social as well as individual aspect because individual use increasingly bumps up against, and is limited, conditioned, and created by, the

---

4 See also the environmentalist view of Durning (1992:37-48); for or a statement by a philosopher about the relativity of well being and the desire to consume, see Lichtenberg (1998:155-175).

surrounding social environment. This is particularly true of position in the status hierarchy (the ultimate "economic good"), where by definition wants are always scarce and a shortage of satisfied winners in the distribution competition always persists and "economic failure" is chronic. Hirsch calls this the social scarcity of positional goods. The growth of unregulated self-interest has actually weakened the market system by damaging its moral underpinnings of self-control: as bourgeois objectives of comfort and status spread downward through the social scale the short-term political legitimacy of the system is reinforced, but the long-term frustration of an ever increasing population is guaranteed. Unregulated self-interest has harmed traditional human goods such as sociability; it has induced commodity fetishism and commercialization of more areas of culture, even as palpable economic growth demonstrably fails to increase overall human satisfaction (Hirsh 1976:111-114). It creates struggles for the redistribution of wealth that are irresolvable. The underlying difficulty is that self-interest is incomplete as a social organizing device, for it operates effectively only in coordination with some social organizing principle (and this does not necessarily mean a collectivist state) which qualifies and regulates self-interest.

Frank (1985, 1999) pursued similar arguments, which can be summarized in the following points:

- Psychological studies show that prestige and status competition tend to have a major impact on human social life and consequent economic behavior.
- The perception of status and success is relational, depending fluidly on the whole environment of shifting social "standards" (Frank 1985:3-38).
- Status competition is probably a product of evolutionary psychology and biology, therefore deeply rooted in the human mind.
- Unregulated status competition is disruptive and destructive for the following three reasons: a) Unregulated status competition is non-finite: Unlike basic biological scarcity, which can be solved, because of its inherent nature status competition cannot be brought to any conclusion. When economic growth is motivated for this reason it will end in frustration and disappointment because the effort on the "positional treadmill" is inherently interminable. b) When individual status competition gets out of control, it results in a diversion of resources and in underinvestment in socially shared goods (transportation, policing, education) which become increasingly expensive to both individuals and the larger society because of waste. Excessive competition causes a reduction in inconspicuous consumption and sacrifices in the sphere of public/collective spending. Trickle-down economics and high economic inequalities are associated with lower economic growth and greater social inefficiences. The principle is "smart for one, dumb for all" as conflict between the interests of the individual and the group exagggerates patterns of conspicuous consumption and status competition (Frank 1999: 48-63, 146,

172, 227-259). c) Unregulated competition has knock-on effects, such as exaggerating the role of very small qualitative differences when competition goes into action in the top levels of markets, resulting in "winner-take-all" markets (Frank 1985: 132-153).

- Finally, normally all traditional ethical systems try to limit the role of money in society in order to restrict the damage caused by uncontrolled competition's escalating expenditure levels (Frank 1985: 192-213).

Both Hirsch and Frank point out that the phenomenon of the social creation of desire has been ignored by neo-classical economics.

4 The Impact of Wide-open Globalization (i.e. Unregulated Competition) on Cultural Variety

In examining any question of lost cultural variety and the leveling of differences, perhaps the one key issue is this point about status competition. Nothing does more to reduce local variety and level cultural differences than the recent global regime of mass consumer competition and insatiability.

Of course, transnational consumerism in nothing new. It has a long history among the elites of imperial regimes throughout the world ranging back to ancient times. In the West, transnational consumerism began to spread among middle classes beginning about the time, for example, of the Dutch empire.

What is different now, at the beginning of the 21st century, is the ever-increasing scale of this consumerism, an increase which seems to have led to a qualitative alteration. When we talk about "globalization" today we are talking about the aggressive, universal expansion of a certain kind of status competition, associated with a certain kind of social aesthetics and even morality. An effect of globalization is thus to alter traditional, more local status hierarchies and to situate everyone in the world on the same positional treadmill. This set of conditions is unprecedented. And perhaps it is too obvious to note, but one of the main discomforts of recent globalization, which many environmentalists and anti-colonialists have noted, is also that it tends to spread a distinctively American ethos and aesthetics of consumption around the world and turn it into a kind of dominating imaginative standard.

Thus cultural critics of globalization are not wrong: in many ways, in its current form, "globalization" is not about economics at all, but about the invasion of values, and perhaps (from a critical perspective) even about ethical incompleteness or failure in the aggressors' own business and ethical culture.

5 Can We Imagine Some Kind of More Comprehensive Moral Reintegration?

We are not very close to a consensus which might incorporate not only the issues of mixed economy, corporate ethics, and sustainability, but also these other understandings concerning cultural relativity, the value of inconspicuous consumption, and the disruptiveness of excessive competitition. Indeed, if one attends to these latter three types of usually neglected, but quite scientific, arguments (and excluding, of course, the matter of economic development for the one-third of humanity which is still desperately poor) it is difficult to escape the conclusion that for two thirds of the globe – for the majority of humanity which is not actually desperately poor – globalization is not primarily about human happiness and well-being at all. It is only about a regime of accelerated growth and competition per se.

In the mainstream business literature, these brutal scientific matters – the cultural relativity of perception, the real conditions of typical human well being, and the treadmill of status competition – are hardly discussed. A disturbing fact about the current mainstream world discourse on economics is the disconnection between, on the one hand, even the most progressive mainstream business ethics, and on the other hand, what we know quite scientifically about cultural relativity, about "happiness" and "well-being," and about the dangers of unregulated competition. It seems that the globalized leadership culture has a paradoxical relation to the anthropological, religious and psychological facts: it knows about cultural relativity, but subverts it; it knows about the traditional disciplines enforced by religious traditions, but undermines them; and it knows about the evils of status and prestige competion, but it accelerates and exaggerates them.

Of course, there is an even larger disconnection between progressive business ethics and the skeptical attitudes about business which have been prevalent in historical religious traditions, even when people in those traditions were faced with conditions of scarcity. (Such remarks are not dependent on any single religion: all of the traditional ones have deep resources for dealing with the problem of self-control and its relation to society.)

A contemporary ethical critique of the overall picture can be found in parts of the "simple living" school of thought, represented for example by the American philosopher Robert Segal. Segal (1999:81-82) summarizes the dominant economic paradigm as follows:

- The good life is to found in the satisfaction of our desires, in particular desires that can be satisfied through material consumption.
- The economy contributes to the good life by providing consumers with the goods and services they desire.

- Work (along with land, capital and information) is an input within the productive process, as well as the central means through which people earn the income which allows them to purchase the good and services produced.
- Successful performance of the economy is best understood as the sustained expansion of goods and services (i.e. economic growth).
- Efficiency is primarily a matter of achieving maximum outputs (goods and services) with any level of resource input.

The alternate paradigm, in contrast, is this:

- The good life is a form of "simple living." It is found primarily in meaningful activity and the simple pleasures of friends and family. It requires an abundance of time to do things right.
- The economy contributes to a good life by providing goods and services to meet core needs, by offering meaningful forms of activity, and by providing economic security. Once core needs have been met, the consumption of goods and services is of secondary importance.
- Work is itself a central arena in which the good life is either found or lost. Work is not a mere means to income or productive output; at its best it is an opportunity for people to engage their highest qualities and creativities in ways that are of value to others. The kinds of work opportunities a society has to offer are its real outputs, the forms of life it makes available.
- Economic performance should be evaluated not in terms of economic growth but by looking at the levels of need satisfaction, levels of leisure, levels of security, and quality of work roles.
- Efficiency is primarily a matter of achieving high levels of need satisfaction at low levels of labor time or at low levels of income.

Commentators have noted, however, that such an alternate paradigm cannot work as a unilateral reform enacted only by individuals or small communities. Movements rooted in such individual effort and decision have a weak history of success because they do not reorganize the overall socio-economic framework and disposition of consumption practices (Shi 1985). It is impossible to deal with status competition on an individual basis, without the assistance of regulatory social norms.

Problems of getting a moral balance between self and society are, of course, the stock in trade of historical religious traditions. For the purposes here, it would be helpful to think of "religion" not so much as some kind of theological system of strange and possibly irrational beliefs, but as a socially shared control system to deal with mapping the experiences of individual selves in such a way as to prevent the uncontrollability of anxiety and desire. In the Buddhist tradition, for example, such ideas are not just implicit, but are quite explicit.

And thus from the point of view of the religious historian, one of the implications of "secularization" – setting aside all the theological issues – is that the secularized individual in practice often has no systematic way, rooted in prior human experience and sociality, for responding to the positional treadmill. Yet as the general moral seriousness and sobriety of historical religious traditions suggest, this task of getting control over the anxiety and desire of individual selves, and moderating the balance between individual and society, is a difficult one. Indeed, if individual hypercompetitiveness is product of some kind of evolutionary psychological history with overtones of biological maladaptation in modern societies, controlling the self-society relationship is on a par with struggling against the tendency of human beings to overemphasize sex, to crave overeating, or to become addicted to narcotics – in another words, it is a pervasive challenge.

We do not know what is going to happen in the coming century. Will it be a return to scarcity and the moral disciplines associate with scarcity? Will it be the dis-topian onset of scarcity without discipline? Will science pull more technological rabbits out of the hat, which will enable the continuing expansion of the influence of the global culture of insatiability, with the loss of variety and the leveling which accompanies it? Or, probably, will we enter an era of some extremely complex, tense mixture of cultures both of consumer insatiability and of genuine scarcity, which has already been observed in the bitter rhetorical conflicts between "north" and "south".

And yet we have an enormous body of historical experience in dealing with these problems, if we would only integrate it properly into everything else we know about economics, politics and technology. The future scientific study of economics and business has an ever-increasing responsibility to integrate critical perspectives from other disciplines of knowledge in a more sophisticated manner. We must reduce the prevalence of what can be called "idiot savant" behavior in global economic thinking, which can be defined as the application of enormous technical cleverness to the accomplishment of goals which are humanly meaningless or doubtful. Anthropology and biology, psychology and history show us that many different cultural forms can "work" within a given set of economic constraints, even when those constraints are fairly tight in low-tech societies. The diversity of choices made has as much to do with social aesthetics (rooted in history and religious traditions) as with alleged material "necessity". Mainstream business and economic thought about culture has tended to ignore such basic facts and instead to continue to serve as an expression of certain competitive forms of social aesthetics (and power) over other forms.

An anecdote about silk from wild cocoons was offered at the beginning, an anecdote illustrating a unity of concerns not only about market life, business ethics, and sustainability, but also about epistemological fluidity, the social source of happiness, and the dangers of asocial competition. The caveat was that such levels of integration may belong to the past. But do they really belong only to the past? What else can we afford to seek in the future?

References

Arimoto M. (1997), *Shûkyô Shakaishi no Kôsô – Shinshû Monto no Shinkô to Seikatsu* [Conceiving a religious social history – religiosity and lifeways among Shin Buddhist followers], Tokyo: Yoshikawa Kobunkan.

Business for Social Responsibility (2000), *Introduction to Corporate Social Responsibility*, www.bsr.org.

Caux Round Table (2000a), *Core Beliefs*, www.cauxroundtable.org/COR_BEL.HTM.

Caux Round Table (2000b), *History & Meetings*, www.cauxroundtable.org /HISTORY.HTM.

Crocker, D. A. & Linden, T. (eds.) (1998), *Ethics of Consumption: The Good Life, Justice and Global Stewardship*, New York: Rowman and Littlefield.

Durning, A. T. (1992), *How Much is Enough? The Consumer Society and the Future of the Earth*, New York: W.W. Norton.

Frank, R. H. (1985), *Choosing the Right Pond: Human Behavior and the Quest for Status*, New York: Oxford University Press.

Frank, R. H. (1999), *Luxury Fever: Why Money Fails to Satisfy in an Era of Excess*, New York: The Free Press.

Hirsh, F. (1976), *Social Limits to Growth*, Cambridge: Harvard University Press.

Lane, R. (2000), *The Loss of Hapiness in Market Democracies*, New Haven: Yale University Press.

Lane, R. (1998), The Road Not Taken: Friendship, Consumerism, and Happiness, in: Crocker, D. A. & Linden, T. (eds.), *Ethics of Consumption: The Good Life, Justice and Global Stewardship*, New York: Rowman and Littlefield: 218-248.

Lichtenberg, J. (1998), Consuming Because Others Consume, in: Crocker, D. A. & Linden, T. (eds.), *Ethics of Consumption: The Good Life, Justice and Global Stewardship*, New York: Rowman and Littlefield: 155-175.

Rosenblatt, R. (ed.) (1999), *Consuming Desires: Consumption, Culture, and the Pursuit of Happiness*, Washington, DC: Island Press.

Segal, J. M. (1999), *Graceful Simplicity: Toward a Philosophy and Politics of Simple Living*, New York: Henry Holt.

Sen, A. (2000), *Development As Freedom*, New York: Knopf.

Sen, A. (1983), Poor, Relatively Speaking, in: *Oxford Economic Papers* 35: 153-169.

Shi, D. E. (1985), *The Simple Life: Plain Living and High Thinking in American Culture*, New York: Oxford University Press.

Cosmocorporations and Cosmoconsumers: A Note on the Identity Management of German and Japanese Transnationals

Sierk A. Horn

1 Geocentrism: Feeling the Spirit

Symbols of the ongoing globalization can hardly be ignored: Advertising banners at airports such as Hong Kong International/Chek Lap Kok, Tokyo Narita or Frankfurt Rhein-Main signal passengers that they have finally reached "Marlboro-Country". Product placement is no longer limited to regional efforts. With the appearance of their new models in the John Woo-movie "Mission Impossible 2" the German automobile-producers Audi and Porsche target an international audience. Even advertising, once outpost of a phalanx of regional managers, is no longer bound to regional restraints. New Information-Technologies, World Wide Web and Multilingual Interfaces are forebearers of time- and spaceless marketing-possibilities.

One might wonder, what is going on here? Has the 1980s and 1990s mandala of the "Think global, act local"-approach lost its appeal to executives of transnational corporations? Given recent statements of top-executives one thing becomes clear: Corporate philosophies are more than ever dominated by geocentric mind-sets: J. Gogels, advisor to Mercedes Benz, speaks of the "Global Mercedes Benz-Community". P. H. Knight, CEO of sports-giant Nike, compares the employees with an international sports-team. M. Garlette, vice president of the Swiss based Nestlé-concern, praises the international "Nestlé spirit". During the planned merger of Deutsche Bank and Dresdner Bank CEO Breuer promised a bright future as a "Global Powerhouse". Certainly, companies still face a global up-hill battle and are far away from being a true cosmocorporation[1].

---

1 Studies reveal that "Global Players" are still closely connected to their country of origin (Doremus et al. 1998:140). Focussing on the human-resource-management of corporations Adler and Ghadar show the boundaries of global carrier paths. In what they call the "invisible ceiling" the promotion of local staff is limited to the position of country managers. The level of top-executives is dominated by country of origin-managers (quoted in: Meffert & Bolz 1998:287). Interviews with executives showed however that companies are preparing steps towards a more globalized human-resource-management.

But push- and pull-factors such as global sourcing, the shortening of innovation-circles or the rapid development of technology force companies to rethink their once successful ethnocentric strategies. Due to these driving parameters of globalization, corporations have to operate increasingly from a global perspective. The era of country of origin-strategies once highlighted by a "Made in..." seems to come to an end. Instead there is evidence that companies rely more than ever on "Made by..."-concepts (e.g. "Made by Mercedes-Benz" or "Made by BMW"). The perception of "Digital Dream Kid"-products, with their worldwide appeal, is no longer dominated by any regional origin. They simply become "a Sony". At the end of last decade the marketers dream of Theodore Levitt's "Global Village" has for many companies finally become true.

Based on falling telecommunication and transportation costs not only cosmoscorporations are evolving. The synchronisation of consumer behavior, the development of international customer orientation systems or the global demand for global products signal the emergence of cosmoconsumers, too. In an interview a top-executive of a well-known IT-corporation mentioned, that "the customers are already global, we – the company – are on our way of getting global". Regardless of the localization, this new consumer orders software via internet from the USA, plays video-games online with friends in Australia or leaves WAP-messages on a mobile phone in Okinawa from his computer in Europe. The dimensions of this new global system with cosmocorporations, cosmoconsumers and cosmoproducts are hardly to foresee. This evolving "One World Vision" can be illustrated by a Japanese girl visiting Los Angeles: Thinking of "*Makudonarudo*" as a Japanese company, she could hardly believe that McDonald's also exists in the United States (Friedman 1999:238). This example depicts converging value systems (especially of young consumers), in which a corporate identity or a product identity can no longer be associated with a specific region or country. Next to distinct regional or local orientation systems there is a co-evolutionary shift towards cosmopolitic values influencing future consumer behavior. This evolving cosmopolitan view[2] will form the basis of geocentric marketing strategies.

2 Marketing in the Cosmoarena

There is a growing need for international marketing strategies that reflect not only ethnocentric or polycentric premises but focus also on the converging mind sets of consumers. In the light of these developments basic marketing knowledge of

[2] Friedman (1999) illustrates the impact of the globalization by means of interviews and case studies. His multidimensional approach sheds light on the paradox of this evolving global value system on the one hand and the necessity of distinct local affinities on the other hand.

adjusting product- and communication-strategies to the local markets has to be reconsidered. Core competences have to be validated across borders. Intercultural or "hybrid" key values of products that take shared consumer beliefs into account have to be deducted and integrated into geocentric marketing strategies. For an increasing number of products traditional marketing wisdom on how consumer behavior in country X and country Y is different or how the diverging consumer needs can be met seem to be relicts of the past.

Instead of focussing on the heterogenity product managers will have to comprehend the evolving homogenity of markets and consumers. What are the communalities of the consumer value system in country X and country Y? Which key values of a product are transnationally valid? Which product identity is shared by the consumers in country X and country Y? Questions like these will form the basis of future success. The creation of "hybrid" corporate or product identities sheds light on the far-reaching scope of geocentric strategies and stresses the importance of a proactive rather than a reactive course towards globalization. Consider the following examples of the dynamics and multidimensionalities of international marketing approaches:

- According to E. Bernard, executive of Nestlé Japan, the Nestlé product portfolio consists of 700 local brands, 140 regional brands and 35 global brands. Labeling standards, branding-policies and design-guidelines of global brands are centralized in the headquarter of Vevey, Switzerland. Its instant coffee Nescafé Excella for example is based on the key value of "international heritage" and is promoted worldwide with TV-commercials showing the product in slice of life-situations (family scenes/morning coffee). The communication strategy for Nescafé Golden Blend however is localized. Except for an interlude between 1987 and 1989, when Nestlé tried to establish coffee-products as an afternoon beverage in the Japanese market, well-known testimonials promote the Golden Blend brand in Japan. On the level of the corporate identity the slogan "Good food, good life" was developed by its Japanese subsidiary. The definition of this Nestlé-core-competence was accessed by the company network and is now used all over the world. The geocentric "Good food, good life"-competence became integral part of Nestlé's globalization strategy.
- The necessity of intra-organisational exchange of marketing-related information is increasingly emphasized by transnational operating companies. Sharing research methods, brand building investment costs, customer insights, best practices, brand strategy development processes, brand management models, positioning and segmentation models will be the key of developing geocentric marketing strategies (Aaker 2000:309). For instance, Matsushita executives meet on a regular basis to share best practices in different markets. Aaker reports from "Honda-teams", which are sent to regional markets to learn successful practices firsthand. Henkel and Sony at the CEO level and

IBM and Mobil at the brand manager level arrange meetings to gain access to successful brand strategies in different markets. Procter and Gamble established a strategic planning staff aiming at the diffusion of marketing know-how in the companies network (Aaker 2000:313). Sony introduced the European Marketing Support System EIS (Executive Information System), which provides country managers with market insights (e.g. consumer/competitor behavior in other markets, market share) online (Absatzwirtschaft 1993:72). In order to coordinate international marketing efforts companies implement structural and organisational methods such as guidelines, teams or regional communication managers to detect and enforce corporate or product identities on the synergetic basis of "hybrid" key values.

- Marketing research no longer focuses on local customer evaluation. The German Gesellschaft für Konsumforschung (Association of consumer research/GfK) studies the *uniformization* of buying behavior in Europe. In its "Euro Styles"-panel GfK has identified a cluster of 16 consumer-typologies in Europe (Berndt, Altobelli & Sander 1997:265). With the emergence of Eastern European markets consumer research is expanded to Poland, Czech Republic or Slovenia. But not only regional marketing research is conducted. Companies go on to gather consumer information on a worldwide basis. German automobile-producers introduced panel studies in Europe, America and Asia to detect similarities and dissimilarities of the value systems of consumers. A Scandinavian IT-company initiated an international marketing research program to find possible synergies of positioning and segmentation strategies. An American brewery studied consumer-tastes in more than 20 countries in three world-regions to identify the necessity of adapting its products to local preferences (e.g. ingredients, flavor, bottle design).

As the examples above demonstrate the new global system unfolds on two dimensions: The globalization of consumers and the globalization of corporations. There is an increasing synchronisation of consumer behavior, which has to be recognized by the marketing strategies of globalizing companies. Even though local dissimilarities will remain (one has to think of the German beer market with its strong local product identities or the Japanese music industry, in which Japanese bands take a lead in music productions), there is a central tendency of converging mind sets with the World Wide Web, Media over-spill[3] or increased customer mobility as drivers of this consumer revolution. Thus, emerging cosmoconsumer will be demanding cosmoproducts.

---

3 Media are no longer bound to specific regions. With the rise of new communication technology TV-programs such as MTV, CNN or Star TV are operating increasingly on a geocentric level.

Nowadays global brands are neither limited to certain product categories[4] nor exclusively from a certain region (once global products were surprisingly often American, e.g. Coca Cola, Marlboro or Kellog's). For instance, Japanese beer brands such as Kirin, Asahi or Sapporo are en vouge all over the world. Luxury goods such as Montblanc or Gucci sell as well in New York as in Tokyo, Paris or Johannesburg. Mercedes Benz- or BMW-products meet the demands of the consumers worldwide. Of course, the development of a global product or global brand is not a black-or-white strategy. It is rather a matter of degree. Adaptation can take place in a variety of forms: For instance adjusted branding strategies (Procter&Gamble, for instance, uses different brand names in different countries), adjusted packaging or color (e.g. Sony uses transparent packaging in the United States to meet the consumer needs of "seeing what one buys"), adjusted features (e.g. German car-makers offer right hand and left hand steering in Japan), adjusted ingredients (e.g. McDonald's uses chili sauce instead of ketchup in Mexico) or adaptation in size (e.g. a German car seat-manufacturer researches the size of Japanese drivers to adapt the proportions of its products to the safety needs of the Japanese market). In the light of the new global system with its global customers companies strive, however, for more standardized strategies and try to limit the necessary adaptation to local markets.

Understandably Nestlé with its 700 local brands or Gillette with its 800 products sold in more than 200 countries are looking for ways to cut down costs that result from local marketing strategies (e.g. extra expenses for advertising agencies, packaging, promotion, product adaptation). To illustrate on the other hand the cost explosion due to highly diversified marketing strategies look at the following examples:

- The Gillette shampoo series Silkience is based on the same ingredients and formulas, but the French brand name is Soyance, the Italian brand name is Sientel and in Germany the product is called Silience (Kotler 1997:414).
- An American-German car manufacturer targets young, urban, sophisticated females and males (25 to 40 years old, university educated, with a modern, active lifestyle) in Japan, whereas its products rely more on a family-appeal in Germany.
- Nissin Cup Noodles uses a localization approach in advertising-communication, ranging from adapting Japanese commercials (in Germany the award winning "Hungry?"-CM was shown with a fork instead of chopsticks) to totally assimilated communication strategies (e.g. terracotta

4 Even though one might think of fashion- and food-products to be highly culture-bound and therefore influenced by regional preferences, the globalization of these industries is very much advanced. Yamamoto, Prada or Jil Sander, for instance, sell their products to global customers. Hamburgers, Sushi or Frankfurters became part of daily consumation anywhere and thus formed a "global" eating culture.

soldiers for their "*Demae-Itchô*" product-line in Hong Kong) (Sakurai 1998:45).

These companies follow the paradigm of "global consumers and local companies" (*shôhisha ga gurôbaru kigyô ga rôkaru*, Katahira 1998:296), neglecting cost-reduction, possibilities of inter-market synergies and simplification of managing a global brand by means of a more standardized approach.

Yet, many other companies are increasingly involved in standardizing their global marketing strategies, in developing "hybrid" product identities and in positioning as a global partner. In a cross-marketing campaign German Bundespost declares that it "moves worlds", whereas Messe Frankfurt "creates global markets". The newly formed Star Alliance is the "Airline network for earth" and Mitsubishi declares that it is a "healthy, global company" (*Kenzen na gurôbaru entâpuraisu*). These open statements of "going global" or "being global" are signals of the intensifying global competition. Facing foreign competitors on their local markets, many companies have to take a second look at the chances and challenges of the new global system. Global brand leadership – as Aaker (2000:303 ff.) calls the 21st century quest for the intercultural relevance of brands – centers around a distinct brand identity that is valid in all markets[5], supporting and tapping best practices in a company network.

3 Managing "Identity" in the International Context

In relation to the unfolding globalization process, the author conducted a research project on how the driving forces of cosmocorporations and cosmoconsumers are shaped by German and Japanese companies operating transnationally (Horn 2000). Juxtaposing German and Japanese strategies the research takes a fresh look at the dimensions brought forth by globalization. Thus, it aimed at measures taken by German and Japanese companies to manage corporate and product identities in the unfolding global market. From March to June 1999 more than 120 marketing executives in headquarters and local subsidiary companies in Germany and Japan were interviewed[6] on the importance, aims and strategies of global identity management. The geocentric objective of symmetric transparence – cosmo-corporations can no longer be attributed to headquarter activities but have also take into account the company network – was reflected on terms of a four group

5 Future segmentation strategies might be focussing not on regional but on international benefits. To be more precise, product identities could be developed that target customers worldwide in metropolitan or rural areas. In this sense segmentation would rather rely on psycho-demographic benefits than on geographic preferences.

6 Full coverage on the collected data of the research project on German and Japanese transnationals can be found in Horn (2000).

design: German and Japanese headquarters and their subsidiary companies in Japan respectively in Germany. Not only the challenges of local corporate identity strategies[7] were pursued, but also the aspects of the identity management on an international level were integrated into the research. The contributions by the marketing-experts provided new perspectives and useful insights into the challenge of globalization German and Japanese companies face today.

The relevance of an international corporate identity was stressed by German and Japanese executives. In both headquarters and local subsidiary companies, the development of a transnational valid identity system was rated unequivocally important. More than a third of the respondents see in an international identity management a very important factor for future success (38.7%). 46.8% of the German and Japanese executives rated it as an important factor, whereas only 13.7% of the respondents rated the importance of identity management on international markets semi-relevant. Few executives attribute a subordinate role to international corporate identity strategies (less important: 0.8%, invalid: 1.6%). As shown in figure 1 the majority of executives in all groups emphasized the relevance of an identity management in the international context. Significant differences could neither be found between German and Japanese companies nor between headquarters and subsidiary companies. However, Japanese headquarters pay especially attention to identity management in the international context. More than half of the respondents rated this aspect as very important for the future success of their company (51.4%).

The empiric evidence of the relevance of developing an international identity system found in all four groups is supported by the respondents estimation on future perspectives (Will identity-oriented actions with international relevance increase or will they rather decrease?). Again, the majority of marketing-executives emphasized the future importance of a transnationally valid identity: More than three quarters of all respondents rated identity-oriented measures as very increasing or increasing (83.6%). Even though inter-group differences could not be found, the group-evaluation indicated an increasing interest especially in German headquarters (very increasing/increasing: 93.3%). Thus, empiric evidence illustrates the growing importance of identity-oriented measures with international relevance. Clearly, the development of an international identity system will be a key factor in the globalization process of German and Japanese corporations.

---

7 In order to compare the affinities and diversities on the perception of the "One World Vision" not only the groups were divided into headquarters and local subsidiaries. The questionnaire itself also contained a national and international part with an overall number of 153 items.

Figure 1: Importance in the International Context

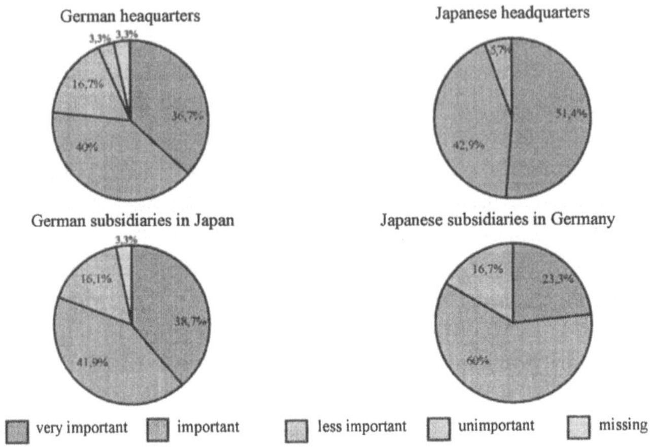

Question: How important is identity management for the future success on inter-national markets?

Source: Horn (2000).

Pinpointing concrete coordination mechanisms the executives were asked, which measures their companies take to support the development of an international identity system. As shown in figure 2 actions pursued by German and Japanese headquarters differ significantly in focus as well as in extent. According to the respondents more than 90% of Japanese corporations rely primarily on intra-organisational exchange of information. Standardization of communication and design-guidelines take also a lead in external coordination mechanisms, followed by prerogative rules on communication topics and content. In comparison, German headquarters concentrate primarily on regulations on communication topics (69%), followed by a coordination-mix of an international target system, design-guidelines, teams to coordinate communication strategies and intra-organisational exchange of information. Surprisingly, in both samples advertising agencies (mix of local agencies, international network) played a minor role.

Figure 2: External Coordination Mechanismus (Headquarters)

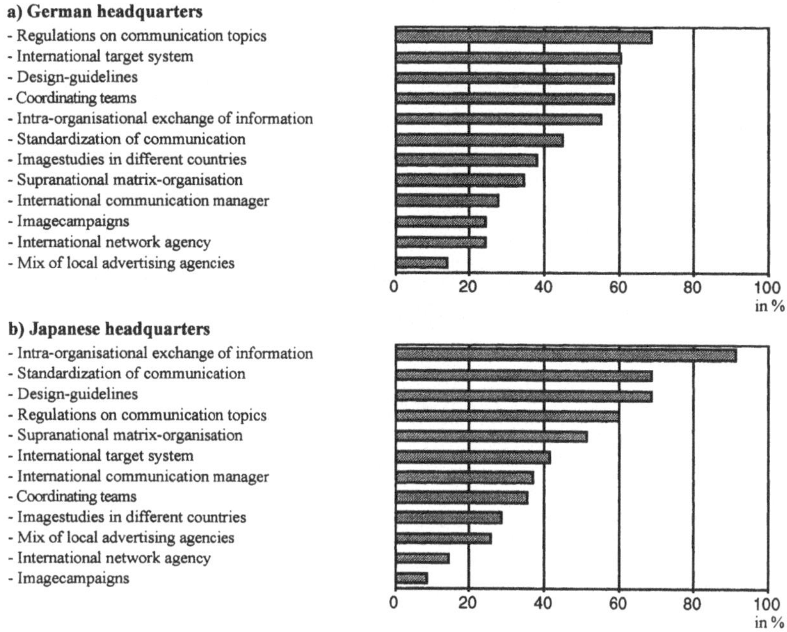

Source: Horn (2000).

The empirical findings illustrate different approaches to coordinate and integrate brand identity on an international level: Japanese corporations try to tap best practices of the company network by means of implementing structures which support intra-organisational information exchange. Whereas the importance of synergies between markets is stressed in this group, German companies emphasize a more one-sided approach of guidelines and regulations with the headquarters in its center. As shown in figure 3 the importance of intra-organisational information exchange was confirmed by the Japanese subsidiary companies, which also takes a predominant role in coordination mechanisms. There is however a distinctive gap between the perceptions of coordination mechanisms in headquarters and local subsidiaries. Even though this gap is particularly evident in Japanese affiliates, respondents of German subsidiary companies, too, rated the implementation-level of coordinating parameters significantly lower as their headquarter-counterparts. Inter-group comparisons indicated significant differences in standardization of communication, regulations on communication topics, intra-organisational information exchange and communication management, in both German and Japanese samples. Empirical evidence refers to a central tendency that formal and structural coordinating measures implemented by German and Japanese headquarters are not equally perceived by their local affiliates.

Figure 3: External Coordination Mechanismus (Subsidiary Companies)

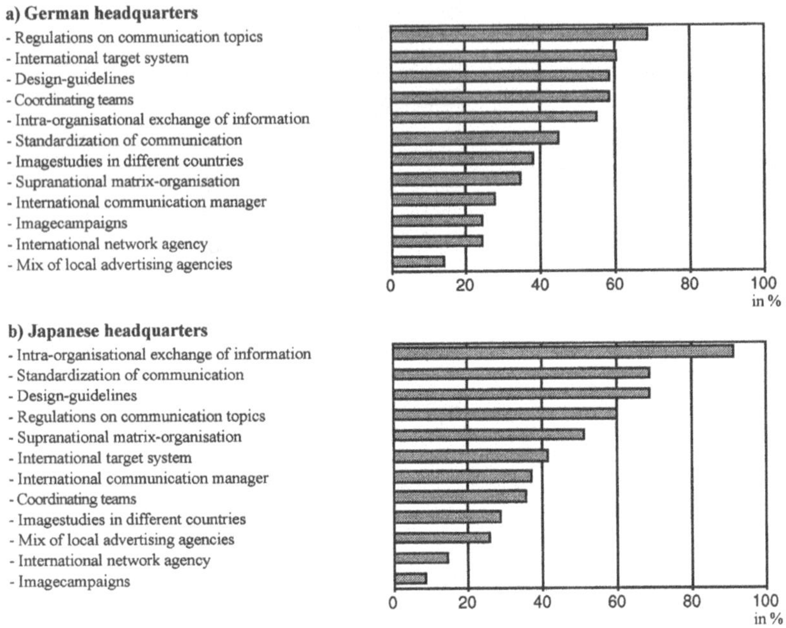

Source: Horn (2000).

4 Coordination and Integration: The "Hybrid" Identity

Discussions on "identity", brand identity or corporate identity, witness a renaissance. Extensive attention was paid to brand image/customer loyalty in the 1980s. Under the auspices of Aaker (1991) perspectives of brand equity were the marketing focal point of the 1990s. The end of last decade however saw a rise in identity-oriented issues. Aoki (1999:36) and Minamiyama (1999:44) postulate for instance a "recursive relationship between customers and brands" (*kokyaku-burandokan no kankeisei*) as the basis of identity building activities. Suyama & Umemoto (2000:248) propose an increasing interest in identity building actions in Japanese companies that seem to withdraw from the "ambiguity" of former marketing strategies. Katahira (1998:81) introduced the "dream" (*yume*) as a key element of future brand building activities. This "dream", "vision" or "mind-identity" – that has to be as vivid as possible – is the core of any brand or corporate identity. Aaker (2000:8) refers openly to the growing importance of identity management. As a new brand imperative he introduces the new paradigm "brand leadership", which is rather strategic than tactical, rather broad focussed than limited and consequently centers on "identity" as the driver of strategy. Hence, a slow shift from reactive to proactive approaches can be seen, reinforcing theories on corporate identity-parameters such as philosophy, core competences, two-way communication or design-guidelines.

With the unfolding global system, however, "identity" can no longer be limited to local or regional activities. The creation and deduction of key values that exceed local markets and project a geocentric scope of relevance seem mandatory for future success in the international market place. The "Marlboro-Country"-strategy with its geocentric definition exemplifies the possibility of a transnational valid core identity. Primed by the emotional cowboy-world, the product developed a distinct appeal that can hardly be challenged by other tobacco manufacturers locally and globally. Based on the controversial Toscani-campaign on social issues, the Italian manufacturer Benetton was able to establish an intelligible corporate identity with geocentric relevance.

Regardless of product or corporate identities the challenges brought forth by the globalization process have to be reflected in "hybrid" key values, that allow geocentric integration and – if necessary – polycentric adaptation. Empirical Research by the author supports the thesis of the relevance of identity management in the new global system. This indicates that the globalization process of German and Japanese corporations will be closely accompanied by identity- related issues. An identity management is regarded as a key factor of successful geocentric strategies. Moreover, the majority of German and Japanese executives expect a significant increase in corporate actions towards establishing an identity from a global perspective. In developing an identity system with transnational, "hybrid" relevance the above mentioned importance of "Made by..."-concepts will further expand. Presently, both German and Japanese companies are implementing a variety of mechanisms, focussing on formal as well as structural coordination of identity strategies. Empirical evidence, however, indicates that there are distinct approaches towards the geocentric integration. German executives stress the importance of a centralized decision process. The coordination profile of the German sample revealed that guidelines and regulations on communication are the main objectives of communication strategies across borders. In comparison, Japanese corporations primarily rely on the exchange of information. Both headquarter and subsidiary executives emphasize coordination mechanisms tapping best practices of the company network. In contrast to the *commanding* system in German corporations *connecting* coordination mechanisms seem to be predominant in Japanese corporations. At the moment, it is impossible to predict which strategy is more promising or will be more successful. The new global system is just unfolding. Yet, we are just beginning to understand its new dimensions of cosmocorporations, cosmoconsumers and cosmoproducts.

References

Aaker, D. (1991), *Managing Brand Equity*, New York: The Free Press.

Aaker, D. (1995), *Building Strong Brands*, New York: The Free Press.

Aaker, D. (2000), *Brand Leadership*, New York: The Free Press.

Aoki, Y. (1999), *Burando Birudingu no Jidai* [The Era of Brand Building], Tokyo: Dentsû Tekku.

Absatzwirtschaft (1993), Das Management der Führungsinformationen, in: *Absatzwirtschaft* April: 70-73.

Berndt, R., Altobelli, C. F. & Sander, M. (1997), *Internationale Marketing-Politik*, Berlin et al.: Springer Verlag.

De Mooji, M. (1997), *Global Marketing and Advertising: Understanding Cultural Paradoxes*, Thousand Oaks: Sage Inc.

Doremus, P., Keller, W. Pauly, L. & Reich, S. (1998), *The Myth of the Global Corporation,* Princeton: Princeton University Press.

Friedman, T. (1999), *The Lexus and the Olive Tree*, London: Harper Collins Publishers.

Horn, S. A. (2000), Strategisches Identitätsmanagement Transnationaler Unternehmen, published on microfiche at Free University Berlin.

Katahira, H. (1998), *Pawâ Burando no Honshitsu* [The Essence of Power Brands], Tokyo: Daiyamondosha.

Katahira, H. (1999), Burando no DNA toshite no Tôsôshin [Conflicts and Brand DNA], in: Egusa T. (ed.), *Burando Kôchiku*, Tokyo: Yûhikaku: 45-62.

Katahira, H. & Sano Y. (1997), Futari no Shôhisha [Two Customers], in: *Kikan Mâketingu Jânaru* 66: 16-30.

Kotler, P. (1997), *Marketing Management*, London: Prentice Hall.

Meffert, H. & Bolz, J. (1998), *Internationales Marketing-Management*, Berlin: Kohlhammer-Edition Marketing.

Minamiyama H. (1999), Senryakuteki Aidentiti Manejimento no Honshitsu [The Essence of Strategic Identity Management], in: *Senden Kaigi* 594: 44-47.

Nonaka, I., Takeuchi, H. & Umemoto K. (1998), *Chishiki Sôzô Kigyô* [The Knowledge Creating Company], Tokyo: Tôyô Keizai Shinpôsha.

Suyama, K. & Umemoto, H. (2000), *Nihongata Burando Yûi Senryaku* [Chances for Japanese Branding], Tokyo: Daiyamondosha.

The Technological Revolution in World Markets: Strategies for Global Company Competitiveness

Carsten Fussan

1 Global Technological Challenges

A new technology-centric economy with different interaction and valuation rules for economic success shapes increasingly the reality of global companies. Technical innovations influence international market structures, value chains, customer interaction and dominant parts of the competitive landscape.

The world is connecting at a dramatic rate, as evidenced by the growth in cross border trade, with exports now constituting over 26% of the world's GDP. At the same time, we are observing sustained economic growth in North America and growing economies in Europe and Asia Pacific. The growth of foreign direct investment is approaching $500 billion. (IBM 2000) Significantly, a growing proportion of investment is related to cross-border mergers and acquisitions – evidence of increasing international trust and openness to deeper economic interdependence. In its core, globalization implies a diminished importance of national borders to the movement of goods, services, capital and talent. (IBM 2000)

The volume of international e-commerce business is estimated up to $7 trillion by 2004, 40% above the most bullish last years estimations (IBM 2000). It is obvious that electronic markets revolutionize context and rationality of international economics in a fundamental way. Companies are forced to implement new technical solutions in their strategies and in their value chains. Aggressive outsourcing becomes a competitive necessity. Integrated value chains become flexible value nets, in which markets begin to substitute for traditional management control. Coupled with the profound shift of value to knowledge work, and the global adoption of free market capitalism, basic assumptions about business must be re-examined. (Knight & Cavusgil 1996, IBM 2000)

Ownership no longer drives asset control – information trumps ownership; and traditional assets are liabilities. Reproduction and distribution cost virtually nothing for information products. Furthermore, equity is replacing cash as the vehicle for acquisitions, minority investments and employee attraction and retention (IBM 2000). Business culture can't cope – social systems, business processes, shared habits create hidden inertia. To be effective, business models, key processes in organizations and measurements must be consistent with the realities of the new economy.

The following figure highlights the major technological trends we are presently facing.

Figure 1: Technology Trends

Technology Trend	Characteristics	Implication on Corporate Competitive Environment
Information-, Computer-Communication Technology	- Convergence of traditionally separated areas: Computer, Communication, Media, Content Technology - Mass markets relevance on global level through price reduction of technical infrastructure and available networking facilities	- General redefinition of international value chain and company interaction networks - New markets and product emergence - R+D and company organization become critical success factor
Internet	- Worldwide accessible infrastructure medium in combination with reliable and cost effective browser and transmittance technology is a basis for new interaction and information forms	- Reduced information costs and new sources of information for companies - New customer relations B2C, B2B - New international networks, e.g. sourcing, sales and community building
Biotechnology	- Precise knowledge of molecular and cellular biology, genetics and biotechnology lead to e.g. bioinformatics biorobotics and combinatoric chemistry	- Emergence of new industries like health care, environmental management, food and non food in vitro production, etc.
Material Technology	- Optimized development of new materials through specific modification of atomar and molecular structures - Micro-Engineering	- Innovation wave and new product emergence - New R+D networks with universities, research centers and companies - Process innovations with new production methods

Source: Own analysis based on Kaounides (1999) and Dandridge & Levenburg (2000).

New technologies influence nearly every segment of the value chain or redefine the value chain as a whole. New markets for newly invented products are emerging or the demand structure is changing due to new fashions or information promoted by the Internet. New products emerge out of R&D results and innovative services start from new ICC-opportunities[1]. Fast changing product life cycles are just one obvious result. The Internet in combination with communication and computer technology allows a more intense relationship with customers. Machine interaction between seller and buyer revolutionize

[1] ICC: Information, Communication, Computer.

distribution and service relationships. Much more individuality can be offered. Due to the revolution of Internet information and research capabilities the buying power of customers increases rapidly. Consequently the cost pressure on international companies rises.

Information transparency is provided by network and search software. Different companies combine production and information processes with ICC innovations in a cost effective way. Because of software and hardware innovation the production processes are more flexible and efficient. Process innovation, the rising complexity of several products and permanent search for sufficient solutions extend the pressure on corporations any size. Global online information access and the related international transparency increase the cost, service, innovation and quality competition on producing companies. (Karagozoglu & Lindell 1998, Jolly et al. 1992)

These aspects are examples of value chain implications. The permanent pressure on each segment of the value chain or the overall cost position results in a rising necessity for strategic redefinition (see figure 2).

Figure 2: Effects of New Technologies on the Value Chain

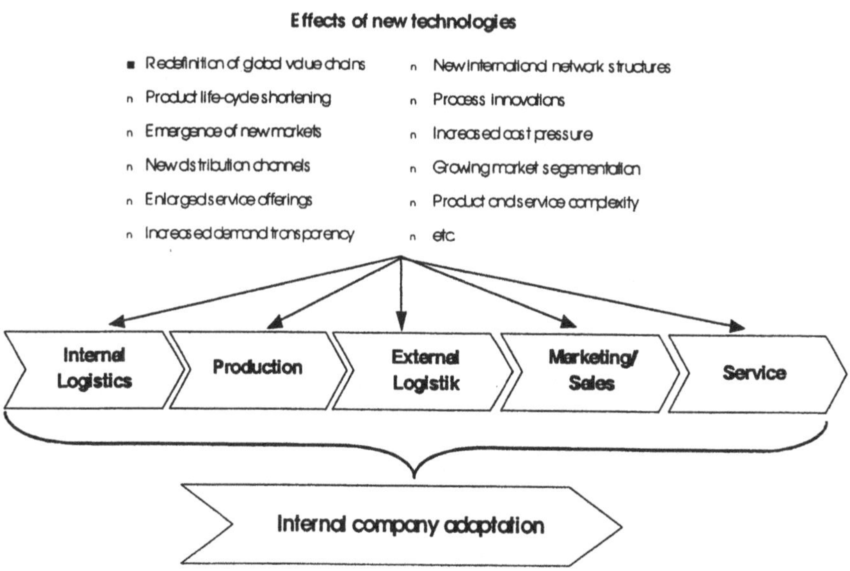

Consequently emerging technologies enlarge the adaptation and innovation pressure on companies. The general value chain is object of potential adjustments or redefinitions. (Tapscott 1996, IFO 1999) International and national strategies are subject of evaluation and only a path near the optimum through the various influencing variables leads to sustainable economic success (see figure 3).

Figure 3: Impact of New Technologies

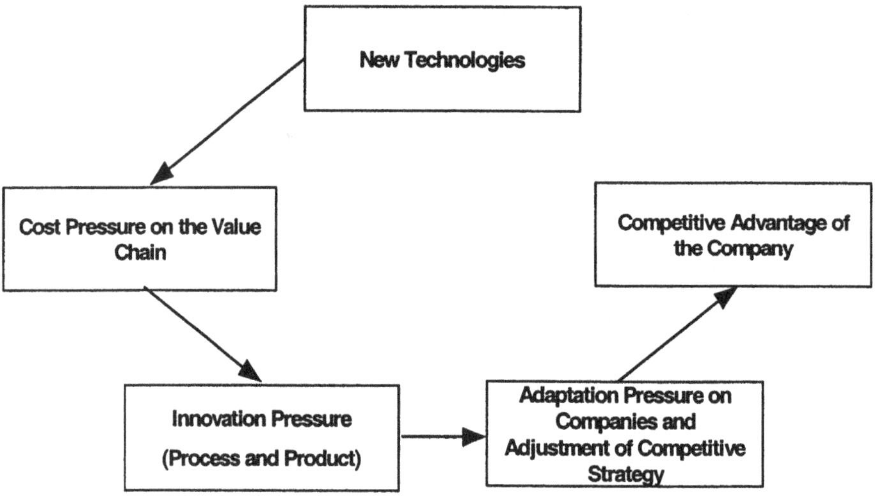

2 Success Factors in International Markets

A set of success factors (see figure 4) for small firms can be deducted from the structure of technological influences. The adaptation and innovation pressure on companies and every segment of their value chain rewards firms with the ability of quick and sophisticated reaction. The dynamism of production and product variability can only be managed if the learning and changing ability of the whole company, especially of the management and the R&D department, is international competitive (Fussan 1997).

Figure 4: Global Success Factors

- Companies adaptation ability
- Innovation competence
- Strong customer relationship
- Segment specific price (unelastic differentiation strategy)
- Global market-leadership strategy
- Use of new technologies for product and process innovation
- Concentration on company specific knowledge and core competencies (strategy of complex differentiation and market barrier assembling)
- International and technology experienced management team
- Permanent review of competitive strategy

Rising complexity and advanced service expectations of customers result in an increasing need for advanced customer relationship management (Österle & Muther 1999). Companies with outstanding client integration anticipate future needs and avoid dead-end productions.

Increasing cost pressure and the general uneasy position of especially small firms in cost-competitive industries (missing economies of scale advantages) strengthens the necessity of a differentiated strategy. Only through value adding additional components a comparison to cost competitive standard products can be avoided (price unelastic strategy, Simon 1996).

Specialization is generally correlated with a niche strategy. In mass markets small firms face strong product and price competition with large companies. In times of international transparency any worldwide niche competitor is in a dangerous position as far as the product is exportable even if the competitors location is distant (Simon 1996, Wolff & Pett 2000). Because of small volumes of niche markets, dominant global market control by producers is necessary for a sustainable position. Specialized firms need a high degree of market control and have to defend it internationally. (Johanson & Vahlne 1977, McDougall & Oviatt 1996). On the other hand, a profitable national niche without the threat of international competition avoids an preventive globalization strategy (Porter 1998).

New technologies with cost advantages must be implemented both in product innovations and process improvements. Extreme cost pressure enforces these tendencies. The precondition for future oriented company development is a current knowledge basis within the firm and the management. Continuous learning and creative improvement of core competencies and innovations is the basis for success. Any specialized knowledge is at the same time an entrance barrier for competitors (Simon 1996). Emerging technologies offer several ways of exploiting innovation advantages in this sense.

The overall success factor "strategy" is widely discussed. The strategic advantage of companies can be enlarged by a quick and strong redefinition of the corporate strategy (Simon 1996) depending on the changing environment and new technological developments. The ability to change is one of the most underestimated barriers to successful development of companies.

3 Adaptation Management – Implications for Strategic Company Reaction

How can companies increase their ability of identifying and setting into action the specific success factors for competition in the new economy?

The different decision-relevant actors within the company's internal environment usually are embedded in a complex structure of personal, technical and knowledge related variables. The conceivable company's repertoire of strategies is related to the intra-structural ability of complexity reduction (Luhmann 1968) of external factors and to the organizational setting of internal strategy and decision development. Consequently competitive strategies of companies are a function of the external variables given. (Porter 1998) But as we know, this relation is complex. Not only the variety of company-strategies in the same economic environment differs but also their degree of simplicity (Miller 1993, Pascale 1989). There is some evidence that simple strategies just concentrating on a few competitive factors like costs, quality, marketing or innovation are as much successful as multifaceted strategies (Miller 1993). As a whole the corporate strategic set as well as its organizational implementation is a source of competitive success.

Consequently the conditions and mechanisms of strategy development and organizational change must be considered. These conditions predefine the success of a strategy by influencing its scope *and* its organizational realization. This interactive organizational part can be described as "adaptation management". It is the source of innovation or agony, it can be the critical process for identifying and implementing success factors in complex and turbulent environments like the present revolutionary technological development.

The core of adaptation management is knowledge and information management. Knowledge management itself can be divided in internal and external knowledge management. Internal knowledge management describes the availability and connection of knowledge within the company. Efficient knowledge software use, personal interaction and innovative data warehousing are keys to optimal internal knowledge integration. External knowledge management includes acquisition of new information and knowledge from different sources like customers, research institutions, competitors, new employees, etc. Another part is external knowledge networking, i.e. institutionalized knowledge and information sharing among organizations with future oriented market focus. The anticipation of future developments and the timely integration of the related critical innovation sources are key elements. In early stages of a new product's life cycle knowledge might be cheap through e.g. patent acquisition or research laboratory cooperation, in later stages it could be roughly expensive due to market valuated M&A transactions.

The second element of adaptation management is the process of intra-company knowledge implementation. Bureaucratic companies most likely have a more complex and rigid way of setting new business aspects into action than a young high tech startup company. Knowledge implementation has to do with structured strategy development, organizational learning, reengineering and change management. Different step models for each of those aspects have been developed and sold by consultancies and scientific publications. Several software solutions help companies with both knowledge management and its implementation.

The most important aspect of adaptation management is the ability of companies to understand and react on their changing economic environment. It includes the internal loops of companies before and after strategy definition. A strategy is the outcome of this process and the general guideline for concrete economic action. The post-action evaluation of the strategy's effect is again a task of adaptation management. In other words adaptation management is a way of complexity reduction of organizations and could be compared with the self-adjusting part of living systems. Figure 5 summarizes the elements of adapatation management.

In general the intra-company complexity of knowledge management and implementation is probably sometimes greater than the environmental complexity. The sustainable balance between investments in necessary knowledge management, successful strategic simplicity and the expected revenue of innovative future markets is the key to success. Simple strategic targeting (Miller 1993) based on an efficient knowledge generation and implementation within a change-oriented organization structure can lead to major success. Companies with such an ability can be seen as highly adaptive.

The expertise in adaptability is a combination of different company actors and systems. The more adaptable a company is the more efficient its change processes are. The efficiency of adaptation management is determined by the synergetic combination of individual cognition, organizational support and perception (Schirmer 1992). Practically, a highly innovative company in an R&D intensive environment could be adaptive-efficient with a lot of organizational slack (Staehle 1991) and room for creativity. On the other hand, a very complex adaptable company structure for a simple economic environment could be highly inefficient.

Figure 5: Adaptation Management

Knowledge Management	**Strategy Implementation Management**
• Knowledge input (Technology Transfer)	• Change Management
• Knowledge availability	• Reengineering
•Intra-company knowledge pooling	• Process Development
• Knowledge integration (Product and process innovation	• IT-infrastructure scoping and implementing
• External knowledge networking	

Consequently the appropriate degree of adaptation complexity depending on the degree of market change and innovation pressure leads to the optimum between managing turbulent environments with a minimum of adjustment costs. The better the adaptation ability of the internal corporate structure is the less transaction costs the company has to calculate for implementing new strategies (Fussan 1997:136).

The permanent pressure of new technologies on the value chain results consequently in an competitive advantage for fast adapting companies. Their cost position for reconstructing the value chain or for creating product or process innovations is below slow adapting competitor's with significantly larger amounts of redundant costs.

The central part for implementing several success factors for new technology influenced markets is adaptation management with its core elements knowledge and change management for reengineering. The future relevance of this approach will be defined mostly by the overall competitive situation in world markets. The more the cost and innovation pressure rises the more efficient adaptation management plays an important role.

4 Global Perspectives

The influence of technological change in world markets defines new international solutions for integrating different value chains. The markets are more linked together, interaction mechanisms are defined by new technology like the Internet, less by personal and cultural influenced aspects. International internet e-trading platforms ignore cultural defined preferences of the involved actors. New international network structures are implemented mostly by a new generation of scientists and managers with a more or less comparable technological background – consequently with an equalized socialization structure.

In the last years the degree of market prohibition and protection by trade borders or political barriers has been reduced (Moen 2000; Madsen & Servais 1997). The more the world markets are linked together and the more international trade takes place the less we observe cultural defined specific trade practices. A hard cost competition dominates international interests and closed cultural habits are weakened. More and more culture neutralized international trade and negotiation standards are accepted.

Nevertheless the internal structures of corporate organization and decision are widely untouched by international equalization. Korean style of internal communication or strategy definition can be seen as significantly different to American or European habits for example (Hofstede 1993). As a result the way companies manage their internal adaptation processes is different. Finally the degree of adaptation ability and the volume of related internal transaction costs must be competitive to international players. Excellent Japanese companies for example have a comparable decision time or an adequate creativity level to western competitors of the same level (Fussan 1997).

The market pressure of new technologies tend to equalize cultural differences on the surface of international corporate interaction and trade but leave the internal structures widely untouched. Firms manage their internal adaptation processes with high cultural individuality but compete with high standardized mechanisms. The cost position for adaptation must be fairly competitive, the way of moving towards this point is cultural specific.

This conclusion can be applied to different parts of the industry or to different companies. There is no unique way of optimal adaptation management. Adaptation management is a specific process related to the special sociological environment of every company. Standardized methods or software products of optimizing the adaptation management ability of companies are excellent tools for constructing individuality. The result counts, not the way to achieve it.

References

Dandridge, T. & Levenburg, N. M. (2000), High-tech Potential? An Exploratory Study of Very Small Firm's Usage of the Internet, in: *International Small Business Journal* 18,2: 81-91.

Fussan, C. (1997), *Wettbewerbsvorteile durch Unternehmensevolution*, Wiesbaden: Gabler Verlag.

Hofstede, G. (1993). Die Bedeutung von Kultur und ihren Dimensionen im internationalen Management, in: Haller, M. et al. (eds.), *Globalisierung der Wirtschaft. Einwirkungen auf die Betriebswirtschaftslehre*, Bern: Akademie Verlag: 127-148.

IBM (2000), *Global Market Trends 2000 – IBM Corporate Strategy*, New York & San Francisco: IBM.

IFO (1999), *Globalisierung und neue Informations- und Kommunikationstechnologien*, ifo-Schnelldienst 25/99.

Johanson, J. & Vahlne, J.-E. (1977), The Internationalization Process of the Firm: A Model of Knowledge Development and Increasing Foreign Commitments, in: *Journal of International Business Studies* 8, 1: 23-32.

Jolly et. al. (1992), Challenging the Incumbents: How High-technology Start-ups Compete Globally, in: *Journal of Strategic Change* 1: 71-82.

Kaounides, L. C. (1999), Science, Technology and Global Competitive Advantage, in: *International Studies of Management & Organization* 29,1: 53-79.

Karagozoglu, N. & Lindell, M. (1998), Internationalization of Small and Medium-Sized Technology-Bases Firms: An Exploratory Study, in: *Journal of Small Business Management* 36,1: 44-59.

Knight, G. A. & Cavusgil, S. T. (1996), The Born Global Firm: A Challenge to Traditional Internationalisation Theory, in: *Advances in international Marketing* 8: 11-26.

Luhmann, N. (1968), *Zweckbegriff und Systemrationalität*, Tübingen: Mohr Verlag.

McDougall, P.P. & Oviatt, B. M. (1996), Internationalization, Strategic Change, and Performance: A Follow–up Study, in: *Journal of Business Venturing* 11: 23-40.

Madsen, T. K. & Servais, P. (1997), The Internationalization of Born Globals – An Evolutionary Process?, in: *International Business Review* 6, 6: 561-583.

Miller, D. (1993), The Architecture of Simplicity, in: *Academy of Management Review* 18: 116-138.

Moen, Ö. (2000), The Relationship Between Firm, Size, Competitive Advantages and Export Performance Revisited, in: *International Small Business Journal* 18, 1: 53-72.

Österle, H. & Muther, A. (1999), Radikale Kundenzentrierung im Informationszeitalter, in: *IOManagement* 9: 36-41.

Pascale, R.T. (1989), *Managing on the Edge*, New York: Simon & Shuster.

Porter, M. E. (1998), *On Competition*, Boston: Harvard Business School Press.

Schirmer, L. (1992), *Arbeitsverhalten von Managern: Bestandsaufnahme, Kritik und Weiterentwicklung der Aktivitätsforschung*, Wiesbaden: Deutscher Universitäts Verlag.

Simon, H. (1996), *Die heimlichen Gewinner* (Hidden Champions), Frankfurt & New York: Campus Verlag.

Staehle, W. H. (1991), Redundanz, Slack und lose Koppelung in Organisationen: Eine Verschwendung von Ressourcen?, in: Staehle, W.H. & Sydow, K. (eds.): *Managementforschung I*, Berlin & New York: DeGruyter.

Tapscott, D. (1996), *The Digital Economy*, New York: McGraw-Hill.

Wolff, J. A. & Pett, T. L. (2000), Internationalization of Small Firms: An Examination of Export Competitive Patterns, Firm Size, and Export Performance, in: *Journal of Small Business Management* 4: 34-47.

DaimlerChrysler's Strategy Towards Asia[1]

Karin Funke

1 Introduction

Globalization at DaimlerChrysler is nothing really new. It is a logical strategic initiative to pursue growth. A global company is therefore one, that makes optimal use of the business opportunities which other countries and regions offer. This paper intends to give a brief empirical overview of DaimlerChrysler activities in Asia as part of its global strategy.

2 Overview of the DaimlerChrysler Group

Daimler-Benz had its main business focus on Europe but with the merger of Daimler-Benz and Chrysler Corp. into DaimlerChrysler the new company became a global player. Today, DaimlerChrysler is one of the world's leading automotive, transportation and services companies. Its passenger car brands include Mercedes-Benz, Chrysler, Jeep®, Dodge and Smart. Commercial vehicles are produced under the Mercedes-Benz, Freightliner, Sterling, Thomas Built and Setra brands. The group also manufactures aircraft and equipment at DaimlerChrysler Aerospace (EADS) and offers financial and other services through DaimlerChrysler Services (debis). With 466,900 employees, DaimlerChrysler achieved revenues of 150.0 billion Euro ($151.0 billion) in 1999 and is therefore in terms of revenues the third largest worldwide vehicle manufacturer behind GM and Ford.

In 1999 roughly 64% of the total revenues were derived from passenger car vehicle and 17% from commercial vehicle sales. With almost 90% of the total revenues coming from vehicle sales these divisions are the focus of interest for the following analysis. In order to understand DaimlerChrysler's movements towards Asia it is necessary to briefly outline the passenger car development in the region.

---

1 Recent events have been forcing DaimlerChrysler to rethink its global activities. This paper discusses all measures taken before October 2000.

Table 1: Overview of the DC Group in the Main Markets (1999)

	NAFTA	EU	Asia/Australia	Total
Employees	160,000	271,000	5,520	466,940
Revenues	87,083	49,960	5,664	149,985

Note: Revenues are in Million Euro.

Source: DaimlerChrysler.

3 Passenger Car Development in the Asian Region

Forecasts for the next decade show that the Asian countries will recover from the crisis of 1997; the expected economic recovery is going to be a long-lasting upward trend. This outlook and the limited market growth in the "traditional" DaimlerChrysler core regions NAFTA and Western-Europe are the drivers for the car manufacturer to invest in Asia.

Table 2: Development of Passenger Vehicle Market 2000-2010

Region	Market Growth
Western Europe	-1%
NAFTA	+0%
USA	-3%
Latin America	+111%
Asia	+64%
Japan	+14%
Rest of World	+97%
World Total	+23%

Source: DaimlerChrysler

As demonstrated in table 2 the growth rate for passenger cars in Asia is 64%, whereas it is stagnating in the NAFTA region and even negative in America and Western Europe.

Looking at the regional distribution of the revenues in 1999 (see figure 1), almost 90% of DaimlerChrysler's revenues were generated in NAFTA and Europe. This figure clearly shows that revenues are regionally extremely unbalanced.

Figure 1: Regional Distribution of GDP Compared with DC Total Revenue

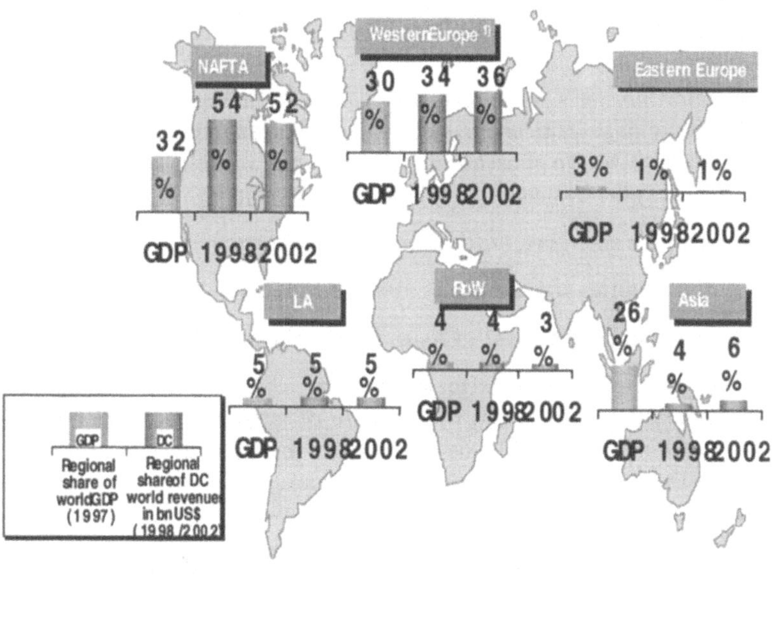

Source: DaimlerChrysler.

Like all other markets across the world the Asian markets are highly competitive: Ford and GM already implemented their expansion strategies in Asia. Both have shares in Japanese partners and thus extended their operational basis in Asia. Ford acquired a 33.4% interest in Mazda in 1994; GM which already holds a 49% stake in Isuzu linked up with Suzuki (10%) and acquired this year 20% of Fuji Heavy (Subaru) for $1,4 billion. Furthermore, Renault bought 37% of Nissan and 70.1% of Samsung Motor.

Not only the passenger car side shows high growth rates – the commercial vehicle side does as well. The commercial vehicle business in Asia for instance already accounts for more than 40% of the world's commercial vehicle market while DaimlerChrysler's commercial vehicle division in 1999 sold less than 3% of its vehicles in Asia.

Having outlined the general development of the Asian vehicle development, let me now elaborate on the approach DaimlerChrysler chose for Asia.

4 DaimlerChrysler's Asian Strategy

In 1998, DaimlerChrysler's Asian revenues of Euro 5.1 billion accounted for only 3.9% of the total global DaimlerChrysler´s sales, whereas Asia contributed nearly 25% to the world GDP. To subsequently increase the market share in the Asian region, DaimlerChrysler evaluated the following three options:

- exporting into the emerging markets,
- building new factories and companies in the regions or
- forming an alliance or purchase an Asian automobile manufacturer

DaimlerChrysler already exports to some Asian countries on a completely-knocked-down basis (CKD). However, because of tariff and non-tariff barriers exports are sometimes impossible, or import taxes may double or even triple the price of a car. The second option requires the carmaker to invest in the start-up of production and to build an entirely new sales & marketing network.

In the DaimlerChrysler Board of Management the decision was therefore taken to form an alliance with an Asian partner. In 1999, the German-American car manufacturer started negotiations with Nissan, mainly because of its strong position within the commercial vehicle business. During a three months period both parties assessed the strategic and financial options of a global co-operation. However, the integration of Daimler-Benz and Chrysler had the utmost priority. One year later – after the integration process had been completed – DaimlerChrysler chose Mitsubishi Motors as alliance partner.

4.1 DaimlerChrysler's Alliance with Mitsubishi Motors

On March 27th 2000, DaimlerChrysler and Mitsubishi Motors signed the Letter of Intent to form an alliance regarding the design, development, production and distribution of passenger cars as well as light commercial vehicles. With this letter it has been agreed that DaimlerChrysler will acquire a 34% stake in MMC through a capital increase.

DaimlerChrysler pursues two main strategy goals with this alliance: to strengthen its presence in Asia and to enhance its competence in small cars.

4.1.1 Presence in Asia

Mitsubishi Motors has an excellent distribution network throughout Asia and the highest market shares in some parts of the region. In the fast growing ASEAN countries, Mitsubishi Motors is the clear market leader with 26% market share (see figure 2). DaimlerChrysler and MMC will have a combined market share of about 10.8% in Japan and 9.4% in the other parts of the Asia Pacific Region.

4.1.2 Small Car Competence

Mitsubishi Motors has many years of experience and fundamental technological know-how in building small cars. DaimlerChrysler will profit from this expertise in building the second generation of the smart that is the smallest car in DaimlerChrysler's passenger car product portfolio. From 2004, when the co-operation between Volvo and Mitsubishi Motors in Europe ends, the Netherlands Car B.V. (Nedcar), formerly jointly run by Volvo and MMC, will become a 50/50 joint venture of DaimlerChrysler and Mitsubishi Motors instead; it will concentrate on development and production of small cars. The annual capacity within the first year is estimated to be about 300,000 units.

Other considerations to pursue this alliance were:

- expanding and securing current economies of scale;
- ensuring that manufacturing facilities in Latin American and European countries are working at full capacity in the future;
- reducing fleet fuel consumption;
- expansion of the smart product line and
- development of the joint 3l-engine.

The first step towards the new alliance has been the announcement of three board members from DaimlerChrysler, who are in charge of strategic partnerships and alliances in Asia, product planning and marketing as well as for international operations.

Because of the recall problems Mitsubishi Motors is facing since July 2000, DaimlerChrysler and MMC renegotiated the terms of the alliance. The main results were:

- The purchasing price was reduced by 10% from the original price.
- It was agreed that DC can raise its stake unlimited after a three years period of time.
- DC will send a Chief Operating Officer (COO) to MMC.

The new contracts put DC in a much stronger position than before. It is the first time that a foreign car manufacturer has the option to increase its stake in a Japanese car manufacturer without any limits.

Figure 2: Worldwide Presence of MMC

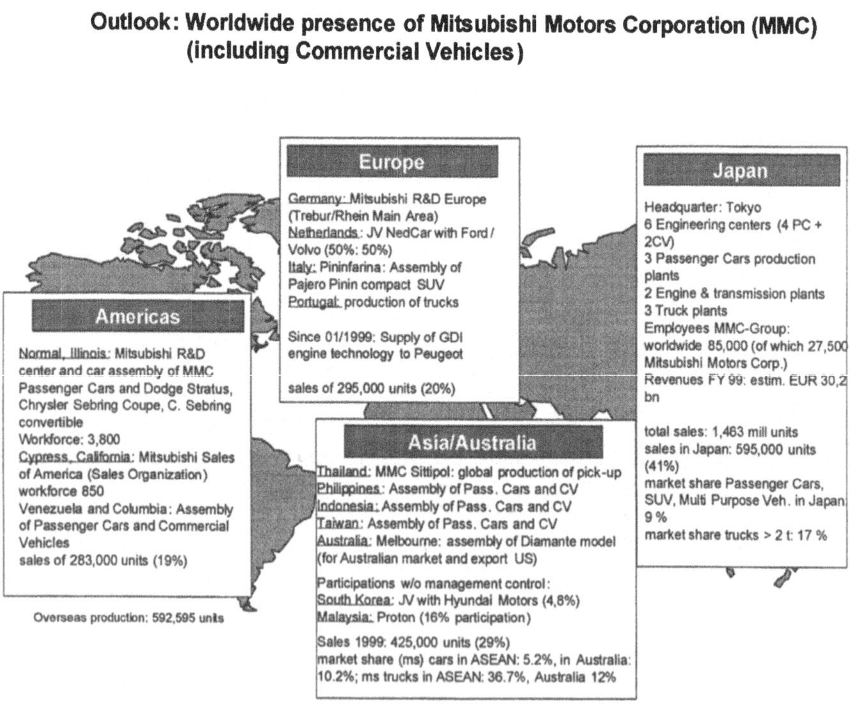

Source: DaimlerChrysler.

4.2 The Alliance with Hyundai Motors

The only real access to the Korean market is through a local business partner. To achieve this, DaimlerChrysler acquired a 10% stake in the Hyundai Motor Company for $428 million.

A letter of intent for this alliance has been signed on June 26th 2000 which specifies the following key areas of cooperation:

- a 50/50 joint venture for the development, production and marketing of commercial vehicles and
- an alliance for the development and production of passenger cars.

Hyundai is the strongest player in the Korean automotive market. The South Korean-based Hyundai Motor Company (HMC) is one of the most successful automotive manufacturers not only in Asia, but worldwide. Together with its subsidiary Kia Motor, in which it acquired a 51% stake in 1998, HMC has a market share of more than 70% in Korea for passenger cars, and – with the brands Kia and Asia – 90% for commercial vehicles. In 1999, HMC achieved consolidated sales of $21.3 billion and an operating profit of $843 million, which makes the company one of the most profitable automotive manufacturers in the world. With an annual production in 1999 of 1.55 million passenger cars and 390,000 commercial vehicles, Hyundai – with Kia/Asia – is the world's No. 11 automotive producer.

Under the terms of the 50/50 commercial vehicle joint venture, Hyundai will contribute its Korean production facilities and distribution network. DaimlerChrysler will provide state-of -the art technology.

The joint venture will involve the production in Korea of DaimlerChrysler's commercial vehicles as well as sales and marketing for its products. In addition it will utilize the company's respective global distribution capabilities to increase market share.

To reduce costs, DaimlerChrysler and Hyundai will also cooperate in the areas of research, product development and global supply chain management. Additional joint ventures are under consideration in areas such as financial services.

Together with Hyundai and Mitsubishi Motors DaimlerChrysler will – by the year 2004 – achieve a market share of 12.7% in Japan, 73% in Korea and 27,6% in the rest of the Asia Pacific region (see table 3).

Table 3: DaimlerChrysler's Global Market Shares (2004)

	NAFTA	Latin America	Western Europe	Africa	Korea	Japan	Rest of Asia
DC	16.8	1.9	6.2	2.9	–	0.9	1.2
MMC	1.4	2.8	1.5	4.6	–	11.8	8.2
HMC	1.7	0.5	1.9	0.5	73	–	18.2
Total	19.9	5.2	9.6	8	73	12.7	27.6

Source: DaimlerChrysler

5 Summary

The stagnating European and US passenger and commercial vehicle markets are the driving forces for an automobile manufacturer to invest in Asian markets, which show steady growth potential.

So far the German-American carmaker has generated over 90% of its revenues in its traditional European and American core markets. The high growth rates of the Asian markets made an investment in Asia necessary, if the company does not want to miss out the opportunities of these regions. Hence DaimlerChrysler decided to form alliances for the following reasons:

- Time: the operational business can start immediately after the contracts have been signed.
- Access: through the alliance partner the foreign company gets access to its local and regional distribution system (sales & marketing network).
- Know-how: DaimlerChrysler will profit from the know-how and experience which MMC and Hyundai have gained in the development of small cars.
- Efficiency: An extended worldwide production network will help ensure that all production facilities worldwide will be working at full capacity.

Although I have stated in the beginning that globalization is nothing really new for DaimlerChrysler, the presence of the company in Asia did not reflect the (growing) importance of this region. With the new alliances outlined above, DaimlerChrysler will be able to achieve its target of 20% to 25% revenue in this region (in 1999: 4%). The success of the alliances will depend on how fast new organizational structures will be implemented, how efficient project teams will work and how effective top-managers will steer and monitor these alliance processes. One of the most critical factors will be the cultural issue all managers deal with. By implementing these new alliances DaimlerChrysler has become a true global player.

JAPAN AND GLOBALIZATION:
WHO SHAPES WHOM?

Mirroring Consensus

Joop A. Stam

1 Introduction

Mirroring Consensus is a cooperative research project in which the universities of Rotterdam, Tilburg, Nijmegen and Maastricht have been involved.[1] This project has been one of the many activities to celebrate the commemoration of 400 years relations between Japan and the Netherlands and focusses on the analysis of business practices of Japanese companies in the Netherlands and Dutch companies in Japan. This study concerns consensus and decision making and is based upon the following considerations.

Japanese society is known to be consensus oriented and Japanese enterprises emphasize harmonious relations among their employees in a family-like fashion. In the Netherlands we come across a similar consensus orientation in society, often labeled as "poldermodel". This "poldermodel" refers to the practice of broad consultation among the major stakeholders in social, political and economic live with the aim to generate agreement about policies, problems and solutions. This model of consensus building has dominated Dutch society for a long time and is said to be one of the main factors behind the current economic boom.

Taking into consideration the differences in national cultures between Japan and the Netherlands as clarified e.g. by Hofstede (1997), the question of meaning and content of this joint consensus orientation arises. And in a more practical sense, when Japanese and Dutch are cooperating, for example in joint ventures or subsidiaries in Japan or the Netherlands, how beneficial is this joint consensus orientation for dealing with the obvious cultural differences.

The shared importance of consensus in Japanese and Dutch society stimulated us to focus on the impact of this consensus orientation on decision-making in Japanese companies in The Netherlands and Dutch companies in Japan. By making an analysis of both setting and process of consensus building in decision

---

1 This article is a revised version of the presentation by the author of the findings of the research project at the symposium *Mirroring Consensus*, held on June 2 and 3, 2000 in Maastricht. The field research has been executed by Arjan Keizer and Satoshi Takahashi of the Rotterdam Institute of Modern Asian Studies of Erasmus University Rotterdam under supervision of the author, in cooperation with Niels Noorderhaven of Tilburg University, Jos Bender of Nijmegen University and Hiroshi Kumon of Hosei University.

making in companies we assumed to be able to better understand the differences and its consequences but also learn how Dutch and Japanese employees deal with the differences in day to day company life.

To make comparisons between experiences in Japan and the Netherlands, to mirror these experiences, we visited seven Japanese companies in the Netherlands and four Dutch companies in Japan. Altogether we were able to interview more than sixty people, from CEOs to managers and regular employees. As this project was executed within the framework of the celebration of 400 years Dutch-Japanese relations, we were able to secure the support of both the Japanese and Dutch business communities and the full cooperation of all participants. The results of the project have been published in the book *Mirroring Consensus* (Benders et al. 2000). This article is a revised edition of the presentation of the findings of our study at a symposium devoted to a discussion on cross-cultural issues in business.

2 Decision-Making in Japan and the Netherlands

A vast amount of literature on decision-making in Japanese companies indicates that, first and foremost, the preservation of harmonious relations in the organization, *wa*, is of crucial importance. Managers of Japanese companies see it as their task to stimulate and motivate people to work together harmoniously (Hasegawa 1986). This task is to some extent facilitated by the strong group orientation prevalent in Japanese society. Or more explicitly, the interest of the individual is subordinated to that of the collective, the group, and the company can benefit from this characteristic for lining up its employees behind its plans and policies

Secondly, before introducing changes into the organization it is absolutely necessary to consult all relevant parties. The instruments often used for this purpose, is the so-called *ringi-system*; a procedure to collect all information necessary to make a balanced proposal but also to sound out the opinions of the departments and sections involved and to prepare for the implementation of the decision. The circulation of a document, the so-called *ringi-sho* serves to administer the process and simultaneously creates opportunity to echo consent or dissent among the employees.

In order to get the support of all relevant parties, an informal method of persuasion, called *nemawashi* or root turning, is used. The term *nemawashi* refers to the gentle technique used in Japanese gardening for moving plants and trees, loosening the tree step by step from its soil without damaging the roots. In reality, however, the *nemawashi* part of decision-making in Japanese companies quite often turns out to be a process of hard bargaining and arm-twisting which takes place during and particularly after office hours. In essence *nemawashi* prepares the way for a common understanding of the issues, the problems and the solutions.

Whereas the *ringi* procedure predominantly concerns the managerial and administrative levels of the company, at shopfloor level we come across the practice of extensive reporting, communicating and discussion, *hôkoku - renraku - sôdan*, abbreviated to *hôrensô*, in order to keep each other informed, discuss the consequences of the decisions and accommodate their implementation

In sum, decision-making in a Japanese setting requires a proper understanding of the issues or problems. To that end facts and figures as many and as detailed as possible are collected. Secondly, there should be a shared understanding of the problem and a common feeling about the solution. This part involves personal emotions and requires heart to heart talks, in Japanese *isshin-denshin*. Whenever there is this shared feeling and understanding among the participants, a quick and unconditional execution will result.

This high degree of participation in decision-making looks very sympathetic but should not be taken at face value. The authority and responsibility to take decisions in Japanese companies clearly lies with top management. There is no freedom of action *below* in the organization without confirmation from *above* but there is a lot of discussion and exchange of information. In Japanese companies good managers are those who listen patiently and get their way but do not force their opinion on their subordinates in a direct fashion. As a matter of fact they elicit support for their case by appealing both to the head and the heart.

Whereas consensus decision-making in Japanese companies has been documented elaborately, this is much less the case for Dutch companies (d'Iribarne 1989, Lawrence 1991, Van Dijk & Punch 1993, Pot 1998). The Netherlands is usually not portrayed as a group-oriented, consensus seeking society in the Japanese fashion. On the contrary, individualism and personal freedom are cherished strongly. And yet consensus in decision-making is favored. Apparently, individualism and consensus do not exclude each other. At face value the consensus-seeking behavior in the Netherlands seems to be more pragmatic than ideological.

It is common knowledge that people in the Netherlands distrust authority. Managers or superiors in general can not rely on their authority merely based upon their position in the hierarchy. Throughout history power and authority has been challenged and met with suspicion. And yet the Dutch have relied very much on authority for survival. The meticulous organization of the water management system and unrivaled authority of the water boards of the Low Countries is a point in case.

However, when a Dutch manager or a boss wants to get the support of his subordinates he can not claim it but he has to organize it through consultation.

The right to participate in the discussion, to voice one's opinion, is strongly developed in The Netherlands and is defended vigorously. In the Dutch context a good manager is "the voice of reason"; he should reach his goals by presenting objective facts in a rational way and convince his people, win their trust as a real professional. He should show compassion and respect, be prepared to give and to take. Compromise is the key leading to consensus. Obviously, this type of consensus decision-making flourishes in a well organized setting, in a works council or other types of platforms which create the opportunity to discuss the issues, explain the positions and persuade the antagonists. Once persuasion has been achieved loyal cooperation follows.

In sum, literature on decision-making indicates that the consensus orientation in Japanese companies can be related to the eagerness to preserve harmony within the organization and this can be linked to the pseudo-family character of the Japanese firm, while in the Netherlands consensus is often the result of pragmatism among the parties involved, taking in consideration objective facts and mutual respect for each others view. In the Japanese company rank and position enhance the authority of the manager but in the Dutch case a manager should have a good and convincing story.

3 Japanese Decision-Making in the Netherlands, Dutch Decision-Making in Japan

In the fieldstudy of our research project *Mirroring Consensus* we addressed the intriguing questions: how do Japanese companies in the Netherlands deal with these Dutch characteristics; to what extent do they adapt to the Dutch style of consensus building and decision-making and conversely, how much adaptation do we see among Dutch companies in Japan. A detailed account and analysis of the interviews with Japanese and Dutch/European employees of all ranks in the company hierarchy has been published in the conference edition of the project (Benders et al. 2000). In this contribution we will particularly concentrate on the comparison and mirror the experiences, by looking at the decision setting and the decision process in Japanese companies in the Netherlands and Dutch companies in Japan.

3.1 The Decision Setting

Both Japanese companies in the Netherlands and Dutch companies in Japan are in general relatively small in size. With a few exceptions, most companies do not have more than 100 employees in total. This means that the distance between managers and local personnel tends to be small and the relations informal.

Consequently, in the Netherlands we do not come across large formalized decision-making procedures à la *ringi*.

Moreover, in most cases headquarters in Japan tend to have a strong say in whatever is happening at the Japanese subsidiaries in the Netherlands and this makes the decision making process relatively simple. One does not have to spend a lot of time on discussing issues when the directions from above are clear and decisive. Obviously, this does not concurs well with the locally hired manager for whom it is difficult to accept that sound professional advise and judgement based upon local experience is overruled by some vague prescriptions from far away headquarters in Tokyo. Exemplary is the case of a local finance manager who was asked to prepare the financing of an investment plan. In the best professional tradition he shopped around among banks and institutions for the best deal. His proposal with a detailed advice was faxed to Tokyo but rejected. Why? Tokyo preferred to honor the long-term relationship with the traditional bank over the best business deal. The result was three weeks of work and efforts wasted and a desillusioned local manager.

Another interesting issue is the link between job description, responsibility and authority. Dutch enterprises generally work with clear job descriptions, demarcating individual authority and responsibility. Most Japanese companies in the Netherlands have introduced individual job descriptions as well and thus so-called boundary discussions about tasks can be avoided. However, this does not mean that in the eyes of Japanese managers Dutch employees are exempted from responsibility for what their colleagues are doing. The Japanese manager, who has been brought up with the idea that there is a joint responsibility for the total results of the organization, can not accept a narrowly defined individual responsibility. This issue of individual versus collective responsibility is a real issue but should not be exaggerated. Just like in other local companies two types of employees can be discerned: those of the so-called "9 to 5 type" who prefer to stick to their formal individual responsibility and work during the prescribed time, and the more ambitious and highly capable employees who tend to go beyond their task related responsibility and spend more time and energy to the organization than required. Most Japanese companies accept this split as a fact of life. In general, clear job descriptions diminish the need for lengthy discussions and *nemawashi* type of consultations. This means speedier decisions, but it is impossible to overlook due process. As soon as Dutch employees have the feeling that they are not involved and properly informed or excluded from the discussion, problems will arise.

Finally, the intermediary role of middle management should be mentioned. In Japanese companies managers at the top are formally endowed with authority but they depend heavily on the expertise of middle management. Through this expertise middle management in Japan has clout and control beyond its formal authority. The dependency relation between top and middle management also applies to Japanese companies in the Netherlands. In general a good understanding with and active involvement of local middle management appears to be the recipe for successful operation.

3.2 The Decision Process

In order to make decisions extensive exchange of information and communication with colleagues about the issues, problems and options for solution is the rule. Here we see substantial differences between the Japanese approach and the Dutch way of doing. In Japanese companies in the Netherlands we witness a broad collection of all relevant and sometimes irrelevant information and a subsequent analysis and discussion. To the Dutch participants in this process there often seems to be an overkill, at least an inefficiency.

Dutch managers and employees tend to be selective in information gathering and focus on their own functional field. In addition, they tend to consider information "private property" and a source of power or influence. While Japanese employees are widely informed and broadly documented, Dutch personnel in general has a more thorough knowledge of issues and likes to show that in formal meetings. They have a reputation to be quite frank but this apparently stimulates Japanese managers as well to speak up for themselves and boost their morale.

In Japanese companies in the Netherlands informal communication, both during and after office hours, is used for information exchange and building a common understanding about issues and problems. No formal meeting is scheduled without a preceding informal meeting in which views and standpoints are carefully considered so that unexspected events or embarrassments can be avoided. In practice these informal meetings also function as an instrument to let off steam and express the inexpressable. Although strong views and opinions might be ventilated, at the end both Japanese and Dutch participants are prepared to settle for a compromise. Dutch companies in Japan follow this practice of pre-meeting discussions as well and formal meetings are mainly conducted to communicate the results and reinforce the team spirit.

In sum, we have witnessed a lot of adaptative behaviour of both Japanese and Dutch employees of Japanese companies in the Netherlands in order to avoid confrontation. This pattern of mutual adaptation is less explicit in Dutch companies in Japan. Since the majority of the employees there are Japanese and only a few expatriates are working with them, they have opted for doing it the Japanese way.

4 Reflections

The objective of this project was to clarify and qualify consensus and decision making in Japanese companies in the Netherlands and Dutch companies in Japan by mirroring the experiences. In the following we will reflect on our findings sofar.

Interviewees were not able to see substantial differences in content between Dutch and Japanese consensus. However, when we focus on the process of achieving consensus there are major differences. The Dutch like to listen to opinions and views, collect information to substantiate their position and finally make a decision, preferably based on consensus but if needed based on a majority vote. Even when matters are discussed at length, it is clear from the outset who is authorized to take the final decision. The authority and personal responsibility of managers in Dutch organizations reduces the need to always make decisions by full consensus.

Japanese managers tend to emphasize the collective responsibility for the results of the organization, even though they acknowledge individual responsibility. Consensus about goal and process is rule. Continuous information gathering and wide consultations are part of this process of consensus building; it reduces uncertainty and enhances the collective responsibility among the people involved. Authority is diffuse even though top management is required to confirm all actions. The formal responsibility is located at the top but control on the process is in the hands of middle management. This mutual dependency between top and middle management is both the strenght and a weakness of the Japanese governance structure. It is strong in periods of stability, weak in periods of adversity when guidance is needed.

Another interesting observation emerging from our fieldresearch is the time allowed to spend on discussion. Everybody agrees that it takes time to convince your colleague, but how much does it require exactly. Here we find a difference between Japanese and Dutch participants. The Dutch tend to come to conclusions much faster, even when they are not completely satisfied. They might even change their opinion later if a better solution is offered. Efficient use of time seems to be the rule of the game.

Japanese on the contrary take their time. They check and double check their information before taking a decision. As one of the Dutch interviewees put it: "The Japanese approach is one of trial and error but then without the errors." Consensus means full support without any doubt. Effectiveness in stead of efficiency is the norm and in the end this approach often tends to pay off because, as our Dutch spokesman conceded: "Often we say we have achieved consensus but then we open the discussion again because we have forgotten something." In that way the time gained is lost again.

Finally, for consensus building steering and guidance appears to be a hot issue. When company goals, strategy and tactics are clear and well defined, management in Japan is usually capable of getting everyone quickly in line. The ensuing discussions within the organization then mostly concentrate around how to complete the tasks from a company perspective. This, to Dutch interviewees, sounds too much like a hidden agenda and negates the professional input of employees. Open exchange of opinions and views without a preset conclusion is preferred above the psychological exercise to get all noses in the same direction.

5 Concluding Remarks

First of all, we can conclude that both Japanese and Dutch employees agree that consensus seeking is an essential element in their day to day company life. They might disagree about style or approach to achieve consensus but they consider it key to success for Dutch-Japanese cooperation.

Secondly, in all organizations we observed active adaptation of behavior among Dutch and Japanese employees. That is what intelligent people do when they have a joint interest in solving a common problem . Individual employees adapt to new circumstances and the young employees quicker than the older generation but also organizations adapt. In general, we see a stronger combination of Japanese and Dutch elements in Japanese subsidiaries in The Netherlands than in Dutch companies in Japan. Japanese expatriates, new in the Netherlands, sometimes do not recognize their own company and have the idea to have landed in a foreign company. The Japanese subsidiary has often well-blended in the Dutch local environment even though it might still have a Japanese character. Dutch managers in Japan have the same experience. But in that case the dominance of local Japanese employees tends to dictate the way of management and adaptation usually means compliance with Japanese practice.

At the outset of our study on consensus we choose decision-making as our target for research. When we compare styles of decision-making, the Japanese style can be labelled comprehensive. All possible information is taken into account and no decision is taken before the complete picture is clear and all details have been filled in. This involves many people and therefore procedures are carried out carefully. At the end the proper decision will emerge and is accepted by everyone involved. Effectiveness is the objective; inefficiencies during the process are taken for granted.

The Dutch decision-making style can be characterized as pragmatic. Facts and figures are the basis of discussion but once an agreement on essentials has been reached, Dutch managers tend to neglect further discussion on details and consequently they might run into trouble when situations change. Consensus is important but not a psychological necessity. They can live with a compromise or even an authoritaritative decision, provided the argumentation is sound. Efficiency in the decision-making process is the rule even at the cost of some loss of quality.

References

Aoki, M. (1990), Towards an Economic Model of the Japanese Firm, in: *Journal of Economic Literature*, 21,1: 1-27.

Benders, J., Noorderhaven, N., Keizer, A., Kumon, H. & Stam, J. (eds.) (2000), *Mirroring Consensus. Decision-making in Japanese-Dutch Business*, Utrecht: Lemma Publishers.

Fentener van Vlissingen, C. (1986), Project Management and Culture: Two case-studies of Dutch-Japanese industrial projects, in: Stam, J. (ed.), *Industrial Cooperation between Europe and Japan*, Rotterdam: Donner Boeken: 115-136.

Hasegawa, K. (1986), *Japanese-style Management: An Insider's Analysis*, New York: Kodansha International.

Hofstede, G. (1997), *Cultures and Organizations. Software of the Mind*, New York: McGraw-Hill.

d'Iribarne, Ph. (1989), *La Logique de l'Honneur; Gestion des entreprises et traditions nationals*, Paris: Editions du Seuil.

Lawrence, P. (1991), *Management in the Netherlands*, Oxford: Clarendon Press.

Pot, F. (1998), *Continuity and Change of Human Resource Management*, Ph.D.-thesis, Rotterdam: Tinbergen Institute.

Van Dijk, N. & Punch, M. (1993), Open Borders, Closed Circles: Management and Organization in the Netherlands, in: Hickson, D. (ed.), *Management in Western Europe: Society, Culture and Organization in Twelve Nations*, Berlin: DeGruyter: 167-190.

Visser, J, & Hemelrijck, A. (1997), *"A Dutch Miracle": Job Growth, Welfare Reform and Corporatism in the Netherlands*, Amsterdam: Amsterdam University Press.

Transformation of the German Production System "After Japan" in the 1990s

Ulrich Jürgens

1 Introduction: The German Production Model

In the 1990s a massive wave of restructuring of production systems affecting almost all industrial sectors swept through Germany. Production concepts which had been developed in Germany during the 1970s and 1980s and had been regarded by many as the manifestation of a specific German production model gave way to lean production concepts based on the "Japanese model", the Toyota production system.

The principles of mass production still served as a basis for the German production model of the period from 1975 to 1985. Under the impact of the first oil crisis and rising unemployment, however, a range of labour reforms and production modernization programmes were developed in close co-operation between employers' associations, Unions and the state. Many of the new concepts developed during this stage were inspired by Swedish work experiments but because of the specific German training system providing the industry with especially skilled workers ("Facharbeiter"), quite different solutions were sought. The German approach supported a high degree of autonomy, time sovereignty and self-responsibility of shop-floor workers believing this to be the paradigm for future-oriented forms of work in the industry as a whole.

The profile of this system can be outlined by the following five points:

- **Process organization** in Germany basically followed the same mass production principles as in America. Due to smaller company sizes and production runs, however, less emphasis was given to economies of scale. As in America, performance was regulated through Taylorist standard-setting methods coupled with incentive pay-schemes on the basis of rules and procedures co-determined by the Unions and the works councils. Supervisory control was executed via the distinct German "Meister" (master craftsman) system which mixes elements of personnel supervision and engineering expertise.
- As in America, **job design** was centered on individual jobs. The impact of the European debate on socio-technical system design as well as the humanization of work programme of the German government, however, moved job design

into the very centre of work reforms in the 1970s. New forms of work aiming at job enlargement and enrichment and the de-coupling of human work from the immediate pressure of machinery or assembly lines were introduced.

- **Improvement and process innovation** lay in the realm of the experts, production planners and industrial engineers. Technology was regarded as the main driver of improvement. Collective agreements on the introduction of new technology protected individual workers against the rationalization effects of such an improvement on employment and wage levels.

- **Human resource policies** were based on the principles of long-term employment stability and vocational training. School-leavers were trained half the time by the companies which offer them a temporary contract and half the time at public vocational training schools. Unskilled and semi-skilled job categories were regarded as obsolete. Production departments increasingly hired skilled workers who were assigned to ordinary production jobs while the tripartite vocational training system introduced new training curricula for skilled workers to be assigned to production jobs in charge of new production technology. The skilled workers were regarded as the "winners of rationalization" (Kern & Schumann 1989:94).

- **Social cohesion** and consensus were regarded as a major source of productivity. Therefore a system of interrelated internal and external institutions of conflict resolution was developed. This system was based on mutual responsibilities: employers accepted that they had social responsibilities in areas such as training, ergonomics, quality of work etc. while state actors were ready to support the bargaining partners, i.e. the companies, to solve their problems.

The contrast to the American production approach is evident. A major differentiating factor comes from a national policy emphasis on vocational skill formation. Raising the skills of the blue- and the white-collar workers is regarded as a central goal to be assured by state policy. The dynamic center of the German system thus is its skill base. The "dual" system of private-public apprenticeship training provides basic skills. Due to the fact that the upper positions in the career structure – the "Meister" (master craftsman with a diploma), technicians and engineers – have mostly served a "Facharbeiter" (skilled worker) apprenticeship, a common background of skills and experiences exists among blue- and white-collar employees which fosters company-wide communication and co-operation. The "Facharbeiter" has often been identified with (neo-)craftswork. This is wrong. As it can be seen from the curricula especially after the modernization in the mid-1980s, apprenticeship training for industrial jobs rather aims at creating "little engineers" than classical craftsmen or artisans. The situation in the small and medium companies of the machine tool industry has often been cited as an example for the virtuousness of this system. Labour policy institutions at the industry and the national level played an important role in shaping the system of skill formation.

The classical argument, of course, for promoting apprenticeship training which leads to a skilled worker's certificate was to support labour market mobility and reduce the dependence of workers on individual employers and industries. With the diffusion of the system of mass production in Germany the argument gained ground that a better skilled workforce could allow for different forms of work in mass production and thereby help to avoid some of the negative effects of the "American model". The expectation was that hoarding skills in areas such as assembly line work would eventually enable the company to use new technologies more efficiently than in other countries. Apprenticeship training made further headway with the rise of unemployment after the first oil shock. Offering an apprenticeship to school-leavers reduces the problem of youth unemployment which – on the background of historical experience – has almost become a national goal. Thus the issue of apprenticeship training is seen as a prime indicator of the social responsibility of companies. Since the second half of the 1970s it has become a quasi-right of each school-leaver to receive an apprenticeship training after finishing school (however, not necessarily in the aspired industry) and it has become a ritual each year that politicians knock the companies' doors to provide more training positions for school-leavers. As a result the vast majority of secondary school-leavers receives some kind of apprenticeship.

With the experience of the "oil crisis" in mind and in view of the technical development in the area of microelectronics, the labour policy actors at different levels came to a number of agreements in the second half of the 1970s. On the whole, these can be regarded as a national pact between Capital and Labour: in exchange for increased flexibility and acceptance of new technology in the interest of employers, workers gained employment and a certain degree of wage protection, more apprenticeship training and increased works council participation in work design matters. National government supported this pact by various legislative programmes in the fields of co-determination, labour market and social security policies.

The German production approach seemed to usher in a golden age with these labour conditions. A "virtuous circle" was to emerge making best use of Germany's skill potential which was fully exploited by "intelligent work structures" producing diversified quality products (DQP) which met the new consumer trends. Therefore, high prices could be obtained which in turn enabled companies to pay the comparatively higher wages of the German production sites.

This virtuous circle was diligently worked out by Sorge & Streeck (1988) and was often propagated as the foundation of the German model which explained its relative success during the 1980s. And there can be no doubt that German companies during this period pursued a policy of diversified quality production, which many have continued in the 1990s. As comparative research has shown

German companies tend to aim at the higher price segments of their product markets. This holds true not just for the well-known cases of the automobile and machine tool industry, but also for the textiles industry as well as for precision engineering and food processing industries (Broadberry & Wagner 1996). In the debate about the German model, however, the following factors were often overlooked: Firstly, while concepts of "intelligent" forms of work were widely discussed, the reality lagged far behind. This was true in particular for organizational concepts such as the introduction of teamwork, cross-functional project organization and supplier and customer integration. The emphasis was laid on process technology, in particular on computer integrated manufacturing (CIM). Yet, as in America it turned out that productivity effects expected from CIM more than often did not materialize. Secondly, the high value of the Dollar during the first phase of Reaganomics made German high-quality high-priced products quite affordable in America, thereby creating strong demand in support of the DQP strategy. And thirdly, the fact that the Japanese production system was able to produce quality and diversity at much lower costs than the German system had not been taken into account.

However, by the end of the 1980s it had become clear that the German model in fact had triggered a vicious circle: the concentration on high-priced quality products supported a trend towards complex and complicated "over-engineered" products and a fixation on technology-driven solutions. It also supported a rather scientific orientation in the areas of quality control – quality was "inspected in" and not "built in". There were no bottom-up improvement activities to exploit the potential of skilled workers deployed in production. There were no systematic efforts for influencing the product design in the early stages of product development in order to alleviate production problems and improve the manufacturability of the products. As a consequence the technology was much too complicated and even under the advantageous skill conditions problems abounded; thus the productivity effects did not suffice to reduce the costs. This put further pressure on the companies to cut down labour costs, especially in the semi-skilled areas, thereby furthering the neglect of non-technology related improvement potential there.

2 Lean Production in Germany

The frustration with this vicious circle can explain some of the enthusiasm the lean production "revolution" aroused in Germany at the beginning of the 1990s. In contrast to the resilience of Japan, German companies in the 1990s were ready for drastic rethinking and restructuring of their production model. Compared with America and other European countries this readiness for change came comparatively late due to the fact that Germany's economy had fared well through the 1980s, which of course had supported the belief in the "German model". An attitude of complacency prevailed during the 1980s, and German companies lacked the experience of direct Japanese investments which had already become a catalyst of change in the American and British economies during these years.

The propagation of the "lean production model" by Womack et al. (1990) which had been developed in the context of the international Motor Vehicle Programme of the Massachusetts Institute of Technology and had been published just in time when a new orientation was looked for did indeed play a major role in the reorientation during the early 1990s:

- The central concepts of process organization of the **"lean production model"** were adopted by the majority of German companies in the course of the 1990s; however, in many cases in a hesitating and gradual way. They were implemented mostly by seeking to compromise with existing practices or building them into new approaches. One example of **hybridization of Japanese concepts** with new approaches is the restructuring of supplier relations. The introduction of just-in-time supplier concepts was combined with new approaches of modularization. Supplier responsibilities in Germany thus went further than in Japan (Fujimoto 1999). Also, buffer minimization, just-in-time principles, quality management and so forth were introduced, following – in most cases – the prescription of the lean production system, the model of which is the Toyota production system.
- **Job design** now emphasized teamwork, moving away from the traditional approach of separating the tasks of direct production, quality inspection and repair work which had been a major cost-driver in the previous system. In contrast to concepts of new forms of work which had evolved from the humanization of work debate focussing on group work – with a high degree of responsibility, time sovereignty, opportunities for skill development and democratic forms of self-regulation within a group – mostly "structurally-conservative" solutions now prevailed (Kuhlmann & Schumann 1997). This went along with the abolishment of most of the long-cycle work operations which had been introduced during the 1980s (Jürgens 1997).
- The involvement of the workforce in **improvement activities** beyond the traditional suggestion systems also belongs to new management methods based on the lean production model. However, the dominant position of experts remains. With regard to technology a more cautious and incremental approach can be observed. Work-sharing and employment agreements concerning protection against plant closures as well as against rationalization effects have been reconfirmed on company and industry level. However, due to increasing uncertainties related with the process of globalization, mergers and acquisitions and a stronger shareholder value orientation, the credibility of this critical linkage between Capital and Labour has been decreasing.

- Despite the continuous pressure for rationalization, the commitment to long-term employment security has remained strong in **human resource policies**. Companies and employers' federations, however, have taken advantage of labour's weakened position (on the background of record-high unemployment rates) in demanding concessions. Even though it is difficult to validate, the "long-term orientation" of employment is on the retreat and the proportion of employees leased or with time-limited contracts is increasing.
- Little change occurred on the dimension of **social and industrial relations** at plant and firm levels. Most restructuring programmes were carried out jointly by works councils and management, even when they were connected with major workforce reductions. Due to early retirement programmes and work time reductions to 35 hours per week (and even less in the case of some companies, like VW with 28.8 hours) mass redundancies and dismissals could be avoided in many cases.

On the whole, these changes were to a large extent conceived as a "common project" of company management and works councils supported by collective agreements between Unions and employers' associations which allowed for more flexibility especially regarding working time. During this period the established institutions of collective bargaining demonstrated their ability to adapt and innovate, even though at times with pain (Turner 1997).

Is it justified to speak of a transformation of the German production model in view of these changes? The answer must be ambiguous: On the one hand new principles regarding process organization and job design were adopted. It seems as if they need some time to sink in. Thus, it can be observed that the more recent a factory reorganization occurred the purer lean production or Japan-oriented concepts are implemented. A good example in this regard is the introduction of the pull-cords which allow workers to stop the line in order to prevent quality problems which have so far been installed only in few German assembly plants (first at Opel's East-German Eisenach plant, at Porsche's and recently at Daimler-Chrysler's plant in Rastatt). On the other hand, principles of rank-and-file-based improvement systems and self-regulation of performance affecting the role of the experts never really caught on and are on the retreat again in some companies (Springer 1999, 1997). Finally, the institutions of labour politics (collective bargaining, works council system, co-determination) remained largely unchanged despite the continuous pressure resulting from the debate about high production costs in Germnay.

These changes of the German production regime were quite clearly influenced by concepts of non-German origin. In most cases Japanese companies or Japanese transplants were the benchmark (Womack & Jones 1996:189-218). A direct interaction with Japanese companies or consultants nevertheless remained the exception. The American influence on the German restructuring programme was considerable. Firstly, American multinationals were in many cases at the forefront of introducing new concepts. An example already mentioned is Opel's assembly plant in Eisenach (Jürgens 1998). Secondly, the experience of German supplier companies interacting with Japanese transplants in America (and Britain) had a great impact; and a third influence of paramount importance came via mostly American consultant firms. German companies during the 1990s were particularly keen clients of these companies. It cannot come as a surprise that for these consultants German peculiarities like the system of co-determination, the skilled workers and the apprenticeship training system – still seen by many as distinct strengths that should be preserved (Roth 1997) – were regarded with scepticism.

The continuity of consensus in the area of industrial relations is remarkable. Despite an increased problem load due to German unification, collective agreements between the Unions and employers' associations supported the introduction of more flexible forms of production operations, and on company level works councils and management usually agreed even on far-reaching change programmes, often in the framework of so-called location protection ("Standortsicherungs"-) agreements.

3 Conclusion: The German Catch-up

The situation of the 1980s was marked by an extreme imbalance in the performance of production regimes with a clear and dramatic superiority of the Japanese system. This situation was reflected by MIT's study (Womack et al. 1990); its data on performance differences between Japanese and American or European production systems caused shock waves in Western countries. In the late 1980s the process of adopting Japanese concepts intensified and became more systematic recognizing the complementarities between various elements of the Japanese production model. Survey research about the diffusion of the various "methods" ranging from just-in-time delivery, total quality control, Kaizen, teamwork and so forth show little difference today between Western and Japanese companies. There can be little doubt that these measures contributed to the fact that the German companies have caught up considerably in mastering the *cost-plus-quality-plus-flexibility* interrelationship which is the key to the Japanese production excellence. In addition the supplier-base for parts, process equipment and services has been restructured and process chains newly defined. While it is true that this restructuring process has not yet ended, the gaps have obviously been narrowed. The Western production systems have become more competitive and their vulnerability – measured for instance by the break-even point – has been reduced. Another result of this catch-up is that companies have broadened their capabilities to opt for a certain product market strategy. As it has been described above, the German model in the 1980s thrived upon the strategy of product upgrading and profited from the price premium they could charge for these products. However, as quality statistics show (for instance the J. D. Powers index in the auto industry) the differences in terms of quality have become very small between companies in general, and German companies are far from regularly occupying top ranks in the quality performance "leagues" (Andersen Consulting 1994). At the same time German companies have caught up in terms of cost competitiveness, often through building production networks including low-cost production sites in the East and through reaching bargains in employment agreements between Unions and employer's federations.

A shift toward the Japanese-inspired lean production concept clearly has taken place in the areas of process organization, process control and supplier relations. There can be no doubt that for the central principles of process control, just-in-time delivery, total quality management and continuous improvement which are today regarded as global production standards Japanese companies, in particular their American and European transplants, have remained the benchmark. In view of their increasingly international structures and globalization strategies car makers and the major supplier companies are seeking to standardize their production system and in doing so they will level out national or plant-specific variations. A prominent example for this is the implementation of the Chrysler Operating System (COS) since the mid-1990s developed explicitly after the Toyota production system. Its central elements are just-in-time supply and buffer minimization, team organization and quality responsibility of direct workers, standard operating procedures and so forth. The interest in a standardized production system on company level, a correlate of the globalization process, thus has been driving production system design in the direction of the Japanese model. Convergence tendencies also prevail in the area of job design as witnessed by the fact that many companies scrapped the production systems they had set up under the influence of Swedish work concepts in the 1980s. Thus the assembly line with short work cycles and standardized job operations has returned as an almost unchallenged element of modern best practice production systems. The Japanese influence can be observed also in the emphasis on standardizing operations, decentralizing quality responsibility and emphasizing continuous improvement.

The notion of convergence may however be misleading. The debate about teamwork shows that the broad diffusion of elements of the Japanese system should not be regarded as an indication for an unqualified convergence of the national production models. Although teamwork has become almost a standard feature of Western production systems there are wide differences as to the meaning of teamwork and its organizational characteristics. One might argue from the background of the Swedish and German debate about new forms of work, whether the term "teamwork" should be used at all in the context of the Japanese production model (Sey 1998, Nomura & Jürgens 1995). The notion of teamwork encompasses widely different forms of work organization and performance regulation and these differences are still very much related to national contexts as research carried out in the mid 1990s has shown (Durand et al. 1999).

Another example of prevailing national differences are improvement activities. Process improvement factually still lies mostly in the responsibility of experts in Germany. Finally, in the area of human resource development, skill formation and labour relations signs can hardly be observed indicating a trend towards convergence between any of the three production models. Skill formation is still focusing on technically specialized front-loaded ("fachliche") skills in the German context. Japanese personnel development systems, i.e. the complex of skill formation, career structure, job rotation and personnel appraisal, have not been implemented in Germany.

Although it can be summarized that many of the management concepts that characterize the Japanese production model have been formally adopted by German companies, production models still hinge very much on their traditional core elements. The diffusion of certain elements or methods cannot be seen as an indication of convergence of the German production system and the Japanese model. Speaking of convergence or divergence, the wide diffusion of Japan-inspired concepts seems to indicate at least that forces of convergence seem stronger in the 1990s than those of divergence. At the same time new "challenges" arise which force changes in all production systems including the success model of the recent past, the Japanese.

References

Broadberry, S. N. & Wagner, K. (1996), Human Capital and Productivity in Manufacturing During the 20th Century: Britain, Germany and the United States, in: Crafts, N. & van Ark, B. (eds.), *Quantitative Aspects of Post-war European Growth*, Cambridge: Cambridge University Press.

Durand, J.-P., Stewart, P. & Castillo, J. J. (eds.) (1999), *Teamwork in the Automobile Industry: Radical Change or Passing Fashion?*, Houndmills: Macmillan Business.

Fujimoto, T. (1999), *The Evolution of A Manufacturing System at Toyota*, New York, Oxford: Oxford University Press.

Jürgens, U. (1998), Implanting Change: The Role of "Indigenous Transplants" in Transforming the German Productive Model, in: Boyer, R. et al. (eds.), *Between Imitation and Innovation: The Transfer and Hybridisation of Productive Models in the International Automobile Industry*, Oxford: Oxford University Press: 319-341.

Jürgens, U. (1997), Rolling Back Cycle Times: The Rennaisance of the Classic Assembly Line in Final Assembly, in: Shimokawa, K., Jürgens, U. & Fujimoto, T. (eds.), *Transforming Automobile Assembly. Experience in Automation and Work Organisation*, Berlin: Springer-Verlag: 255-273.

Kern, H. & Schumann, M. (1989), New Concepts of Production in West-German Plants, in: Katzenstein, P. J. (ed.), *Industry and Politics in West-Germany. Toward the Third Republic*, Ithaka, London: Cornell University Press: 87-110.

Kuhlmann, M. & Schumann, M. (1997), Patterns of Work Organisation in the German Automobile Industry, in: Shimokawa, K., Jürgens, U. & Fujimoto, T. (eds.), *Transforming Automobile Assembly. Experience in Automation and Work Organisation*, Berlin: Springer-Verlag: 289-304.

Nomura, M. & Jürgens, U. (1995), *Binnenstrukturen des japanischen Produktivitätserfolgs. Arbeitsbeziehungen und Leistungsregulierung in zwei japanischen Automobilunternehmen*, Berlin: edition sigma.

Roth, S. (1997), Labour's Perspective on Lean Production, in: Kochan, T. A. et al. (eds.), *After Lean Production. Evolving Employment Practices in the World Auto Industry*, Ithaka, London: Cornell University Press: 117-136.

Sey, A. (1998), Zur empirischen Aufarbeitung von Gruppenarbeit in Japan, in: Altmann, N. et al. (eds.), *Innovative Arbeitspolitik? Zur qualifizierten Produktionsarbeit in Japan*, Frankfurt, New York: Campus Verlag: 291-303.

Sorge, A. & Streeck, W. (1988), Industrial Relations and Technical Change: The Case for an Extended Perspective, in: Hyman, R. & Streeck, W. (eds.), *New Technology and Industrial Relations*, Oxford: Basil Blackwell: 19-47.

Springer, R. (1999), *Rückkehr zum Taylorismus? Arbeitspolitik in der Automobilindustrie am Scheideweg*, Frankfurt, New York: Campus Verlag.

Springer, R. (1997), Krise der Arbeitswissenschaft, in: *Leistung und Lohn*, December 1997: 3-14.

Turner, L. (ed.) (1997), *Negotiating the New Germany – Can Social Partnership Survive?*, Ithaca, London: ILR Press.

Womack, J. P., Jones, D. T. & Roos, D. (1990), *The Machine that Changed the World*, New York: Rawson.

Womack, J. P. & Jones, D. T. (1996), *Lean Thinking. Banish Waste and Create Wealth in Your Corporation*, New York: Simon & Schuster.

On the Policy of Reserving Different Currencies after the Asian Crisis

Yoshiaki Takahashi

1 Introduction

How do financial managers of East Asian firms escape from the impacts of a sudden change in the exchange rate between dollar and yen such as it happened in the Asian currency crisis in July 1997? This article is aimed to discuss the policy of reserving different currencies that financial managers of East Asian firms should take after the Asian currency crisis, in order to counterbalance the effects of erratic changes of the exchange rate between dollar and yen. Based on the analysis of the structure of Japan's foreign trade with East Asian countries and the impact of the dollar/yen rate, the author proposes that each country of East Asia should have its own currency basket containing a different proportion of yen, dollar, and euro.

2 The Causes of the Asian Currency and Financial Crisis in 1997

Three points have been discussed as the causes of the Asian currency crisis that began from the devaluation of the Thai Baht on July 2nd 1997. The first is the sudden and rapid outflow of large amounts of short-term private capital, which was a direct cause for the crisis. However, we have to point out the underlying cause that most East Asian countries had not organized their own financial system properly, and thus depended on foreign short-term capital. These countries also did not observe and control the inflow of the short-term capital. The high economic growth rates of East Asia countries were supported by private capital from foreign countries, which in turn was financed from off-shore markets or free financial markets. On these special markets, the regulation for tax, financing and foreign exchange were extremely lax and the markets were separated from the domestic financial markets.

The second reason for the Asian crisis is that most East Asian countries continuously stuck with the policy of a dollar peg system even during a period when the exchange rate of the dollar declined after May 1995. Under the system of pegged currencies, financial investors could realize riskless profits by arbitrage operations between countries with low and countries with high interest rates. This is the reason for the inflow of short-term capital after May 1995 (weak dollar), which induced over-investment and speculative bubbles. After 1997 (strong dollar), the outflow of this capital from Thailand, Korea and the other East Asian countries caused the burst of these bubble economies.

The third reason is related to the structural economic problems of Asian countries. The most important issue is that domestic enterprises on one hand could not accumulate technology and production skill during the years of high economic growth. On the other hand, wage level increased higher than the increase of labour productivity during the high economic growth (JETRO 1998:35-36). These problems and other economic structural issues led to a constant deficit of foreign trade, especially with Japan. In periods of strong yen (*endaka*), the trade deficit decreased, while it increased in periods of weak yen (*enyasu*). In order to explain the relation of the trade deficit and the currency crisis in these countries, Japan's foreign trade with East Asian countries should be analyzed.

3 Japan's Foreign Trade with East Asian Countries

3.1 General Trends of Japanese Exports and Imports

Though Japanese exports to the world decreased, the share of Japanese exports to East Asian countries[1] has increased about 11%, from 29.6% in 1990 to 40.6% in 1997. The share of imports from East Asian countries (especially from ASEAN and China) to Japan has also increased about 8% from 26.6% to 34.7% in the same period. Concerning trade balances, Japan has always registered a large surplus ($106 billion in 1995, $61 billion in 1996 and $82 billion in 1997) in total trade with East Asia, though it has registered deficits with China (JETRO 1998:63&68). Especially, Japan's trade surplus has been large with Korea, Thailand, Indonesia and the Philippines which had to face severe economic crisis when the Yen was depreciated in 1997. Therefore, these countries should reconsider whether it was right to continue the dollar peg system at that time.

1 East Asian countries refer to NIEs = Korea, Taiwan, Singapore and Hong Kong, ASEAN = Thailand, Malaysia, Indonesia and Philippine, and China.

3.2 Structure of Japan's Exports and Imports

What kind of goods are exported and imported by Japan? According to the White Paper on Foreign Trade by MITI in 1998, the share of capital goods (machinery and equipment) and parts and machine tools in Japan's total exports has increased by about 10%, whereas the share of durable consumer goods (automobiles, household electric equipment and so on) has decreased by about 10%. The share of export of machine tools and parts to East Asian regions has increased from 33% in 1988 to 45.8% in 1996, but the share of export of these goods to the USA in contrast has decreased from 35.7% to 30.3% during the same period. Concerning the value of machine tools and parts exported from Japan to East Asian countries, the value of these goods to China, ASEAN and NIEs has increased four times, about two times and 1.5 times respectively from 1990 to 1996 (MITI 1997:54-56).

Parallel to the increase of export of capital goods and parts and machine tools, the value of import of these goods also has increased from 11.9% in 1988 to 22.8% in 1996 and from 5.9% to 12.2% during the same period, respectively (see figure 1). Looking at the regional distribution of the import, imports from East Asia increased from 26.1% in 1988 to 45.3% in 1996, whereas the share of imports from the USA decreased by about 12%, from 52.8% to 40.2%, and from Europe by 8%, from 19.7% to 11.5% between 1988 and 1996 (see figure 2) (MITI 1997:54-56).

These facts mean that:

1) The share of Japanese foreign trade with East Asian countries has been constantly growing.

2) The increased amount of Japanese foreign trade with East Asia has been originated from intra-firm trade between Japanese subsidiaries abroad and domestic mother companies.

This means that exchange rate fluctuations of dollar/yen rate have a big impact on the trade balance of East Asian countries as well as Japanese daughter companies located in the East Asian region.

Figure 1: Share of Capital Goods, Maschine Tools and Parts to Japanese Total Import

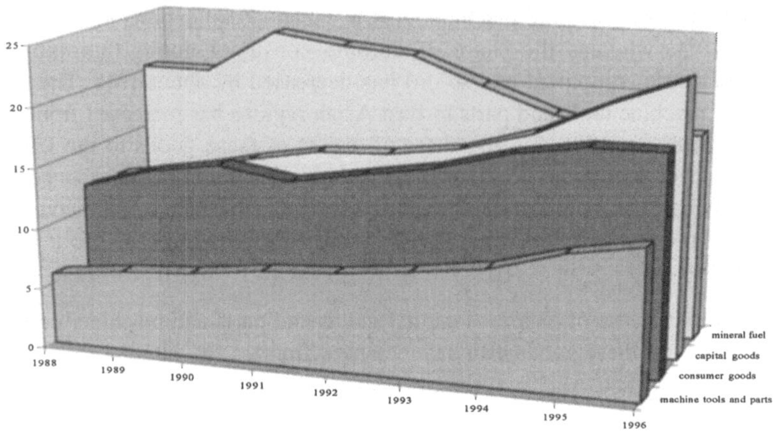

Source: The Ministry of Trade and Industry (MITI), *White Paper of Trade and Industry 1998*, Toyko: MITI: 56.

Figure 2: Japanese Share of Import of Machine Tools and Parts from Different Countries

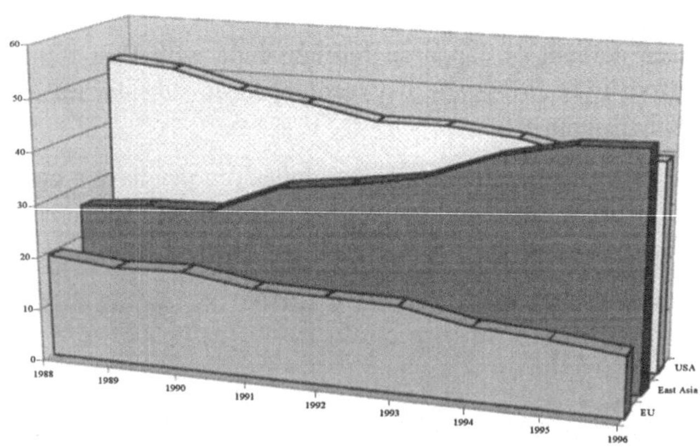

Source: The Ministry of Trade and Industry (MITI), *White Paper of Trade and Industry 1998*, Tokyo: MITI: 58.

4 The Trade Balances of Some Selected East Asian Countries

Here, we will show the situation of foreign trade of Korea and Taiwan, Thailand and Malaysia, and China.

Korea runs trade surpluses with ASEAN countries and China, but on the other hand it has a large trade deficit with Japan, America, Middle and South America, the Near and Middle East. As a result, the total trade deficit amounted to $8.4 billion including a deficit of $13 billion with Japan in 1997. Thus, South Korea's economy is increasingly intertwined with ASEAN countries and China (JETRO 1998).

In contrast to Korea, Taiwan registerd a $7 billion surplus in 1997. Though the value of imports from Japan and Europe exceeds the value of export to both regions (resulting in a $17 billion trade deficit with Japan and a $3 billion trade deficit with the EU), Taiwan enjoys a trade surplus from the other regions. Taiwan has also strong interdependence with East Asia, especially with Hong Kong and China (JETRO 1998).

Thailand, too, has registered a fairly large trade deficit (117 billion baht) including a 221 billion baht trade deficit with Japan. Thailand has transformed itself from an importing to an exporting country for NIEs and ASEAN countries between 1991 and 1997, and strengthened the economic relations with ASEAN, NIEs and Japan. Due to an increase of wages, Thailand has now to face a strong competition from China in several industries like cloths, shoes and sundry goods (JETRO 1998).

Compared with Thailand, Malaysia registered a little trade surplus (0.4 billion ringgit) in 1997. Though Malaysia registered a 20 billion ringgit trade deficit with Japan and a 4 billion ringgit trade deficit with Korea it has large trade surpluses with Singapore and Hong Kong in 1997. Because of no trade deficit, Malaysia did not face any serious crisis like Thailand (JETRO 1998).

China's situation of foreign trade is different from Thailand and Malaysia. While China registered a $13 billion deficit with Taiwan and a $5 billion deficit with Korea in 1997, China has a total trade surplus of $40 billion (including a $36 billion surplus with Hong Kong, a $16 billion surplus with the USA and a $2 billion with Japan). These figures of Chinese foreign trade show that China could escape from the serious currency crisis in spite of taking Dollar peg system on foreign trade. (JETRO 1998).

From the analysis of the trade balances of selected East Asian countries, we can conclude that the trade deficits of Korea and Thailand had direct impacts on their economic and currency crises, because the currency crisis did not occur in Taiwan and China which could enjoy trade surpluses. However, to answer the question why the currency crisis hit Indonesia which had a trade surplus, further analysis is necessary.

5 Three Types of Japanese Imports from East Asian Countries

Analyzing the kinds of goods imported from East Asian countries to Japan, we can distinguish three types. The first is the import from the NIEs countries (Korea, Taiwan, Hong Kong and Singapore) where Japan has increased the share of import of machinery, and machine tool and parts. From Korea, Japan increased the share of import of machinery and semiconductor from 16.7% in 1991 to 29.7% in 1997, while the share of import of textile goods and fish decreased from 18.9% and 8.9% in 1991 to 5.9% and 6.4% in 1997, respectively. From Taiwan, Japan increased the share of import of machinery and semiconductors from 20% in 1991 to 41% in 1997, while the share of fish and meats were decreased from 12% and 11% in 1991 to 6% and 2% in 1997, respectively. (JETRO 1998)

From Hong Kong Japan increased the share of import of machinery and semiconductors from 15% in 1991 to 32% in 1997, while the share of textile and precious metals were decreased from 24% and 10% in 1991 to 12% and 5% in 1997, receptively. Finally, from Singapore, the share of different office machines and equipment, and semiconductors was increased from 32% in 1991 to 63% in 1997, while the share of petroleum products was decreased from 33% in 1991 to 8% in 1997. (JETRO 1998)

The second type of import is imports from Thailand and Malaysia to Japan where the share of import of machinery increased on one hand and the share of import of goods like natural gas, natural rubber and food (fish and meats) remained more or less constant on the other hand. In the case of import to Japan from Malaysia, the share of machinery increased from 15% in 1991 to 37% in 1997 and the share of imports of timber, natural gas and crude oil decreased only marginally (the share of imports of the timber, natural gas and crude oil were still 9%, 17% and 4% respectively to the total import in 1997). In the case of import from Thailand to Japan, the share of machinery increased from 20% in 1991 to 33% in 1997, while the shares of fish, natural rubber and chicken meats remained fairly constant (12%, 7% and 4% in 1997, respectively). (JETRO 1997)

The third type is imports from Indonesia and China to Japan where the share of import of machinery to the total import increased gradually (at low levels), while the share of the import of goods like crude oil, natural gas, plywood, textile and fish gradually decreased (at high levels of 30% to 50% of the total imports from both countries). In the case of import from Indonesia to Japan, the share of import of machinery was only 6% in 1997, while the share of import of crude oil, natural gas, plywood and fish still was 24%, 14%, 11% and 8% to the total import, respectively. In the case of import from China to Japan, the share of import of machinery increased from 5% in 1991 to 17% in 1997, while the share of import of textiles, crude oil, and fish stayed rather unchanged at 25%, 4% and 5% in 1997 (Kokuseisha 1998).

From the above analysis of the three types of imports to Japan from East Asian countries, we can conclude that the industries of Korea and Taiwan have been economically highly developed and competitive with those of Japan, because the share of import of machinery and semiconductors from the two countries has increased. In contrast to Korea and Taiwan, the industries of China and Indonesia have not been so highly developed and competitive, rather they have been substitutive to Japanese economy, because the share of import of textile, crude oil, and fish have not decreased.

6 Necessity and Possibility of an Asian Currency Block

6.1 The Exchange Rate Between Yen and Dollar and the Asian Economic Performance

According to the research of the Nomura Research Institute (NRI), extreme fluctuations of the dollar/yen rate triggered the Asian economic crisis. Asian high economic growth coincided with the phase of yen appreciation (*endaka*) in the period from 1991 to 1995, whereas low economic growth coincided with the phase of cheap yen (*enyasu*) during 1989 and 1990 and after 1996 (see figure 3).

Figure 3: Economic Growth Rates of Asian Countries in Accordance with Japan's FDI into East Asia and the Yen/Dollar Exchange Rate's Movements (%)

Note: Asian Countries includes the NIEs, the ASEAN-countries and China.

Source: Kwan, S. (1998), *Asian Currency Crisis: From the Stand of View of Japanese Yen and Chinese Yuan*, Tokyo: NRI: 4.

Thus, Asian economic activities have expanded in the phase of strong yen against the dollar, while the economy activities have conversed in the phase of weak yen. Therefore, East Asian countries with trade deficit with Japan should reserve more yen. However, according to C. H. Kwan, a research fellow of the NRI, it was a popular opinion among East Asian countries to follow a currency exchange policy of a dollar peg system for the purpose of achieving high economic growth. This opinion was an unreliable myth that was proved false in the Asian currency crisis after July 1997. In fact, most East Asian countries except Malaysia and China had to abandon the dollar peg system after the crisis of 1997 (Kwan 1998:4).

6.2 Necessity and Possibility of an Asian Currency Block

With a deepened division of labour and close trade and economic relations among East Asian countries, a large devaluation of an East Asian currency must necessarily cause the devaluation of its surrounding countries' currencies. To avoid hedge risk of currency exchange rate, the countries of the East Asian region must be economically and financially cooperative. One of the cooperative systems to be considered at present is to build an Asian Currency Block. Even if it is impossible to immediately create a common currency block in East Asian region like Euro in the European Union, discussions of a "Common Currency Unit" or the Asian Currency Block have been begun.

I will introduce two approaches towards a currency block in this section, and discuss the currency basket system reserved by East Asian countries on the next section.

The first approach is the proposal of a APEC Common Currency Unit (C.C.U.) asserted by K. Kondo, the executive director of Japan External Trade Organization (JETRO), in 1995 before the Asian currency crisis. His concept of the currency consists of 5 factors:

1) C.C.U. will be defined as monetary cocktail including dollar, yen, Chinese yuan, Korean won and Thai baht.
2) The composition share of the C.C.U. will be decided by the APEC Finance Minister meeting.
3) The APEC Secretariat will publish every day the calculated C.C.U. rate against dollar, yen, and others.
4) C.C.U. will be used, for the time being, only for "numeraire (the standard of the currency exchange)". So it will be a pure calculation unit and will have no substance as an asset.
5) C.C.U. will be used in the APEC as denomination unit for trade and investment. The monetary authorities will promote, but will not force, the use

> of C.C.U. They will leave its use totally up to the initiative of private parties involved in trade and direct investment. (Kondo 1996: 211-212).

However, Kondo does not explain why Chinese yuan, Korean won and Thai baht (besides dollar and yen) are included, whereas on the other hand Malaysia ringgit and Indonesian rupiah are not selected.

T. Murase who worked in a Japanese bank located in Europe and Hong Kong for a long time has asserted another approach. He proposes to build a currency basket peg system and an Asian currency fund for stable exchange rates with the long-term aim to build a stable Asian Currency Block.

According to his explanation, the currency basket peg system means that exchange rates of regional countries will be fixed at a definite relation of their currency, or restricted to fluctuations within a definite span. The European Monetary System (EMS) before the introduction of Euro was a highly developed currency basket peg system where the common currency, "the ecu", was anchored as a standard currency. Compared with it, Murase makes a proposal that a relatively simple basket currency system consisting of dollar, yen and euro should be discussed in the East Asian region after the currency crisis. The shares of these three currencies in the basket of the East Asian countries depend upon their export and import shares. (Murase 1999: 276-278)

Murase proposes three steps to build a stable Asian Currency block and finally the Asian Monetary System. The first step is to build a common currency basket. The second step is to add other Asian currencies and give the characteristics of an "Asian Currency Unit (ACU)" to the common basket. In the second step, the currencies' shares should be as follows: 30% yen, 30% Asian currencies, 20% dollar and 20% euro. To reach the second step, Asian countries must improve their economic and financial systems, and have to build an Asian Currency Cooperation Fund. It will take 10 years to reach this step. The third step is that "ACU" (composed from yen and other Asian currencies) will become an currency by its own such the dollar and the euro. Murase thinks it will take about 30 years for East Asian countries to reach the third step (Murase 1999:281-282).

7 Present Currency Reserving Systems

7.1 Currency Basket System

What currency reserving policy should East Asian countries take on the condition of erratic fluctuations of the dollar/yen rate besides the common basket system, Asian Currency Cooperation Fund and Asian Currency Unit (ACU)? From the analysis shown in figure 3, Kwan asserts that each Asian country will have to consider a stable relation not only between its own currency and the dollar, but also between its own currency and the yen. These countries should individually take a currency basket system. The currency basket system means that every country designs its own currency policy in the relation with two or three foreign currencies in order to stabilize its currency. Take the example of the Korean currency basket which relates to the dollar and the yen. It is supposed that Korea has a basket which is composed of 70% yen and 30% dollar. If the yen appreciates by 10% against the dollar, the Korean won is thus appreciated by 7% against the dollar, The basket system of two or three currencies is similar to a fixed exchange rate system because the exchange rate of one currency in relation to two or three other currencies is fixed on the weighted average (Kwan 1999).

7.2 Structure of Currency Baskets

Kwan continues to discuss merits and demerits of a strong (weak) yen for each Asian country. According to his explanation, Korea and Taiwan, whose economic development level is high and competitive with Japan, can profit from a strong yen by increasing their exports, but accordingly suffer from a weak yen. In contrast to these countries, China and Indonesia, whose economic development level is low and whose exports are uncompetitive but rather substitutive to Japanese ones, are hardly influenced at all. As a result, Kwan makes a proposal that Korea and Taiwan shall reserve 70% or 60% yen and 30% or 40% dollar in their baskets, while China and Indonesia shall reserve 10% yen or 90% dollar in their baskets, and Thailand and Malaysia shall reserve 30% yen and 70% dollar in their baskets (Kwan 1999).

This proposal is different from Murase's that each country of East Asian region should have the same basket aiming at building the Asian Currency Block. The core point of Kwan's approach is that each country has to consider the proportion of yen and dollar independently based on its economic and trade conditions. Moreover, not only each country but also each firms can reserve a different proportion of currencies in its basket, in accordance with regional, economic and trade conditions.

Therefore, it is important for the financial manager of East Asian firms to follow a targeted policy of reserving different currencies, considering each item of their firm's trade.

8 Concluding Remarks

It is very difficult for East Asian countries to realize an integrated economic area like European Union, which needed over fifty years of political and economical integration, because the level of economic development – besides cultural differences –is very different. At the present, councils and meetings on economic cooperation within the East Asian region have been organized. There are among others the Asian-Pacific Economic Cooperation (APEC, inaugurated in 1989), the ASEAN Regional Forum (agreed on in 1993), and the Asia-Euro Summit Meeting (first held in 1996).

China, Japan and Korea do not belong to any free trade agreement, while all other major advanced countries of the world do. However, the time is ripe for free investment agreements between Singapore and Japan, and between Korea and Japan. The free investment agreement between Singapore and Japan has been concluded in the middle of 2000, and the free investment agreement between Korea and Japan will also be concluded in 2000. According to the framework of agreement with Korea proposed by Japanese government, the following issues are extended:

1) Both countries guarantee same and equal treatment of foreign firms to domestic firms.

2) The host country is forbidden to compel foreign firms to procure materials from domestic firms, to export from its local factory, and to transfer technologies to domestic firms.

3) Both countries guarantee the right of tangible and intangible intellectual property.

However, the author thinks that Japanese firms and the government should consider a reasonable trade balance and more technology transfer for the promotion of competition and cooperation between Japan and Korea.

With these bilateral agreements and China's admission into the World Trade Organization (WTO), the possibility of organizing economic cooperation in the East Asia draws closer.

References

JETRO (1998), *Jetoro Hakusho* [White Paper of JETRO], Tokyo:JETRO.

Kokuseisha (1998), *Nihon no Alamanaku* [Almanac of Japan], Tokyo: Kokuseisha.

Kondo, T. (1996), *International Monetary System and APEC*, Tokyo: Printing Unit of the Minister of Finance.

Kwan, C.H. (1998), *Asian Currency Crisis: From the Viewpoint of Japanese Yen and Chines Yuan*, Toyko: NRI.

Kwan, C.H. (1999), Asian Currency Baskets, in: *Nihon Keizai Shimbun* August 26th 1999.

Murase, T. (1999), *Stable Asian Currency Block: The Role of Japanese Yen*, Tokyo: Keisô Shobô.

A Current Picture of Internet and E-Commerce in Asia

Kerstin Teicher

1 Introduction

Is Asia online already? How do Internet usage and Internet commerce transactions look like in Asia? Is it different to the western world? Is there one common pattern in Asia at all?

A number of obstacles are frequently mentioned why e-commerce potential for the Asian region should be low:

- Behavioral or cultural barriers such as resistance to credit card payment over the Internet or preference of Asians for face to face buying.
- Infrastructural barriers such as high telecom access charges, small base of installed PCs, low telephone penetration rate, low credit card ownership, low discretionary incomes with many people living in subsistence mode who cannot afford Internet access.
- In some countries, especially in China, but also in Singapore and Vietnam, government or legal restrictions are quoted as a big barrier for Internet and e-commerce.

In fact, in comparison to other countries three big differences of the Internet in Asia can be observed:

- **Internet penetration**: The channels of access are different in Asia with rather low Internet penetration resulting from home PCs but with a very early adaptation of accessing the Internet via mobile devices as well as from "Internet cafes".
- **Consumer behavior** in Asia is specific with a highly entertainment/electronic enthusiastic population.
- **Approach to e-commerce** is different: Companies offer online shopping services by adapting to some of these requirements or characteristics.

This article gives examples for these three main issues arguing that there is a big potential for Internet based commercial transactions (e-commerce) which might take in Asia rather the form of m-commerce, i.e. transactions done via mobile devices. Moreover, this article focusses on business-to-consumer e-commerce.

2 Internet Penetration

If the traditional calculation for Internet penetration and e-commerce potential (based on fixed line telephone penetration and PC ownership in households) is conducted for Asia, for most countries the results are rather poor. In most Asian countries (except for Japan, Korea, Taiwan), both measures are low in comparison to advanced western countries such as Germany or America (see figure 1).

Figure 1: Fixed Line and PC Penetration in Selected Asian Countries

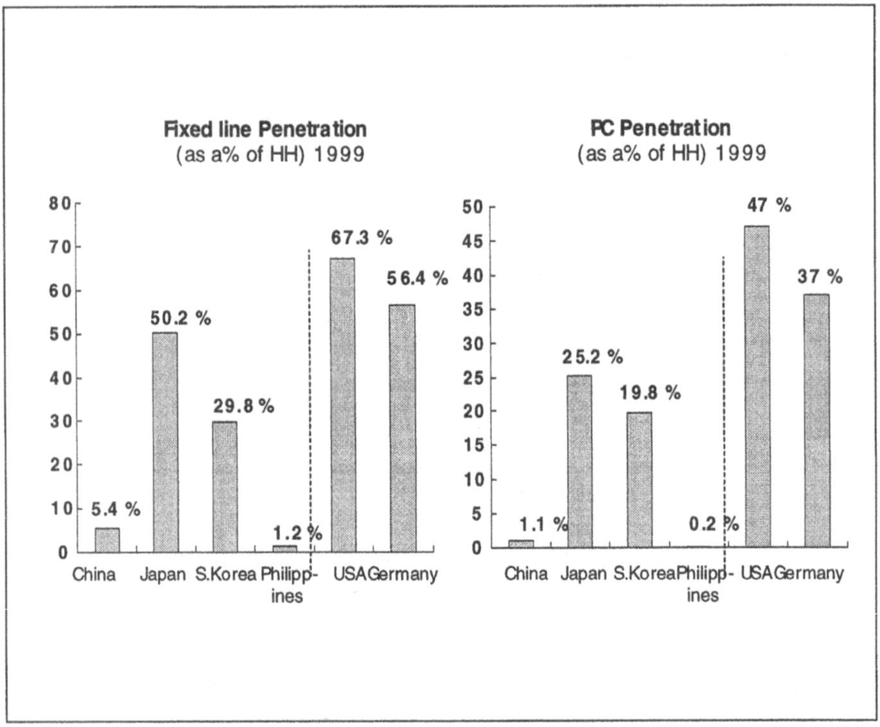

Source: Teicher.

However, in mid 1999, NUA estimated the total worldwide number of Internet users at 333 million, with a share of the Asian region of 23% or approximately 75.5 million users, following Europe's share of 28% and America's of 43% (see figure 2) (Nua Internet Surveys, August 2000).

Figure 2: Number of Internet Users Worldwide as of Mid 1999 (in Millions)

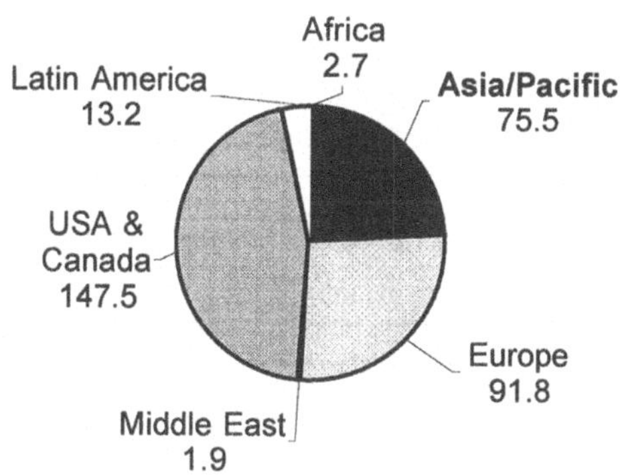

Source: Teicher, based on Nua Internet Surveys, August 2000.

By country, this breaks down as follows (see also table 1): Whereas the percentage of Internet users in most Asian countries is low (e.g. 1.3% in China), the absolute numbers already are as high as in the western world. The difference of the total numbers of Internet users in Asia in figure 1 and table 2 are due to different times (one is from late 1999, the other from 2000), indicating the rapid growth of this industry in which numbers are usually valid only for a very limited time frame. However, for illustration reasons, numbers are given in this article.

How is this rapid growth possible without any comparable increase in fixed line and PC penetration rates? A large part comes indeed from the growth of mobile phone penetration. Asia's current mobile phone subscribers outnumber Internet users nearly four to one. Although Europe is still leading in terms of numbers of subscribers (215 million), Asia-Pacific is second already, and the region is the fastest growing mobile phone market in the world, expected to reach approximately 400 million users until 2004/5, more than the EU or America have inhabitants (Asiaweek, July 2000, Morgan Stanley Dean Witter, *Asian Wireless Internet*, October 2000; see also table 1).

In China, for example, fewer than 10 million telephone lines existed in 1990. Today there are 125 million lines. However, mobile phones are multiplying even faster, from 5 million mobile-phone users in 1995 to over 70 million today. More mobile handsets will be sold in China in 2000 than in either the United States or

Japan. The same is true for Internet growth: In 1995, there were fewer than 50,000 Internet-users in China. If statistics from the state China Internet Network Information Centre are to be believed, there were 2.1 million users at the beginning of 1999 and 8.9 million at its end. By August 2000, the number already had risen to 17 million (The Economist, July 22nd 2000, NUA Internet Survey, July 2000).

Table 1: Number of Internet and Mobile Phone Users in Asia (as of early 2000)

Country	Internet users	Internet users (% of population)	Mobile phone users	Mobile users (% of population)
Australia	7,000,000	36.8%	9,000,000	47.7%
China	16,900,000	1.3%	75,000,000	5.8%
Hong Kong	1,800,000	32.1%	3,000,000	53.6%
India	4,500,000	0.5%	18,000,000	1.8%
Japan	27,000,000	21.4%	56,000,000	44.4%
Malaysia	600,000	2.9%	3,000,000	14.6%
Newzealand	1,300,000	35.1%	2,000,000	54.1%
Philippines	1,000,000	1.4%	1,800,000	2.5%
Singapore	1,700,000	56.7%	1,800,000	58.3%
SouthKorea	15,300,000	33.3%	27,500,000	59.8%
Taiwan	6,400,000	29.6%	13,000,000	60.2%
Thailand	1,000,000	1.7%	2,500,000	4.2%
Rest*	2,400,000	0.7%	1,000,000	0.3%
Sum	84,600,000		213,600,000	

* Bangladesh, Bhutan, Brunei, Cambodia, North Korea, Laos, Maledives, Mongolia, Myanmar, Nepal, Pakistan, Sri Lanka, Vietnam: partly estimates.

Source: Teicher, based on Nua Internet Surveys, August 2000 and other sources.

Given these numbers it becomes obvious, that m-commerce has a very good basis in Asia-Pacific. This region accounts for 98% of the world's wireless Internet browsing, with 5.9 million users! Especially in Japan, already more Japanese users access the Internet through mobile devices than through PCs (PR Newswire, August 3rd 2000).

3 Consumer Behavior

One general remark on consumer behavior in Asia is that the people are very affectionate to entertainment (e.g. having very high TV penetration rate and high viewership in all Asian countries), to games and electronics. This is an exellent basis for Internet usage in general and can potentially translate in significant e-commerce revenues. A few examples shall illustrate this:

- Japan: When Sony sold 3,000 pieces of its robot pet "Aibo" over the Internet in Japan as early as June 1999 for Y250,000 per piece, it was sold out within 20 minutes.
- Japan: Subscribers to NTT DoCoMo's pioneering I-Mode service on August 6th 2000 passed the 10 million mark, up from less than a million a year ago (see also chapter 4 and figure 3).
- Philippines: This country with a mere 2-3 million mobile phone subscribers is already second only to Nordic countries in terms of absolute numbers of text messages (SMS) sent daily.
- South Korea: Six months after SK Telecom launched wireless Internet services, more than 15% of its subscriber base was using the Internet.
- South Korea: More than 50% of brokerage is done online in mid 2000.
- South Korea and Japan: Customers, many of them teenagers and young adults, are not buying with their mobiles what might be expected from a western perspective; digital entertainment such as Pokemons (used as mobile phone screen displays), daily horoscopes, and karaoke music generate the most wireless traffic in Japan and Korea. The second most-popular category is information such as news headlines and stock prices. Online banking, ticket sales, book sales and others generate less than 10% of traffic (Asiaweek, July 2000).
- China: Although the average income is very low, the top 10% of the population consists of 130 million people (exceeding Germany's total population) who can afford to purchase new technologies and services. Chinese mobile phone users spend in average US$39 per month for their service, which is only 8% lower than the average monthly bill of American consumers (International Herald Tribune, June 19th 2000). 14% of Chinese Internet users have already purchased online.

- In countries with still small Internet penetration rates, "Internet cafes" are booming. They offer cheap Internet access with the opportunity to meet other people.

Another reason for the boom of Internet cafes in Asia is the fact that they offer Internet access for people with lower income as well as young people without computer ownership, whereas the middle and upper-income class usually access the Internet from their homes. Therefore, the argument that the rise of Internet usage will deepen the so-called Digital Divide, the gap between the rich who can afford to pay for Internet access and the poor who do not have the means to access the Internet, cannot be stated unchallenged.

Although it is impossible to exactly estimate the number of Internet cafes in Asia – as well as in the rest of the world – because in most countries the operators are not obliged to register (in China, however, Internet cafes are required to register with the government), most estimations assume that at least 30,000 Internet cafes are in operation in Asia. They usually offer Internet access at very low rates.

For example, a big majority of Internet users in Indonesia uses the Internet either at the office or at Internet cafes, of which in Jakarta alone exist about 500 (The Jakarta Post, July 2nd 2000). Even in a underdeveloped country like Mongolia, the capital Ulan Bator has over 40 Internet cafes which have sprung up across the city within just two years. And in most provincial capitals satellite Internet access is available in local libraries, financed by the Soros Foundation (Newsday, July 24th 2000). In the Philippines, the company PhilWeb plans to build 1,255 "Cyberworld cafes" in affiliate schools and related organisations by December 2000. In both Korea and India more than 10,000 Internet cafes already exist (in Korea they are called "PC rooms").

4 Approach to E-Commerce

As mentioned above, specific consumer behaviours can be observed in Asia. Unsurprisingly, most players in the market for e-commerce adopt very well to these characteristics:

- Online shopping malls ("Cyber malls") attract a large number of users offering a comprehensive shopping experience displaying a large variety of products and offering the opportunity for online chatting or "auctioning". For example, 87% of Korean Internet users have visited one of the 800 online shopping malls; in Japan, among the web sites most frequently visited are shopping malls like Recruit's "I-Size" or DNP's cybermall.
- After online purchase, many companies, especially in Japan, let consumers choose between postal, courier service delivery or pick-up of the ordered items

at convenience stores. In the latter case, two main problems associated with e-commerce are solved: a) the consumer can pick up the product whenever he likes at a place he usually passes by anyway on the way home and b) the consumer can pay cash upon delivery (COD).

- M-commerce has this commercial advantage over the regular Internet as well – mobile phone companies can act as a universal clearing-house for accepting payments and settling bills (Asiaweek, July 2000). Japan's mobile giant NTT DoCoMo for example already invoices Internet commerce transactions done via its I-mode service through its monthly mobile phone invoice.

E-commerce revenues in Asia so far have been quite low but are estimated to grow tremendously in 2000. Online sales in China totaled just US$6.6 million in 1999 but could grow by 500% in 2000. In the rest of Asia, they reached US$1.5 billion in Japan and US$720 million in South Korea, with the rest of Asia totalling US$180 million, according to the Boston Consulting Group (International Herald Tribune, June 19th 2000).

5 I-Mode – an Example

Indeed, NTT DoCoMo's I-mode is a very good example for the impact mobile Internet access will have on markets and consumer behavior.

Mobile phone companies might benefit most from the rise of the Internet: encouraging customers not just to talk but to surf the Internet increases minutes of use, and creates new revenue streams as well: DoCoMo gets up to a 12% commission of the subscription fees that content providers charge their customers, a kind of toll for being listed on the official I-mode portal. DoCoMo also gets a 9% commission on all sales (Asiaweek, July 2000). The Japanese market is characterized by very rapid adoption of mobile Internet and 3G licenses have already been issued. Japan is expected to implement the world's first commercial 3G network in the second quarter of 2001, and Ericsson has already been selected as 3G supplier by NTT DoCoMo and Japan Telecom.

Technically, unlike WAP phones, I-mode uses a system based on the Internet lingua franca HTML that allows users to access regular websites without dialing-up each time since they are "always online", yet, only the transferred data has to be paid for.

More than these technical, strategical and business issues, I-mode is a lifestyle tool in Japan; it can be adapted to suit their owners – girls download snips of favorite pop melodies to replace the normal ringing tone, have little characters live on their screens and so forth – and it is used virtually everywhere. And different to western countries, mobile phone ringing in business meetings or in restaurants is usually not considered impolite in Asia.

Figure 3: Overview of the Mobile Internet Service "I-Mode" in Japan

Data

- **I-mode** is one Japanese Internet mode for Mobiles (different to WAP), user is always "online"
- Provider: NTT DoCoMo
- **Start**: February 99
- IDO and DDI followed with own services (45.000 or 100.000 customers)
- **More than 600 pages** with I-mode start pages; other Web address can be put in by URL
- All pages in HTML-Format
- **Customers**: 7,600,000 (July 00)
- **Cost**:
  - Basic Charge: ¥1200 /month
  - E-mail: 0.9 ¥-4.2 ¥ (15 letters, 250 characters)
  - Mobile Banking: 20-50 ¥ per transaction
  - Handy: 10-35.000 ¥
- **Transmission rate**: 9.600 bps
- **IP-Partner**: Fuji Bank, Lawson Ticket, Asahi Shimbun, Kinokuniya u.a. (actually 200)

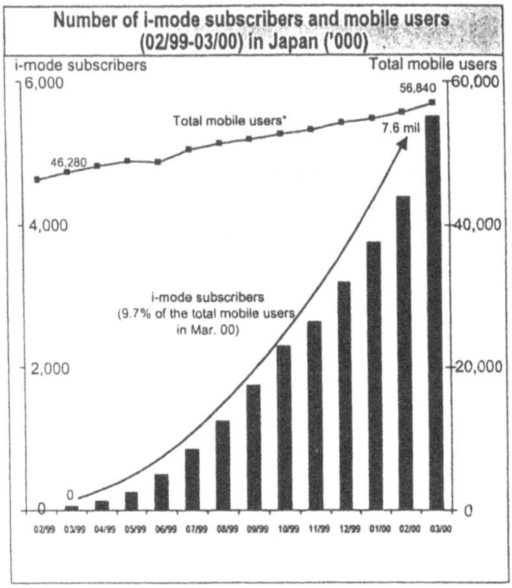

* including subscribers of PHS

Source: Teicher

Moreover, NTT DoCoMo plans – as the first company in the world – to launch wireless service with the "third generation" technology called W-CDMA, enabling users to send and receive far more data at high speeds, including photos and moving images. It also wants to export its service internationally on a large scale: it has already teamed up with Sun, Microsoft, and others, and has taken a stake in Hutchison Telephone Co. of Hong Kong in December. NTT DoCoMo's President Keiji Tachikawa said that the investment aims at promoting I-mode in Asia. In May, Hutchison Telephone began testing I-mode services in Hong Kong. NTT also invested US$3.8 billion in KPN Mobile NV of the Netherlands and is already in talks to export I-mode to South Korea.

Additionally, NTT DoCoMo is teaming up with Sony. I-mode users will be able to download games to their phone, play them and upload them to their Playstation (AP Online, August 1st 2000). With AOL NTT DoCoMo has reached an agreement to make AOL's online content and e-mail service accessible via DoCoMo's I-mode phones. Under the accord, NTT DoCoMo and AOL will each invest US$100 million in AOL Japan Inc., a joint venture between AOL, the trading firm Mitsui and Co. and the newspaper publisher Nihon Keizai Shimbun Inc., for a combined stake of 80% (Jiji Press, August 1st 2000). This way, NTT DoCoMo tries to establish a strong network to push its technology further.

But also in other countries, companies that offer Internet access via mobile phones are very active: In Taiwan, for example, the leading mobile phone company Taiwan Cellular Corp. invested US$6.6 million in a WAP portal, which so far includes 67 affiliated content providers selling more than 200 items. Merchandise on sale includes daily electronic horoscopes, CDs, flowers, fast food and even vacation packages.

6 Internet Players in Asia

Like the rest of the world, Asia has witnessed a Internet boom which is accompanied by venture companies that specialize in investing in Internet companies. The most prominent examples are Softbank of Japan and PCCW of Hong Kong which both have made a fortune by investing in companies like Yahoo!Japan and others in the late 1990s.

As anywhere else, Internet in Asia began with portals, but real e-commerce activities such as online book or media shops, online-Banking, auctioning, etc. started soon thereafter.

Especially China has seen a huge number of portals coming to life. The number of Chinese web sites doubled in the six month from December 1999 to June 2000 totalling more than 27,000. Most portals consist of a large number of vertical genre sites, ranging from life style oriented sites, games and entertainment to financial information. Many of these companies are incorporated outside mainland China due to the still existing restrictions of foreign ownership. They have thus attracted a variety of investors, like investment banks, companies like AOL and others.

The second half of 2000 was – like elsewhere – a phase of consolidation as start-up companies faced funding problems. Especially portals now are desperately looking for additional money, and those that are listed already on stock exchanges have suffered big losses in their stock prices. Most experts estimate that only the two or three biggest and most successful portals in China will survive. Strong contenders are the following portals:

- **Sina.com**'s is currently the number one portal, and its key strengths is in reporting headline news. It is the equivalent of the Yahoo to runner ups Netease and Sohu, since they all have been pure portals and launched two to three years ago. The company has strong growth in traffic.

- **Netease** is currently the number three portal. Its strength has been and still is in its strong community. It has been able to build up a strong following based on the traditional community tools of chat, message boards, bbs. Netease listed on NASDAQ and looks to dislodge Sina.com from the number one spot by embarking on a massive advertising campaign. News Corp is one of the investors in Netease

- **163.net** (currently number six) and **263.net** (currently number four) both evolved from government related areas: 163.net was formerly owned by Guangzhou Telecom before it was privatized and bought out by another group led by some investment bankers. The web site is strong in providing free email to users in the Guangzhou region. 263.net was formed as a joint-venture between a Beijing paging company and Beijing Telecom. Similar to 163.net, its first service was free email and it was very popular with users in the Beijing area.

Regarding pure e-commerce companies, in most Asian countries it started with online book and music selling as well as with auctioning and in some countries (e.g. Korea) with online banking or broking. One key characteristic of e-commerce in Asia is, however, that there are very few foreign (western) e-commerce players so far. In Korea, Samsung, which operates one of the countries biggest cybermalls, has alliances both with Amazon and Kinokuniya of Japan for selling books online at lower prices than in conventional book stores (even including delivery charges). However, the alliance with Amazon is more an "affiliate deal" without any real presence of Amazon. Amazon has put a lot of efforts into a market entry in Japan too, but so far failed owing to a number of reasons, of which two only for illustration will be mentioned here:

- First of all, foreign companies have to deal with the difficulty of Asian language which in the Internet world indeed is a big problem as the technology to display those non-alphabet characters has to be so-called "double-byte" capable which requires additional development.

- Second, as the wholesale structures in the publishing industry in most Asian countries is rather complex, it is very difficult to get access to books since it is almost impossible to acquire books from literally thousands of publishers.

Usually, online book shops in Asia have their roots in a number of different industries: book shops, publishers, pure e-commerce companies, sometimes wholesalers and in Japan also a few logistic service companies and in China some state owned publishers and book shops.

In Japan, more than 90 online book shops exist. The retailer Kinokuniya has opened the first one (in September 1996) and is still operating the largest one. Other online book shops include the wholesalers Nippan and Tohan, logistic companies such as Kuroneko and Skysoft, retailers like Maruzen, and many others. As late as in June 2000, the first foreign online media shop, Bertelsmann's "BOL" was able to launch in Japan with a Japanese site. Thereafter, Amazon increased its own efforts and finally launched its first Japanese store in November 2000. However, it has to cooperate with the rather third class wholesaler Osakaya.

Competition in online book and media selling has been dramatically increasing in Japan since then: Most online shops have lowered their delivery fees; BOL and Amazon are even offering delivery free of charge until the end of 2000. Although this has increased orders significantly, such cost-intensive marketing increases further the financial pressure on e-commerce companies in the high-cost country Japan.

In all countries, the success of e-commerce or other online activities cannot yet be measured and needs to be proven over time.

7 Summary and Outlook

Although the half of the world's total population lives in the Asia-Pacific region, it is implausible to expect an according share of e-commerce revenues in the near future as the overall income per capita is still very low. Nevertheless, as argued in this paper, there is a big potential for e-commerce: if only 10% of the Chinese and Indian population use e-commerce services the total number of users will equal the entire American population.

Although this article mentions a number of idiosyncratic characteristics, it is not meant to emphasize how different Asia is. On the contrary, under a long-term perspective, it is very likely that East and West will meet in the world of Internet and e- and m-commerce, but having taken a different way there. Chances are high that the current high mobile penetration rates of many Asian countries transform into future high Internet penetration rates (see figure 4).

Japan, Korea, Taiwan and Hong Kong are the most developed countries in Asia for e-commerce and Internet usage, with China and India representing major growth opportunities. All of them offer big opportunities in m-commerce as well.

Figure 4: Potential Future Development of Asian Countries

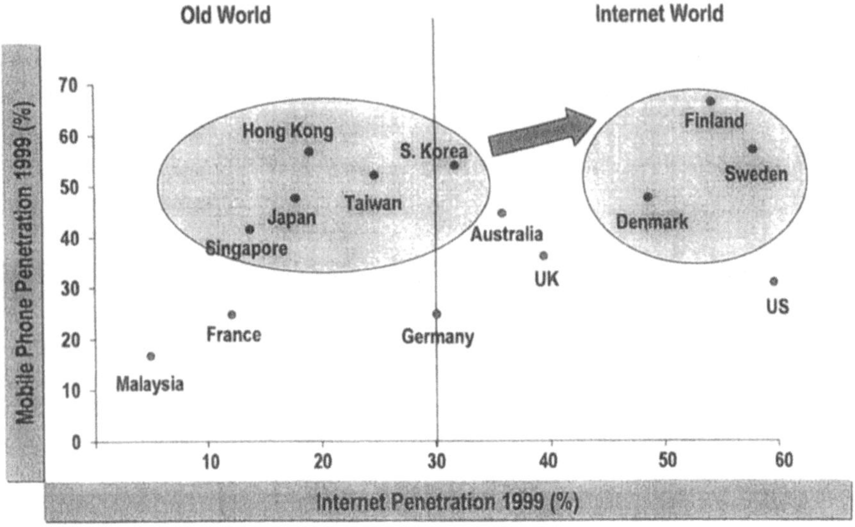

Source: Teicher

Strategy and Localisation in China

Dieter Beschorner & Marc-Oliver Thurner

1 The Situation: China's Economy and Regulatory System

With the death of Chairman Mao Zedong in 1976 and the subsequent rise of Deng Xiaoping as the new leader of new communist party, a new chapter began – not only for China but also for the world economy. Since the proclamation of the People's Republic of China in 1949, the regime's policy had left a country with a more than doubled headcount (Hermann-Pillath & Lackner 1998:616), a centrally planned and state-owned economy, and a complete generation (the current manager generation) hindered from education during the cultural revolution era.

The Open Door Policy, adopted in 1979, was the liberal approach proclaimed by a group around Deng Xiaoping that was meant to lead China out of its poverty. Deng Xiaoping's stated objective was to open China's economy to the outside world and quadruple the Chinese gross national product until the year 2000.

In the early 1980s, foreign companies were primarily confined to some fourteen special economic zones and the principal coastal cities where the Chinese government was experimenting with change. Later, this geographic limitation to access to China has been gradually relaxed and further provinces were partially opened up for investment.

The Open Door Policy programs initiated what should become the beginning of a new industrial age in China. For most multinational corporations it meant the discovery of the Chinese market. One of the main reasons of granting western companies access to China's markets was that the Government leaders had recognised that the country was unable to finance the rate and style of development needed. Domestically, it was not able to generate a sufficient surplus for investment, and internationally, it was strapped by a lack of foreign exchange (Steidlmeier 1995:18). China attained Deng Xiaoping's goal in 1995, when the Chinese GNP reached RMB5,760 billion, five years ahead of target (Brahm & Daoran 1996:3).

Today, China is facing several problems that are challenging the leadership's ability to secure the stability of the country. Growth of economic power is still an imperative. But almost on every frontier the remains of the centrally planned economy deteriorate the progress in economic development (Business Week 1999:29).

The main concerns are:

- a slowing economy,
- growing unemployment,
- widespread unrest,
- financial meltdown of the state banks,
- corruption,
- housing problems and
- the bankrupt state-owned enterprises.

With continued economic growth, income disparities have emerged practically spliting the country into two classes: urban and rural citizens. Beyond that, there is also a division into two geographies: the more developed economic zones[1] and the rest of the country (see also figure 1). If this tendency prevails, this growing inequality may become a potential social time bomb. This development is also a result of the uneven geographic distribution of foreign direct investment in China, which was primarily directed into cities in economic zones. During the 1985-1992 period, the twelve coastal provinces attracted approximately 90 percent of total FDI inflows (Broadman & Sun 1997:5).

To sustain growth and avoid deterioration China is depending on a continued inflow of capital and knowledge. So far the Overseas Chinese have proven to be instrumental in this respect. But after the Asian crisis and the high profile bankruptcy of GITIC in the end of 1998, the enthusiasm for investment in China has suffered significantly. To regain credibility and improved access to outside markets the anticipated membership in the World Trade Organisation is seen as the key to the future.

But China's leaders have also recognised the necessity to focus on high value added industry sectors for a sustainable economic development and to ensure competitiveness in the years to come. The Government institutions are fostering the development of certain industries that are considered "strategic" – e.g. biotechnology and semiconductors. In these industry sectors, the Universities as well as Chinese private companies are provided with all necessary resources – seeking world leadership and ultimately dominance.

---

1 Economic zones here include the five state-level special economic zones, several dozen economic and technological development zones, high-technology development zones and free-trade zones, as well as countless sub zones, city- and count-level zones, and industrial parks which are spread across the country.

Figure 1: The GDP per Capita Map – Coastal Wealth and Hinterland Poverty

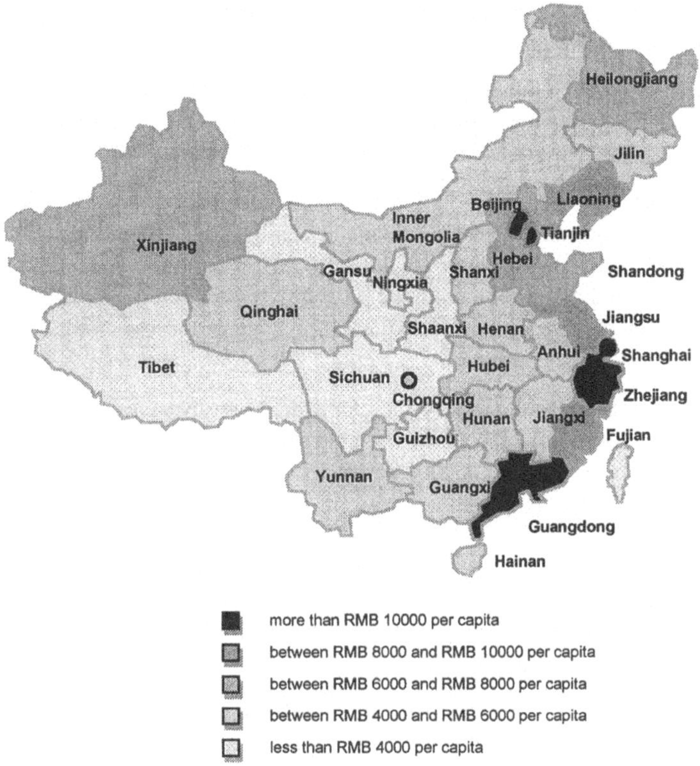

Note: 1 RMB ≈ 0.12 USD

Source: Statistical Yearbook of China 1998.

2 MNCs Strategy and Localisation in China

For multinational companies with significant local operations the term "localisation" has become the mantra for business leaders within recent years. Localisation is a decisive factor of a China strategy that qualifies the balance between investment and utility. But localisation is not only a question of choice – it is the result of circumstances and available corporate assets. This balance is unique for each company – greatly influenced by the company's degree of competitive advantage in the Chinese market. However, forming a clear strategy requires a comprehensive analysis of all factors driving localisation.

The general idea of "going local" is that the expatriate organisation, formed as an indispensable import-supporting beachhead to build a new organisation on foreign territory, is converging towards a local company.

The first phase in this development process is the set-up of a new organisation by creating a legal entity, transfer technology, deploy management and technical expatriates, and provide capital to a new institution.

In the second phase, this entry vehicle is developing towards a company with a more local character along the "five dimensions of localisation": human resources, production, local sourcing of materials and components, research and development and management control. The extent – scale and scope – and the time horizon reflect the corporate strategy as they determine the competitive position of the multinational company.

The last phase, though rarely desired by the managers from overseas, would be a Chinese company with merely foreign ownership. The main motives for "going local" are generally:

- cost reduction – the effort to increase the operational effectiveness and competitiveness,
- market competence – the need to better approach the market through capturing institutional knowledge and by creating a more stable environment (e.g. through less short-term expatriates), and
- easing Government pressure – as a result of official and unofficial policies regarding investment and product sales in China (e.g. "buy local" policies) many MNCs have decided to become a *local* company to be able to compete. This pressure is generally seen to decrease the more local a company is.

Starting from these motives, two different forms of localisation can be derived:

a) operational localisation, incorporating the need to reduce cost and increase the market competence of a company, and

b) corporate image localisation, where the measures are aimed at meeting Government policies

As a result, Government policies significantly influence the competitive position and are a significant factor that influences the country strategy for China.

In the quest for improved operational effectiveness, the localisation efforts in the *five dimensions of localisation* have proven to bear distinctively different characteristics:

2.1 Production: Local Value Added vs. Import

The Chinese government has long been enforcing a technology transfer and local production in China. In many markets this was done through hefty import tariffs (e.g. 100% and more for automotive imports) and "buy local" policies, enforced by managers obeying commands, motivated by patriotism, driven by cronyism or a combination of all three rationales.

These circumstances were forcing – and to a degree still force – multinational companies to shift production to China to ensure the market access. The extent to which the localisation of operations has been carried out varies widely. Hence, the primary question to be asked is whether investment in China is definitively necessary – and if, to what extent.

For a multinational corporation manufacturing in China – let alone the difficulties related hereto – is generally expensive and connected with a high risk of failure. It usually takes large investment amounts that sometimes duplicate capacity already available in more mature markets.

On the positive side, investing in a China operation often provides invaluable advantages such as preferred market access, better understanding of the market and improved acceptance by Chinese authorities. It is seen as an effort to build a long-term relation with China that cannot be achieved otherwise.

In order to assess the localisation level that MNCs have chosen with respect to transferring manufacturing expertise and production capacity to China, the concept of Local Value Added (LVA) is of great importance. The LVA is designed as a principle measure of localised production. It is used to compare a multinational company's effort of shifting the value creation process to China (see figure 2).

The level of LVA is an expression of the basic strategic posture of multinational companies in China. It has effects on required investment and the financial return of China operations.

The key factor determining the range of the options – in terms of localisation – available to the China Centre (i.e. the corporate headquarters of a MNC's China operations) is the competitive advantage (e.g. technological leadership) of a product or service. With a strong competitive advantage the need to localise the operations is less critical compared to a weaker position due to China's need and desire for state-of-the-art products. To compete head-to-head with local companies requires low cost, high quality and high volume manufacturing facilities with a large investment and high systematic risk.

Figure 2: The China Exposure Balance

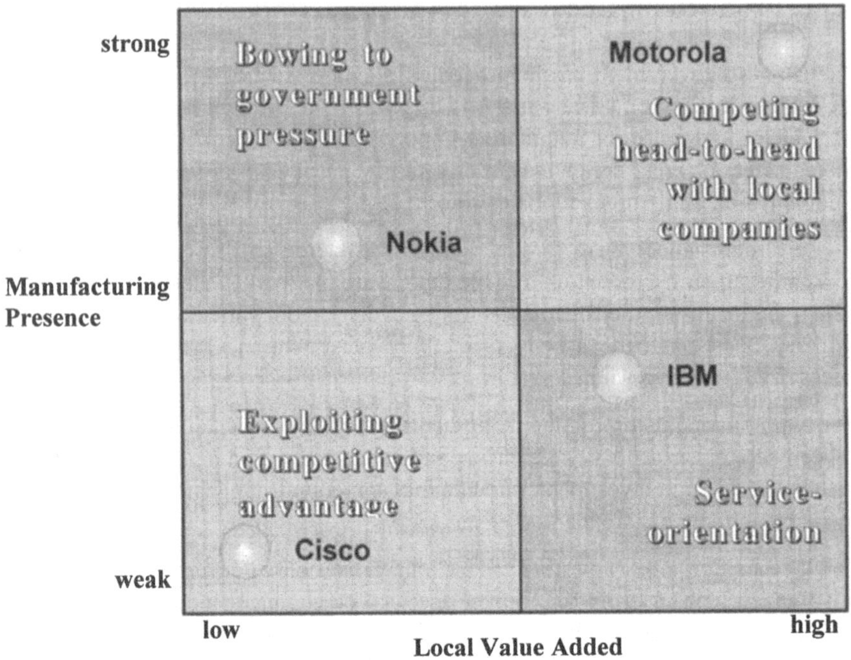

Note: Manufacturing presence can be measured with the local production vs. import ratio, Local Value Added can be approximated using the local content level; The positions of the four companies are estimated on the basis of publicly available information.

Source: Own analysis, interviews.

MNCs need to understand the balance between the local value added and import, and the relation of this posture to competitive advantage (e.g. the level of technological advantage to competitors). To a large extent this relationship restricts the opportunities to manoeuvre. A weak manufacturing presence and a business that is primarily confined to import means a strategy of *exploiting the competitive advantage* to optimise the profit stream. A low percentage of LVA combined with a strong existing manufacturing presence is often the result of *bowing to government pressure*, for example as a result to imposed tariffs or taxes, hindering the company to import its products and implying an insufficient competitive advantage. A company in the latter position should thoroughly examine whether its organisational abilities are fully exploited.

2.2 Human Resources: Cut Costs and Foster Institutional Memory

Human resources have, without a doubt, become a key element of localisation measures of multinationals in China. It is an important step to boost the morale of local employees and lower operating cost. Experience shows that companies that have specified a target localisation rate and time horizon are more likely of succeeding to reach their objective (HLCOR 1998:5). However, the financial necessity to replace costly expatriates with a cheaper local labour force is hard to manage. It takes extensive training programs, high salaries, appealing corporate culture and image to attract and retain high-potential employees.

2.3 Local Sourcing: The Currency Hedge

Local sourcing of materials and components is still playing a minor role for MNCs. An advantage of a higher local sourcing level is that in case of a possible devaluation of the Chinese currency, a high degree of locally sourced materials could partly hedge against an unpleasant competitive backdrop in relation to local Chinese companies. Whereas the quality of locally sourced materials and components is a serious problem in some industries, another reason for unwillingness to further localise the value chain seems to be the MNCs policy to utilise existing overseas capacity of materials and components production. A side effect of importing materials and components to Chinese manufacturing facilities is the opportunity to use transfer pricing to create a more efficient profit structure.

2.4 Research and Development

Research and Development is a relatively new topic for MNCs in China. To date, the activities of MNCs have been mostly focused on adaptation of international products for the Chinese market. The government is encouraging MNCs to go beyond this stage but a lack of skilled researchers in many areas in combination with home base R&D sites defending their budget is making further steps difficult. Moreover, the lack of enforcement of intellectual property rights is a major concern for proprietary technology protection and therewith a threat to the competitiveness of MNC products and services.

2.5 Management Control

Most MNCs manage their China operations on the short leash. Partly lacking trust in local managers or because individual capability is still insufficient, local management is granted only operational authority. The resulting dissatisfaction of local key managers – confronted with the impression of being second class employees and soon hitting a glass ceiling – not seldom leads to high turnover rates in important positions that invariably lead to organisational instability. This is particularly disruptive on the top management level. In contrast, the few MNCs that have been able to install a high quality local top management with inspiring leaders who serve as a role model for the individual employee had great influence on the success of an organisation.

The localisation of control and the empowerment of local employees is an important ingredient for a more flexible organisation. Understanding the environmental dynamics of the arising competitive landscape combined with the ability to judge which part of the organisation has to be localised is certainly a key factor to form a China strategy.

The competition will become even more intense in the future, when the multinational corporations will fight each other for the few profitable positions available for foreign companies in their industries. Strategy, its implementation in management and organisation, and the corporate assets will ultimate determine which companies will survive.

3 Case Study: The Chinese Market for Telecom Switching Equipment

The Chinese telecommunications equipment market is one of the most competitive markets in the world (The Economist 1998) – with the digital-switching equipment segment at its core. After conveniently exporting to China in the 1980s, MNCs have soon been forced to enter joint ventures with Chinese partners and manufacture their products locally.

Since the mid 1990s, private Chinese domestic companies, such as Huawei Technologies, Zhongxing, and Datang, are seriously challenging the multinational companies' share of the Chinese telecom equipment market. Within just 5 years from 1993 to 1998, domestic suppliers increased their collective share of the switching business from 7% to more than 41% (The Economist Intelligence Unit 1998:5). This shift has been supported through a more liberal approach to entrepreneurship and strong (financial, technological and "buy local") support by the Chinese Government (see figure 3).

Figure 3: The Result of the "Government Support" in the Telecom Equipment Sector

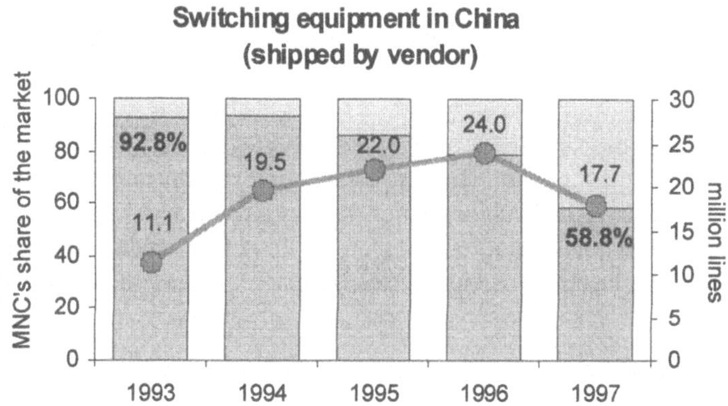

Note: Left scale: MNCs share of the market, right scale: million lines.

Source: The Economist Intelligence Unit (1998), Who Needs Competition?, in: *Business China*, October 12th,1998: 4.

3.1 Three Major Obstacles for MNC's Profitability in Telecom Equipment

Firstly, a major problem for MNCs is that today's technology of Chinese domestic companies is, to a large degree, either acquired through MNC's direct transfer (into JVs), reverse engineering of products, or technological support by leading Chinese Universities (which in turn get their know-how from co-operating with MNCs in Research and Development projects). This enables Chinese domestic companies to sell products 10-20% below that of their MNC competitors (The Economist 1998). Without the heavy R&D overhead of MNCs, Chinese companies have a lower cost base and are able to drive the prices down.

Secondly, the buy-local-policy is showing its effect in declining accessible market share for foreign companies and importers. The Ministry of Information Industry (before April 1998: the Ministry of Post and Telecoms) officials publicly endorsed this policy of preferred buying from Chinese domestic companies at several occasions (Financial Times 1999). In 1998, 60% of telecom equipment, so the authorities, has been purchased from local companies (The Economist 1998). In practice, this policy basically consists of three stages (The Economist Intelligence Unit 1998:5):

1) Purchase from local vendor provided that their equipment is up to scratch.

2) If it is not, buy instead from foreign-invested joint ventures.

3) And when all else fails, buy imported.

With such distinction between foreign and domestic suppliers, the competitive environment is strongly distorted and will inevitably result in the exit of several MNCs.

Thirdly, Chinese companies are said to be practically buying market share. Financially safe, as the government has already chosen those companies to be China's role models, many of these high-tech private companies now receive government directed loans and generous credit lines from state banks to cover their expenses. The incentive is clearly to gain market share – no matter at what cost.

3.2 What Will the Future Bring?

If China's authorities continue to distort the competitive environment, MNCs will inevitably have to rethink their local operations. High volumes, localised production and a crowded market have driven prices down to razor-thin margins (The Economist Intelligence Unit 1998:5). With cut-throat competition, prices for exchanges in China can be as little as half of the price for comparable equipment elsewhere – which is one of the reasons why half of the 16 large telecom MNCs are said to be loosing money in this market. Some MNCs, such as Fujitsu and NEC, have already scaled back in China; two or more big western names could be forced to retrench in the next couple of years (The Economist 1998).

4 Conclusion and Outlook

It is certainly time for multinational companies to review their China operations. This must begin with a critical view back – in order to learn from past experiences. MNCs have to put more effort in researching the environment and developing a strategy for the most challenging market of the next decade. Understanding the strategic posture including localisation must be part of this assessment.

The Chinese economic environment is at a critical point in the year 2000. The difficult transition from a centrally planned to a socialist market economy is causing pain and discomfort among the people. Many MNCs, hit by fierce competition and low demand, have reacted to the economic slowdown by either consolidating or divesting business projects.

The obstacles for multinational corporations are twofold: one main problem is that the MNCs have difficulty to manage their operations in China, the other is that their life is getting harder through the emerging domestic competitors, a economic slowdown and a markedly more hostile regulatory environment.

Developing a clear country strategy must be the first priority for the many multinational companies in China that came without a plan. Principally, MNCs have to re-think China along the following imperatives:

- Identify and use competitive advantage in China.
- Adjust the operating paradigm to meet the environmental situation.
- Create flexibility for the China Centre.
- Form a diversified organisation.
- Demonstrate corporate commitment.

All these points are related to the analysis of localisation, but they also deserve a wider scope of thought and analysis in themselves, in order to form a clear strategy.

The scope of this paper is limited to a single but important aspect of running business operations in China. Strategy has many aspects and further research is possible in virtually every field mentioned, such as empirical studies on strategic patterns or management styles of organisational structures. But as quite often in this dynamic environment, the results expire very quickly. MNCs in China will face a difficult environment in the years to come. But companies that are prepared for tumultuous times in the Chinese market by having a clear strategy and a capable, informed organisation have fair chances to emerge as global leaders.

References

Alberts, L.H. (1997), The Keys to Winning in China, in: *Mercer Management Journal* 8: 83-91.

A.T.Kearney (1997), *Global Companies in China*, A.T.Kearney White Paper, Chicago: A.T. Kearney.

A.T.Kearney (1998), *Global Investment in China*, A.T.Kearney White Paper, Chicago: A.T. Kearney.

Ayala, J. & Lai, R. (1996), China's Consumer Market: A Huge Opportunity to Fail?, in: *The McKinsey Quarterly* 3: 56-71.

Baldinger, P. (1998), *Distribution of Goods in China: Regulatory Framework and Business Options*, Washington: The US-China Business Council.

Beschorner, D., Lesko, M., & Schweinbenz, A. (1995), German Environmental Technologies in the PRC, in: *Management International Review* 35, Special Issue, 1995/1: 53-63.

Business Week (1999), China: What's going wrong?, in: *Business Week*, February 22nd, 1999: 28-31.

Brahm, L. & Daoran L. (1996), *The Business Guide to China*, Singapore: Butterworth-Heinemann Asia.

Broadman, H. & Sun, X. (1997), *The Distribution of Foreign Direct Investment in China*, Policy Research Working Paper, No. 1720, Washington: The World Bank.

Chao, J. (1998), Factors Affecting the Competitiveness of China-Based Companies, in: *Competitive Intelligence Review* 9,3: 39-44.

Chan, W.-K., Perez, J., Perkins, A. & Shu, M. (1997), China's Retail Markets are Evolving More Quickly than Companies Anticipate, in: *The McKinsey Quarterly* 2: 206-211.

Financial Times (1999), China: Top Official to Head Unicom, in: *Financial Times*, February 2nd 1999.

Hang Lung Center for Organizational Research (1998), *What Makes Localization Work?*, Hong Kong University of Science and Technology, Newsletter – Autumn Issue: Hong Kong: 4-5.

Herrmann-Pillath, C. & Lackner, M. (1998), *Länderbericht China – Politik, Wirtschaft und Gesellschaft im chinesischen Kulturraum*, Bonn: Bundeszentrale für politische Bildung Schriftenreihe 351.

Hsieh, T. (1996), Prospering Through Relationships in Asia, in: *The McKinsey Quarterly* 4: 4-13.

Lasserre, P. (1997), *Joint-Venturing in Asia Pacific – A Survey*, Paris: INSEAD Euro-Asia Centre Research Series.

MacMurray, T. & Woetzel, J. (1994), The Challenge Facing China's State-Owned Enterprises, in: *The McKinsey Quarterly* 2: 61-74.

Meier, J. & Shaw S. (1993), Second Generation MNCs in China, in: *The McKinsey Quarterly* 4: 3-16.

Ministery of Foreign Trade and Economic Cooperation (1995), *The China Investment Guide 5th Ed.*, Hong Kong: Pearson Professional.

Overholt, W. H. (1994), China's High Road to Economic Development, in: *The McKinsey Quarterly* 1: 121-132.

Roehrig, M. (1994), *Foreign Joint Ventures in Contemporary China*, New York: St.Martin's Press.

Roland Berger & Partner (1998), *Success Analysis of German Direct Investments in the P.R.China – Results of a Representative Study*, München: Roland Berger China Competence Centre.

Schütte, H. (1997), *Regionalisation of Global Thinking: Strategy and Organisation of European MNCs in Asia*, INSEAD Working Papers 97/04/ABA.

State Statistical Bureau (of the People's Republic of China) (1998), *China Statistical Yearbook*, Beijing: China Statistical Publishing House.

Steidlmeier, P. (1995), *Strategic Management of the China Venture*, Westport: Quorum Books.

The Economist (1998), Chinese Companies: Silicon Valley, PRC, in: *The Economist*, June 27th 1998.

The Economist Intelligence Unit (1998), Who Needs Competition?, in: *Business China*, October 12th 1998.

Tse, E. (1998a), Competing in China: An Integrated Approach, in: *Strategy & Business* 13,4: 13-23.

Tse, E. (1998b), The Right Way to Achieve Profitable Growth in the Chinese Consumer Market, in: *Strategy & Business* 11,2: 10-21.

Thurner, M.-O. (1999), *Strategies for Multinationals in China*, Diplom thesis, University of Ulm, September 1999.

Vanhonacker, W. (1997), Entering China: An Unconventional Approach, in: *Harvard Business Review*, March-April 1997: 130-140.

Weidenbaum, M. (1998), The Bamboo Network: Asia's Family-Run Conglomerates, in: *Strategy & Business* 10,2: 59-65.

Yan, R. (1998), Short-term results: The Litmus Test for Success in China, in: *Harvard Business Review*, September-October 1998: 61-75.

EPILOGUE

Is There a Japanese Economic Crisis?

Johan Galtung

I am not going to say no. But I might like to be more careful with that expression, "economic crisis", than most of the commentators. They tend to take it for granted that there is a crisis, seem to be under no obligation whatsoever to define a term before they indulge in using it, to the point that it takes on a life of its own. It came into life fall 1997, grew rapaciously, has now attained monster status driving people around in a frenzy, till – I have seen this many times – some St. George somewhere stands up and kills the dragon. In no way does that mean that the crisis goes away, only that the term "crisis" has outlived its usefulness. Nobody gets excited any longer, let's find something new to excite us. No term can hope for more than a couple of years; the life expectancy for most of them is far shorter. Reality has nothing, or very little, to do with it.

For me crisis has to do with human beings suffering, or with highly probable, imminent suffering. Economic crisis means that they suffer because the economy – global, national, local and/or personal – does not provide for basic needs, livelihood, sustenance. Sooner or later being under-fed, under-clad, under-sheltered shows up as illness (as opposed to wellness, being healthy). We read it as morbidity and mortality statistics.

It may not affect all of society. As there are diseases caused by too little money, there are also diseases related to too much money. The basic economic crisis, what I shall call Crisis I, is the crisis suffered by those unable to satisfy the basic material needs for food, clothing, shelter and medical services. But it often passes under-reported because it hits people at the bottom of society, and changes slowly, if at all.

Comparing GNP per capita status and HDI status (UN Human Development Index based on child mortality, life expectancy and literacy) countries may be high on one and low on the other, depending on their economic priorities. High on both are most first world countries; high on GNP per capita and low on HDI would be many oil countries; low on GNP per capita and high on HDI would be the ex-socialist countries as long as they can live off past investment in health and education. Low on both would be very sad countries at the bottom of the third world. That is crisis.

Let us first take note that Japan is in the most privileged category, so the situation cannot be that bad. Let us also take note that the number of people in Japan suffering from being under-fed, clad and sheltered is minimal; there is little or no sign of Crisis I. Nor is there any sign that Crisis I is coming. Further, let us take note that no country can sustain super-growth forever. Japanese growth rates have gone down through the 1990s; 1998's growth rate was -1.1%. Is that a crisis when people are not truly suffering? Or, could it be a sign that Japan has become too rich, needing some downsizing?

For a person slimmed down by flagrant poverty, putting on weight is a sign of health. After some time, however, he may be very happy with negative growth, known as slimming. There is an optimum. Nowhere in economic theory do we find any indication of how much is enough, showing the miserable intellectual state of that "science". It could also be a warning that we have been programmed for ever-lasting growth come what may, and cry crisis when that crazy program is incompatible with reality. Changing the program might help. How about switching from economic growth to social growth, spiritual growth, for instance?

From 1988 to 1994 Japan's economic growth rate declined from 6.2% to 0.6%; well below the world average of 3.1%. Draw a line on a sheet of paper and -1.1% is a reasonable prediction. From 1957 to 1993 the Japanese GDP per capita increased from $336 to $33,849. Fantastic, but can we expect that phenomenal increase in material accumulation to go on forever? The Japanese weekly wages were $657, well above Germany $508, UK $420, US $354 – and China: $9. Again, do we have any reason to believe that the sky is the limit given that we live in a finite world?

From 1960 to 1990 the average Japanese family size dropped from 4.14 to 2.99 and the trend continues downward. Households with no children went up from 45% to 67%. At the same time there is the famous aging: from 1920-1994 the percentage of the population from 0-14 decreased 20 percentage points and the population 65 and above increased 9%. Of course, that also accounts for very many of the households without children: they left the nest long time ago.

But does this constitute a crisis? Or, is the crisis in our mind because we assume without any further reflection that material value can only be produced by the younger generation, and then be distributed to older generation via social security, welfare or whatever we choose to call it? In the old days perhaps yes, long time ago, when so much production was related to sheer physical strength, from hunting to electro-mechanical industry. But in the electronic age, in a highly tertiarized society, this kind of thinking is simply outdated nonsense. Most tasks require light touches. We could turn the whole thing around. We could say: how about valuing experience-intensive work more and youthful muscular agility less?

There is no way the young can catch up with the old in experience. There is no course in experience, except life itself. The young may say, OK, but we have the education just behind us, fresh in mind, we can apply the most recent insights! Your schooling is about a century old! The answer is obvious: it is easier for the older generation in a society with a good system for continuing education to catch up with "the most recent insights" (e.g., by plugging into the Internet) than for the younger generation to catch up on experience. And, maybe many things go wrong when "the most recent insight" is practiced by those with least experience; like the proverbial scene at the world's stock exchanges: juveniles out of some MBA school playing with capital resources as if they were sport games cheer-leaders. A little experience might have taught them what the consequences could be when money changes hands that quickly.

However, the argument here is not age fascism in reverse, discriminating against the young rather than the old. But how about shifting the work upward in the age structure if this is where the population is moving anyhow? Japan has a venerable tradition: the retirement job. And one more retirement job after that. And then more education for the younger generation? Maybe more problematic. A real problem for Japan is not an economic crisis but an educational crisis: students passing through universities almost untouched by deep knowledge. Imagine they stayed longer at the universities and started really studying? Imagine they all had a year of travel paid by society? In other words, take the "retirement" early, as a preparation for life, and let those who want to continue producing do so, not retiring them prematurely and forcibly.

Having said all this, there is of course no denial that there are problems in the Japanese economy. Whether banker incompetence, or inability to adjust to a possible downward turn in demand even for excellent Japanese products (itself a sign of incompetence) remains perhaps to be seen. Another possibility is that the loosening of Ministry of Finance supervision turns Japan from the problems of bureaucratic rigidity to the problems of company greed and wishes for quick profits. Still another problem could be the new wave of US-trained (particularly Harvard) Japanese economists, presumably more monetarist and supply-side oriented – a combination that could easily lead to overprotection and shifts in focus from real to finance economy.

But there are deeper domestic and geopolitical forces at work. Some years ago, I, like so many others, made an analysis of "The Japanese Industrialization Model". Post-Meiji Japan was seen in terms of giant corporation-building with capital-accumulation and bureaucracy-building with power-accumulation, in a sense typical of Western-inspired "modernization". But then a basic point: the ability to overcome contradictions that have impeded smooth modernization in so many other countries: between bureaucracy and corporation, between labor and capital, and between labor-intensive and capital-intensive production. The West has suffered from the tendency to make a choice, either one or the other horn of these dilemmas. Western socialism, from Bismarck to Thatcher-Reagan, privileged the bureaucracy-labor combination, and mainstream Western capitalism has always privileged the corporation-capital combination. Both of them saw progress/modernization as the victory of capital-intensive over labor-intensive production, from artisanry to automation.

That preference had a hidden advantage: the gradual abolition of a "dangerous" working class that favored the bureaucracy-labor combination. Economists designed models, linking increases of wages to increases in labor productivity, in other words, paying the working class to abolish itself.

In the West politics was defined for a good century in terms of these two options, referred to as "left" and "right", respectively. Some space emerged for an option in the middle, social democracy, possibly the most successful option, using bureaucracy for distribution and corporation for growth.

The point made, then, was that Japan went beyond these contradictions using Oriental, both-and eclecticism as the key. Bureaucracy and corporations entered patterns of cooperation unheard of in the West (with the possible exception of France), enacted by MITI-Keidanren. Labor and capital also entered patterns of cooperation within the same company, with bonuses, consultation, solidarity in times of crisis, etc. And the labor-intensive element was brought into capital-intensive production through a very high element of artisan, rather than automated, finishing touches to the production process. Rather than losing political and other energies Japan transcended the contradictions creating new patterns of modernity. General Oriental eclecticism as opposed to Western dualism, could be drawn upon for both-and production processes, Confucianism and (mahayana) Buddhism could be drawn upon for the combination of verticality (responsibility and discipline) and collectivism (solidarity) characteristic of the Japanese company, and shinto (less militarized after the Pacific War) provided an overarching umbrella for the two branches of modernity.

The basic point in the study was the contradictions created by overcoming contradictions, however. Japan was a tremendous economic success, for these and other reasons. Successes are admired, sometimes imitated, rarely loved. The study, hence, focused on the losers, and the contradictions between them and the towering success of the state-capital combination, much more integrated than in Western countries (again, with the possible exception of France). The following losers were identified:

- the population, bogged down by the state-capital combination, unable to play one against the other, like in the West,
- women, exploited in a heavily male-dominated society,
- small companies, at the bottom of the production process,
- modernized Western countries, their modern products outcompeted by Japanese products higher on quality/price and

- traditional non-Western countries, their traditional products being outcompeted by Japanese products higher on quality/price.

So, the study concludes with the words: "Nothing, however, lasts forever in this world. So, where are the vulnerable points. There are costs – who pays the bill?"

The bill is presented, in the first run, to the population as heavy democracy deficits, to marginalized women, to small, underpaid companies, to outcompeted Western companies and to countless workers in the third world threatened by ingenious rice cookers, scooters, outboard engines and what not. Many collapse. Others, in the first run Japan's neighbors, even China, imitated Japan, copying the structures, trying to draw on their cultures for legitimation. Still others, like the USA, mobilizes its defenses, introduces "voluntary constraint", sees their own trade deficit as "unfair trade practice", and so on.

In short, actio produces reactio. The test of the world was taken by surprise by Japanese ingenuity and originality; Japan is then taken by surprise by the reactions to this creativity. A part of these reactions is the glee, the triumph, in the Western press at every and any sign of economic troubles for Japan. But how could it be otherwise? In the 1970s and the 1980s Japan suffered from triumphalism, lecturing the USA in the same arrogant way as the USA is now lecturing Japan. And just as the USA in those heady decades was busy studying what they believed to be manuals of Japanese management, Japan is now learning what they think are the tricks of Harvard Business School etc. Both underestimate the structural-cultural context.

Western naivety, talking about the "21st century as the Japanese century" is understandable. Western dualism predisposes people to think that change is forever. Is there a corresponding Japanese naivety? Oriental yin-yang thinking should predispose them for more cyclical thinking; "OK, we came up, there was a downturn, that is normal, there will soon be an upswing." Or, could it be that Japan has become so "americanized" that they combine their "worst case analysis" with "worst case forever"? In that case a spiritual crisis exacerbates the economic crisis.

Then, the contradictions created inside Japan. A democracy deficit becomes intolerable against a general background of modernization, and the obvious prediction is the emergence of a strong civil society based on NGOs and on local authorities. The marginalization of women becomes equally intolerable and the obvious prediction would be that they find outlets in the civil society. And the small companies? Obvious prediction: they try to become big. Or else, they collapse.

In the 1980s I gave courses on world economics to IBM and to Shell managers, two major transnational corporations. Often asked how those corporations would stand up against Japan, my forecast ran about as follows: "Shell has nothing to fear as long as it sticks to low levels of processing; the Japanese comparative advantage is in very high levels of processing and quality/price ratios. For that reason IBM might one day be controlled by Japan." A counter-argument was that IBM to a large extent was run like a Japanese company with life long employment practically speaking guaranteed. And my counter-argument was that this would make a Japanese take-over easier.

I was right about Shell, wrong about IBM that was in a crisis in the late 1980s. What I had not foreseen was that they would get out of the crisis firing about half of their employees, rehiring some on a contract basis, getting into black. Japan is now doing some of the same being even more a traitor to their tradition, possibly driving some managers into corruptive practices to help save some of the jobs.

At one of those workshops I met a Briton who had been training British managers about business/trade with Japan, telling them about savings ratios, investment horizons, etc. He, in turn, had met a Japanese training Japanese managers in what to expect in the West. They exchanged notes, and the Japanese expressed his admiration for the British approach. "And how do you train them?" "Well, I basically use two books in order to understand the West," the Japanese said. "One is the Christian Bible. And the other is a book by someone called Gibbon, The Decline and Fall of the Roman Empire." Well, well. We haven't seen the end of the story, yet. Maybe all empires collapse?

References

Galtung, J. (1971), Social Structure, Education Structure and Life-Long Education: the Case of Japan, in: Ben-David, J., Dore, R., Faure, E. & Reischauer, E. O. (eds.), *Reviews of National Policy for Education: Japan*, Paris: OECD: 131-152.

Galtung, J. (1970), *Paths of Development: a Diachronic Analysis of Development in Japan*, Oslo: PRIO.

Galtung, J. (1972), Human Resources and Socio-Economic Growth: a Case Study of Japan, in: Gostkowski, Z. (ed.), *Toward a System of Human Resources Indicators for Less Developed Countries*, Warsaw: Polish Academy of Sciences: 217-235.

Galtung, J. (1983), On the Possible Decline and Fall of Japan: The Limits to Transcendence of Contradictions, in: *East Asia – International Review of Economic, Political, and Social Development I*, Frankfurt: 1-26.

APPENDICES

Political-Cultural Aspects of the German Reunification Experience – Possible Implications for Korea?

Ulrich Albrecht

Dedication:
The following paper is dedicated to Professor Sung-Jo Park, my distinguished colleague at the Otto-Suhr-Institute. When I thought what I could submit for a Festschrift in honouring his 65th birthday, I rapidly came to the conclusion that a writing reflecting German unification experiences would be most appropriate. I clearly recall Sung-Jo Parks enthusiastic interest in the process of German unification. In the year 1990 I found myself quite unexpectedly in the position of head of planning in the Ministry for Foreign Affairs in the outgoing German Democratic Republic (the title was an euphemism, actually the main job was to prepare for the GDR part in the 2+4 negotiations). My colleague Park took a very active interest in what I was doing over there. We repeatedly met in those month, discussing e.g. potential Korean investment into the debilitating GDR economy. Since this time, there was a series of academic meetings and conferences, many of them organized by Sung-Jo Park, about the topic what Korea could learn from the German unification experience. This ended up in a formal cooperation scheme between the Free University of Berlin and Seoul National University to promote studies about the new great project, Korean reunification[1] *I remain impressed how Sung-Jo Park energetically propelled Korean-German encounters about the unification issue, and thus I submit this piece to my fellow patriot and colleague with the sincere hope that he in person will witness unification of the two Koreas in the years ahead.*

1 Disposition

The concept of political culture will be used in the following in order to portray both the East and West German societies and the collective experience of reunification, with a view to possible repercussions for the case of Korea. Beyond the formalities of bringing unification about (in the German case three treaties, the

1 See e.g. SNU-FUB Joint Conference, The Political and Socio-Economic Challenges of Korean Unification: Lessons from Germany's Post-Unification Experience, Seoul 1996.

one about economic and currency unification, the negotiations about "domestic" unification, ending in the Schaeuble-Krauss agreement, plus the 2+4 agreement about the external aspects of reunification), the mental problems of associating two different political units and cultures into one emerged as the most formidable challenge.

The specific notion used here has been formulated by Archie Brown (1984) in his seminal book *Political Culture and Communist Studies*. Originally developed as part of a broader discourse about democracy, Brown in the late 1960s introduced this research concept into the study of communism. Because the concept has been applied both to democratic *and* communist societies, it will be well suited to assess the political-cultural dimensions of unifying the populace from two such systems.

In contrast to the more common traditional institution-oriented approach in the study of communist societies, the political culture concept allows for a study of subjects and their role in society, as well as for the historical and the socio-cultural conditioning which took place particularly in communist states. Thus, the definition used here for political culture encompasses values influenced by historical experience, sociological and cultural factors, attitudes and bodies of knowledge. There are both objective dimensions (such as institutional frameworks, hidden and declared rules of conduct, the position of an individual in society) and subjective ones (e.g. personal political attitudes, behavior in society, or individual value orientations).

The collective experience of all Germans – and the ensuing collective memories in this country – can be generally described as follows. In the beginning, in the wake of state reunification, there was widespread euphoria. East Germans, with the falling-down of the Berlin Wall, unexpectedly enjoyed the new freedom to travel whereever they wanted to (East German embassies in this summer suddenly had to cope with the diplomatically unconventional task to supply spare parts of broken-down *Trabbis* and other cars of East-German design in places as far as Spain or Turkey). East German citizens in addition engulfed into the joys of consumption which became accessible after the introduction of the Deutschmark. As it should be reminded, economic and currency union preceded political reunification. It may be a typical German approach that German unification was economy-lead. And the early euphoria about unification had a very materialist dimension.

Euphoria was followed by increasing disenchantment, mainly because of the disappointing economic and social development post-unification (again a strong materialist element). Whilst large amounts of public finance were transferred to the East, averaging DM150 to 190 billion annually, a gap opened between the well-to-do part of the population and the poor. Private capital did not take up the challenge by these generous public investments, mainly into infrastructure. Now it becomes more and more difficult to believe that the (West) German taxpayer is willing to continue with these large money transfers. In the decade since 1984, which spans unification, the share of poors living on public money has risen in West Germany to 7.5 percent of the population. In East Germany, the share of the poor has doubled within two years in the first half of this decade. The collapse of the *Kombinate* (East German's large concerns) made hundreds of thousands workers redundant, among them mostly women and older employees. State employees in East Germany were generally dismissed, not only because of alleged former Party memberships. If two systems unite, one can't simply double the size of central government by accepting all public employees from both sides. The lion's share of GDR diplomats and other top personnel of the East German Government lost their job. The *Bundeswehr* (West Germany's army) took, on time-limited contracts, around 10,000 of the East German National People's Army, which numbered 170,000 before unification. And there was certainly no continuity in employment for the nearly 100,000 employees of the *Stasi* (state security) or the great number of SED Party officials – they all lost their jobs. The newly unemployed and – as they are called in Germany – frustrated loosers of unification, *Vereinigungsverlierer*, form by now a significant part of the electorate, having remarkable repercussions for the German political system and German political culture.

There is also atmospheric alienation between Westerners and Easterners, and suddenly there was the slogan of the "resurrection of the Wall in the minds" of people. West Germans pouring into the new Eastern provinces, or *Wessis* for short, became dubbed *Besserwessis*, better-to-know *Wessis*, and vice versa Easterners (*Ossis*) who complained more and more about their disappointing fate were viewed by Westerners as *sissy easties*, contemporaries who appeared somewhat badly fitted for life in a modern Western society.

The mutual misgivings and the lack of understanding has been intensively researched (Wiesenthal 1998). One of the biggest surveys polled 1022 Easterners and 2025 Westerners and was carried out by the University of Leipzig and the USUMA opinion research institute in Berlin (Brähler & Richter 1995).

The tested persons respond to 40 questions about their personal feelings, their day-to-day behavior, and how they perceive their social environment. Eastern and Western responses significantly differ in 15 of the 40 items asked. Five responses reflect the finding that East Germans are more inclined to find social contact than their West German equivalents, and that they see themselves better socially interconnected than the West Germans, who by contrast stress distance in social contacts. East Germans are oriented towards communities and small groups, reflecting the micro-milieus of the communist past. West Germans are more individualistic according to this survey.

The self-esteem of Easterners and Westerners in Germany after unification shows also great differences. Easterners are more self-critical, even self-pitying, whilst this kind of self-criticism is hardly seen among West Germans. The "self" of the average East German seems to be less protected and more vulnerable by mismood and conflict than this is the case on the side of the Wessis. In addition, Easties see themselves more estranged than their Western counterparts - reflecting again the socialisation and experience of the GDR past.

The Germans in general believe that the next generation will be facing a harder life, that unemployment is going to rise, and especially the younger persons polled are pessimistic with regard to successes in efforts to preserve the environment. A clear majority of all Germans shares the opinion that it remains important to have a public discourse about the Nazi past. There is a higher number of East Germans than West Germans who support this view. This finding brings in an empirical as well as a conceptual notion: the collective memories of a group. Markovits & Reich (1997) in their seminal study about German collective memories[2] come to the conclusion that this conundrum shapes German foreign policy to a greater extent than the still dominating school of realism can explain.

2 The Political Culture of the Outgoing GDR

There was for years a West German research community about East Germany's affairs. [3] The very existence of *DDR-Forschung*, GDR research, was important for West Germany for featherbedding the change, *die Wende*, and reunification.

Nevertheless, research about East Germany was partly wrong. A broadly accepted hypothesis in West German research has been that the GDR was modernising, and that the requirements ensuing with modernisation would lead to an opening of the system towards more political participation, flexibility, and possibly democratisation. Looking at the experience of the 1980s, the opposite turned out to be true. The East German political leadership – very much in contrast to a groundswell within the party – blocked modernisation (a striking parallel to the present North Korean stalemate). The more competent policy directions for the adaptation of the GDR economy and society were needed, the more the holders of power proved incapable to cast appropriate decisions. Their sole aspiration was to stay in power. There were no mechanisms providing corrective action which could have lead to "reform from within" (Lemke 1991:11-15).

The ensuing political culture in the former GDR has in fact been a dualistic culture. The official legitimation strategies of the Party form one sphere, and the numerous micro-milieus among the populace under *real-existing socialism* form

2 The very concept was developed by the reknown French Sociologist Maurice Halbwachs (*La Mémoire collective*), written in 1925. The manuscript was found after the death of Halbwachs in a German concentration camp in 1945.

3 I have got the impression during repeated stints at Korean universities that there is no parallel academic research community in South Korea which continuously deals with North Korean affairs on a permanent base.

the other sphere. The notion of "micro-milieus" refers to small societal spaces not accessible for state and party politics (families, friends and so forth). In addition, leisure time activities were used for private political debates uncontrolled by the Party. It will be interesting to learn whether the North Korean society developed comparable schemes of day-to-day survival.

This dualistic political culture in former East Germany was characterized by severe contradictions. The Party leadership permantly called on the "active members of society" to join in contributing to the build-up of a modern (socialist) society. In fact, activity from below was only wanted to the degree which was found compatible with Party objectives. Beginning in kindergarten, the young generation was taught to adopt to a prescribed agenda - and not to reflect, i.a., about desirable changes in the GDR.

These positions became manifest in the contradicting requirements especially in political socialisation. As it appears by now, the reach of the authoritarian Party system into the micro-milieus of GDR citizens was much more limited as assumed both on the side of the rulers and on the side of Western analysts. These micro-milieus proved to be enormously stable over time. They provided for private spaces, in which West German TV broadcasts were discussed, where rumours and political information were exchanged, and where independent attitudes and opinions were developed. Mistrust with the State Party claiming to be the herald of peace grew during the Polish crisis in the early eighties (when an invasion into Poland by Warsaw Pact forces seemed to be imminent) and during the intermediate-range missile crisis which soon followed, leading to the gradual formation of an independent peace movement in the GDR. In parallel – and possibly even more remarkable – an independent environmetal movement emerged in East Germany – citizens became more and more suspicious about the handling of environmental issues by Party authorities. Resistance against the state developed firstly in narrow policy fields. But in the end, the dissenters succeeded and the communist regime collapsed.

The experience of successful resistance – of having been able to tobble the communist regime in 1989 – was particularly motivating during the great change (*die Wende*), i.e. during the early month around unification day. But the political activists of this period soon became marginalized in German political affairs. For the political scientist, especially experts on revolutions, it was no surprise to see that a revolution within the revolution took place in East Germany.

3 A Post-Communist Party in the German Democracy

Like other post-communist societies, East Germany is confronted with the revival of a follow-up party to the former communist party, in the German case the PDS (*Partei des Demokratischen Sozialismus*). Due to the fact that the PDS hardly attracts voters in West Germany, the party does not muster the strength in the vote which its sister parties enjoy, e.g. in Poland. But earlier assumptions that the ex-communist party would disappear during the transition phase and that its clients would be absorbed by the socialdemocrats or even by conservative parties were falsified as well. Presently the PDS is number two in the new *Länder* (former GDR), behind the Christian democrats (who amalgamated the puppet CDU of the GDR with the formidable West German CDU). The PDS is now seen as a regional party with a solid base in the former GDR.

This does by no means imply that the PDS is a fully accepted force in German political life. There remains a deep split in the political arena. This became evident when after the 1994 general election accidentally the most senior member of parliament (who traditionally presides over the opening session of the Bundestag and who is entitled to deliver the opening address) happened to be a PDS deputy. He was a popular writer who did not have a record as a staunch Party member. According to tradition, parlamentarians raise from their seat when the acting president of the Parliament enters the room. But in 1999 – to the amazement of the nation watching the ceremony on TV – the non-PDS members of Parliament remained seated when their president went in. This episode is prototypical: German political life is still split about the issue how to deal with the post-communists. Parliamentarian exchanges of other parties with the PDS are stiff-lipped. The PDS does not have full political rights (e.g. it is not being represented in the Parliamentarian body which supervises the German secret service). Yet, it seems likely that the PDS will loose this pariah status over time, and that Germans, like their former communist neighbour countries, learn to accomodate with the post-communists among them.

4 Collective Memories and Their Role in the Political Culture

The concept of collective memories focusses on historical experiences that influence in a specific manner politics and ideology of a society. Thus, political cultures can be best understood by studying the collective memories of a given society. As Archie Brown stresses: the experience of history remains a key variable for understanding national characteristics: "Previous political experience [remains] the most relevant to the formation of the political culture of the society." (Brown 1984:16)

Markovits & Reich recently have highlighted the concept of collective memories:

> We differentiate between history and collective memory, and show that it is mainly the latter – in its multiplicity, murkiness, its malleability – that is a formidable influence on the ideology of reluctance that shapes German foreign policy. (Markovits & Reich 1997:9)

In a more general manner the two authors discern the notion in the following way:

> The politics of collective memory – impossible to quantify, hard to measure with the methods of survey research, yet still very real – is a major ingredient of the political arena, the public discourse, and the policy setting in every country. It circumscribes the acceptable. It defines such key ingredients as pride, shame, fear, revenge, and comfort for al large number of a country's citizens. It is central to an understanding of the forces of nationalism. (Markovits & Reich 1997:9)

In societies which experience enforced social change, such as Germany, collective memories apparently play an important role, owing to the disturbant times a majority of citizens has to face. "Pride" and "shame" were indeed for citizens of the former GDR shaking issues: what about the pride about the "socialist accomplishments" (and the gold medals in olympic games which once went with them)? "Fear" and "revenge" are also at stake: those 100,000 Stasi employees – and twice that number of year-long informers – are uneasy and afraid. The trials about *state crimes*, certainly conducted in full accordance with the law, are viewed in those circles as "justice of the victors", and thus discredited. There is great bitternes among the former functional elites of the former GDR, who find themselves ousted and who have finally to realize that the society in united Germany does not need them.

There is a unique development with regard to the collective memories of East Germans post-unification. A specific nostalgia, or *Ostalgia*, has been emerging among large parts of the East German population. Social security under communism, cheap healthcare and job security suddenly appear in a golden light. The slogan emerged that there was not everything bad in the former GDR.

5 The Ugly Interference: Right-Wing Militancy in Reunited Germany

Germany's neighbours, the world community, and the Germans themselves have noted with surprise the emergence of a militant rightist movement after unification. There have been Nazis in West Germany all the time. But these extremist groupings remained peripheral to the political process, their action was limited to heavy propaganda in the internet and the occasional smearing of Jewish memoria with swastikas. The fall of communism in East Germany apparently unleashed a new kind of right extremist activities: anti-personal violence, against foreigners, asylum-seekers and their homes. This seems to be rather unique to the German course of development. As the writer Gyorgy Conrad, the Hungarian president of the German Academy of Fine Arts, states: "We also have a militant right in Hungary, but they don't kill people."

Militancy against foreigners is particulyarly brutal in East Germany, the former communist part of the divided country. During the state-socialist years the internationalist propaganda of the regime certainly rejected any charges that there might be problems with foreigners. The files of the Stasi, the state security agency, however show that there has been indeed violence against foreigners in the GDR, and that there even existed some sort of Nazi rightism – it was duly repressed.

After the fall of the East German communist regime and the disappearance of repression those rightist aspirations suddenly gained unexpected freedom to act. It should be noted that the average GDR citizen had a much slimmer chance to meet foreigners than his fellow compatriot in West Germany. But it would be naive to assume that East Germans would be more friendly to foreigners. To the contrary, East German youngsters chased preferably those few foreigners which happened to live in their country as contract workers, namely Vietnamese and Mozambicans. It remains hard to reject the notion that these poor victims of hatred were surrogate objects of a collective resent.

For a European observer it remains impossible to predict whether in the case of Korean unification a part of the North Korean populace would comparably veer to the right, engaging into extreme Korean nationalism. But it is reasonable to state that the end of communist rule may encourage extreme nationalism.

6 Findings

One particular feature of recent German political culture is the linkage between basic political changes and generational political attitudes. The two authors Greiffenhagen (1979:27) see a "comparatively high generational fragmentation" in political attitudes because of the dense sequence of ruptures in German history. The end of the monarchy in 1918 was followed by a short-lived democracy lasting 13 years, which was superseded by twelve years of Hitlerism. The East Germans then experienced 40 years of communist rule and try by now to adjust to democracy. These political ruptures also leave their imprint on the German collective memory.

This profile of rapid changes of political settings may be not representative for other societies. But it will support the claim that political cultures tend to be focussed upon specific generations in societies which undergo enforced social change. Generational changes will then have direct repercussions for the political culture. This means that the notion of political culture should be understood in a specific way in societies such as the German or Korean one, where rapid social change is occuring.

What are the potential lessons for the Korean case? According to the German experience the unbeloved communist past of East Germany will leave strong footprints onto the unified country. There will be loosers (and winners) after possible unification, and this divide will strongly influence the political culture of the new Korea. Koreans also will learn that the most difficult part in reunification will lie in the field of societal relations between the North and the South. Sufficient attention towards issues of the collective memories of Koreans will facilitate this process, as the preceding German case demonstrates.

References

Brähler, E. & Richter, H. E. (1995), Deutsche Befindlichkeiten im Ost-West-Vergleich, in: *psychosozial* 18,1: 7-20.

Brown, A. (ed.) (1984), *Political Culture and Communist Studies*, London: Macmillan.

Brown, A. & Gray, J. (eds.) (1984), *Political Culture and Political Change in Communist States*, 2nd ed., London: Macmillan.

Greiffenhagen, M. & S. (1979), *Ein schwieriges Vaterland*, Frankfurt: Fischer.

Lemke, C. (1991), *Die Ursachen des Umbruchs 1989. Politische Sozialisation in der ehemaligen DDR*, Opladen: Leske+Budrich.

Markovits, A. S. & Reich, S. (1997), *The German Predicament. Memory and Power in the New Europe*, Ithaca, London: Cornell University Press.

Munske, B. (1993), *The Two Plus Four Negotiations from a German-German Perspective*, Münster, Hamburg: Lit.

Wiesenthal, H. (1998), Post-Unification Dissatisfaction, in: *German Politics* 7,2: 1-30.

Applied Sciences and Global Technology Transfer – A Challenge for Universities

Gerhard Ackermann & Wolfgang Jahnke

1 Actual Demands in Germany for Collaboration between Industry and University

1.1 Flexibility of Study Course Programs

Society demands from universities to educate students on the purpose to get – for instance – highly qualified engineers with state of the art knowledge in their special professional fields. Therefore every technical university has to adjust the study course offers according to actual changes in the professions. Twenty years ago nobody thought of installing multimedia study courses, today every technical university has one. Two years ago our university, the University of Applied Sciences Berlin, installed the study course program "International Technology Transfer Management", a postgraduate Master of Science study course. Intensive market research had shown the national and international demand for such an offer. This expensive study course is financed by the fees of the participants, who know very well that they will have a better chance in their personal professional development by successfully passing this unique and internationally qualifying study course. The final thesis of this master course is usually written in close co-operation with the industry – and a lot of companies are eager to get acquainted with this type of internationally oriented engineers. Our university has also installed a "Collaboration Committee of Economy and University", where representatives of companies and universities can discuss their mutual expectations. Having this forum of exchanging and creating ideas about how to educate engineers for the society of today and tomorrow is essential for a successful public private partnership. We are co-operating in this Committee with managers of Siemens, Schering, IBM, Landesbank Berlin, Telekom, BSR, Lausitzer Rundschau Druckerei and DaimlerChrysler.

1.2 Development of Technology in German SMEs

More than 80% of German enterprises are small and medium-sized enterprises (SME). These companies usually cannot afford the knowledge and equipment for developing their own technologies or to create innovations and apply actual results of scientific research. Yet, they have to do just this in order to maintain their competitiveness. To solve this dilemma the 140 public German Universities of Applied Sciences are co-operating with SMEs, offering capabilities in the above mentioned areas. Our university offers its capacities in the following way: Out of our 7000 students more than 1500 are permanently working or researching in firms (internship, thesis), guided by 300 professors; in our 100 laboratories test programs are run for SMEs by members of our staff, professors and engineers. Planning of manufacturing operations and assembly lines or developing and modernising products are examples of this collaboration. What becomes quite clear is typical for Germany: Our University of Applied Sciences is a needed and accepted partner for Berlin's economy with its more than 6000 manufacturing companies; this is also an essential factor for a successful public private partnership.

1.3 Entrepreneurship has a Nucleus at University

Founding new companies needs entrepreneurs. These entrepreneurs need management and business knowledge as well as innovative ideas to start their own companies. Our university offers an incubator system supporting this nucleus of a growing economy; this incubator system consists of an educational program including coaching and the offer of office space and laboratory facilities in the start-up situation.

It goes without saying that during our coaching and educating support we demonstrate the chances of global views and activities in the start-up situation of a successful company.

2 Partnerships between German and Foreign Universities as a Part of the Educational Program

2.1 International Co-operation of German Universities

To educate students in a way that global thinking becomes selfevident means to establish the consciousness of global equality and the willingness to co-operate with partners world-wide. This is supported by the German government, by the DAAD and the German embassies world-wide.

In 1996 our university started the "East Asia Co-operation Centre", headed by professors of the Free University of Berlin and of our university. This co-operation is a basic element of establishing well functioning university contacts especially to South Korea, Japan, China and the Asian part of Russia. The mutual enforcing activities of two Berlin universities are very successful as both German partners are fitting very well to each other: on the one hand the more academic approach of Japanese and East Asian studies by Prof. Sung-Jo Park from the East Asian Institute at the Free University of Berlin and on the other hand the more practical approach of applied science in research and technology development in the field of industrial engineering by Prof. Wolfgang Jahnke (from the department of mechanical engineering at our university).

The results are partnerships with eleven Asian Universities to exchange staff members and students continuously. Additionally we established mutual research activities and technology transfer concepts including initiating and accompanying joint activities of industry from Germany and Asia.

2.2 Internationalisation of German Universities as Part of the Educational Program

Very practical steps can be taken to introduce ideas of international co-operation into German universities: Besides the co-operation with foreign partner universities we should introduce international degrees like the Master degree, we should offer more and more seminars, postgraduate and even regular study courses in English and we should recruit our students internationally. We should have a percentage of at least 15% foreign students at our universities. Another very practical step in the same direction is establishing mutual study courses, especially for postgraduate programs. This includes a special credit point system to value single study courses and degrees of both universities that participants obtain by graduation of the study course. Our university has established the postgraduate master course "International Project Management in Civil Engineering" in collaboration with the British University of Newcastle. Here, we give students the chance to study in Germany and in Britain. These students are really internationally educated. Other study course programs of our university include at least one semester in a foreign country. This has a long tradition at our university extending to the early beginning in 1823, the year of our foundation by Peter Lenné, the famous horticulture architect.

3 Advantages and Necessities of International Technology Transfer

3.1 Survival Strategy for High Tech Companies

Usually high tech products have a small national market. But globalisation may open the market, sometimes unexpectedly fast. Let's look at an example:

"Rapid Prototyping" is a sophisticated scientific way of simulation ahead of realization. But it needs – like every business – a minimum of turnover to reach the economic break-even within a reasonable range of time. Rapid Prototyping calls on know-how for CAD simulation as well as on know-how and expensive equipment for the manufacturing process of creating the model out of the CAD program. A co-operation between the Keimyung University in Daegu, South Korea, and our university, the University of Applied Sciences Berlin, offered the platform to successfully practice entrepreneurship in this high tech field, using the technology transfer co-operation between universities located in South Korea and Germany as well as the market of both countries for a successful start-up of this worldborne entrepreneur activity. This strategy of enlarging the market is convincing.

3.2 The Role of Universities in International Technology Transfer Activities

Universities should initiate, support and establish international technology transfer activities. This means to accept the catalytic role of universities within a globally interchanging world. Sometimes special organisations like Fraunhofer Gesellschaft in Germany or KITECH in South Korea take care of international technology transfer activities. This support is welcome, but closer and direct contacts are better. Our universities have therefore co-founded the N.E.W.S.-group, consisting of eleven universities from different countries and continents, aiming at international technology transfer between companies via universities. The general secretary of this N.E.W.S.-group is Prof. Dr. Sung-Jo Park, co-ordinating all these international technology transfer activities with outstanding success. He has created with N.E.W.S. a win-win-situation for all three actors, universities, industry and government. The N.E.W.S.-group fosters the communication between the three actors improving the awareness that new methods to apply research findings are part of technology transfer programs via universities.

Worüber sprechen wir? Eine japanologische Überlegung am Beispiel von „Betrieb“ und „Gewerkschaft“

Wolfgang Seifert

1 Einleitung

Wenn sich deutschsprachige Sozialwissenschaftler vergleichend mit Arbeit und industriellen Beziehungen in Japan beschäftigen, sehen sie sich unvermeidlich auch terminologischen Problemen gegenüber. Die Ausgangsfrage dabei lautet: Gibt es für die mit den deutschsprachigen Grundbegriffen bezeichneten Phänomene der hiesigen Arbeitswelt Entsprechungen in Japan? Man sollte annehmen, daß dies zweifelsohne der Fall ist, da es sich schließlich in beiden Ländern gleichermaßen um hochentwickelte, kapitalistisch verfaßte Industriegesellschaften handelt. Und in der Tat: Kapital und Arbeit; Vermögen und Einkommen; Kapitaleigentum, Management und Lohnarbeit; Arbeiter und Angestellte; Unternehmensleitung und Belegschaftsvertretung; Arbeitgeberverbände und Gewerkschaften; kollektive und individuelle Arbeitnehmerrechte; partizipatives Management und Gruppenarbeit – diese Institutionen und Strukturen, um nur einige wenige herauszugreifen, finden wir in beiden Gesellschaften. Allerdings zeigt sich bei näherem Hinsehen, daß die Unterschiede in der Sache doch erheblich sind und nach adäquatem Ausdruck verlangen, nach Spezifizierungen, Charakterisierungen oder eben, weil kurz und prägnant, nach anderen Termini. Nur durch präzise Charakterisierung können Mißverständnisse vermieden werden. Sich auf die Suche nach adäquaten Termini zu begeben, bedeutet nun aber nicht, bei japanischen Institutionen, Strukturen und Prozessen die betreffenden japanischen Begriffe einzuführen und damit eventuell zu unterstellen, es handele sich um singuläre Phänomene, die nur in Japan anzutreffen sind und für die es anderswo kein Äquivalent gäbe.

Welche Probleme einen erwarten, wenn man sich der industriellen Arbeitswelt Japans forschend und beschreibend nähert, soll hier an einem ausgewählten Beispiel illustriert werden. Im Zentrum steht der Begriff „Gewerkschaft“. Längst schon ist in westlichen Ländern bekannt – und in Deutschland war dabei Sung-Jo Park ein Pionier (Park 1983) –, daß Gewerkschaften in Japan etwas anderes sind als Gewerkschaften in der ehemaligen und heutigen Bundesrepublik. Aber was sind sie dann? Zwar handelt es sich beide Male um Interessenvertretungen abhängig Beschäftigter, doch bezieht sich zunächst einmal der Umfang der gewerkschaftlichen Mitgliedschaft im Falle Japans auf den Betrieb bzw. das Unternehmen, in Deutschland jedoch auf einen Industriezweig. Hierzulande sind die größten und wichtigsten Gewerkschaften nach dem Industrieverbandsprinzip aufgebaut, so daß sie hinsichtlich ihrer Organisationsform als „Industriegewerkschaften" bezeichnet werden, und zwar häufig auch dann, wenn sie Arbeitnehmer in nicht-industriellen Wirtschaftszweigen organisieren. Demgegenüber spricht man im japanischen Fall von „Betriebsgewerkschaften" oder „Unternehmensgewerkschaften". Ist nun „Betriebsgewerkschaft" dasselbe wie „Unternehmensgewerkschaft", so daß es legitim wäre, beide Begriffe synonym zu gebrauchen? Und gibt es Institutionen, die dem deutschen dualen System der Interessenvertretung mit seinen beiden Arenen der Tarifautonomie und Betriebsverfassung, sowie seinen Akteuren auf Arbeitnehmerseite, der Industriegewerkschaft und des Betriebsrates, entsprechen?

In der deutschsprachigen Fachliteratur zu den industriellen Beziehungen in Japan bzw. zum Vergleich zwischen den Systemen beider Länder findet sich häufig der synonyme Gebrauch. So heißt es in der vorzüglichen Studie von Tokunaga et al. über japanisches Personalmanagement:

> 90% der organisierten Arbeitskräfte in Japan sind in (1988 ca. 72.000) Betriebsgewerkschaften organisiert (JIL 1989; diese verteilen sich auf 32.000 Unternehmen). (...) Die meisten Betriebsgewerkschaften (wir benutzen diesen Begriff synonym mit dem der Unternehmensgewerkschaft) gehören Branchenföderationen (...) an. (Tokunaga et al. 1991:236-237)

Von „Betriebsgewerkschaften" spricht auch Bergmann (1990) in seiner Studie zum japanischen Fall. Die nicht ausführlich auf Japan eingehenden Darstellungen enthalten zumeist ebenfalls diesen Begriff. Müller-Jentsch beispielsweise schreibt:

> (...) nicht zuletzt begründet die Existenz von betrieblichen Arbeitsmärkten, insbesondere in Großbetrieben, eine materielle Basis für die Bildung von Betriebsgewerkschaften. Anders als in den USA und in Japan, wo Betriebsgewerkschaften die Regel sind, blieben in Deutschland betriebsgebundene Gewerkschaften – obwohl von Unternehmerseite zeitweise (bis 1918) stark gefördert – die Ausnahme. (Müller-Jentsch 1997:106)

Hier wird demgegenüber vorgeschlagen, daß man um der Klarheit willen beide nicht ohne Grund verschiedenen Wörter beibehalten, ihre semantische Differenz herausarbeiten und sie jeweils inhaltlich bestimmen sollte. Es geht zunächst um das Verständnis der deutschen und dann um das Verständnis der japanischen Termini, sowie um ihren Realgehalt. Zum Schluß soll begründet werden, warum ich die Übersetzung „Unternehmensgewerkschaft" für plausibel halte. Die Entstehungsgeschichte der Unternehmensgewerkschaft in Japan; die Existenz mehrerer Unternehmensgewerkschaften im selben Unternehmen; Arbeitskonflikte, die trotz dieser Organisationsform stattgefunden haben; nicht-gewerkschaftliche Formen der Interessenvertretung im Unternehmen – all dies ist nicht Gegenstand der folgenden Bemerkungen.

2 „Betrieb“ und „Unternehmen“ im Deutschen und im Japanischen

Bei der inhaltlichen Bestimmung von „Betriebs-“ und „Unternehmensgewerkschaft“ stoßen wir zunächst auf die spezifizierenden Bestandteile „Betrieb“ und „Unternehmen“. Welche Differenz verbirgt sich zwischen den beiden Wörtern im Deutschen? Unstrittig spielt der Begriff „Betrieb“ in der Industrie-, Betriebs- und Arbeitssoziologie eine zentrale Rolle. Was aber bedeutet „Betrieb“, und sind im Deutschen „Betrieb“ und „Unternehmen“ bzw. „Unternehmung“ dasselbe? Falls ja, wäre schließlich auch der synonyme Gebrauch der Zusammensetzungen „Betriebsgewerkschaft“ und „Unternehmensgewerkschaft“ legitim.

Eine beliebig herausgegriffene lexikalische Erklärung von „Betrieb“ lautet:

> [Der Betrieb ist eine] organisierte Wirtschaftseinheit, in der durch den Einsatz von Produktionsfaktoren für den Markt Güter produziert oder Dienstleistungen erbracht werden. Im Unterschied zum Unternehmen versteht man Betrieb i.d.R. als techn. Einheit. (Meyers Neues Lexikon 1994)

Demgegenüber lautet die Erklärung für „Unternehmen“:

> Unternehmen (Unternehmung), die rechtl. und organisator. Gestaltungseinheit der Betriebe in marktwirtschaftl. Wirtschaftssystemen, die sich aus der Zielsetzung des Unternehmers ergibt, langfristig das Gewinnmaximum durch Erstellen und Verwerten von Leistungen zu erreichen. In der Betriebswirtschaftslehre werden U. und Betrieb meistens dadurch unterschieden, daß das U. als rechtl., finanzielle oder Verwaltungseinheit und der Betrieb als techn. Einheit definiert wird. (Meyers Neues Lexikon 1994)

Diesen Definitionen ist gemeinsam, daß es sich beidesmal um eine bestimmte „organisierte Wirtschaftseinheit“ handelt. In beiden Wörtern werden also lediglich verschiedene Aspekte derselben Sache in den Vordergrund gerückt: im Falle von „Betrieb“ der Aspekt der technischen (auch organisatorischen) Einheit, im Falle von „Unternehmen“ der rechtliche, finanzielle (auch steuerliche) und administrative Aspekt. Eine derartige „organisierte Wirtschaftseinheit“ wird in der wissenschaftlichen Forschung zum Gegenstand der Betriebswirtschaftslehre. Offenkundig hat sich aber in der Praxis auch des wissenschaftlichen Sprachgebrauchs der synonyme Gebrauch beider Wörter eingeschliffen. Auf die Hervorhebung eines der erwähnten Aspekte, die ja die Wortwahl entscheiden könnte, wird zumeist verzichtet.

Diese Nachlässigkeit im Deutschen hat Folgen für die präzise Bestimmung unterschiedlich akzentuierter Phänomene in anderen Gesellschaften, insbesondere in Japan. Es fällt nämlich oben bei der Nennung der verschiedenen Aspekte jener „organisierten Wirtschaftseinheit“, die mit „Betrieb“ bzw. „Unternehmen“ bezeichnet wird, auf, daß ihre soziale Seite nicht genannt wurde. Gerade sie ist es aber, die den Soziologen interessiert. Max Weber hat hierzu – veröffentlicht erstmals 1922 – grundsätzliche Überlegungen angestellt:

> Es ist häufig und mit Recht beanstandet worden, daß in der nationalökonomischen Terminologie ‚Betrieb' und ‚Unternehmung' oft nicht getrennt werden. ‚Betrieb' ist auf dem Gebiet des wirtschaftlich orientierten Handelns an sich eine technische, die Art der kontinuierlichen Verbindung bestimmter Arbeitsleistungen untereinander und mit sachlichen Beschaffungsmitteln bezeichnende Kategorie. (...) Der Gegensatz zu ‚Unternehmen': einer Art der wirtschaftlichen Orientierung (am Gewinn) ist dagegen: ‚Haushalt' (Orientierung an Bedarfsdeckung). (Weber 1980:63-64)

Schon für Weber ist also bei „Betrieb" im Rahmen von wirtschaftlichem Handeln – es gibt den „Betrieb" auch in anderen Bereichen des Handelns, beispielsweise in der Politik – der technische Aspekt das Charakteristische. Der „Betrieb" bildet keinen Gegensatz zum „Unternehmen", sondern ist sozusagen dessen technische Grundlage oder sein technisch-materielles und zugleich soziales Substrat, ohne das es nicht existieren kann. Dem „Unternehmen" setzt Weber, dem es auf die Art der Orientierung des wirtschaftlichen Handelns ankommt, vielmehr den „Haushalt" entgegen. Anschließend geht er jedoch auf die uns hier interessierende Differenz ein und arbeitet sie folgendermaßen heraus:

> Passend (weil eindeutig) ist aber (...) der Ausdruck ‚Erwerbsbetrieb' statt: kontinuierliches Erwerbsunternehmen nur für den einfachsten Fall des Zusammenfallens der technischen Betriebseinheit mit der Unternehmungseinheit. Es können aber in der Verkehrswirtschaft mehrere, technisch gesonderte, ‚Betriebe' zu einer Unternehmungseinheit verbunden sein. (...) Wo nur von ‚Betrieb' die Rede ist, soll jedenfalls darunter immer jene technisch – in Anlagen, Arbeitsmitteln, Arbeitskräften und (eventuell: heterokephaler und heteronomer) technischer Leitung – gesonderte Einheit verstanden werden, die es ja auch in der kommunistischen Wirtschaft (...) gibt. Der Ausdruck ‚Erwerbsbetrieb' soll fortan nur da verwendet werden, wo technische und ökonomische (Unternehmungs-) Einheit identisch sind. (Weber 1980:64)

In diesem Zusammenhang wendet sich Weber dann seinem eigentlichen Interesse zu: den drei Arten, „wie innerhalb einer Menschengruppe Leistung und Arbeit sich vollziehen können", und charakterisiert diese als 1. technisch, 2. sozial und 3. ökonomisch (Weber 1980:62-63&65ff.). Festzuhalten ist demnach, daß der Soziologe das am Gewinn orientierte wirtschaftliche Handeln – das unternehmerische Handeln – nie allein unter ökonomischem Aspekt betrachtet, sondern ihn stets auch die technische und soziale Dimension interessieren.

In der heutigen Umgangssprache wie auch in der Wissenschaftssprache des Deutschen wird jedoch, wie bereits erwähnt, diese Differenzierung zwischen „Betrieb" und „Unternehmen" kaum mehr durchgehalten. Ist sie deshalb schon irrelevant? Nach Wahrig bedeutet „Betrieb" heutzutage 1. eine Einheit von zusammenwirkenden Personen und Produktionsmitteln zum Hervorbringen von Gütern und Leistungen, und 2. im engeren Sinne, die dazu nötige räumlich-technische Anlage, also Fabrik, größere Werkstatt, Geschäft, Büro (Wahrig Deutsches Wörterbuch 1986). In der ersten Bedeutung fällt „Betrieb" mit „Unternehmen" zusammen. Max Weber allerdings würde nur dort, wo ein Unternehmen aus lediglich einem einzigen Betrieb („Betrieb" im engeren Sinne) besteht, den Begriff „Erwerbsbetrieb" zulassen – und ihn nur dort synonym mit „Unternehmen" benutzen. Meiner Ansicht nach sollten wir uns der differenzierenden Weberschen Terminologie bedienen, wenn wir über Japan, seine Unternehmen und Gewerkschaften sprechen.

Kennt nun das Japanische ebenso wie das Deutsche die Doppelbedeutung von „Betrieb" im Sinne Webers oder auch im Sinne der heutigen lexikalischen Definition beispielsweise in Wahrig Deutsches Wörterbuch, wie wir sie oben zitiert haben? Glücklicherweise nein. Dem „Betrieb" in der Bedeutung von räumlich-technischer Einheit entspricht im Japanischen *jigyôsho*. Durch den Bestandteil *sho* (= *tokoro*: Ort) wird bereits der räumliche Aspekt der „organisierten Wirtschaftseinheit" angezeigt. Das Pendant des deutschen Wortes „Betrieb" in der Bedeutung von „Betriebsführung", „Management", „unternehmerisches Handeln" – sie fehlt bei Wahrig, nicht jedoch bei Weber – ist dagegen das japanische Wort *keiei*. Von diesem wird beispielsweise *keieisha*: „Manager" abgeleitet, ebenso *keieigaku*: „Betriebswirtschaftslehre". „Japanisches Management" heißt dementsprechend im Japanischen *nihonteki keiei*. Wenn bei „Betrieb" allerdings der ökonomische Aspekt jener Art von wirtschaftlicher Organisationseinheit, die oben bei Weber als „Unternehmen" (Unternehmung) benannt wurde, betont werden soll, dann wird dafür im Japanischen *kigyô* gewählt. Im Deutschen haben wir übrigens ein Kriterium für die Unterscheidung zwischen den beiden Hauptbedeutungen von „Betrieb": Wo das Wort nämlich im Sinne von „Management" gebraucht wird, kann man keinen Plural bilden; wird „Betrieb" dagegen im Sinne von „räumlich-technischer Organisationseinheit" gebraucht, so kann sehr wohl der Plural gebildet werden. Ein Beispiel dafür ist der Satz: „Dieses Unternehmen verfügt über mehrere Betriebe." Festzuhalten ist jedenfalls, daß durch die sprachliche Differenzierung zwischen *keiei*, *kigyô* und *jigyôsho* im Japanischen Missverständnisse, wie sie im Deutschen wegen des vagen Charakters des Wortes „Betrieb" leicht aufkommen können, vermieden werden.[1]

Erstaunlicherweise wird diese, phonetisch und schriftlich mit drei völlig verschiedenen Grundbestandteilen arbeitende Differenzierungsmöglichkeit umgekehrt von japanischer Seite an einem bestimmten Punkt regelmäßig aufgegeben.

---

[1] Ein vor wenigen Jahren erschienenes deutsch-japanisches Wörterbuch ist darüber hinaus noch genauer: Für „Betrieb" in seinen zwei Hauptbedeutungen werden zwei Gruppen von japanischen Wörtern angegeben: erstens, *keieitai*, *kigyô* und *keieitai no tatemono* in der Bedeutung der organisierten Wirtschaftseinheit, das zuletzt genannte japanische Wort in der Bedeutung der räumlich-technischen Einheit im Sinne des entsprechenden Gebäudes; zweitens *keiei*, *eigyô* und *sôgyô* in der Bedeutung von Management und Betrieb (im Singular). (Kenkyûshas Deutsch-Japanisches Wörterbuch 1996)

Bei der Beschreibung der industriellen Beziehungen in Deutschland wird nämlich die deutsche Institution des „Betriebsrates" immer wieder mit *keiei kyôgikai* oder auch *keiei hyôgikai* übersetzt.[2] Dieser Fehler, der zu Mißverständnisse führen muß, scheint seit langem mitgeschleppt zu werden, obgleich es Versuche gegeben hat, ihn zu überwinden (Kishida 1978). Die mit *keiei* operierenden japanischen Wörter legen – zumal bei isoliertem Gebrauch – nahe, daß das Management als Akteur (*keiei-gawa*) entweder alleine oder zusammen mit der Belegschaftsvertretung im deutschen Betriebsrat vertreten sei. Bekanntlich ist das Gegenteil der Fall: Es ist dort nur die Belegschaft vertreten, denn Betriebsräte als einzelne Personen (Gremienmitglieder) wie auch als Gremien sind Interessenvertreter der Belegschaft, oder sollten es sein. Daß es überhaupt zu dieser mißverständlichen Übersetzung des deutschen Wortes „Betriebsrat" kommen kann, liegt daran, daß man japanischerseits zumeist wortwörtlich übersetzt, d.h. vom deutschen Wort „Betrieb" ausgeht, und nicht von der Sache, also von „Belegschaftsvertretung". Für „Betrieb" aber fand man zumindest in älteren deutsch-japanischen Wörterbüchern an erster Stelle *keiei* (Kimura-Sagara's Deutsch Japanisches Wörterbuch 1963). Möglicherweise hielt man auch deshalb an *keiei kyôgikai* fest, weil sich das Wort inzwischen eingebürgert hatte, und nahm lieber seine Mehrdeutigkeit in Kauf, als danach zu fragen, worin sein wesentlicher Inhalt besteht. Die Antwort darauf hätte zu einer Neuprägung führen müssen, da es eine dem deutschen Betriebsrat völlig äquivalente Institution in Japan nicht gibt.

3 Der Begriff „Gewerkschaft" im Deutschen und im Japanischen

Im deutschen Wort „Gewerkschaft" steckt noch der Hinweis auf die Entstehungsphase der Gewerkschaften. Der Bestandteil „Gewerk" verweist darauf, daß es sich ursprünglich um einen Zusammenschluß (union) der Beschäftigten (potenziell aller Beschäftigten) in einem Beruf oder Berufszweig (trade) handelte. Gemeint sind mit „Beschäftigte" lohnabhängig Beschäftigte. Im Verlauf der Entwicklung der Gewerkschaftsbewegung ist die Beschränkung einer Gewerkschaft auf ein bestimmtes „Gewerk" im Sinne eines Berufes obsolet geworden. Entscheidend wurde vielmehr der Industriezweig oder die Branche innerhalb eines solchen. In der Industriesoziologie und Gewerkschaftsforschung spielte dann bei der Typenbildung das Kriterium der Arbeitsmarktbezogenheit eine wichtige Rolle. Hiernach sind insbesondere die folgenden, in der Realität verschiedener nationaler Systeme industrieller Beziehungen am häufigsten auftretenden Gewerkschaftstypen gebildet worden:

---

2 Zwei von zahllosen Beispielen für diesen Wortgebrauch in japanischen Untersuchungen der industriellen Beziehungen in Deutschland seien hier herausgegriffen: Kumazawa (1989:114-117) und – aus jüngster Zeit – Ôshige (2000).

a) Betriebsgewerkschaft (auch: Werksverein),

b) Berufsgewerkschaft,

c) Industriegewerkschaft,

d) allgemeine Gewerkschaft.

Auch Standesorganisationen wie die der Angestellten oder der Beamten, die sich von Arbeitnehmerorganisationen abgrenzen wollten, tragen mitunter die Bezeichnung „Gewerkschaft" in ihrem Namen. Dies wäre Typ e): Gewerkschaften als Standesorganisationen.

Das japanische Wort für „Gewerkschaft" ist *rôdô kumiai*, wobei die Einzelbestandteile *rôdô* „Arbeit" (genauer: „Lohnarbeit") und *kumiai* „Genossenschaft" bedeuten. Dem Wort *kumiai* wird spezifierend *rôdô* vorangestellt, weil es natürlich noch andere Arten von Genossenschaften gibt. Man denke im Hinblick auf Japan vor allem an die dort noch bedeutenden Agrargenossenschaften (*nôgyô kumiai*) und die Genossenschaften im Baugewerbe. In beiden Fällen setzt sich die Mitgliedschaft aus selbständigen (Klein-) Unternehmern zusammen, so daß wir es im Ergebnis gerade mit dem Gegenteil von „Gewerkschaft" im Sinne eines Zusammenschlusses von (Lohn-)abhängig Beschäftigen zu tun haben. *Rôdô kumiai* müßte wörtlich eigentlich mit „Arbeits-" bzw. „Arbeitergenossenschaft" ins Deutsche übersetzt werden, wird jedoch tatsächlich im Sinne von „Gewerkschaft" gebraucht. Die Entsprechungen zu den deutschen Begriffen für die vier ersten Organisationsformen von „Gewerkschaft" lauten im Japanischen (wobei der Bestandteil *rôdô* vor *kumiai* jeweils eingefügt werden kann):

a) *kigyô-betsu kumiai* („Betriebsgewerkschaft" oder „Unternehmensgewerkschaft")

b) *shokugyô-betsu kumiai* (Berufsgewerkschaft)

c) *sangyô-betsu kumiai* (Industriegewerkschaft)

d) *ippan kumiai* oder – als Lehnwort aus dem Englischen – *zeneraru yunion* (allgemeine Gewerkschaft).

Allgemein läßt sich behaupten: Welche Gewerkschaftsform in einer Gesellschaft dominiert, hängt von der Form der Industrialisierung, den wirtschafts- und sozialhistorischen Voraussetzungen, den politischen und rechtlichen Gestaltungsinitiativen der gesellschaftlichen Kräfte, sowie von geistigen und praktischen Einflüssen aus dem Ausland ab. Für Deutschland gilt, daß sich das Industrieverbandsprinzip und damit die Form der Industriegewerkschaft weitgehend durchgesetzt haben, während für Japan die Forschung darin übereinstimmt, daß sich dort die „Betriebsgewerkschaft" bzw. „Unternehmensgewerkschaft" als die beherrschende Form erwiesen hat. Es gibt natürlich auch in Japan Gewerkschaftsorganisationen auf der Ebene von Branchen oder Industriezweigen. Weil sich jedoch Aufgaben und Funktionen der gewerkschaftlichen Zusammenschlüsse auf dieser Ebene zwischen Japan und Deutschland wesentlich unterscheiden, wäre es falsch, für den japanischen Fall denselben Begriff wie in Deutschland – also „Industriegewerkschaften“ – zu benutzen. Im japanischen Fall handelt es sich auf dieser Ebene um Föderationen von Einzelgewerkschaften. Diese Föderationen besitzen keine Tariffähigkeit. Um die Differenz in der Sache schon im Wort auszudrücken, habe ich den Begriff „Branchenföderation“ (d.h. Föderation von Unternehmensgewerkschaften in einer Branche bzw. einem Industriezweig) in die Diskussion eingebracht und setze die Sache damit auch sprachlich von „Industriegewerkschaft“ ab. Das japanische *tan'itsu sangyô-betsu rôdô kumiai* (abgekürzt: *tansan*) sollte man also mit „Branchenföderation“ wiedergeben.

4 „Betriebsgewerkschaft“ oder „Unternehmensgewerkschaft“?

Wenn wir untersuchen, welche Merkmale die Gewerkschaftsform hat, die mit „Betriebsgewerkschaft“ bzw. „Unternehmensgewerkschaft“ bezeichnet wird, und wenn wir ferner den entsprechenden japanischen Fachbegriff aufschlüsseln, sollte es möglich sein, zu einer adäquaten Übersetzung zu gelangen. Diesen Weg habe ich bei der Festlegung der von mir selbst einzusetzenden Terminologie beschritten, als ich, unzufrieden mit der Mehrdeutigkeit des zur Bezeichnung des japanischen Falles am häufigsten benutzten deutschen Wortes „Betriebsgewerkschaft“, zunächst danach fragte, welches japanische Wort für die dort dominierende Gewerkschaftsform verwendet wird. Es zeigte sich, daß nicht nur in der Fachwelt, sondern auch darüber hinaus allgemein *kigyô-betsu* (*rôdô*) *kumiai* (seltener auch: *kigyô-nai rôdô kumiai*) gebraucht wird. Dabei wird das hier in der Mitte stehende Wort *rôdô* zwecks Vereinfachung meistens weggelassen.

Oben wurden *rôdô* und *kumiai* bereits erklärt. Die Bedeutung des dritten Bestandteils des Begriffs – *kigyô* – ist eindeutig: „Unternehmen“ (Unternehmung). Das Suffix -betsu bedeutet: „je nach“, bezeichnet also die Ebene, hier also enterprise level bzw. enterprise-based. Vom Japanischen her gesehen, kann es folglich nur eine richtige Übersetzung für die Spezifizierung *kigyô-betsu* (*rôdô*) *kumiai* geben, und diese lautet: „Unternehmensgewerkschaft“, bzw. für das seltener gebrauchte *kigyô-nai* (*rôdô*) *kumiai*: „unternehmensinterne Gewerkschaft“. In den Übersetzungen der auf den japanischen Fall bezogenen Fachtexte vom Japanischen ins Englische wird hierfür enterprise-based union oder kürzer: enterprise union gewählt. (Kawanishi 1984:543, Inagami 1988)

4.1 Merkmale der Unternehmensgewerkschaft

Welche sachlichen Umstände werden nun mit diesem Begriff bezeichnet? Anders gefragt, welches sind die charakteristischen Merkmale der *kigyô-betsu* (*rôdô*) *kumiai*? Neben der traditionellen und allgemeinen Funktionsbestimmung von Gewerkschaft überhaupt – Erhaltung und Verbesserung der Arbeitsbedingungen ihrer Mitglieder – wäre hier zunächst auf den Organisationsbereich hinzuweisen. Die *kigyô-betsu kumiai* organisiert die Belegschaft eines Unternehmens in den Grenzen und auf Basis desselben, reicht folglich nicht über das jeweilige Unternehmen hinaus. Alle Stammarbeitnehmer sind in ihr organisiert, unabhängig davon, welche Tätigkeit sie ausüben, welchen Schulabschluß sie haben und ob sie Arbeiter oder Angestellte sind, sofern ihre Position nur unterhalb der Ebene des Abteilungsleiters (*kachô*) liegt. Irregulär Beschäftigte wie etwa Temporärbeschäftigte und Teilzeitarbeitnehmer können keine Gewerkschaftsmitglieder werden. Außerdem gilt, daß die einzelnen Stammarbeitnehmer individuell Gewerkschaftsmitglied nur in „ihrer" Unternehmensgewerkschaft werden können. Mitglied einer übergeordneten gewerkschaftlichen Organisation – etwa einer Organisation auf Branchen- oder Industriezweigebene – zu werden ist ihnen verwehrt. Ihre Beiträge führen sie folglich auch nur an die Unternehmensgewerkschaft ab, und zwar in den Großunternehmen in der Regel in Form des automatischen Abzugs von der Lohn- bzw. Gehaltszahlung. Ferner herrscht in den japanischen Unternehmensgewerkschaften das Prinzip der Zwangsmitgliedschaft für reguläre Arbeitnehmer vor, die automatisch mit dem Eintritt ins betreffende Unternehmen beginnt und mit ihrem Ausscheiden – aus welchen Gründen auch immer dies erfolgt – endet (union-shop system). Die freigestellten Arbeitnehmer unter den Funktionären der *kigyô-betsu kumiai* behalten als Hauptamtliche ihre Zugehörigkeit zum Unternehmen bei; die Dauer ihrer Amtszeit bemißt sich nach der Dauer ihrer Betriebszugehörigkeit (Hisamoto 1994:14-15). Die Unternehmensgewerkschaft ist ferner autonom in ihren Entscheidungen, finanziell unabhängig, und in ihrer Willensbildung, in der Wahl ihrer Funktionäre und in ihren Finanzen gegenüber Gewerkschaftsorganisationen auf höheren Ebenen selbständig (Shirai 1982). Letzteres sind wiederum Kriterien, die auch in den allgemeinen Definitionen von „Gewerkschaft" enthalten sind, unabhängig von einem bestimmten nationalen Systems der industriellen Beziehungen.

4.2 Die beiden Organisationsformen der Unternehmensgewerkschaft

Wenn *rôdô kumiai* „Gewerkschaft" heißt und *kigyô-betsu kumiai* „Unternehmensgewerkschaft" bzw. „Betriebsgewerkschaft", sollten wir nochmals auf den dritten Bestandteil *kigyô* zurückkommen. Innerhalb des Typus der Unternehmensgewerkschaft sind nämlich zwei Organisationsformen zu unterscheiden. Das Kriterium dafür ist, ob es sich um eine Gewerkschaft handelt, die alleine im

Unternehmen besteht, oder um einen Verband von mehreren gewerkschaftlichen Organisationen im Unternehmen. Der „Unternehmensgewerkschaft" können also zwei Sub-Typen subsumiert werden. Der erste bezeichnet den Fall, daß nur eine einzige Gewerkschaftsorganisation im Unternehmen existiert, unabhängig davon, ob das betreffende Unternehmen nun über einen oder mehrere Betriebe (Fabriken, Werke, Betriebsstätten, Dienststellen o.ä.) verfügt. Der spezifizierende Unterbegriff lautet dann im Japanischen *tan'itsu soshiki* (*rôdô*) *kumiai.* Im Deutschen wäre dies sinngemäß wiederzugeben mit „Einzel-Unternehmensgewerkschaft". Dieser Fall tritt meistens – aber nicht immer – dort auf, wo ein Unternehmen aus einem einzigen Betrieb besteht, folglich Unternehmen und technisch-räumliche Einheit deckungsgleich sind.

Wenn dagegen mehrere Gewerkschaftsorganisationen in einem Unternehmen existieren, und zwar jeweils eine Gewerkschaftsorganisation für jeden Betrieb, spricht man von *tan'i soshiki* (*rôdô*) *kumiai.* Eine brauchbare deutsche Übersetzung hierfür wäre wohl „Kombinierte Unternehmensgewerkschaft", weil damit ausgedrückt wird, daß diese Unternehmensgewerkschaft aus mehreren Einheiten (*tan'i*), nämlich Einheiten auf Betriebsebene, besteht. Hier bilden also mehrere Betriebe (*jigyôsho*) in ihrer Gesamtheit, unter einheitlicher unternehmerischer Leitung stehend, das Unternehmen. Jeder Betrieb hat eine eigene, relativ selbständige Gewerkschaftsorganisation, die dann passend als „Betriebsgewerkschaft" (*jigyôsho-betsu kumiai*) bezeichnet wird. Auch hier gibt es natürlich die Unternehmensgewerkschaft, die jetzt aber eine „zusammengesetzte Unternehmensgewerkschaft" ist. Für eine derartige „zusammengesetzte" oder „kombinierte Unternehmensgewerkschaft" wird in der japanischen Fachsprache mitunter auch ein weiterer Fachausdruck benutzt: *kigyôren.* Er besagt, daß man es in einem Unternehmen mit einem „Verbund mehrerer Betriebsgewerkschaften" (*jigyôsho-betsu kumiai no rengôtai*) zu tun hat (Hisamoto 1994:15). Daß im Japanischen in beiden Fällen das Wort *rôdô kumiai* (= Gewerkschaft) benutzt wird, zeigt an, daß wir es rechtlich in beiden Fällen mit mehr oder weniger selbständigen Gewerkschaften zu tun haben. Mit *kigyôren* wird von Fall zu Fall auch ein Verbund der Betriebsgewerkschaften von (ökonomisch beherrschten) Zulieferbetrieben oder Tochterunternehmen eines (ökonomisch beherrschenden) Hauptunternehmens (z.B. in einer vertikal affiliierten Zulieferkette: Keiretsu) bezeichnet, auch wenn diese Zulieferbetriebe und Tochterunternehmen formal unabhängig sind.

Entscheidend dafür, ob für Gewerkschaftsorganisationen auf der Ebene des Betriebes – im Sinne eines von mehreren Betrieben, die zu einem Unternehmen gehören – der Begriff „Gewerkschaft" überhaupt verwendet werden sollte, ist meines Erachtens das Kriterium der Tariffähigkeit, anders gesagt: der Fähigkeit, Kollektivverhandlungen führen und Kollektivverträge abschließen zu können. Nur dann, wenn eine „Betriebsgewerkschaft" im gerade beschriebenen Sinne so unabhängig von der ihr übergeordneten „Unternehmensgewerkschaft" ist, daß sie in ihrem Organisationsbereich tariffähig ist, sollte von „Gewerkschaft" gesprochen werden. Fälle mit in dieser Hinsicht relativ unabhängigen „Betriebsgewerkschaften" gibt es nun aber durchaus. Hisamoto zitiert eine Untersuchung des Arbeitsministeriums über Kollektivverhandlungen und Arbeitskonflikte von 1987, in der festgestellt wird:

> Unter den [Unternehmens-]Gewerkschaften, die Kollektivverhandlungen durchführen, beträgt der Anteil der Fälle, in denen nur die betreffende Gewerkschaft alleine solche Verhandlungen durchführt, 83 Prozent; dagegen beträgt der Anteil jener Fälle, in denen die betreffende Gewerkschaft zusammen mit einer übergeordneten, aber unternehmensinternen Gewerkschaftsorganisation solche Verhandlungen durchführt, rund 18 Prozent. (Hisamoto 1994:14)

Hieraus können wir schließen, daß in jenem Jahr über vier Fünftel der Unternehmensgewerkschaften sog. „Einzel-Unternehmensgewerkschaften" waren, während sog. „kombinierte Unternehmensgewerkschaften" etwas weniger als ein Fünftel ausmachten. Bei einer Klassifizierung der erfaßten Unternehmen nach Größenklassen ergibt sich aus derselben Untersuchung eine etwas andere Gewichtung. Es zeigt sich, daß von Großunternehmen ab 5.000 Beschäftigten die dort bestehenden Gewerkschaften zu 38% Kollektivverhandlungen zusammen mit einer übergeordneten, jedoch unternehmensinternen Gewerkschaftsorganisation durchführten. „Zusammen mit" bedeutet, daß sie alleine eben nicht tariffähig sind, obwohl sie als „Gewerkschaften" bezeichnet werden. Daraus ist zu folgern, daß besonders in Großunternehmen mit mehreren Betrieben häufig mehrere „Betriebsgewerkschaften" existieren, die jedoch bei Kollektiverhandlungen mit der Unternehmensleitung im Verbund und geschlossen, nämlich als Einheiten einer „Unternehmensgewerkschaft", auftreten. Weiterhin können wir den Schluß ziehen, daß in den Großunternehmen „Kombinierte Unternehmensgewerkschaften" häufiger vorkommen als in mittleren und kleinen Unternehmen. Ohnehin ist bekannt, daß Gewerkschaften in Japan weit überwiegend in Großunternehmen existieren.

Auch bei der statistischen Zählung spielen diese Verhältnisse eine Rolle. So wird vom Arbeitsministerium seit 1953 die Anzahl der Gewerkschaften stets zweifach erhoben: Zum einen werden Unternehmensgewerkschaften gezählt, die „Einzel-Unternehmensgewerkschaften" sind, zum andern Unternehmensgewerkschaften, die „Kombinierte Unternehmensgewerkschaften" sind. Doch im zweiten Fall werden deren Einheiten, die Betriebsgewerkschaften, addiert. Daher kommt es, daß die Anzahl der „Kombinierten Unternehmensgewerkschaften" regelmäßig höher liegt, so beispielsweise für 1990 bei 72.000 „kombinierten", gegenüber 33.000 „Einzel-Unternehmensgewerkschaften". Anders ausgedrückt: Bei zehn Einzel-Unternehmensgewerkschaften schlagen alle zehn als Unternehmensgewerkschaften statistisch zu Buche. Ob aber bei zehn Betriebsgewerkschaften, die zusammen einen Verbund in einem Unternehmen und damit eine Unternehmensgewerkschaft bilden, alle zehn als Gewerkschaften zu Buche schlagen, hängt davon ab, ob sie alle jeweils über eigene Tariffähigkeit verfügen. Sollten nämlich diese zehn Betriebsgewerkschaften in Kollektivverhandlungen als ein Verbund auftreten, werden sie in der erwähnten Statistik als eine „kombinierte Unternehmensgewerkschaft" gezählt. Wenn einige der zehn Betriebsgewerkschaften bei Kollektivverhandlungen als ein Verbund auftreten, andere jedoch eigene Tariffähigkeit besitzen, so werden der Verbund als eine Unternehmensgewerkschaft und die Betriebsgewerkschaften zusätzlich gezählt.

4.3 Wie sollte *kigyô-betsu kumiai* ins Deutsche übersetzt werden?

In der deutschsprachigen Fachliteratur finden wir mehrere Übersetzungsvarianten des japanischen *kigyô-betsu kumiai*. Deren Vor- und Nachteile seien kurz erläutert.

4.3.1 „Firmengewerkschaft" bzw. „Hausgewerkschaft"

Relativ oft kommt „Firmengewerkschaft" bzw. company union als Übersetzungsvariante vor. Dies hat seine Berechtigung insofern, als „Firma" und „Unternehmen", aber auch company, firm und enterprise häufig synonym gebraucht werden. So spricht beispielsweise K. Ôshige in seiner jüngst erschienenen Studie von „Firmengewerkschaften" (Ôshige 1999:139ff.). Er begründet diese Wortwahl wie folgt:

> Hier nehme ich ‚Firmengewerkschaften' für die Bezeichnung der japanischen Gewerkschaften. Die Ausdrücke (...) ‚Betriebsgewerkschaften' und ‚Unternehmensgewerkschaften' können den Eindruck wecken, daß sich die Gewerkschaften auf bestimmte Ebenen in der Unternehmensstruktur beziehen und können somit zum Mißverständnis führen. Die Bezeichnung ‚Firmengewerkschaften' ist dank ihrer unklaren Bezugnahme von diesem Eindruck frei und stellt trotzdem den internen Charakter ausreichend dar. (Ôshige 1999:141)

Über diese Begründung läßt sich sicherlich diskutieren, doch bleiben für mich Zweifel. In einem anderen Kontext warnt Kawanishi jedoch vor diesem Wortgebrauch:

> However, one sign of the uninformed observer is the tendency to equate Japanese unionism with enterprise unionism, and the enterprise union with the company union. For some reason the view seems common that Japan's enterprise unions are established on the principle that all employees of a given firm will automatically join that firm's enterprise union. (Kawanishi 1992:XV)

In dieser Sicht fallen nämlich all jene Fälle heraus, in welchen es zwei oder mehrere Unternehmensgewerkschaften im selben Unternehmen gibt, die bei der Organisierung von Belegschaftsangehörigen konkurrieren.

Gegen die Variante „Firmengewerkschaft" sprechen drei weitere Einwände: Erstens, der Ausdruck „Firmengewerkschaft" kommt gefährlich nahe an „Hausgewerkschaft" (house union) heran, also an eine Gewerkschaftsform, die nicht mehr die für jede Gewerkschaft, welche diesen Namen verdient, notwendige Selbständigkeit und Unabhängigkeit besitzt.[3] Aber auch company union kann bei rein negativer Auslegung sogar als „gelbe Gewerkschaft", als eine vom Management geschaffene und von ihm ausgehaltene Gewerkschaft (japanisch: *goyô kumiai*), verstanden werden, und wird es häufig auch so. Zweitens, die lokalen Unterorganisationen der *kigyô-betsu kumiai* auf der Ebene des einzelnen Betriebes, Werkes, der Dienststelle usw. können so sprachlich nicht mehr differenziert ausgedrückt werden. Schließlich wäre noch zu bedenken, daß das englische company union die Assoziation an company man nahe legt; damit scheint company union wie dieser ein Werk der Unternehmensleitung bzw. des Managements zu sein.

4.3.2 „Betriebsgewerkschaft"

Fragen wir danach, ob es im Japanischen ein Wort für „Betriebsgewerkschaft" gibt, so fällt die Antwort keineswegs eindeutig aus. Wenn von deutscher Seite das deutsche „Betriebsgewerkschaft" für den japanischen Fall benutzt wird, der Sache nach aber die Unternehmensgewerkschaft gemeint ist, so dürfte an originaler Stelle, d.h. im japanischen Text bzw. beim Hinweis auf Japan von japanischer Seite, mit großer Wahrscheinlichkeit *kigyô-betsu* (*rôdô*) *kumiai* gestanden haben. Wo das deutsche Wort „Betriebsgewerkschaft" an Stelle von „Unternehmensgewerkschaft" gewählt wurde, gerät man jedoch in Verlegenheit, wenn jene gewerkschaftliche Organisationsform, die nicht auf Ebene eines Unternehmens, sondern auf Ebene der zu diesem gehörenden Betriebe organisiert ist, bezeichnen werden muß. Im Japanischen kann das terminologische Dilemma mittels der erwähnten Spezifizierung von *kigyô-betsu* (*rôdô*) *kumiai* in „Einzel-Unternehmensgewerkschaft" und „Kombinierte Unternehmensgewerkschaft" gelöst werden. Die Übersetzungsvariante „Betriebsgewerkschaft" für *kigyô-betsu kumiai* führt dagegen unweigerlich zu Mißverständnissen, solange sie nicht von einer ausführlichen Erläuterung begleitet ist. Daher sollte der Begriff „Betriebsgewerkschaft" besser nur für die gewerkschaftliche Organisation in einer „räumlich-technischen Anlage" – in einem Betrieb, einem Werk, einer Dienststelle – eines mehrere Betriebe umfassenden Unternehmens reserviert werden. Eine solche gewerkschaftliche Organisationseinheit auf Ebene eines Betriebes kann durchaus eine gewisse Selbständigkeit im Verhältnis zur Unternehmensgewerkschaft, zu der sie gehört, besitzen, ohne jedoch tariffähig zu sein. (Seifert 1997:43-50)

---

[3] Diese Konnotation darf hingegen nicht auf die sog. „Haustarifverträge" – beispielsweise beim deutschen VW-Konzern – ausgedehnt werden.

4.3.3 „Unternehmensgewerkschaft“

Die japanische Unternehmensgewerkschaft setzt qua Organisationsform andere Rahmenbedingungen für das Denken und Verhalten ihrer Mitglieder, wenn auch diese Setzung an sich nicht schon über ihr Schicksal und das ihrer Mitglieder entscheidet (Kawanishi 1992). In der großen Mehrzahl der Fälle – so jedenfalls der Befund der kritischen Industrie- und Arbeitssoziologie in Japan – gibt das Unternehmen als Wirtschaftssubjekt und Rechtseinheit (und zwar in der Regel als juristische Person) nicht nur dem gewerkschaftlichen Organisationsumfang die Grenzen vor, sondern richtet auch stärker, als es unternehmensübergreifende Gewerkschaften tun, das Denken und Verhalten der Gewerkschaftsmitglieder, also aller Stammbelegschaftsmitglieder, auf den ökonomischen Aspekt ihrer Existenz als Beschäftigte aus. Die Gewerkschaftsmitglieder denken in diesem Fall weit eher „betriebswirtschaftlich“, d.h. auf die Perspektiven und das Wohlergehen des Unternehmens bezogen, als dann, wenn sie Mitglieder einer Industriegewerkschaft wären. Sie verfügen allerdings auch kaum über die Möglichkeit kollektiver Interessenvertretung außerhalb des Unternehmens und können sich dort nicht auf eine von ihnen unterstützte Organisation beziehen, wie dies in Deutschland mit seinen Industriegewerkschaften im Prinzip der Fall ist. Daraus folgt auch, daß sich in Deutschland multiple Loyalitäten in Bezug auf Arbeitnehmerinteressen entwickeln können, nämlich einmal gegenüber dem Betriebsrat als Belegschaftsvertretung im Unternehmen, und zum anderen gegenüber der Gewerkschaft als einer unternehmensübergreifenden Organisation. Verglichen mit der Macht der ökonomischen Bedingungen, unter denen das Unternehmen agiert, und der suggestiven Kraft des „betriebswirtschaftlichen Denkens“ ist der Einfluß der sozialen Beziehungen am Arbeitsplatz und im einzelnen Betrieb (Betrieb als technisch-räumliche, aber auch soziale Einheit) wohl eher als schwach einzuschätzen. Wenn die formale Organisierung dieser sozialen Beziehungen in Gruppen, Teams, Zirkeln etc. durch das Management der interpersonalen „Unterfütterung“ der betriebswirtschaftlichen Imperative dient, so die gleichfalls vorhandenen informellen sozialen Beziehungen und informellen Gruppen etc. der Kompensation für die Arbeitslast. Allerdings: die Unternehmensgewerkschaft gibt es nicht. Es kommt, um ein Gesamturteil über die „performance“ der Unternehmensgewerkschaft fällen zu können, auf die systematische Auswertung vieler Einzel-Analysen an.

5 Terminologische Spitzfindigkeiten?

Warum haben wir uns ausführlich mit terminologischen Fragen, die hier zugleich Fragen der Übersetzung sind, beschäftigt? Der Grund dafür dürfte nach dem Gesagten auf der Hand liegen: Terminologische Differenzen bezeichnen Unterschiede in der Sache, und deshalb kommt es auf den präzisen Gebrauch der

Termini an. In der Bundesrepublik sind seit Jahren Tendenzen zur „Verbetrieblichung“ der Arbeitsbeziehungen zu beobachten, wobei es keineswegs nur um den Flächentarif und seine Aushöhlung geht. Sie sind Gegenstand zahlreicher tiefschürfender Untersuchungen geworden. Wie immer man diese Tendenzen einschätzen mag – fest steht wohl, daß den Betriebsräten in der Zukunft wachsende Bedeutung zukommen wird. Der Betriebsrat im System der deutschen industriellen Beziehungen, also die gesetzlich abgesicherte Belegschaftsvertretung im Unternehmen, weist in seinen Funktionen durchaus Parallelen zur japanischen Unternehmensgewerkschaft auf, und ist doch in seiner Organisationsstruktur völlig verschieden. Schon durch das Betriebsverfassungsgesetz ist er auf rechtlicher Ebene auch auf das Wohl des Betriebes (hier im Sinne von „Unternehmen“) verpflichtet. Im Betriebsverfassungsgesetz § 2, Abs. (1) heißt es:

> Arbeitgeber und Betriebsrat arbeiten unter Beachtung der geltenden Tarifverträge vertrauensvoll und im Zusammenwirken mit den im Betrieb vertretenen Gewerkschaften und Arbeitgebervereinigungen zum Wohl der Arbeitnehmer und des Betriebs zusammen. (Betriebsverfassungsgesetz von 1988)

Auf der Ebene der Satzungsanalyse finden sich in den Satzungen japanischer Unternehmensgewerkschaften teilweise ähnlich klingende Bestimmungen. Für eine vergleichende Realanalyse der Interessenvertretung der Belegschaft müßten allerdings auch japanische Unternehmen untersucht werden, in denen eine Unternehmensgewerkschaft nicht existiert, es aber gleichwohl andere Formen der Belegschaftsvertretung (*jûgyôin daihyô soshiki*) gibt, wie z.B. eine Beschäftigtenorganisation (*jûgyôin soshiki*) der Stammbelegschaft (Seifert 2000). Ebenso wichtig für die zukünftige Forschung erscheint angesichts der Flexibilierung der unternehmerischen Organisationsformen, ihrer Auswirkungen auf den Organisationsbereich von Belegschaftsvertretungen und angesichts der Pluralisierung der Beschäftigungsformen die Frage nach dem Schicksal des deutschen Betriebsrates (Benz-Overhage & Klebe 2000). Diese ist unmittelbar mit der anstehenden Reform des Betriebsverfassungsgesetzes verknüpft, über die bereits heftig debattiert wird. Wegen der neuen Strukturen in der Ökonomik dürfte es also fortan noch schwieriger werden, bei der sachlichen Beschreibung auch terminologische Genauigkeit im deutsch-japanischen Vergleich industrieller Beziehungen zu erreichen.

Welches ist die Schlußfolgerung aus den Überlegungen zu der Frage, nach welchen Kriterien die Terminologie in deutschsprachigen Untersuchungen zur Arbeitswelt und ihren Strukturen in Japan geschaffen werden sollte? Grob gesagt, bestehen zwei Wege: Die erste besteht darin, den japanischen Begriff, der für die Sache bereits „vor Ort“ geprägt worden ist, ins Deutsche zu übersetzen. Dagegen wird bei der zweiten Möglichkeit zunächst der in der japanischen Gesellschaft entstandene Realgehalt der Sache erfaßt und davon ausgehend nach einem passenden Begriff gesucht. Der zweite Weg ist meines Erachtens vorzuziehen. Man wird sich dann bei unserem Beispiel der *kigyô-betsu kumiai* für jene

Übersetzungsvariante entscheiden, die auf die stärkste der Realitäten abhebt – das Unternehmen – und deshalb jene andere, zwar „neutral" klingende, in Wirklichkeit aber die räumlich-technische Einheit einschließlich ihrer sozialen Organisation nahelegende Variante nicht länger in Betracht ziehen.

References

Benz-Overhage, K. & Klebe, T. (2000), Was ist künftig ein Betrieb? Überlegungen zu einer modernen Unternehmensverfassung, in: *Arbeitsrecht im Betrieb* 1/2000.

Bergmann, J. (1990), *Rationalisierungsdynamik und Betriebsgemeinschaft. Die Rolle der japanischen Betriebsgewerkschaften*, München: Rainer Hampp Verlag.

Hisamoto, N. (1994), Kigyô-betsu Kumiai, in: *Nihon Rôdô Kenkyû Zasshi* 408: 14-15.

Inagami, T. (1988), Kigyô-betsu Kumiai, in: Mita, M. et al. (Hrsg.), *Shakaigaku Jiten* [Sozialwissenschaftliches Lexikon], Tokyo: Kôbundô: 180-181

Kawanishi, H. (1992), *Enterprise Unionism in Japan*, London, New York: Kegan Paul International.

Kawanishi, H. (1984), Sangyô, in: Kitagawa et al. (Hg.), *Gendai Shakaigaku Jiten* [Sozialwissenschaftliches Lexikon], Tokyo: Yûshindô: 541-554.

Kishida, S. (1978), *Keiei Sanka no Shakaigakuteki Kenkyû* [Sozialwissenschaftliche Forschung zur Managementbeteiligung], Tokyo: Kyôikusha.

Kumazawa, M. (1989), Nihonteki Keiei to Yôroppa Rôdôsha [Japanisches Management and Europäische Arbeiter] in: Kumazawa, M. (Hg.), *Nihonteki Keiei no Meian* [Licht und Schatten des Japanischen Managements], Tokyo: Chikuma shobô: 114-117,

Müller-Jentsch, W. (1997), *Soziologie der Industriellen Beziehungen. Eine Einführung*, 2. erw. Auflage, Frankfurt, New York: Campus.

Ôshige, K. (2000), Doitsu ni Okeru Jigyôsho Reberu no Rieki Daihyô-sei [Das System der Interessenvertretung auf Ebene des einzelnen Betriebes in Deutschland], in: *Rôdô Shakaigaku Kenkyû*, 2: 1-54.

Ôshige, K. (1999), *Konvergenz der Interessenvertretungen durch Globalisierung? Ein Vergleich der Funktionsmechanismen der Arbeitnehmerinteressenvertretungssysteme in Deutschland und Japan am Beispiel der Elektroindustrie*, Frankfurt a.M.: Peter Lang.

Park, S. J. (1983), Japan, in: Mielke, S. (Hg.), *Internationales Gewerkschaftshandbuch*, Opladen: Leske + Budrich: 621-643,

Seifert, W. (2000), Beteiligung von Belegschaftsvertretungen in Deutschland und Japan – Grundzüge eines Forschungsprojekts, in: *Miyagi Gakuin Joshi Daigaku Jinbun Shakai Kagaku Ronsô* 9: 1-22.

Seifert, W. (1997), *Gewerkschaften in der japanischen Politik von 1970 bis 1990 – der dritte Partner?* Opladen: Westdeutscher Verlag.

Shirai, T. (1982), *Die japanische Betriebsgewerkschaft*, Bochum: Studienverlag N. Brockmeyer.

Tokunaga, S. et al. (1991), *Japanisches Personalmanagement – ein anderer Weg?* Frankfurt, New York: Campus.

Weber, M. (1980), *Wirtschaft und Gesellschaft: Grundriss der verstehenden Soziologie*, 5. rev. Aufl. Tübingen: Mohr.

The Authors

Gerhard Ackermann is professor at the Berlin University of Applied Sciences. He is the president of the same university.

Ulrich Albrecht is professor of peace and conflict studies at the department for political sciences, Freie Universität Berlin. He has served as vice president of Freie Universität Berlin in 1981 and 1982. He has also been consultant to the department for disarmament affairs at United Nations headquarters and head of planning at the Ministry of Foreign Affairs of the outgoing German Democratic Republic in 1990. He has published numerous books and articles in the field of peace and conflict studies, security and disarmament issues and German re-unification.

Galen Amstutz is professor at the Edwin O. Reischauer Institute of Japanese Studies, Harvard University and public program administrator at the same institute. He is also the editor of *Tsûshin*, the bilingual newsletter of the Reischauer Institute. He received his Ph.D. in religion and East Asian studies from Princeton University. His publications include *Interpreting Amida: Orientalism and History in the Study of Pure Land Buddhism* (New York: State University of New York Press, 1997).

Enno Berndt is associate professor at the College for Business Administration, Ritsumeikan University in Kyoto and senior research advisor to the Social and Technology Research Group of DaimlerChrysler AG. He is also visiting associate professor at the Global Information and Telecommunication Institute of the Waseda University in Tokyo. His research interests lie in the area of corporate culture and human resource management. He has published widely in these areas including *Doitsu kara mita Nihonteki Keiei no Kiki* [The Crisis of Japanese Management from a German Perspective] (Tokyo: Kodansha, 1995).

Dieter Beschorner has studied electrical engineering and economics at the Technical University of Munich, where he got his doctoral degree in 1976. He taught at the Universities of Bamberg, Speyer, Vienna and Freiburg. Since 1992, he is professor at the University of Ulm in Germany. His principal areas of research include international management, controllership and environmental studies. He has published various books and papers in these fields. He is also the Chairman of the Board of the Humboldt Studies Centre of Humanities and Philosophy at the University of Ulm.

Reinhard Drifte is professor of Japanese studies at the University of Newcastle upon Tyne; he received his Ph.D. from the Ruhr-Universität Bochum, Germany. He has published over 100 articles and book chapters on many aspects of Japanese foreign and security policies, security and arms control issues in Northeast Asia and EU-East Asia relations. His main publications include: *Japan's Foreign Policy in the 1990s. From Economic Superpower to What Power?* (London/Oxford: Macmillan, St. Antony's Series and New York: St. Martin's Press, 1996) and *Japan's Quest for a Permanent Security Council Seat. A Matter of Pride or Justice?* (London/Oxford: Macmillan, St. Antony's Series and New York: St. Martin's Press, 1999).

Peter Duus is William H. Bonsall Professor of History at Stanford University. He received his Ph.D. in History from Harvard University in 1964. Over the years he has written on a variety of subjects, from Japanese feudalism to Taisho politics. His most recent work has focused on Japan as an imperialist power (*The Abacus and the Sword: The Japanese Penetration of Korea*) and as a semicolonized country (*The Japanese Discovery of America: A History with Documents*). He has also edited Volume 6 of *The Cambridge History of Japan* and has written *Modern Japan*, a textbook on modern Japanese history.

Sam Dzever has the chair in international marketing and strategy at Telemark University College, Norway. He has a Ph.D. in marketing from The University of Strathclyde (Britain) and a Doctor of Economics in industrial organization from the University of Linköping (Sweden). He has published eight books and research monographs as well as numerous articles in leading international journals. His latest books include: *Le Comportement d'Achat Industriel* [Industrial Buying Behavior] (Paris: Economica, 1996), *Perspectives on Economic Integration and Business Strategy in the Asia-Pacific Region* (London: Macmillan, 1997) and *China and India: Economic Performance and Business Strategies of Firms in the Mid-1990s* (London: Macmillan, 1999).

Gesine Foljanty-Jost studied political science, sociology and Japanese studies at the universities of Bonn, Tokyo (Tôdai) and Berlin (Freie Universität), received her M.A. in Japanese studies and her doctoral degree in political science from Freie Universität Berlin. Since 1992, she is professor and director of the institute of Japanese studies at Halle University; she has been a visiting professor at Tokyo University in 1999. Her major fields of research are environmental and educational policies in Japan. She has published widely in these areas.

Furthermore, she has held leading positions in several research organizations including chairwoman of the Association of Social Scientific Research of Japan between 1988 and 1997, chairwoman of the European Japan Experts Association between 1996 and 1998, and deputy chairwoman of the German Association of Asian Studies.

Karin Funke is head of public relations of DaimlerChrysler AG in Asia. She received her doctoral degree in Japanese studies from Freie University Berlin in 1996. She has worked two years for BMW in Munich before joining DaimlerChrysler in 1998.

Carsten Fussan is senior consultant at IBM Global Services specialized on e-business strategy. Previous positions have been those of consultant for Deloitte Consulting and head of strategic planning and participation department of a WestLB investment banking subsidiary. He studied business administration at Freie Universität Berlin and got his doctoral degree in economics in 1997. His major publications include *Competitive Advantages and Company Evolution* (Wiesbaden: Gabler, 1997).

Johan Galtung is currently distinguished professor of peace studies at the University of Hawaii, Universität Witten/Herdecke, Germany and Universitetet i Tromsö, Norway. He established the International Peace Research Institute, Oslo (PRIO) in 1959 and the Journal of Peace Research in 1964. His international academic career has spanned five continents, a dozen major positions and over 30 visiting professorships. He is a consultant to several UN agencies and has recently founded "Transcend", a global network of experts trained in conflict analysis who do field work in various trouble spots. He has published hundreds of articles and more than 70 books, including recently *Human Rights in Another Key* (Polity, 1994) and (with Daisaku Ikeda) *Choose Peace* (Pluto, 1995). He holds numerous honorary degrees and awards, among them the Right Livelihood Award.

Kurt Görger is director and head of East Asia Group of Bankgesellschaft Berlin AG. He studied business administration at Freie Universität Berlin and spent five years at Freie Universität Berlin between 1972 and 1977 as assistant professor. Since 1979 he has been working for Berliner Bank, which was merged into its Holding Company Bankgesellschaft Berlin in 1999.

András Hernádi is a senior research fellow at the Institute for World Economics of the Hungarian Academy of Sciences, and Director of the Japan, East and Southeast Asia Research Centre of the same institute. He received his Ph.D. in economics from the Budapest University of Economics. His main fields of research include Japan and the Asia-Pacific region, and consumption in the world economy. He has authored and edited several books and numerous articles on these topics. His main publications include *The Pacific Region: Sources of Growth, Development Paths, Co-operation* (Budapest: Kossuth, 1982) and *Could a New Consumer Identity Emerge? A New Approach to the Theory and Practice of Consumption* (Budapest: IWE, 1999).

Arne Holzhausen is assistant professor at the Institute for East Asian Studies of Freie Universität Berlin. His principal areas of research are employment, management and industrial structures in Japan. His publications include *Das Japanische Beschäftigungssystem in der Krise* [The Japanese Employment System in Crisis] (Wiesbaden: Gabler, 1998) and the co-authored book *Keiretsu am Ende?* [Keiretsu at an End?] (Hagen: ISL, 1999).

Sierk Horn is assistant professor at the Institute for East Asian Studies of Freie Universität Berlin since May 2000 after being visiting research scholar at the University of Tokyo, Faculty of Economics, from 1998 to 2000. He received his Ph.D. in Japanology from Freie Universität Berlin in July 2000. His research interests cover Japanese advertising, Japanese marketing concepts, communication and psychology.

Wolfgang Jahnke is professor of technical engineering at the Berlin University of Applied Sciences. He is the vice-president of the same university.

Ulrich Jürgens studied economics and political science at Freie Universität Berlin from 1965 to 1969. He was assistant professor of political science at the same university between 1969 and 1977. Since 1977 he has been a research fellow at the Social Science Research Center Berlin (WZB) and since 1989 he is adjunct professor at the Institute for Political Science of the Freie Universität Berlin. From 1989 until 1999 he was deputy director of the research unit "Regulation of Work" at the WZB and since January 2000 he is head of this research unit. At the WZB he conducts international comparative research in the fields of industrial policies, work organization and organizational development with a focus on the automotive industry.

Paul Kevenhörster is professor of political science as well as director of the Institute of Political Science at Westfälische Wilhelms-Universität Münster, Germany. He received his doctoral degree in political science from the University of Cologne and has been visiting professor – among others – at Sophia University Tokyo and Nippon University Tokyo. He has published numerous books and articles on the political system of Japan, development policies and the political impacts of information technology. His main publications include *Das politische System Japans* [The Japanese Political System] (Köln-Opladen, 1969), *Politik im elektronischen Zeitalter. Politische Wirkungen der Informationstechnik* [Political Impacts of Modern Information Technology] (Baden-Baden, 1984) and *Politik und Gesellschaft in Japan* [Politics and Society in Japan] (Mannheim, 1993).

John B. Kidd was educated in the UK and worked for several major UK organisations before returning to University scholarship. In the Universities of Birmingham and now at the Aston Business School his research has focused on the development of IT usage in Small and Medium Enterprises; the management of projects; and the softer management issues which concerns multinational joint ventures, especially between Asian and European companies. He has held visiting professorships in several European Universities, and in the China Europe International Business School, Shanghai.

Takeo Kikkawa is professor of Japanese business history at the Institute of Social Science, University of Tokyo. His main publications in English include *Policies for Competitiveness: Experiences of Industrial Economies During the "Golden Age of Capitalism"* (with Hideaki Miyajima and Takashi Hikino) (Oxford: Oxford University Press, 1999).

Kazuo Koike is professor of labour studies at Hosei University Tokyo. His principal areas of research include the cross-cultural comparison of industrial relations and employment systems. He has published widely on these topics, among others *Understanding Industrial Relations in Modern Japan* (New York, London: Macmillan, 1988).

Ilse Lenz is professor of gender studies at Ruhr-Universität Bochum, Germany. She has been visiting professor at the Institute of Gender Studies, Ochanomizu University (1994) and at the Institute of Social Science, University of Tokyo; she has also served as speaker of the women's section of the German Sociological Association (1995-1999). Her main fields of research are gender and work, gender and globalization, women's movements, gender and ethnicity and feminist theory between structural and postmodern approaches; these issues are followed in a comparative perspective (mainly Germany and Japan). She has published widely in these areas and is the co-editor of the series *Geschlecht und Gesellschaft* [Gender and Society] of Leske+Budrich publishers.

Andrè Metzner is currently researcher at DaimlerChrysler's Society and Technology Research Group Berlin. He studied sociology and organization studies at Humboldt Universität Berlin and Essex University, Britain, from 1990 to 1995. He held a research position at Humboldt Universität Berlin from 1995 to 1996. He has published several papers and articles on subjects such as organizational problems and the future of the automobile.

Shinobu Muramatsu is professor of business administration as well as dean of the faculty of business administration at Soka University, Japan. His research interests lie in the areas of business finance and M&A strategies. His main publications include *Corporate Restructuring and M&A* (in Japanese) (Tokyo: Dobunkan, 1999).

Michio Nitta is professor at the Institute of Social Science, University of Tokyo. His major fields of research are comparative studies in employment and industrial relations. His main publications in English include *Knowledge Driven Work* (as co-author) (Oxford: Oxford University Press, 1998).

Annette Schad-Seifert is M.A. and Ph.D. graduate in Japanese studies from Freie Universität Berlin. She has been assistant professor at the Institute for East Asian Studies of Freie Universität Berlin from 1990 to 1996. Since 1997 she is associate professor in the Japanology department of the East Asian Institute at the University of Leipzig. Her main fields of research are the history of social and political ideas in modern Japan, and contemporary cultural and gender studies of Japan. She is author of *Sozialwissenschaftliches Denken in der japanischen Aufklärung – Positionen zur "modernen bürgerlichen Gesellschaft" bei Fukuzawa Yukichi* [Ideas of Social Sciences in the Japanese Enlightenment – Fukuzawa Yukichi's Discourse on Modern Civil Society] (Leipzig: Leipziger Universitätsverlag, 1999) and is currently working on a book on the history of manliness and masculinity in Japan.

Wolfgang Seifert is professor of Japanese studies at the University of Heidelberg. He received his doctoral degree in political sciences from the University of Frankfurt am Main, Germany, in 1975. His research areas concern politics and political ideas of modern Japan, industrial relations and the process of modernization. He has published widely on these topics; his main publications include *Gewerkschaften in der japanischen Politik von 1970 bis 1990: Der dritte Partner?* [Unions in Japanese politics from 1970 to 1990: The Third Partner?] (Opladen: Westdeutscher Verlag, 1997). In addition, he has translated several books from Japanese and received the "Japan Foundation Translator Price" in 2000.

Kazuo Shibagaki is professor of economics at Musashi University, Japan, and professor emeritus at the University of Tokyo where he worked over 30 years at the Institute of Social Science. He has been a guest professor at Freie Universität Berlin and the Copenhagen Business School. He has published numerous books and articles on the Japanese economy, including recently *Chishikijin no Shikaku toshite no Keizaigaku* [Economics as a Qualification to Become an Intellectual] and *Gendai Shihonshugi no Ronri* [The Logic of Contemporary Capitalism].

Joop A. Stam is professor of Asian economy and management, especially Japan, at the School of Economics, Erasmus University Rotterdam. His research interests concern human resource management, management of technology and SME in Pacific Asia. Currently he is chairman of the Euro-Asia Management Studies Association.

J.A.A. Stockwin has been Nissan Professor of Modern Japanese Studies and Director of the Nissan Institute of Japanese Studies at the University of Oxford, where he is also a Fellow of St. Antony's College, since 1982. He took his first degree, in Philosophy, Politics and Economics, from the University of Oxford and his Ph.D. from the Australian National University in Canberra, where he taught in the Department of Political Science between 1964 and 1981. His publications include *The Japanese Socialist Party and Neutralism* (1968), *Dynamic and Immobilist Politics in Japan* (editor and joint author, 1988), and *Governing Japan: Divided Politics in a Major Economy* (1999). He has had visiting fellowships at the Institute of Social Science, Tokyo University, and elsewhere.

Yoshiaki Takahashi is professor of business administration at Chuo University Tokyo. He is board member of the Japan Society of Business Administration and deputy chairman of the Euro-Asia Management Studies Association. His main publications include *Management Strategies of Multinational Corporations in Asian Markets*.

Kerstin Teicher received a doctoral degree in business administration from the University of Kassel, following her Master's degrees in business administration and Japanese studies at Freie Universität Berlin. She has worked several years as a consultant with A.T. Kearney; her current position is that of a vice-president at the Asia Development Center of Bertelsmann AG.

Marc-Oliver Thurner holds a Masters degree in Business Mathematics of the University of Ulm where he focused on Competitive Strategy and Finance. During research for his Thesis paper on Multinational Companies in China, he worked two months in a Joint Venture of Fresenius AG and five months for Siemens Ltd., China. He is now working for Merrill Lynch & Co., Inc in the Mergers & Acquisitions department.

Malcolm Trevor took his first degree, in modern languages, from the University of Oxford, his Diploma in social anthropology from the University College London and his Ph.D. from the London School of Economics. He has worked several years in Japan before finishing as European General Manager at the EU-Japan Centre for Industrial Co-operation in Tokyo in 1991 to 1996. He has been a lecturer in Japanese political economy at the College of Europe (Bruges) from 1997 to 1999. His major fields of interest are management of Japanese firms and Japan's political economy. His main publications include *Japan's Reluctant Multinationals* (1983), and *Manufacturers and Suppliers in Britain and Japan* (1988). He is currently working on a book on Japan's political economy.

The manufacturer's authorised representative in the EU is Springer Nature Customer Service Centre GmbH, Europaplatz 3, 69115 Heidelberg, Germany. If you have any concerns regarding our products, please contact ProductSafety@springernature.com

Printed and bound by CPI Group (UK) Ltd, Croydon, CR0 4YY
22/09/2026
02220988-0007